HISTORY OF THE ENGLISH CALVINISTIC BAPTISTS
1771–1892

History of the English Calvinistic Baptists
1771–1892

From John Gill to C. H. Spurgeon

Robert W. Oliver

THE BANNER OF TRUTH TRUST

THE BANNER OF TRUTH TRUST
3 Murrayfield Road, Edinburgh EH12 6EL, UK
P.O. Box 621, Carlisle, PA 17013, USA

© Robert W. Oliver 2006

ISBN–10: 0 85151 920 2
ISBN–13: 978 0 85151 920 3

Typeset in 11/14 pt Bulmer MT at the
Banner of Truth Trust, Edinburgh
Printed and bound in the U.S.A.
by Versa Press, Inc.
East Peoria, IL

For
Rachel

who has supported me throughout all
the lengthy years of this project
and in all the years before

Contents

Foreword *by Dr Michael A. G. Haykin*	xi
Preface	xiii
Introduction	xvii
PART ONE: THE EIGHTEENTH-CENTURY HERITAGE	1
1. The Legacy of John Gill	3
2. Blessing in the Cotswolds	16
3. Three Noteworthy Leaders	30
4. The Communion Controversy 1772–1781	58
5. The Gospel Worthy of All Acceptation	89
6. Antinomianism	112
7. William Huntington's Controversy with the Particular Baptists	132
PART TWO: WHEN GOOD MEN DIFFER	147
8. Andrew Fuller and Abraham Booth	149
9. William Gadsby	173
10. John Stevens	200
PART THREE: RE-ALIGNMENT	229
11. Moves Towards Open Communion	231
12. The Beginnings of the Strict Baptist Magazines	260
13. Joseph Charles Philpot	288
14. Organizations	312
15. Charles Haddon Spurgeon	337

Appendices:

A. John Collett Ryland, Daniel Turner, Robert Robinson, and the Communion Controversy, 1772–81 — 357
B. Andrew Fuller and the Atonement — 361
C. Letter from Dr J. H. Philpot to Mr Dickinson, 25 March 1931 — 367

Bibliography — 369
Index of Names — 393
Index of Places — 401
Index of Subjects — 405

Endpapers: The River Lark at Isleham Ferry, Cambridgeshire, where C. H. Spurgeon was baptized on 1st May 1850, painted in watercolours by his son, Thomas Spurgeon.

Illustrations
(centre pages)

1. John Gill (1697–1771).
2. The Baptist Chapel, Bourton-on-the-Water.
3. The manse built for Benjamin Beddome, now the Old Manse Hotel, Bourton-on-the-Water.
4. John Collett Ryland, Sr. (1723–92).
5. Robert Hall, Sr. (1728–91).
6. Abraham Booth (1734–1806).
7. Robert Robinson (1735–90).
8. Caleb Evans (1737–91).
9. Andrew Fuller (1754–1815).
10. William Huntington (1745–1813).
11. John Ryland, Jr. (1753–1825).
12. John Thomas, Andrew Fuller, William Carey, William Ward, and Joshua Marshman, key figures in the fledgling Particular Baptist Missionary Society.
13. William Gadsby (1773–1844).
14. John Stevens (1776–1847).
15. Robert Hall, Jr. (1764–1831).
16. Joseph Kinghorn (1766–1832).
17. John Warburton (1776–1857).
18. John Kershaw (1792–1870).
19. Joseph Charles Philpot (1802–69).
20. Joseph Ivimey (1773–1834).
21. James Wells (1803–72) and Surrey Tabernacle, Southwark.
22. C. H. Spurgeon (1834–92).

Foreword

THIS BOOK on the history of the English Calvinistic Baptist community during the latter third of the eighteenth century and the bulk of the following century deals with a subject that has become, I confess, one that is extremely dear to my heart. In this community I have found not only theological wisdom and spiritual inspiration for the Christian life, but numerous men and women who held theological and spiritual convictions that I judge to be as close to Scripture as those of any Christians in the history of the church. I am therefore thrilled to be able to write a Foreword to this masterful book by Dr Oliver that provides a piquant study of this community.

The book deals not only with the well-known figures in this community's history – theological giants like John Gill, Andrew Fuller, William Gadsby and Charles Spurgeon – but also with lesser-known lights, men like the hymn writer Benjamin Beddome, the eccentric John Collett Ryland, Abraham Booth, and John Stevens. Wide and deep reading in the writings of these men has given Oliver an excellent grasp of their various theological perspectives. The amount of space given to Booth is especially important since, though largely forgotten today, he was widely regarded by his fellow Baptists as their leading theologian in the late eighteenth century.

No Christian community is without its controversies, and the Calvinistic Baptists in the period covered by Oliver are no exception. Even-handedly and with one eye always on the Calvinistic Baptist roots in the seventeenth century – well summed up by the *Second London Confession of Faith* (1689) – Oliver details the controversies that at times wracked this community. Who may take the Lord's Supper? What is the role of the law in the Christian life? Is there biblical warrant for making free offers of the gospel to all and sundry? None of these issues

[xi]

is a minor matter and none should be ignored by Christians today. The thinking of these Baptist worthies is therefore still of great value.

Unlike some contemporary historians, Oliver is rightly convinced that the development of the Strict and Particular strand of this community in the nineteenth century is not a stagnant backwater that is best forgotten. Even though the churches of this persuasion were not as balanced as their seventeenth and eighteenth-century forebears, there was a spiritual vitality to this group that needs remembering and Oliver has given us a rich overview of the thought and activities of these Calvinistic Baptists.

Finally, this period of English Baptist history covered by Dr Oliver is marked by a distinct note of poignancy. Reading of the differences between Booth and Fuller or the failure of the London Strict and Particular Baptists to regard Spurgeon as a close ally, for example, cannot but convey something of the sadness of the church's life in a world marred by sin. May those of us who claim the words of this community as our spiritual heritage take heed and leave a better witness.

MICHAEL A. G. HAYKIN
2005

Preface

THIS BOOK is based on a doctoral dissertation submitted to the Council for National Academic Awards in 1986 under the title, 'The Emergence of a Strict and Particular Baptist Community among the English Calvinistic Baptists from 1770 to 1850'. I had hoped that it would appear as a book many years ago, but other responsibilities intervened. The original research project developed over a period of several years after I had been asked to write and lecture on various aspects of English Calvinistic Dissent. I felt the need to explore the connections between a number of men and movements. I also wished to explore in depth something of my own theological roots. I had been brought up in a village congregation that was able to harmonize features of what may be described as the Stevens and Gadsby traditions among the Strict Baptists. By the time that I embarked on this research project neither of these traditions completely reflected my own convictions, although I could see elements of great value in both. I had been drawn increasingly to an older Particular Baptist statement of faith, the *Baptist Confession* of 1689.

In the years since the original dissertation was submitted other research projects have been completed and published. These include Dr Kenneth Dix's *Strict and Particular*, which focuses on the Strict Baptists and takes the story beyond the period covered by this work. I have tried to relate the central figures of my study to developments in the wider Particular Baptist context. Another recent and important contribution to this field of study is Dr Ian J. Shaw's *High Calvinists in Action*, which discusses the significant social work of William Gadsby and James Wells, both of whom appear in my book. The focus of my concentration has been on the doctrinal and pastoral issues of these years, although I have not ignored issues of social involvement.

History of the English Calvinistic Baptists, 1771–1892

I owe a debt of gratitude to many people without whose help this work would have been impossible. My supervisors, Dr H. H. Rowdon, then of London Bible College, and the Rev. Dr B. R. White of Regent's Park College, Oxford, both gave wise counsel and unfailing encouragement. It was Dr White who urged me to pursue my subject in the wider Particular Baptist context.

My research required the study of an abundance of long-forgotten printed material as well as manuscript sources. I am grateful for access to that treasure house of Baptist source material, the Angus Library, Regent's Park College, Oxford. Its librarians have been most helpful. The supplies of the Bodleian Library, Oxford; the British Library; Bristol Baptist College Library; Dr Williams's Library, and the Evangelical Library have supplemented the riches of the Angus. Particularly exciting was the discovery of a long-lost pamphlet by John Collett Ryland in the Northamptonshire Central Library. To the librarians of all of these institutions I am grateful. Mr Norman Hopkins of Egerton, Kent, most kindly made me an extended loan of a collection of rare tracts. The Rev. Roger Prime of Beccles gave me access to the archives of the Suffolk and Norfolk Association of Strict Baptist Churches. To these friends and the many people who directed me to single works or were willing to discuss my work I owe a great debt. It seems invidious to single out individuals, but I must mention the late Kenneth Howard, then of Bethersden, Kent, and the Rev. R. P. Roberts, a fellow researcher in the Angus Library, both of whom stimulated me and helpfully criticised my ideas. The expenses necessarily incurred in this work were eased by the generosity of two ancient Dissenting institutions, the Dr Williams Trust and the Particular Baptist Fund.

The elders and church members of the Old Baptist Chapel, Bradford on Avon not only bore with me, but encouraged me in my historical research. Amongst these I must record my especial thanks to my brother-in-law, the late Terry Ladd, who spent more hours than I dare consider putting the dissertation through his word processor at a time when I understood nothing about computers. My debt to him for his labour and patience is incalculable.

Preface and Acknowledgements

The original research would never have been possible without the encouragement and support of my wife, Rachel, my daughter, Naomi, and my son, Paul. They have shown an unfailing depth of understanding especially during those frequent times when I was away from them, spending many hours engaged in historical research. Rachel's forbearance has continued during the long period in which the work has been revised for wider publication.

Since the completion of the dissertation I have experienced the kind but firm pressure of Iain Murray to turn it into a book. My long delays have tried his patience, but our friendship has endured.

ROBERT W. OLIVER
2005

Introduction

THE AIM OF THIS BOOK is to trace the story of the English Calvinistic Baptists from the death of John Gill in 1771 to that of Charles Haddon Spurgeon in 1892.

In the seventeenth century two distinct denominations emerged out of English Separatism. Although they shared a belief that baptism should be administered only to persons professing faith in Jesus Christ, they differed in origin, organization, and doctrine. Most significantly the General Baptists were Arminian while the Particular Baptists were Calvinist.

1. THE *1689 CONFESSION OF FAITH*

In 1644 a group of Particular Baptist churches in London published a *Confession of Faith* which clearly testified to the Calvinistic doctrines of grace. Although published by churches in the nation's capital, this *Confession* also expressed the convictions of a number of other churches spread across the country. The *1644 Confession* went out of print during the turbulent time of the mid-seventeenth century. Various questions were then being raised which the authors of the *1644 Confession* had not foreseen or anticipated. A more detailed statement of Baptist faith was needed and this, because of persecution, was published anonymously in 1677. The passing of the Toleration Act in 1689 gave a measure of religious liberty to those who dissented from the Church of England, and the Particular Baptists took this opportunity to call a General Assembly of their churches in 1689. This was the occasion to commend the *1677 Confession* to the churches as a definitive statement of Particular Baptist beliefs.[1] This *1689 Confession*, sometimes referred

---

[1] *Confession of Faith Put forth by the Elders and Brethren of Many Congregations of Christians (baptized upon Profession of their Faith) in London and the Country,*

to as the *Second London Confession*, was a Baptist adaptation of the *Savoy Declaration* drawn up by the Independents in 1658, which in turn was a slightly edited revision of the *Westminster Confession* of 1647.

The compilers of the *1689 Confession* clearly wished to identify as far as possible with the teaching of these two earlier statements. The introduction to the 1677 draft of the *Confession* explains their intention 'to convince all that we have no itch to clog religion with new words, but do readily acquiesce in that form of sound words, which hath been in consent with the holy scriptures, used by others before us'.[2]

The prefatory statement to the 1689 edition explained that it was issued in the name of 'the Ministers and Messengers of and concerned for, upwards of one hundred baptized congregations in England and Wales, denying Arminianism'.[3] The Particular Baptists thus made it clear that they were not General Baptists. In their understanding of the doctrines of salvation they were closer to the Independents and Presbyterians than they were to the General Baptists.

By the 1670s there was a division of opinion among the Particular Baptists over the issue of whether communion should be 'closed' or 'open'. The closed- or strict-communion churches insisted that only persons baptized on a profession of faith could be admitted to communion at the Lord's Supper. The open-communion churches believed that faith in Jesus Christ was the only qualification for admission to communion. On this issue the compilers of the 1677 *Confession* explained, 'We . . . are not of full accord among ourselves.' The *Confession* insisted on neither practice.[4] Throughout the eighteenth century both open- and strict-communion churches could be found among the Particular

---

1677. Reprinted in William Lumpkin, *Baptist Confessions of Faith*, 1969 [revised edition, 1980], Judson Press, Valley Forge, USA, pp. 241–95. Many subsequent editions have appeared. In this book the title, *1689 Confession*, is used and references will be to chapters in Roman and paragraphs in Arabic numerals.

[2] Lumpkin, *Confessions*, p. 245.   [3] Ibid, p. 238

[4] *Confession*, 1677 edition, pp. 137–8. For a fuller discussion of this debate see B. R. White, 'Open and Closed Membership among English and Welsh Baptists', *Baptist Quarterly*, 24, 1972, pp. 330–4.

Introduction

Baptists although strict communion appears to have been the practice of the majority of these churches.

2. THE *CONFESSION* IN THE EIGHTEENTH CENTURY

New editions of the *1689 Confession* continued to appear regularly until the fifth edition appeared in 1720.[5] Thereafter, there seems to have been no further English edition until 1790, when it was re-published by John Rippon.[6] Subsequently, there were at least three editions in the nineteenth century.[7] During the seventy years period between 1720 and 1790, the *Confession* seems to have fallen out of favour in the London area and among churches which were being influenced by new emphases associated with the teaching of John Gill. However, in 1733 the Western Association, representing churches in Gloucestershire, Wiltshire, and the South West, reaffirmed its adherence to the *Confession* and in the proceedings of that Association there are repeated references to it over the next eleven years.[8] So then, while the *Confession* had received the commendation of a representative Assembly in 1689, the evidence that it had long been neglected in other parts of the country prepares us for the discovery that certain aspects of its theology had been modified.

[5] Lumpkin, op. cit., p. 239, lists editions in 1689, 1693, 1714, and 1720.

[6] Lumpkin, *Confessions*, dates Rippon's edition as 1791, but Rippon himself listed it among books and pamphlets by Baptists published in 1790, J. Rippon, *Baptist Annual Register*, Vol. 1, London, 1790, p. 124. The copy in the Angus Library, Regent's Park College, Oxford, believed to be the Rippon edition, has no date of publication.

[7] The Angus Library contains editions published in 1809 [London], 1851 [Manchester], and 1855 [London, published by C. H. Spurgeon].

[8] 'Records of the Western Association 1733–44', deposited in the Angus Library, Regent's Park College, Oxford. Roger Hayden has recently shown that the *Confession* continued to be a vital influence in the Western Churches and in those areas influenced by the Bristol Baptist Academy. He does however seem to downplay the influence of Gill and Brine outside the London area. Events in the Midlands in the 1780s were to demonstrate that that influence was strong in the middle of the century; Roger Hayden, 'Evangelical Calvinism among Eighteenth Century British Baptists with particular reference to Bernard Foskett, Hugh and Caleb Evans and the Bristol Academy', Ph.D. thesis, University of Keele, 1991.

[xix]

3. The Emergence of the Strict and Particular Baptists

During the nineteenth century the English Particular Baptists passed through a state of flux. In 1813 the Baptist Union was formed on a Calvinistic basis of faith for the promotion of co-operation between Particular Baptist churches throughout the nation. By the end of that century it was an association of both Calvinistic and Arminian churches. Such an alliance only became possible because of seismic changes that had taken place among the Particular Baptists. Shortly before the alliance of the two groups was formalized, John Clifford, the General Baptist leader, wrote, 'We were never further from Calvinism than we are today.'[9]

Such radical changes were totally unacceptable to a considerable minority who stood apart from the Union and became known as Strict and Particular Baptists. A superficial reading of history portrays them as traditionalists left behind by their more progressive brethren. This interpretation misses something of the vitality of their life and piety. They were intensely interested in Christian doctrine and discussed it vigorously, but it was doctrine to be experienced and lived that excited their concerns. They shared the rich legacy of Christian experience which flowed from the eighteenth-century Evangelical Revival. With Joseph Hart, whose hymns they highly esteemed, they agreed:

> Vain is all our best devotion,
> If on false foundations built;
> True religion's more than notion,
> Something must be known and felt.

The Strict and Particular Baptists were also influenced by the spirit of their age and, like other Particular Baptists, experienced certain changes. These were not always for the better. While they loved and preached the doctrines of grace, they did not always reflect the full-orbed Puritan theology of the Particular Baptist founding fathers. For this reason it is necessary to consider the teaching of John Gill and his associates. In

---

[9] Quoted, A. C. Underwood, *History of the English Baptists*, 1961, p. 215. Compare Underwood's statement: 'No confession of faith was asked for or given by either party.'

Introduction

many respect the influence of Gill was beneficial, but there were areas where it was not and these marked a departure from the *1689 Confession*. Historians have not always appreciated this. Writing in the early twentieth century, an eminent Baptist historian, W. T. Whitley, suggested that the men who wished to promote and maintain the distinctive teachings of Gill and his friend John Brine in the nineteenth century were also upholders of the *1689 Confession*.[10] Closer examination of the evidence makes it clear that the supporters of the *Confession* were usually evangelistic Calvinists who were not happy with some aspects of Gill's teaching.

It seems that many Particular Baptists lost sight of the balanced teaching of their seventeenth-century predecessors and their modified theology impoverished their Christian experience and church life. One purpose of this book is to call attention to the theology of the *1689 Confession* and to show how vital it has been to the spiritual well being of the English Calvinistic Baptist churches. One of the few nineteenth-century leaders who emphasized the teaching of the *Confession* was Charles Haddon Spurgeon. It is one of the tragedies of nineteenth-century church history that the Strict and Particular Baptists, who should have been the most loyal associates of Spurgeon in his struggles against the compromises which resulted from the widespread acceptance of Arminianism, were in fact suspicious of him. The chapters that follow will seek to explain why this situation developed.

To understand the situation that pertained among the Particular Baptist churches of the nineteenth century we must turn our attention to developments among the Particular Baptists of the late eighteenth century.

---

[10] W. J. Whitley, *History of the British Baptists*, London, 1923, p. 306. Whitley also says of these people, 'By 1850 they had so secluded themselves that they had ceased to be a drag on others or to be of any general importance.' Ibid.

PART ONE

THE EIGHTEENTH-CENTURY INHERITANCE

1

The Legacy of John Gill

I. John Gill, Baptist Theologian

John Gill, the leading Particular Baptist theologian of his day, was the pastor of Horsleydown Baptist Church in Southwark from 1720 until 1771. Born into a home where the gospel was loved, he was taken from childhood to the Baptist meeting in Kettering, Northamptonshire. There he was converted at the age of twelve and baptized when he was nineteen. Almost immediately he began to preach in the churches in that area.[1]

Gill came to London at a time when orthodox Christianity was being questioned. In these years a reaction against the intolerance of an earlier age was leading to a breakdown of discipline in many of the churches. Although Arminianism had gained a foothold in England in the previous century, men were now questioning the orthodox doctrine of the Trinity. The old Arian heresy, which denied Christ's essential deity, was gaining ground, as was Socinianism, which was an even more extreme form of this teaching. Weakening of doctrine is seldom restricted to a single issue. An anonymous writer in 1732 described some alarming developments among the Dissenters:

> It is very often first manifested in their attacking the divine decrees by applauding the doctrine of universal redemption as a sentiment that is full of benevolence; from thence they appear fond of pleading the cause

---

[1] Biographies include: John Rippon, *A Brief Memoir of the Life and Writing of the Late Rev. John Gill, D.D.* [1809], repr. Harrisburg, Va, Gano Books, 1992; George M. Ella, *John Gill and the Cause of God and Truth*, Go Publications, Egglestone, Co. Durham, 1995; Robert W. Oliver, 'John Gill: His Life and Ministry', in Michael A. G. Haykin, ed., *The Life and Thought of John Gill (1697–1771)*, Brill, Leiden, 1997.

[3]

of the heathens, and of the possibility of salvation merely by the light of nature in a sincere improvement of the powers and faculties of men; and by degrees these charitable sentiments produce a small opinion of revelation, and of the necessity of it in order to salvation ... No wonder they became hereupon sceptics and amongst other truths the doctrine of the Trinity is with them a matter of jest and ridicule.[2]

In the face of such heresies John Gill emerged as a powerful advocate of orthodoxy. He also wrote a detailed defence of the doctrines of grace, *The Cause of God and Truth*. He was called upon to defend Baptist principles and to defend Dissenters generally against the charge of schism. His *magnum opus* was his *Exposition of the Old and New Testaments*. The *New Testament* began to appear in folio volumes in 1746. The last volume of the *Old Testament* was completed in 1765. With the completion of this work Gill became the first person to complete a verse by verse commentary on the whole of Scripture in the English language. His commentary was followed by a *Body of Divinity*, a systematic theology which was finished in 1770. Gill's writings brought him to the attention of a public far beyond that of the London Particular Baptist churches. The completion of his *Exposition of the New Testament* was the occasion when the University of Aberdeen made him a Doctor of Divinity. Professor Osborn of Aberdeen explained that this was 'on account of the honest and learned defence of the true sense of the Holy Scriptures against the profane attacks of Deists and Infidels, and the reputation of his other works'.[3]

2. Doctrinal Developments

Gill's role in the defence of the faith at a time when it was seriously challenged should not be overlooked or underestimated. Sadly, however, there were areas in his teaching which led to modifications of Particular Baptist theology and had serious implications for the future. The Horsleydown congregation in London, to which he was called in his

---

[2] 'View of the Dissenting Interest in London of the Presbyterian and Independent Denominations from the year 1695 to the 25 of December 1731', Unpublished manuscript in Dr Williams's Library, London, MS. 38.18., pp. 82-3. Quoted by permission. On Socinianism, see also the footnote on pp. 51-2.

[3] Rippon, *Memoir*, p. 59.

The Legacy of John Gill

mid-twenties, occupied a prominent place among the Particular Baptist churches. Its wooden meeting house in Goat Yard held almost a thousand worshippers. It had been served by Benjamin Keach until his death in 1704, and after that by Keach's son-in-law, Benjamin Stinton. Keach had been one of the Particular Baptist leaders of the previous century and had played a prominent part in the affairs of the 1689 Assembly. Although he had died in 1704, the memory of his ministry was still dear when Gill paid his first visit to the congregation. His successor Benjamin Stinton died suddenly in 1719 and it was as the protégé of another son-in-law of Keach, Thomas Crosby, that John Gill came to London.[4]

In 1697 Keach had drawn up a *Covenant and Articles of Faith* for the church, based on the *1689 Confession*.[5] Between the time of Gill's call to the pastorate (September 1719) and his ordination (March 1720) the church passed through a time of uncertainty, when a number of members left. In October 1719 Gill's supporters re-affirmed Keach's *Covenant*, possibly to emphasize their legitimacy as Keach's old church.[6] While it is unlikely that Gill had by then arrived at his final theological convictions, he must have become increasingly uneasy with Keach's *Confession* with the passing of the years.[7] This became evident in 1729 when Gill presented a new doctrinal statement to the church. This *Declaration of Faith and Practice* was approved, copied into the church book, and printed by order of the church.[8]

Gill's *Declaration*, consisting of twelve articles of faith, is shorter than Keach's *Confession*, but its omissions are significant. Following the *1689*

---

[4] Rippon, *Memoir*. I have discussed these events in greater detail in 'The Life and Ministry of John Gill', pp 12–17.

[5] Benjamin Keach, *A Short Confession of Faith Containing the Substance of All the Fundamental Articles in the Larger Confession Put Forth by All the Elders of the Baptized Churches Owning Personal Election and Final Perseverance*, London, 1697, after referred to as Keach's *Confession*.

[6] B. R. White, 'John Gill in London, 1719–1729, A Biographical Fragment', *Baptist Quarterly*, 23, 1967–8, pp. 72–9, gives an illuminating account of the way in which Gill escaped from Keach's shadow and from dependence upon the Keach family. See also Oliver, 'John Gill: His Life and Ministry', pp. 17–18.

[7] B. R. White, 'John Gill in London', pp. 82ff.   [8] Ibid., p. 87.

Confession, Keach had taught the free offer of the gospel,[9] which he included under the heading of effectual calling. Gill excluded all reference to the gospel offer from his *Declaration*, although he did not explicitly reject it, as did some nineteenth-century statements.[10] It is reasonable to assume that in 1729 some members of Gill's church still viewed this matter as they had done, when Keach's *Covenant* was re-affirmed in 1719, but Gill was clearly preparing the way for the acceptance of other views.

Possibly of even greater significance is Gill's treatment of justification. In this he made no reference to faith at all. This was a significant departure from both the *1689 Confession* and Keach's *Covenant*.[11] Events were to show that Gill believed that the justification of the elect is from eternity. However, his careful wording of this article in the *Declaration* made it possible to believe either justification by faith or justification from eternity. He wrote:

> We believe that the justification of God's elect is only by the righteousness of Christ imputed to them, without the consideration of any works of righteousness done by them and that the full and free pardon of all their sins and transgressions, past, present and to come is only by the blood of Christ according to the riches of his grace.[12]

Gill's words are significant. In 1730 he published a small work on justification, which plunged him into controversy. The cause of the contention was that the larger part of the work was devoted to arguing the case for eternal justification. Many years later in his work *A Complete Body of Doctrinal and Practical Divinity* he declared, 'God's will, decree or

---

[9] 'He doth persuade and enable us to imbrace [sic] Jesus Christ freely as he is offered in the Gospel.' Keach, *Articles*, p. 12.

[10] For example [J. Gadsby], *Rules and Articles of a Particular Baptist Church*, London, 1852, XV, p. 6. 'We deny offers of grace and every doctrine and sentiment that tends to rob the Lord Jesus Christ of his glory.' This doctrinal statement, published by J. Gadsby, reflected the thinking of Gospel Standard churches and was published for their use. See Chapter 11.

[11] *1689 Confession*, XI, 2, 'Faith thus receiving and resting on Christ and his righteousness is the alone instrument of justification.'

[12] J. Gill, *Declaration of Faith and Practice*, London, 1764, pp. 8–9.

purpose to justify his elect, is the eternal justification of them'.[13] The doctrine of eternal justification had been fiercely debated in the previous century when it was associated with antinomianism. However, following the position adopted by the *Westminster Confession* and the *Savoy Declaration*, the *1689 Confession* firmly rejected this doctrine, stating instead that men

> are not justified personally until the Holy Spirit doth in due time actually apply Christ unto them.[14]

The question was also raised during the deliberations of the 1689 Assembly and again bluntly dismissed.

> None can be said to be actually reconciled, justified or adopted, until they are really implanted into Jesus Christ by faith.[15]

There is thus a clear divergence between the teachings of the *1689 Confession* and John Gill, who taught that believers had been eternally united to Christ before the Fall, eternally justified, and eternally adopted.[16]

Gill taught that justification is an eternal act of God, very closely linked with his election of sinners. He wrote, 'It does not begin to take place in time, or at believing, but is antecedent to any act of faith.'[17]

Gill seems to work on the assumption that since the decree to elect is election, so the decree to justify is justification. If such an analogy were true it might be argued that the decree to create is creation and the decree to redeem is redemption. This error can only lead to evangelistic and pastoral confusion. Faith, instead of being directed towards Christ as the sinner's only hope, becomes a belief by the elect sinner that he is justified. To some extent Gill safeguarded his hearers from such a rationalistic view because he believed that conversion involved the conviction of sin, creating a deep sense of personal need which, under the teaching of the Holy

---

[13] John Gill, *The Doctrine of Justification by the Righteousness of Christ Stated and Maintained*, 1756 [1730], p. 52.

[14] *1689 Confession*, XI, 4.

[15] Quoted in Joseph Ivimey, *A History of the English Baptists* (4 vols., 1811–30), vol. 1, p. 495; hereafter *HEB*.

[16] Gill, *Body of Divinity*., pp. 198, 201. [17] Ibid., p. 203.

Spirit, would lead on to an assurance of salvation as sinners looked to Christ revealed in the gospel.[18]

Gill's teaching on justification is closely linked to his doctrine of the Covenant. In his *Body of Doctrinal Divinity* he devoted considerable attention to the Covenant of Grace.[19] At first sight it might appear that Gill emphasized a doctrine which lay at the heart of the teaching of so many Calvinistic preachers of the seventeenth century, both Baptist and Paedobaptist. These earlier theologians have often been described as Federalists. Thomas B. Ascol has helpfully defined Federalism as 'an attempt to define divine truth in terms of the covenant relationships which God has established with men'.[20] While Gill's language may be similar to that of the Federalists, he took the Covenant of Grace back into the divine decree and taught that the Covenant is an arrangement between the three Persons of the Trinity, made before the Fall, equating it with what theologians have often described as the Covenant of Redemption. By contrast the *1689 Confession,* following Westminster and Savoy, declared:

> Man having brought himself under the curse of the law by his fall, it pleased the Lord to make a covenant of grace, wherein he freely offereth unto sinners life and salvation by Jesus Christ, requiring of them faith in him, that they may be saved; and promising to give unto all those that are ordained to eternal life his Holy Spirit to make them willing and able to believe.[21]

---

[18] In a very helpful article on the doctrine of eternal justification in *Reformation Today,168*, March/April 1999, Earl Blackburn warns that in the USA some teachers of this doctrine have minimized 'effectual calling and vital experimental union with Christ. Biblical experience is soon passed by or minimized'. This did not happen among the people described in this book because of their strong emphasis on experimental godliness.

[19] *Body of Divinity*, pp. 209-50. See also pp. 345-60. The *Body of Divinity* consists of 'A Body of Doctrinal Divinity' and a shorter 'Body of Practical Divinity'.

[20] Thomas B. Ascol, 'The Doctrine of Grace; A Critical Analysis of Federalism in the Theologies of John Gill and Andrew Fuller', Ph.D. thesis presented to Southwestern Baptist Theological Seminary, Fort Worth, Texas, 1989, p. 1.

[21] *1689 Confession*, VII, 2.

The Legacy of John Gill

Ascol wrote: 'Gill so closely identifies the council [the Covenant of Redemption] with the covenant of grace that the distinctions between them are virtually meaningless. This results in the inevitable tendency to collapse salvation history back into eternity – an error which seventeenth century federalism diligently seeks to avoid.'[22]

Having transferred the Covenant of Grace from time to eternity, Gill could ignore the reference to the free offer of 'life and salvation by Jesus Christ' taught in earlier Confessions of Faith. In another context he wrote:

> That there are universal offers of grace and salvation made to all men, I utterly deny; nay I deny that they are made to any; no not to God's elect: grace and salvation are promised for them in the everlasting covenant, procured for them by Christ, published and revealed in the gospel, and applied by the Spirit.[23]

In his *Body of Divinity*, Gill had to face the objection that there are many exhortations to sinners in the Bible. His reply was that

> these passages have no respect to spiritual and internal conversion, but to an external reformation of life and manners.[24]

Faced with the accounts of Christ's desire to gather the people of Jerusalem in Matthew 22:37, he replied:

> This gathering is not to be understood of conversion; but of attendance on the ministry of the word under John the Baptist, Christ himself, and his apostles.[25]

Gill's attitude to the gospel offer indicates that he had been influenced by teaching popularized by Joseph Hussey, a Congregational minister in Cambridge earlier in the century. Hussey had published his views in a volume entitled *God's Operations of Grace but No Offers of His Grace*. His teaching proved attractive to beleaguered Dissenters and was carried amongst the Particular Baptists by John Skepp,[26] formerly a member of

[22] Ascol, 'The Doctrine of Grace', p. 77.
[23] Gill, *The Doctrine of Predestination Stated*, London, 1752, p. 29.
[24] Gill, *Body of Divinity*, p. 549.   [25] Ibid., p. 550.
[26] For details of John Skepp, see Walter Wilson, *The History and Antiquities of Dissenting Churches and Meeting Houses in London* (4 vols., 1808-14), vol. 2, pp. 572-4; vol. 4, p. 216.

Hussey's church at Cambridge. Skepp became a Baptist and was called to the pastorate of the Curriers' Hall Church, London. His only work, *Divine Energy*, also taught the non-offer doctrine. It was published posthumously in 1722. John Skepp had presided at Gill's ordination in 1720. Later, Gill was to identify with Skepp's theology by writing a preface to the second edition of *Divine Energy* in 1751.[27] Another link in this story may be John Noble, who preached at Gill's ordination. While Gill was still a preacher in Northamptonshire, Noble had recommended him for a grant from the Particular Baptist Fund. Noble, the pastor of another London church, was known to be opposed to the free offer of the gospel.

Closely linked to the debate about the free offer of the gospel was the question of whether it was the duty of all men to repent and believe in Christ. This question was raised in 1737 in an anonymous pamphlet, *A Modern Question Modestly Answered*, written by Matthias Maurice of Rothwell.[28] Maurice's answer to the question of man's responsibility was that he did have a duty to believe the gospel. He was opposed by Lewis Wayman of Kimbolton[29] and by John Brine,[30] who had been converted under Gill's earlier preaching in Northamptonshire, and who was by this time pastor of Skepp's old church at Curriers' Hall, London. Gill only intervened in the 'Modern Controversy' to defend himself against the charge of Antinomianism.[31] The controversy gave prominence to the views of Gill and Brine and, according to John Ryland, Jr., was of considerable importance.

> Through the influence of Mr Brine and Dr Gill, who both took the negative side of the question [i.e. do men have a duty to repent and believe?]

---

[27] J. Skepp, *Divine Energy, or The Efficacious Operations of the Spirit of God upon the Soul of Man*, [1722] 2nd ed. London, 1751.

[28] G. F. Nuttall argued convincingly for Maurice's authorship, 'Northamptonshire and the *Modern Question*', *Journal of Theological Studies*, *16*, 1965, p.102. On the other hand, John Ryland, Jr, attributed the pamphlet to Gutteridge of Oundle (*Life of Fuller*, London, 1818, p. 5. See also P. Toon, *Hyper-Calvinism*, 1967, pp. 131 ff.

[29] Lewis Wayman, *A Further Enquiry after Truth*, 1738.

[30] John Brine, *A Refutation of Arminian Principles*, 1739.

[31] John Gill, *The Necessity of Good Works unto Salvation*, 1739.

The Legacy of John Gill

(though the latter never wrote on the subject), this opinion spread pretty much among the ministers of the Baptist denomination. And though the controversy had subsided, and was but little known among the people, yet the preachers were too much restrained from imitating our Lord and his apostles, in calling on sinners to 'repent and believe the Gospel'.[32]

In Gill's church in Southwark his *Declaration of Faith and Practice* replaced the older confessions in 1729 and he appears to have been satisfied with this new *Declaration*, for after its inscription in the church book in 1729, only one addition was made.[33] This was a statement strengthening its adherence to the doctrine of the eternal Sonship of Christ and denying the pre-existarian view that Christ's human soul existed before time.[34] This statement was added in 1768. In the same year the church excommunicated a member who rejected the doctrine of Christ's eternal Sonship.[35] Pre-existarian teaching can also be traced back to Joseph Hussey and gained support among Hyper-Calvinists.[36] Clearly Gill was not prepared to follow Hussey into any deviations from orthodox Christology.

Whereas the *1689 Confession* expressed the creed of a denomination, Gill's *Declaration*, of course, expressed only the teaching of a single church. It was, however, an important church, and Gill was to become an

---

[32] J. Ryland, *Life of Andrew Fuller*, London, 1818, p. 5.

[33] J. Rippon asserted that a number of additions were made after the *Declaration* was drawn up. If so, these were presumably added before it was inscribed in the Church Book, as Seymour J. Price could find no trace of alteration to the 1729 version in the Church Book, apart from the alteration mentioned here. 'Dr. Gill's Confession of 1729', *Baptist Quarterly*, 4, 1928–9, pp. 366–71.

[34] This view was developed in High Calvinist circles in the eighteenth century; see P. Toon, 'The Growth of a Supralapsarian Christology', *Evangelical Quarterly*, 29, pp. 23–9. It will be further discussed in Chapter 10.

[35] R. P. Roberts, *London Calvinistic Baptists and the Evangelical Revival*, Richard Owen Roberts Publishers, Wheaton, Illinois, p. 180. For further discussion of Gill's defence of orthodox Christology, see R. W. Oliver, *John Gill, Orthodox Dissenter*, Strict Baptist Historical Society, Dunstable, 1996.

[36] P. Toon, 'The Growth of a Supralapsarian Christology', p. 25. See also Andrew Fuller's statement in the *Life* by John Ryland, p. 38. It was later to be a cause of division among Strict Baptists.

increasingly influential Particular Baptist minister. When the Horsleydown Church ordered the printing of the *Declaration* in 1729, it probably had an eye to a wider readership than the members of its own congregation. Further printings were made in 1739, 1764 and 1768.[37] How many other churches adopted the *Declaration* is impossible to tell.[38] Gill's prestige would have given it a ready acceptance and during those years, described by John Ryland as the time of the 'influence of Mr Brine and Dr Gill', it was probably more widely received as a summary of Particular Baptist beliefs than the old *1689 Confession*.

3. Experimental Religion

Gill's reputation as a theologian has led some to suppose that his teaching was aridly intellectual. No greater mistake could be made. In part this error may have arisen from the fact that Gill's controversial writings attracted much attention in his lifetime and have done so since. Another reason giving rise to this view may be the modern tendency to polarize matters of Christian doctrine and experience. C. H. Spurgeon paid high praise to Gill's experimental teaching in his tribute to his *Commentary on the Song of Solomon*: 'Those who despise it have never read it, or are incapable of elevated spiritual feelings.'[39] In this early work, based on sermons preached in his twenties, Gill explains how by 'a sight of Christ's loveliness . . . a glimpse of the king in his beauty, [the believer's] heart is won and his soul is ravished and drawn forth in love to him'.[40] Gill demonstrates a passionate love for Christ, and he is also enraptured by a realization of Christ's love for his church.

---

[37] Seymour J. Price refers to the 1729 and 1739 printings on the authority of the Horsleydown Church Book, 'Dr. Gill's Confession of 1729', p 367. Copies of the 1764 and 1768 editions are deposited in the Angus Library.

[38] In 1741, the Particular Baptist Church at Smarden, Kent, adopted Gill's *Declaration* as its doctrinal basis. This church has no known connection with Gill or his church. 'Smarden Church Book', transcribed by K. W. H. Howard, Bethersden, Kent, 1981.

[39] C. H. Spurgeon, *Commenting and Commentaries* [1876], repr. London, Banner of Truth, 1969, p. 113.

[40] John Gill, *An Exposition of the Song of Songs* [1729], repr. London, 1854, p. 21.

Moreover she is so [delightful] as she is clothed with his righteousness and adorned with the graces of his Spirit; her countenance is comely; her voice, both in prayer and praise is sweet; her faith and love are ravishing, and her company delightful: in short he takes abundance of satisfaction and pleasure in her: she is all delight to him; her countenance, voice, actions and gesture.[41]

Gill's doctrinal approach to matters of Christian experience is in harmony with the Puritans of the previous century and is healthier than that of some of his nineteenth-century admirers. In a recent study of Gill's spirituality, Dr Gregory A. Wills has argued that

Gill's insistence upon the happiness and pleasure of Christian spirituality bears a striking resemblance to that of his American contemporary, Jonathan Edwards. Like Edwards, Gill made spiritual affections – love, delight, sweetness, pleasure – the heart of Christian life. Believers 'tasted a real sweetness' in Christ's love and delighted in its 'comforts' and 'pleasures' as well as its benefits.[42]

Gill's sermons on the Song of Solomon were preached very early in his London pastorate but in his last major work, the *Body of Divinity*, he also emphasized the importance of experimental Christianity. His mature consideration of this subject appears in the chapter on 'Communion with God', but it also pervades the whole of the section on the 'Worship of God' in which this chapter appears. He writes of a mutual converse with God, which he likens to the experiences of Abraham and Moses:

Something similar to this, is the experience of all the saints, when the Lord appears unto them, and talks with them, and tells them that he has loved them with an everlasting love, and has drawn them to himself with the cords of it; when he visits them, and discloses the secrets of his heart to them, Psalm 25:14, and they talk with him, and speak to him in prayer; they have access through Christ and that with freedom and boldness through his blood and righteousness, and come up even to his seat,

[41] Ibid, p. 273.
[42] Gregory A. Wills, 'A Fire that Burns Within: The Spirituality of John Gill', Michael A .G. Haykin, ed., *John Gill*, p. 195. I am grateful to Dr Wills for his fine study of Gill's spirituality.

and tell him all their mind, make known their requests to him, and pour out their souls before him; much of communion with God lies in prayer, private, family and public.[43]

Like John Owen, Gill argued the possibility of communion with each member of the Trinity. For him such communion is the high point of Christian experience:

> It is beyond all the enjoyments of life, preferable to everything that can be had on earth; the light of God's countenance, his gracious presence, and communion with him, put more joy into the hearts of his people, than the greatest increase of worldly things, it is this which makes wisdom's ways, ways of pleasantness, and her paths, paths of peace; it is this which makes the tabernacles of God amiable and lovely, and a day in his house better than a thousand elsewhere; and because so valuable, hence the apostle John, in an exulting manner, says, *Truly our fellowship is with the Father, and with his Son, Jesus Christ!* 1 John 1:3.[44]

It is to be regretted that admiration of Gill's great gifts must have caused many preachers to evade the biblical calls to the unconverted to repent and to turn to Christ. The consequences of this were serious, not only among the Calvinistic Baptists in his generation but also among those of succeeding generations. Some of his admirers were able to raise themselves above the fatalism to which this system often leads. In some cases, preachers powerfully emphasized the necessity of an experimental knowledge of the great truths of the gospel and thereby caused many hearers to cry to God for salvation. There were others who acknowledged that they had a duty to preach the gospel to every creature but shrank from pressing the claims of Christ directly on their hearers. Sadly others advanced further into fatalism until they embraced what Spurgeon described as 'the soul-destroying system which takes manhood from a man and makes him no more responsible than an ox'. He continued:

> I cannot imagine a more ready instrument in the hands of Satan for the ruin of souls than a minister who tells sinners that it is not their duty to

---

[43] Gill, *Body of Divinity*, p. 848.
[44] Ibid. p, 851.

repent of their sins or to believe in Christ, and who has the arrogance to call himself a gospel minister, while he teaches that God hates some men infinitely and unchangeably for no reason whatever but simply because he chooses to do so. O my brethren! May the Lord save you from the voice of the charmer, and keep you ever deaf to the voice of error.[45]

It is fair to point out that Spurgeon did not charge Gill himself with such extremism. Spurgeon said of Gill that he was 'the Coryphæus [leader of a party] of hyper-Calvinism', significantly adding, 'but if his followers never went beyond their master, they would not go very far astray'.[46]

---

[45] C. H. Spurgeon, *Revival Year Sermons,* London: Banner of Truth, 1959, p. 88.
[46] *Commenting and Commentaries*, p. 9.

2

Blessing in the Cotswolds

Father of mercies, bow Thine ear,
Attentive to our earnest prayer;
We plead for those who plead for Thee,
Successful pleaders may they be!

Let thronging multitudes around,
Hear from their lips the joyful sound;
In humble strains Thy grace adore,
And feel Thy new-creating power.

Let sinners break their massy chains,
Distressed souls forget their pains,
And light through distant realms be spread,
Till Zion rears her drooping head.

Benjamin Beddome

Situated in the valley of the Windrush, one of the loveliest of the Cotswold streams, is the village of Bourton-on-the-Water. Known today as the 'Venice of the Cotswolds', this Gloucestershire village attracts thousands of tourists every year. Probably few are aware of the great work of grace that was wrought in its Baptist chapel during the eighteenth century. This was the scene of a remarkable ministry, the impact of which was felt over a wide area. People from surrounding villages were drawn to the Baptist meeting-house; from Bourton preachers went out to preach the gospel in other places, sometimes with remarkable results; while hymns composed in this small region have been sung in hundreds of congregations throughout the British Isles and North America.

Blessing in the Cotswolds

In the eighteenth century, Bourton was a remote settlement. When in 1771 moves were promoted to enclose the open fields, it was reported that there were six hundred and fifteen inhabitants; of these, eight were farmers, six were farming gentlemen, and four were graziers. In the Middle Ages, the Cotswolds had been a major wool producing area, largely under the control of the great monasteries; but by 1771, there was little evidence of the woollen industry around Bourton, and land in the valley was mainly devoted to general or dairy farming. Only three of the holdings were over two hundred acres. As the Windrush flowed through the village and along the length of the main street, it passed by a fine double-fronted house, built in 1740 as the Baptist manse. This house still stands, but is now a hotel. In 1771, the minister who lived in this fine building was Benjamin Beddome. Since 1741, he had served the congregation that now numbered between five and six hundred people – a figure that almost equalled Bourton's total population! It needs to be noted, however, that many of the congregation came to the meeting-house from the surrounding villages, lying within a twenty-five-mile radius of Bourton. While other Particular Baptist churches were changing their understanding of the doctrines of faith and justification, this church, under Beddome, continued to bear testimony to the doctrinal position of the *1689 Confession*. Benjamin Beddome's ministry at Bourton-on-the-Water (1741–95) provides a vital link to earlier Particular Baptist history, while also offering an important perspective from which we can study a number of significant developments that were to take place later in this story.

1. The Making of a Minister[1]

Benjamin Beddome was born in January 1718 at Henley-in-Arden, Warwickshire. His father, John Beddome, was the pastor of the Baptist Church in nearby Alcester, an office he had held since 1697. In 1714 he married Rachel Brandon, the daughter of a London silversmith. Her

---

[1] For details of Beddome's life see J. Rippon, *Baptist Register*, 2, pp. 314–26 and B. Beddome, *Sermons and Brief Memoir*, London, 1835. I am indebted to Mr Derrick Holmes for the loan of materials on Beddome and for giving me the benefit of his researches.

family claimed descent from Charles Brandon, the sixteenth-century Duke of Suffolk and grandfather of Lady Jane Grey. Rachel herself received a good education at the expense of a wealthy aunt.

Like his wife, John Beddome was a Londoner. He had earlier been a member of Benjamin Keach's church at Horsleydown. By that church he was sent into the work of the ministry and subsequently received a call to Alcester in 1697. He settled in Henley-in-Arden where he bought a large house, partly for his home and partly to be fitted up as a place of worship, presumably as an extension of the work of the Alcester church. In 1711, he was joined by a colleague, Bernard Foskett, previously a surgeon in London. Foskett and Beddome became life-long friends and worked harmoniously together at Alcester until 1719, when Foskett was called to Bristol to become co-pastor of the historic Broadmead Church. At that time Broadmead Church was the home of the denomination's only seminary.

Benjamin was the eldest of five children born to John and Rachel Beddome. When Benjamin was about seven years old, his father accepted a call to become the pastor of the Pithay church in Bristol. Benjamin grew up in Bristol, receiving a good education, and was eventually apprenticed to a surgeon and apothecary. At the Pithay Chapel, Benjamin sat Sunday by Sunday under his father's ministry. John Beddome was reputed to have been a warm and earnest preacher. One of his hearers described him as 'remarkable for his spiritual winning discourses especially to young converts and enquirers',[2] but Benjamin appears to have hardened his heart under his father's preaching, to the great grief of his parents.

A change came suddenly in 1737, as he listened to a visiting minister, Mr Ware of Chesham. The young man now attended the services under a deep sense of the conviction of sin, sitting himself in the back of the gallery to hide his tears. Assurance of salvation did not come immediately, but after it was granted, he recorded his experience in these words:

---

[2] 'Joshua Thomas to John Rippon', c. 1777, manuscript deposited in the Angus Library, Regent's Park College, Oxford.

> 'Tis done; and with transporting joy,
> I read the heaven-inspired lines;
> There mercy spreads its brightest beams,
> And truth, with dazzling lustre shines.
>
> Here's heavenly food for hungry souls,
> And mines of gold to enrich the poor,
> Here's healing balm for every wound,
> A salve for every festering sore.

By the time his apprenticeship was finished Benjamin was convinced that God was calling him into the ministry, although, strangely, he seems to have delayed being baptized and joining the church. For two years he studied under the supervision of his father's old friend, Bernard Foskett, at nearby Broadmead. Completing his studies at Broadmead, he transferred to the Independent Academy in London, then under the leadership and instruction of Abraham Taylor and John Walker. Abraham Taylor had challenged John Gill's teaching on eternal justification and it may be significant that Beddome attended this particular academy. It may also be significant that he did not attend his father's old home church, now pastored by John Gill, but chose instead to sit under the ministry of Samuel Wilson at Prescot Street. Here he was baptized on 27 September 1739. In the following year, the Prescot Street church recognized his call to the Christian ministry. His father seems to have considered that his son's call to preach was somewhat premature and wrote:

> I am sorry that Mr Wilson is in such a hurry to call you to the ministry. It would be time enough just before you came away; but supposing it must be so, I think you should not preach in public above once or twice, at most, at your own place, and nowhere else except Mr Stennett and his people ask you.[3]

Joseph Stennett (1692–1758) was pastor of the church in Little Wild Street, from which Bernard Foskett had been commended to the ministry many years earlier.

---

[3] Quoted, Thomas Brooks, *Pictures from the Past,* London, 1861, p. 23.

2. Blessing at Bourton-on-the-Water

Shortly after his ministerial gifts were recognized, Beddome was invited to preach at the Baptist church in Bourton-on-the-Water. This church seems to have been founded around the year 1655 and for a time was pastored by Anthony Palmer who had been ejected from the parish church of Bourton in 1662. In 1740 the church was looking for a pastor and Beddome was invited to supply the pulpit for an extended period of probation.

Eighteenth-century Baptist churches did not rush to appoint their new pastors and it was more than two years before Beddome was formally ordained to this charge. However, during this initial period of his ministry at Bourton, the church experienced remarkable blessing. In the early months of 1741, about forty people were converted. By 1745 further blessing led to the reception of seventy-three new members.

These blessings coincided with the early days of the Evangelical Revival and the remarkable events in Bourton cannot be isolated from what was happening elsewhere. In May 1741, George Whitefield wrote from nearby Gloucester: 'The LORD works by me day by day . . . the LORD manifested himself in the great congregation there [Bristol], and doth likewise here. Last night we saw and felt his power.'[4]

Although accompanied by most encouraging results, Beddome's early preaching seems to have needed some improvement. His father wrote to him in May 1742:

> I wish from my heart I could prevail with you not to strain your voice so much in the delivery of your sermons; and if you would make them shorter and less crowded with matter, it would be more acceptable and edifying to your hearers, and more safe and easy for yourself. Strive then to comply with this advice, which is given in great affection, and, I think, with judgement. If you deliver the great truths of the gospel with calmness, and with a soft, mellow voice, they will drop as the gentle rain or dew. For the good of souls, then and for your own good strive after this.[5]

---

[4] *Letters of George Whitefield, 1734–1742* [1771], repr. Edinburgh: Banner of Truth, 1976, 'George Whitefield to Mr S.', p. 261.

[5] B. Beddome, *Sermons and Memoir*, 1835, pp. xiv, xv.

A few months later his father repeated his advice, and urged his son not to allow services to extend beyond two hours. Benjamin appears to have accepted his father's wisdom. John Rippon later recalled: 'Though his voice was low, his delivery was forcible and demanded attention. He addressed the hearts and consciences of his hearers. His inventive faculty was extraordinary, and threw an endless variety into his public services. Nature, providence and grace had formed him for eminence in the church of Christ.'

Beddome's ordination took place at Bourton on 23 September 1743, when Bernard Foskett and Joseph Stennett preached. John Beddome did not feel strong enough to travel on horseback the sixty miles from Bristol. The Bourton church saw its membership continue to increase through the first half of their new pastor's ministry. A peak was reached in 1764, when Beddome noted that he had seen one hundred and seventy-six members added to the church in that remarkable year. In 1748 the meeting-house was reconstructed and enlarged, but even this proved insufficient for the rapid growth of the congregation, and a new meeting-house was built in 1764–65. Additions continued throughout the remainder of Beddome's pastorate, although deaths, transfers, and discipline meant that the overall membership declined to one hundred and twenty-three at the time of Beddome's death. While chapel attendance remained at between five and six hundred people, it is clear that fewer people were being converted during the later years of his ministry, a fact that exercised Beddome greatly. However, this trend should not make us conclude that Beddome's usefulness had declined with age.[6]

3. Beddome's Teaching

The library of Benjamin Beddome was bequeathed to the Bourton church, and is now housed in the Angus Library, Regents Park College, Oxford. Its catalogue reveals that it was very well stocked with Puritan books from the previous century, as well as books written by his

[6] M. A. G. Haykin, 'Benjamin Beddome', in Haykin, ed., *The British Particular Baptists, 1638–1910*, vol. 1 (Springfield Missouri, Particular Baptist Press, 1998), pp. 173–4.

eighteenth-century contemporaries. Beddome's own teaching seems to have been close to that of the Particular Baptists of the Puritan era.

Several volumes of Beddome's sermons have survived, although he did not personally prepare any for the press. As part of the preparation of his sermons, he wrote out a fairly full manuscript, which was then expanded in delivery. His sermons are carefully argued and conclude with several points of application.

Beddome's theology was that of the *1689 Confession*. This should not surprise us, for he had grown up at a time when the *Confession*'s teaching was being reasserted in the face of a strong challenge. During the 1730s, Bernard Foskett, with the support of John Beddome, fought against the challenge of Arianism in the Western Association of Particular Baptist Churches. With some difficulty they persuaded the associated churches to adopt the *1689 Confession* as their doctrinal basis. As a result the Arian ministers left the Association.

During his ministry at Bourton-on-the-Water, Benjamin Beddome used *The Baptist Catechism* as a teaching tool for the instruction of the children and adults in the congregation. A Baptist revision of The Westminster *Shorter Catechism*, it reflected the theology of the *1689 Confession*. Beddome's method of using this teaching tool was to follow up each question of the *Catechism* by asking a number of subsidiary questions 'with advantage to the children, and to many grown persons who attended thereupon'. At the instigation of his friends he published the fruit of this work in 1752 under the title, *A Scriptural Exposition of the Baptist Catechism by Way of Question and Answer*. He explained:

> The Paedobaptist churches having long been furnished with many useful and instructive expositions of their catechism, and something of the same nature being wanted amongst those of Baptist persuasion; I was at length induced to compose the following, in imitation of Mr Henry's, which was published with great acceptance several years ago.

He justified his practice of catechizing by a warning drawn from 'the melancholy state of those churches and families where catechizing is entirely thrown aside'. He maintained that many of them 'have degenerated from the faith, and others from the practice of the gospel'. An illustration of his balance and his rejection of Hyper-Calvinism can be seen in his treatment of the doctrine of the effectual call.

What is effectual calling?

Effectual calling is the work of God's Spirit, whereby, convincing us of our sin and misery, enlightening our minds in the knowledge of Christ, and renewing our wills, he doth persuade and enable us to embrace Jesus Christ, freely offered to us in the gospel.

Is there an outward call given to all men?
Yes, *Unto you, O men, I call,* Prov. 8:4.

Does God call by his works of creation?
Yes. For *there is no speech nor language where their voice is not heard,* Psalm 19:3.

And by his works of providence?
Yes. *The LORD's voice crieth unto the city,* Micah 6:9.

And by his word?
Yes. *He sent forth his servants to call them that were bidden,* Matt. 22:3.

And by the common motions of his Spirit?
Yes. *My Spirit shall not always strive with man,* Gen. 6:3.

But is this call always effectual?
No. *They would not come,* Matt. 22:3.

Are the special calls of the Spirit the fruit of electing love?
Yes. *Whom he predestinated, them he also called,* Rom. 8:30.

Are they attended with the mighty power of God?
Yes. *Our gospel came not unto you in word only, but also in power,* 1 Thess. 1:5.

And yet suitable to the nature of man?
Yes. *I drew them with the cords of a man,* Hos. 11:4.

And are they always effectual?
Yes. *They shall come,* John 6:37.[7]

---

[7] Benjamin Beddome, *Scriptural Exposition of the Baptist Catechism*, 2nd Edition, Bristol, 1776, pp. 64–5.

4. Beddome's Hymns

Beddome's hymns have helped to preserve the memory of this noteworthy minister of the gospel and reflect the evangelical Calvinism of the Particular Baptists. He had the unusual practice of composing a new hymn every week with which to conclude the morning service. Each verse was read by the clerk before being sung by the congregation who, of course, would not have had access to a printed copy. After Beddome's death a selection of eight hundred and fifty of his hymns was published. They appeared with an eloquent commendation from Robert Hall, Jr.

Beddome's sense of the transcendence of God appears in the hymn, *Great God! My Maker and my King*:

> Great God! My Maker and my King,
> Of Thee I'll speak, of Thee I'll sing;
> All Thou hast done, and all Thou dost,
> Declare Thee good, proclaim Thee just.
>
> Thy terror and Thy acts of grace;
> Thy threatening rod, and smiling face;
> Thy wounding and Thy healing word;
> A world undone, a world restored;
>
> While these excite my fear and joy,
> While these my tuneful lips employ,
> Accept, O Lord, the humble song,
> The tribute of a trembling tongue.

A hymn on the high priestly work of Christ includes these lines,

> So fair a face bedewed with tears!
> What beauty e'en in grief appears!
> He wept, He bled, He died for you!
> What more, ye saints, could Jesus do?
>
> Still His compassions are the same;
> He knows the frailty of our frame;
> Our heaviest burdens He sustains,
> Shares all our sorrows and our pains.

Beddome's passion for the extension of Christ's kingdom was also expressed in verse:

> Shout, for the blessed Jesus reigns;
> Through distant lands His triumphs spread;
> And sinners freed from endless pains,
> Own Him their Saviour and their Head.
>
> He calls His chosen from afar,
> They all at Zion's gates arrive;
> Those who were dead in sin before,
> By sovereign grace are made alive.
>
> Gentiles and Jews His laws obey;
> Nations remote their offerings bring;
> And unconstrained their homage pay
> To their exalted God and King.
>
> O may His holy church increase,
> His word and Spirit still prevail;
> While angels celebrate His praise,
> And saints His growing glories hail.

Written to reflect the various subjects of his Sunday ministry, Beddome's hymns express a wide variety of themes. Perhaps the most poignant was the one written to be sung after his sermon on the text, 'My times are in thy hand' (*Psa.* 31:15). The hymn began with words more immediately applicable to the author than he could have realized when he first wrote them out:

> My times of sorrow and of joy,
> Great God are in thy hand.

The day after this hymn was first sung, news reached Beddome that his son Benjamin, a promising young man and medical student at Edinburgh, had died of a fever.

5. Wider Influence

Benjamin Beddome's reputation as a preacher spread widely. He regularly attended the meetings of the Midlands Association of Particular

Baptist Churches and on seventeen occasions preached the sermon at their annual gatherings. He also preached in the Northamptonshire area, the centre of another Association. Other churches, not surprisingly, were anxious to secure his services as pastor. In 1748, his father urged him to consider coming to Bristol as his colleague, arguing that a ministry in the city would provide greater opportunity for usefulness; but Benjamin declined the invitation.

Two years later he came under still greater pressure to leave Bourton. Samuel Wilson, his old pastor at Prescot Street, London, died in August 1750. Three months later (November 1750) the Prescot Street Church extended a call to Beddome, sending a separate letter to his Gloucestershire Church requesting the release of their pastor. In its communications, the London Church expressed the fear that it would not be able to continue for long without an able pastor: its members would be drawn away to other churches. Beddome submitted himself to the will of the Bourton Church, pointing out that

> I am solemnly ordained over a people who have treated me with the greatest affection, and many of them have been the seals since I came amongst them – that they have been a long time before unsettled and divided, but are now, through divine mercy harmonious and united – that my labours have been, and, are still, in a measure blest unto them, above a hundred having been added since my first coming amongst them, and four having been proposed this month; in short their hearts seem as much engaged to me as ever, and they will do what they can to make my stay comfortable.

Bourton expressed its sympathy with Prescot Street and assured them of their prayers, but considered that Beddome had been given to them in answer to prayer, and that he had recently recovered from a serious illness in which much prayer for his restoration had been offered, and, above all, that his ministry had been greatly blessed among them. They could not therefore release him. The correspondence continued with suggestions of much greater usefulness in London. Beddome consulted other ministers and a delegation came down from London to meet Beddome, but the Bourton congregation remained steadfast in their attachment to their

Blessing in the Cotswolds

pastor. Beddome's final refusal is interesting. He could consider a move without the church's agreement only if there had been some failure on its part. In this case there had been no failure. He appealed to the writings of the great Puritan John Owen, who declared that 'such removals only are lawful, which are with the free consent of the churches concerned, and with the advice of other churches or their elders with whom they walk in communion'. Beddome added: 'If the prospect of greater usefulness is in itself a sufficient plea for the removal which you press, then it would be impossible for churches of a lower rank ever to be secure of the continuance of their pastors.' The London Church had hinted that if Beddome moved, John Reynolds, a member at Bourton who was assisting Beddome, would be a worthy successor. Beddome argued that Reynolds was already under call from two other churches, and did not feel called to continue in Bourton. Referring to the resolution of his own church, he wrote:

> If my people would have consented to my removal (though I should have had to sacrifice much on account of the great affection I bear them) yet I should have made no scruple of accepting your call. But, as they absolutely refuse it, the will of the Lord be done. I am determined that I will not violently rend myself from them, for I would much rather honour God in a much lower station in which he hath placed me, than intrude myself into a higher without his direction.[8]

This correspondence is of interest for the light it sheds on pastor/church relationships in the eighteenth century. Beddome continued to preach in other churches occasionally, but his influence spread indirectly through those men who were called into the pastoral ministry from the Bourton church.

At least five such men were called into the Christian ministry; three of these, Richard Haynes, John Collett Ryland, and John Reynolds, were converted during the revival of 1741. John Collett Ryland was the first to be called to serve. He was baptized in October 1741, and went to study

---

[8] Thomas Brooks (*Pictures from the Past*, 1861, pp. 30-49) prints the whole correspondence.

at Bristol under Bernard Foskett in 1744, before serving churches in Warwick and Northampton. Ryland's work will be considered in more detail in later chapters.

Richard Haynes, who was baptized in May 1741, was an early convert of the Revival. In 1747, he received permission to preach in other churches after successfully exercising his preaching gifts at Bourton. Haynes lived at Burford, and preached both there and in Oxford, before receiving a call to Bradford on Avon in 1750. Taking up the pastorate there, he had a fruitful ministry until his death in 1768. Although he had no formal ministerial training, the church at Bourton recorded that they considered him to be a 'remarkable' man of 'a savoury spirit'.

John Reynolds was baptized in 1743 at the age of thirteen. He studied the biblical languages with the help of a schoolmaster in Northleach. He then completed a course of further study in Bristol. In 1751, the Bourton Church formally recognized his call to the ministry, and for a number of years he seems to have given occasional ministerial assistance to Beddome. Reynolds also gave periods of extended service to churches in Oxford, Bratton, Cirencester, Cheltenham, and Bromsgrove, although he does not seem to have served as the pastor of any of them. He was described as an earnest and methodical preacher, but was hampered by an injury to his vocal chords. In 1766, he was called to succeed John Brine at Cripplegate, London, where he served until his death in 1792.

The two other men called to the ministry from Bourton Baptist Chapel were Nathaniel Rawlins and Alexander Payne. Rawlins ministered at Trowbridge from 1765 to 1771, and again from 1778 to 1809. Interestingly, Payne had been a preacher among the Methodists, but then renounced Arminianism. He was baptized and joined the Bourton Church, but they were not altogether happy with his ministry. He later served several churches in the Midlands.

At the very end of Beddome's pastorate, Thomas Coles was baptized on 16 August 1795. On 24 August, and still only sixteen, he went to Bristol for ministerial study, just ten days before Beddome's death. Coles's departure for Bristol so soon after becoming a church member may appear to have been somewhat premature. He had however been

Blessing in the Cotswolds

taking detailed notes of Beddome's sermons since he was eleven, and from the age of thirteen read these at a weekly prayer meeting. From Bristol he proceeded to Aberdeen, where he graduated with an MA in 1800. On his completion there he was invited to Cannon Street Church in Birmingham to succeed Samuel Pearce, but declined and instead went to assist Abraham Booth at Prescot Street, London. In 1801 he was called to Bourton, which had been vacant for six years since Beddome's death. Thomas Coles served the church there until his own death in 1840.

Benjamin Beddome's long pastorate at Bourton-on-the-Water ended on 3 September 1795. He served until his death in spite of some years of poor health. In the closing years of his life he received help from two successive ministerial assistants, but he was able to preach almost until the end and was actually composing a hymn just before he died. Over twenty years later Robert Hall, Jr., paid tribute to him:

> Though he spent the principal part of a long life in a village retirement, he was eminent for his colloquial powers, in which he displayed the urbanity of the gentleman and the erudition of the scholar, combined with a more copious vein of Attic salt [refined wit] than any person it has been my lot to know. As a preacher he was universally admired for the piety and unction of his sentiments, the felicity of his arrangement, and the purity, force and simplicity of his language, all of which were recommended by a delivery perfectly natural and graceful.[9]

To Hall's tribute it is important to add that Beddome combined faithfulness to the historic Particular Baptist theology with the evangelical zeal of the eighteenth-century Revival.

---

[9] Robert Hall, *Works*, vol. 4, London, 1833, 'Preface to Beddome's Hymns, 1819', p. 439.

3

Three Noteworthy Leaders

The last quarter of the eighteenth century was marked by a series of lively debates within the Particular Baptist community. The issues raised included the terms of communion, the presentation of the gospel, and the place of the moral law in the life of the believer. These debates were conducted between men who respected one another and who were united by an acceptance of the doctrines of grace and the experimental nature of true Christianity. In this chapter we will be introduced to some of the men who provided leadership among the Particular Baptists during this period. It would be wrong for us to consider them as merely protagonists in the theological debates of their day, for they were all united by a genuine concern for the advancement of Christ's kingdom and they each exercised a significant preaching and pastoral ministry.

1. John Collett Ryland (1723–92)[1]

In 1833, Olinthus Gregory, the biographer of the younger Robert Hall wrote:

> Mr Ryland was a very extraordinary man, whose excellencies and eccentricities were strangely balanced. In him were balanced the ardour and vehemence of Whitefield, with the intrepidity of Luther. His pulpit oratory was of the boldest character, and singularly impressive, when he did not overstep the improprieties of the ministerial function.[2]

---

[1] Published biographies include: William Newman, *Rylandiana: Reminiscences relating to the Rev. John Ryland, A.M. of Northampton*, London, 1835; James Culross, *The Three Rylands*, London, 1897.

[2] Robert Hall, *Works*, vol. 6, 'Brief Memoir of Robert Hall', by Olinthus Gregory, p. 7, London, 1833.

Three Noteworthy Leaders

In 1854, the Independent preacher, William Jay of Bath, recalled his first meeting with Ryland back in 1788. The young man had come up to London to preach for Rowland Hill, when John Ryland, the veteran preacher, called at the house in which he was staying.

> At this moment I did not personally know him. He was singular in appearance: his shoes were square-toed; his wig was five-storied behind; the sleeves of his coat were profusely large and open; and the flaps of his waistcoat encroaching upon his knees. I was struck and awed with his figure; but what could I think when, walking towards me, he laid hold of me by the collar, and shaking his fist in my face, he roared out, 'Young man, if you let the people of Surrey Chapel make you proud, I'll smite you to the ground!' But then, instantly dropping his voice, and taking me by the hand, he made me sit down by his side, and said, 'Sir, nothing can equal the folly of some hearers; they are like apes that hug their young ones to death.' He then mentioned two promising young ministers who had come to town, and had been injured and spoiled by popular caressings; adding other seasonable and useful remarks.[3]

Similar anecdotes of this remarkable man abound. Larger than life, it is not surprising that John Collett Ryland played a significant part in the controversies that were to affect Particular Baptist life at the end of the eighteenth century.

The Rylands had been Dissenters for several generations. John Ryland's grandfather, also John by name, was a Warwickshire farmer and member of the Baptist church at Alcester in the seventeenth century. During the penal times of Charles II and James II, he had to go into hiding on several occasions because of his refusal to attend the parish church; his nonconformity earned him fines of about £1200. John Collett Ryland was a Gloucestershire man, born at Lower Ditchford, near Stow on the Wold. His father, Joseph Ryland, was also a farmer. The family attended the Baptist meeting in Bourton-on-the-Water. John's mother died when he was just five years of age, and in early adolescence he proved to be headstrong and rebellious. He was seventeen years old when Benjamin

---

[3] George Redford and John Angell James, eds., *The Autobiography of William Jay* [1854], repr. Edinburgh: Banner of Truth, 1974, p. 287.

Beddome first came to preach at Bourton Chapel and in the remarkable awakening that followed, he was one of those who were converted. He was baptized and joined the church on 2 October 1741. Almost immediately, he was conscious of a call to the ministry, but his journal indicates a time of intense spiritual exercise: 'I dare not go if [He] does not answer in some way or other.'[4]

His call to the ministry was recognized by the Bourton church, and he was sent to the Bristol Baptist Academy for training under Bernard Foskett, just as his own pastor had been earlier.[5] Ryland did not enjoy his time at Bristol, where Foskett's methods proved too tedious for his restless spirit. However, a later President of the Academy wrote: 'He became an acceptable preacher, an excellent classical scholar, a better mathematician, and a very good Hebraist; he read widely in all directions, and laid a broad and solid foundation for his after acquirements.'[6]

From Bristol, Ryland was called to the pastorate of the Warwick Baptist Church, and there he ministered from 1750 to 1759. At his ordination, one of the officiating ministers was John Brine of London, a prominent Hyper-Calvinist.[7] Ryland was soon to cultivate a close friendship with John Gill,[8] whose system of theology he continued to preach to the end of his life. He seems to have considered the debate over the 'Modern Question'[9] a distraction, and later, when the question of direct appeals to the unconverted was raised, he said, 'Robert Hall, his son and Fuller were busied on it. The devil threw out an empty barrel for them to roll about, while they ought to have been drinking the wine of the

---

[4] Culross, p. 15.

[5] According to Newman, Ryland was more attracted to the teaching of Hugh Evans, Foskett's assistant, ibid., p. 5. Evans was an open communionist, see below pp. 85-6.

[6] Culross, op. cit., p. 16.

[7] Ibid., p. 5. In 1791 Ryland told his friend William Newman that he wished to be buried in Bunhill Fields near his friend Mr Brine, *Rylandiana*, pp. 79, 80. In fact he was buried in Northampton.

[8] Newman referred to 'the unbounded veneration he felt for his friend, Dr Gill.' Ibid., p. 44; cf. pp. v and l56.

[9] See Chapter 1, p. 10.

kingdom. That old dog, lying in the dark, has drawn off many good men to whip syllabub and sift quiddities under pretence of zeal for the truth.'[10]

Ryland's frequently expressed admiration for Gill has often led to the suggestion that he was a Hyper-Calvinist. While that suggestion may be true, his gospel warnings could be very powerful. William Newman, however, recorded the following from a sermon Ryland preached in 1790:

> Avoid two extremes. Some High Calvinists neglect the unconverted; but Paul left no case untouched. He spoke properly and suitably to Felix as well as to Timothy. Some neglect to preach the law, and tell their hearers to accept Christ. O sinners, beware! If Christ says, 'Depart', 'tis all over. Depart into a thousand Aetnas, bursting up for ever and ever. Your souls are within an inch of damnation. I am clear of your blood. If you are condemned, I'll look you in the face at the judgment, and say, 'Lord, I told that man – I told those boys and girls, on 29th of August 1790 – I warned them – they would not believe – and now they stand shivering before thy bar.'

Commenting on this aspect of Ryland's message, Newman stated: 'No words of mine can express the thrilling sensation of horror with which this was heard by many within the congregation.'[11]

Like Gill, Ryland had a profound admiration for the Dutch theologian, Herman Witsius (1636–1708), after whom he named one of his sons. Interestingly, it seems that the only major area of doctrine in which Ryland differed from Gill was that of the terms of communion, and he published nothing on this subject until about a year after Gill's death.

Ryland was to become a major protagonist for open communion, but it is not known when he arrived at this conviction. Interestingly, the letter transferring him from his church in Warwick to the Northampton church in 1759 was distinctly cool.

> As far as we know, [he] has not acted altogether inconsistent with the grace of God, and the profession he made among us.[12]

---

[10] Quoted, op. cit., p. 63.
[11] *Rylandiana*, pp. 73, 74.
[12] Quoted, *Rylandiana*, p. 10.

His friend, William Newman, suggested that this coolness arose from Ryland's disagreement with the Warwick church over their practice of closed communion.[13]

Prior to leaving Warwick, Ryland had cultivated friendships with a number of paedobaptists. Philip Doddridge had invited the young John Ryland to preach for him.[14] For a number of years he also spent two fortnights a year with James Hervey, rector of Weston Favell, near Northampton.[15] After Hervey's death, Ryland developed a friendship with Augustus Montague Toplady, another of the Anglican Evangelical leaders.[16] Following Ryland's move to Enfield in 1785, he preached regularly in the pulpits of Independent and Countess of Huntingdon Connexion chapels,[17] and had associations with Rowland Hill.[18] It was unusual for a Hyper-Calvinist Baptist minister to enjoy so close an association with men of paedobaptist persuasion. Ryland's appreciation of fellowship with those from whom he differed, in his interpretation both of Calvinism[19] and of baptism, helps to explain his impatience with the practice of closed communion. William Jay paid tribute to Ryland's breadth of sympathy:

---

[13] Ibid., p.11. The relevant article of the Warwick church doctrinal statement had clearly been taken from Gill's *Declaration of Faith and Practice* and includes the words, 'those only are to be admitted to the communion of the church, and to participate in all ordinances in it, who upon profession of their faith, have been baptized by immersion', Ibid., p. 10; cf. Gill's *Declaration*, pp. 5-7 above.

[14] Newman, *Rylandiana*, p. 9.

[15] Ibid., p. 7. James Hervey (1713-58) was one of the original members of the Methodist Holy Club in Oxford and an associate of Whitefield and Wesley, See J. C. Ryle, *Christian Leaders of the Last Century*, London, 1891, pp. 328ff.

[16] Thomas Wright, *The Lives of the British Hymn Writers, vol. 2: Augustus M. Toplady and Contemporary Hymn Writers*, Farncombe and Son, London, 1911, pp. 75ff.

[17] Newman, *Rylandiana*, pp. 14,18.

[18] Jay, *Autobiography*, p. 297.

[19] The few published sermons by Hervey indicate his readiness to exhort the unconverted, *The Works of James Hervey*, Edinburgh, n.d., pp. 654, 661, 671. Rowland Hill was clearly no High Calvinist, William Jones, *Memoirs of the Life, Ministry, and Writings of the Rev. Rowland Hill, M.A., to which are added Fifteen Sermons on Important Subjects* (separately paged), London, 1834, pp. 198-200; *Sermons*, pp. 193 and 214.

Three Noteworthy Leaders

Though he was rather high in his doctrinal sentiments, and not entirely friendly to some of Mr Fuller's views, he was not sour or malignant towards others. He was intimate with Mr Whitefield and Mr Rowland Hill, and much attached to many other preachers less sympathetically orthodox than himself; and laboured, as opportunity arose, with them. He was, indeed, a lover of all good men; and while many talked of candour, he exercised it.[20]

From 1759 until 1785 Ryland was pastor of the College Lane Baptist Church, Northampton, in which town he also conducted a boarding school.[21] The Northampton church prospered under his ministry. There were thirty members when he came, but within a year the number doubled. At this time, he would have been at the height of his preaching powers. Robert Hall, Jr., who was later to be considered one of the greatest pulpit orators of his age, recalled:

> In the powers of memory, imagination, and expression I have never yet seen any man to be compared with him. I should despair of conveying to the mind of one who never heard him an adequate idea of the majesty and force of his elocution. Cicero probably had more softness and polish and artificial grace, but Demosthenes himself must have yielded to him in spirit and fire, in overpowering vehemence and grandeur. Perfectly natural, unstudied, unexpected, there were often passages in his sermons sublime and terrible as the overflowing lava of a burning mountain. Everything in his aspect, his voice, and his whole manner was fitted to arrest and to enchain the attention of his audience . . . He was always above other men, and sometimes above himself. When, for instance, he exhibited the face and convulsions of the terrified Belshazzar, and traced the handwriting on the wall, expounding at the same time its awful import, his hearers were breathless, motionless, petrified with horror. When he described Jacob beholding the waggons that Joseph had sent to carry him to Egypt, every heart was melted, and many wept aloud. He governed the spirits of men with a kind of absolute sway, but while he agitated most powerfully the passions of others as a tempest of wind the mountain grove, he had always the command of his own.[22]

[20] Jay, *Autobiography*, p. 293.

[21] Biographical details are taken from William Newman, *Rylandiana*. Newman was Ryland's assistant from 1787 to 1792.   [22] Culross, op.cit. pp. 36, 37.

[35]

Congregations increased and on two occasions the chapel had to be enlarged.[23] From 1781, his son, John, who already was helping him in the school, assisted him in the ministry. In 1786, he removed to Enfield with his school after experiencing some difficulties at Northampton. The nature of these is not now clear, but they may have been financial.[24]

William Jay, who heard Ryland on a number of occasions, considered that his dramatic mode of preaching breached the canons of good taste from time to time. His effective classroom technique may not always have been appropriate for the pulpit. All witnesses agree that Ryland was an excellent schoolmaster, and it is not surprising that a number of ministers entrusted their sons to his care. Samuel Bagster, later a well-known publisher, was a pupil at the school in Northampton and has left us this description:

> The school was large – about ninety boys. It was of celebrity, and justly so. Mr Ryland was assiduous in improving the mental talent when it appeared, and several men became eminent for oratory and scholarship by the education and training imparted there. A short period before my entry, Dr Ryland of Bristol and the renowned Robert Hall had left the school.

Bagster paid the highest tribute to Ryland's influence on his pupils. He was ingenious and unusual in his teaching methods; the school was ruled with a firm but mild hand (the latter not a common feature of eighteenth century education).

> Many eccentricities manifested by Mr Ryland in his mode of tuition and his manner of preaching are present to my memory, which I omit; but this pleasing truth I declare confidently, that on no one occasion could the hearers doubt the purity of his motives: his one aim the eternal benefit of those who listened to his instructions. I owe to him a high tone of moral feeling impressed upon my mind, I believe, by his peculiar mode of imparting instruction.[25]

[23] Culross, op. cit. p. 35.
[24] For a discussion of the end of Ryland's pastorate in Northampton, see Peter Naylor, 'John Collett Ryland', in M. Haykin, *British Particular Baptists, 1*, pp. 198–9. [25] Quoted, Culross, op. cit., pp. 39–41.

Three Noteworthy Leaders

In 1766, a group of the boarders at the school began to meet together for prayer and soon after a number of other boys were awakened, including John Ryland, Jr.. The blessing continued through 1767. A record of this prayer society stated: 'It is noteworthy that a considerable number of the boys trace their awakenings and salvation directly to Mr Ryland and especially to his talks on Saturday evenings.'[26]

John Newton, the Anglican curate at Olney, was introduced to Ryland in 1765, and the two men became friends. Newton paid an annual visit to Northampton where he conducted services in houses. He regularly preached at Ryland's school as well as at a girls' school run by Mrs Martha Trinder, a member of the College Lane Church. In an entry in his diary in September 1774, he recorded:

> Indeed the Lord's work seems to flourish there, and Mr Ryland, amidst the many particularities which give him an Originality of Character beyond most men I ever knew, appears to new and greater advantage every time I see him. The Lord is pleased always to own me to the comfort of the serious young persons in Mrs Trinder's school, of whom I conversed with about 12 this time, who seem very promising.[27]

John Collett Ryland was an outspoken opponent of tyranny. Like many of his fellow Dissenters, he supported the American colonists in the War of Independence. Robert Hall, Jr., who in his later years was to become the best-known champion of open communion, described a conversation between Ryland and his father. It was on the occasion of the younger Robert Hall being taken to Ryland's school for the first time. He reports Ryland as declaring:

> Were I General Washington, I would call together all my brother officers. I would bare my arm and bid every man bare his, that a portion of blood might be extracted, and mingled in one bowl, and swear by him that sitteth upon the Throne and liveth for ever and ever not to sheath the consecrated blade until the freedom of his country was achieved . . . And

---

[26] Quoted Culross, op. cit. p. 53.
[27] Quoted in D. Bruce Hindmarsh, *John Newton and the English Evangelical Tradition*, Eerdmanns, Grand Rapids, 1996, p. 143.

[37]

if after this any one should turn coward or traitor, I should feel it a duty, a pleasure, a luxury, to plunge my weapon in that man's heart.[28]

Later he was to express the same intensity of feeling in his abhorrence of slavery.[29]

John Collett Ryland died triumphantly at Enfield on 14 July 1792. Eight years earlier he had preached one of his most memorable sermons at the burial of Andrew Gifford in Bunhill Fields. The closing words of the sermon on that occasion could equally apply to those who attended Ryland's funeral:

> Ye ministers of Christ, ye people of God, ye surrounding spectators, prepare, prepare to meet this old servant of Christ, at that day, at that hour, when this whole place shall be all nothing but life, and death shall be swallowed up in victory![30]

2. Robert Hall, Senior (1728–91)

In May 1779 the messengers and ministers of the Northamptonshire Association crowded into the College Lane Chapel in Northampton. This association of Particular Baptist Churches had long extended beyond the bounds of the county from which it took its name, and now included churches from Hertfordshire in the south to Nottinghamshire in the north. Its annual meetings were usually well attended, not only by accredited representatives, but also by church members, and even by visitors from other denominations. As well as discussing matters of common concern and listening to reports from all the associated churches, the occasion was always marked by the preaching of an Association sermon. The 1779 Association preacher was Robert Hall, pastor of the village church of Arnesby in Leicestershire. He chose as his text, Isaiah 57:14: 'Cast ye up, cast ye up, prepare the way, take up the stumbling block out

---

[28] Newman, *Rylandiana*, pp. 194–196 quotes Hall's account of Ryland's enthusiastic support for the colonists. Hall commented, 'I trembled at the idea of being left with such a bloody-minded master,' p. 196; cf. Jay, *Autobiography*, pp. 293–4.

[29] Ibid., pp. 294–5

[30] Quoted, Alfred W. Light, *Bunhill Fields*, 2, C. J. Farncombe and Sons, London, 1933, p. 204.

Three Noteworthy Leaders

of the way of my people.' Reflecting on this occasion fifty years later (in 1830), Joseph Ivimey, the Baptist historian, wrote: 'The year 1779 . . . was, I consider, the commencement of a new era in the history of our denomination.'[31] This comment was prompted particularly by Hall's sermon. Two years after it was preached, it was published under the title, *Help to Zion's Travellers; being an attempt to remove various stumbling blocks out of the way, relating to doctrinal and practical religion*. Hall set out to demonstrate that a true understanding of the doctrines of grace is no barrier to gospel preaching. About this book, John Rippon wrote:

> This little volume, which principally contains a vindication of the genuine doctrines of grace from the objections of Socinians, Sabellians, Arminians and Antinomians, has met with considerable approbation from godly, judicious, and learned men of various denominations.

William Carey praised it, saying, 'I do not remember ever to have read any book with such raptures.' Although Hall ranged widely in his sermon, it was remembered particularly for its statement of warm evangelical Calvinism, a message that encouraged preachers to press the claims of the gospel earnestly upon their hearers. As such, it contrasted sharply with a preaching which, although accurate, was too often presented with an indirectness that lacked any engagement with the hearer. Hall declared:

> If anyone should ask, Have I a right to apply to Jesus the Saviour, simply as a poor undone perishing sinner, in whom there appears no good thing? I answer, Yes; the gospel proclamation is, 'Whosoever will, let him come.' 'To you, O men, I call and my voice is to the sons of men', *Prov.* 8:4. The way to Jesus is graciously laid open to everyone who chooses to come to him.[32]

It was of Hall's teaching in this book that John Ryland, Jr., later wrote:

> This excellent man remarked that if the invitations of the gospel are *not indefinite*, or [not] addressed to *sinners* considered simply as *needy* and *guilty*, there can be no foundation for the first act of faith; the sinner can

---

[31] John Rippon, *Baptist Register, 1*, p. 233.
[32] Quoted in Haykin, ed., *The British Particular Baptists,* 1, p. 207.

have no warrant for his application to Christ, unless he knows his election, or proves his regeneration before he has committed his soul to him.[33]

By the time Hall preached his famous sermon at Northampton he had been pastor of the little village church at Arnesby, south of Leicester, for sixteen years. During those years he had become a prominent figure in the affairs of the Northamptonshire Association. He was a Northumbrian, born in 1728 at Stannington, some twelve miles north of Newcastle-upon-Tyne. He was blessed with godly parents; his father was an Anglican and his mother a Presbyterian. Losing his father when he was just eleven years old, he was sent to live with an uncle a few miles away, near Black Heddon. This uncle attended a Presbyterian church, but Robert gained little from the preaching of a minister described by his first biographer as 'the most gross Arminian he ever met with'.

While living with his uncle, a friend told him about a sermon on the torments of hell, preached by the local vicar. Robert was immediately seized by an overwhelming sense of his own guilt, which continued for four years, as he later confessed to John Ryland, Senior. During this period, while working on a farm, he broke his arm twice in quick succession. Painful though these breaks must have been, Hall was suffering under a deeper sense of pain, as John Rippon explains: 'He has repeatedly declared, that all the pain of these broken bones did by no means equal the anguish of his mind. The doleful sound of "damnation, damnation," seemed continually in his ears.' Under the delusion that he must attain to sinless perfection he struggled hopelessly to fit himself to stand before God. In deep despair, he was on the point of committing suicide, but turning to his Bible once more, he read: 'Come now, and let us reason together, saith the LORD; though your sins be as scarlet, they shall be as white as snow; though they be red like crimson, they shall be as wool' (*Isa.* 1:18). Relief was given but he still struggled with uncertainties until May 1748, when he read the words of the apostle Paul in Galatians 4:

---

[33] John Ryland, Preface to Robert Hall, *Help to Zion's Travellers*, 4th edition, London, 1820, pp. vii, viii.

4–5. At last, he understood the gospel, and rejoiced in the wonder of God's love: that God could forgive the guilty and yet not leave their sin unpunished.

> He now was convinced and rejoiced that salvation was of grace indeed, and abhorred the *Arminian* sentiments, which had so long held him in dreadful bondage. He remarked long after to a friend, 'Perhaps, I should have never detested that system as I do, had I not once drunk into it and felt its effects.'[34]

As a result of this change he moved to another Presbyterian church whose minister did preach the gospel. He was soon alarmed by reports of the spread of 'Anabaptist' principles and was not a little annoyed when his older brother, Christopher, joined the Baptist Church at Hamsterley in Durham. He decided to confront his brother's Baptist minister, David Fernie, but further study of this whole question resulted in Robert becoming a Baptist himself! He joined the Baptist Church at Hexham in January 1752, and later that same year, he began to preach with the approval of his church. He was now twenty-four years of age.

Within a year Robert Hall had received a call to the village church at Arnesby, Leicestershire, where he continued until his death in 1791. Life was a struggle in the early years of his ministry there. His friend Andrew Fuller wrote: 'On his first entrance on the ministry his fortitude was exercised in a scene of persecutions and reproaches, which lasted for many years; his worldly prospects at the same time were gloomy and precarious in a high degree, he had a very numerous family and an income extremely limited.'[35] The church could afford to pay only a very small stipend to its minister and the Hall family eventually grew to fourteen children, but Robert and his wife resolved never to run into debt. To support his family Robert farmed a smallholding. In spite of the difficulties he never felt free to consider a move to another church. Andrew Fuller described his preaching; while acknowledging that his friend had received few educational advantages, his preaching was thoughtful and full of unction:

---

[34] Rippon, op. cit., p. 229.   [35] Ibid., p. 239.

Though he was unacquainted with the graces of oratory, and the embellishments of language, scarce any man spoke with a more striking and visible effect ... His eminent piety lent a peculiar unction to the sentiments he delivered, led him to seize the most interesting views of every subject, and turned topics, which in the hands of others would have furnished barren speculation only, into materials for devotion and prayer.[36]

By the 1770s, the writings of Jonathan Edwards were being avidly read by ministers in the English Midlands. Robert Hall quickly became an enthusiastic advocate of the American preacher-theologian. When Andrew Fuller was wrestling with the challenge of Hyper-Calvinism, it was Hall who urged him to study Edwards on *The Freedom of the Will*. As the years passed, his ministry seemed to be increasingly useful, as Fuller was keen to point out:

He had great force without ornament, and grandeur without correctness. His ministry in the hands of God was effectual to the conversion of great numbers; and in this particular he was distinguished in a manner not very common, for the last years of his life were most successful.[37]

In the last years of his life, Hall was blessed with rich communion with God. In a letter to an intimate friend, describing how he had almost died in a snowstorm in December 1783, he added:

Since I saw you, I have had more pleasure in my work, than has been common with me. Indeed (but I beg you not to mention a word of it to anyone), I have had the most blessed half year in my soul, that I ever remember to have enjoyed. The approach of the Sabbaths has been pleasurable to me; my work a sweet reward; and the worship of God in general attended with meltings of heart, and solemn joy. I have thought, though as poor a creature as ever crawled, yet I would not, on the whole, if I could, exchange my relative connection with Christ and consequential state with an Angel, yet I tremble while thus I speak. I would not vaunt, and I dread desertion: but I make free with you, and intreat you to regard the prohibition above.[38]

---

[36] Ibid., p. 238.   [37] Ibid., pp. 238-9.   [38] Ibid., pp. 233-4.

Three Noteworthy Leaders

As the years passed Hall's health became uncertain, but he continued to preach. Just a month before he died, he wrote to a friend:

> The Lord has ever been kind to *timorous, distrustful, ungrateful* ME. I have always dreaded long life, having a shattered memory at best and apprehending that under natural decays I should be *useless indeed;* nay, worse, a cumberer of the ground. But, dear brother, I mention it for your encouragement, though I dread saying too much, or that you should think I am more favoured than I really am; yet, I say, I may venture to mention to *you*, that hitherto my fears have not been verified. I trust the Lord is with me rather more than heretofore; and the word seems blessed to *some*, if not to *many*. We are well attended, in bad weather excepted; and at evening meetings still more and more.

Blessed with these favours from God, Hall continued until Sunday morning, 13 March 1791, when he preached from the words, 'If thou knewest the gift of God, and who it is that saith unto thee, give me to drink; thou wouldest have asked of him, and he would have given thee living water' (*John* 4:10). Many felt that he preached with exceptional power. At the close he gave out Joseph Hart's beautiful hymn, 'The fountain of Christ, LORD help us to sing'. Appropriately it included the lines,

> This fountain, though rich, from charge is quite clear,
> The poorer the wretch, the welcomer here:
> Come needy, come guilty, come loathsome and bare;
> You can't come too filthy; come just as you are.

This earnest evangelistic appeal was an appropriate end to a ministry which had been blessed with the conversion of many. Late that afternoon Hall was taken ill and that same evening, passed peacefully into the immediate presence of his Lord. So died a man described by John Ryland, Jr., as 'one of the wisest and best of men'. Ryland went on to pay tribute to Hall's readiness to respond to Scripture:

> Open to conviction and willing to follow the light of revelation, let it lead him whithersoever it would, he believed that, about fourteen years before his death, he had found a more excellent way of solving some

theological difficulties, than he had adopted in the earlier part of his ministry.[39]

3. ABRAHAM BOOTH (1734–1806)[40]

'As long as the churches of Christ in this country shall continue to cherish a reverential regard for the doctrine of sovereign, rich and free grace, these Volumes will continue to be held in high estimation'; so wrote the editor of the collected writings of Abraham Booth in 1813. In fact, today Abraham Booth is almost forgotten, a sad indication of the change in thought which has swept through the Baptist Churches of Great Britain since the early nineteenth century.

Abraham Booth was born in the small Derbyshire village of Blackwell on 20 May 1734. Within a year of his birth, his father took a small farm on the estate of the Duke of Portland at Annesley Woodhouse, Nottinghamshire. Life was hard for a small tenant farmer. Abraham was the firstborn of what turned out to be a large family. Since there was not much money for education, he spent less than six months at school. Mercifully, his father could read and gave him lessons each evening. This well-intentioned education, however, was necessarily limited, because Abraham had to spend the daylight hours helping his father work the farm. At the age of sixteen, Abraham left the farm in order to learn the trade of stocking weaving. This change of occupation seems to have given him greater opportunity for self-improvement. Thirsting for knowledge, he read whatever books he could find, often late into the night.

Abraham Booth's parents were members of the Church of England, but there is no evidence of any contact with Evangelical Christianity in his early childhood. However, in the middle decades of the century, the area

---

[39] Ryland, Preface to Hall's *Help*, p. vi.

[40] Biographies of Booth include an anonymous 'Memoir' prefixed to his *Works*, vol. 1, 1813; W. Jones, *An Essay on the Life and Writings of Mr Abraham Booth*, Liverpool, 1808. R. A. Coppenger, 'Abraham Booth, 1734–1806: A Study of His Thought and Work', Ph.D. thesis, University of Edinburgh, 1953; E. A. Payne, 'Abraham Booth, 1734–1806', *Baptist Quarterly*, vol. 26, (1975–6), pp. 28–42. R. W. Oliver, 'Abraham Booth', in Haykin, ed., *The British Particular Baptists*, vol. 2.

in which they lived was the scene of a powerful movement of the Holy Spirit. Some miles to the south of Annesley Woodhouse, was the residence of the Countess of Huntingdon at Donington Park. One of her servants, David Taylor, was converted and embarked on a vigorous programme of village evangelism. Samuel Deacon, one of the earliest converts in this evangelistic work, joined him, and the success with which they met must have been beyond their highest expectations. Most of their converts were from the working classes, some of whom were prepared to walk twenty or thirty miles to the meetings. Groups of believers were established in the villages of North Leicestershire, Derbyshire, and Nottinghamshire. The Wesleys may have influenced the early leaders of this movement, since from the beginning they were Arminian in doctrine, although never actually a part of the Wesleyan Methodist organization.

It was from these itinerant preachers that Abraham Booth first heard the gospel and came to faith in Jesus Christ. These Christians were paedobaptists at first, but soon adopted Baptist convictions. In 1755, between sixty and seventy of their members were baptized, including Booth, who was twenty-one years old by this time. Soon after his baptism, Booth began to preach at Melbourne, Longborough, Diseworth, and a number of other villages within a radius of about forty miles of his home. These preaching stations were all part of the outreach of a single church. Retaining Arminian convictions, they formed a General Baptist Church. However, this church had no connections with the old General Baptist denomination, which was fast sinking into Arianism.

The church, with its branches in at least three counties of England, proved to be so unwieldy that its organisation had to be reviewed. It was Booth who urged the establishment of independent local churches. He was then asked to pastor Kirkby Woodhouse, one of the resulting local churches.[41]

---

[40] Booth, *Works*, vol. 1, 'Memoir', p. xxiv.

[41] W. T. Whitley, *A History of the British Baptists*, London, pp. 217-8; A. C. Underwood, *A History of the English Baptists*, London, pp. 149-150; Raymond Brown, *The English Baptists of the Eighteenth Century*, London, pp. 67-68; E. A. Payne, 'Abraham Booth', *Baptist Quarterly*, 26, pp.30-31.

At the age of twenty-four, Abraham married Elizabeth Bowman, the daughter of a neighbouring farmer. She seems to have received a basic education, but he continued to work hard to extend his own. The young couple established a school at Sutton in Ashfield and Abraham continued to pastor his church. It was at this time that Abraham Booth had to face one of the greatest crises of his life. About a year before his baptism he had written a poem, 'Absolute Predestination', in which he attacked the doctrines of predestination and particular redemption. This poem, he later admitted, was written 'in language as replete with contumely and reproach as is to be found in the writings of Wesley or Fletcher.'[42] As he pursued his studies, these early Arminian convictions were shaken. He described his experience:

> The doctrine of sovereign, distinguishing grace, as commonly and justly stated by Calvinists, it must be acknowledged, is too generally exploded. This the writer of these pages knows by experience to his grief and shame. Through the ignorance of his mind, the pride of his heart, and the prejudice of his education, he, in his younger years, often opposed it with much warmth, though with no small weakness; but after an impartial enquiry, and many prayers, he found reason to alter his judgement; he found it to be the doctrine of the Bible, and a dictate of the unerring Spirit. Thus patronized, he received the once obnoxious sentiment, under a full conviction of its being a divine truth.[43]

One of his early biographers conjectured that he was shaken in his early convictions through the reading of James Hervey's *Theron and Aspasio*, although he does not offer firm evidence for this. Whatever the precipitating factors, his friends were soon noting his changed views. Meetings were held between Booth and the leaders of his group of churches, many of whom held his ministry in high esteem. No agreement was possible and so Booth had to resign his pastorate. It is noteworthy that he retained a warm esteem for his former associates right to the very end of his life.

For a short time his preaching ceased; but he was not alone in his convictions. Some of his friends wished to continue under his ministry, and

---

[42] Booth, *Works*, 1, p.xxi.   [43] Ibid, p. xxiii.

Three Noteworthy Leaders

so a hall was rented and licensed in Sutton in Ashfield. There a Particular Baptist Church was established. To this congregation Booth expounded his doctrine in a series of sermons, which later became the basis of his book, *The Reign of Grace*. Opportunities for regular preaching in the towns of Nottingham and Chesterfield followed, and the series was repeated in these places. A number of his friends urged him to publish the sermons. He was under a considerable workload. During the days of the week, he kept his school to support a growing family, and on the Lord's Day, he usually preached three times. Booth eventually wrote out his manuscript, but for private circulation. Publication seemed impossible for an obscure country pastor who was hardly known even among the Particular Baptist churches. Someone described the unpublished manuscript so enthusiastically to Henry Venn, the Evangelical vicar of Huddersfield, that he asked to see it. Immediately perceiving its value, he rode over to Booth's home to meet the author. He insisted that the book must be published. He gave practical help and wrote an introduction to it. Publication gave Booth the opportunity to renounce the only thing he had previously published, his poem, 'Absolute Predestination'. He wrote: 'If considered in a critical light , [it] is despicable; if in a theological view, detestable: as it is an impotent attack on the honour of divine grace, in regard to its glorious freeness; and a bold opposition to the sovereignty of God. So I now consider it, and as such I here renounce it.'[44]

It was the publication of *The Reign of Grace* that unexpectedly brought Abraham Booth to London. Samuel Burford, the pastor of the Prescot Street Church in Whitechapel, London, died unexpectedly in April 1768. At around the same time, members of that church read *The Reign of Grace*. So impressed were they by this unknown Baptist minister's book that they deputed three of their brethren to make the long coach journey to Nottinghamshire to hear him preach. They were not disappointed, and they reported back to the Prescot Street Church that Booth was 'a sound nervous [vigorous] Gospel minister'. An invitation to preach quickly followed, and during June and July 1768, Booth preached

[44] Ibid, p. 4.

for three Sundays at Prescot Street. The church members were drawn to him and decided to invite him for four more Sundays, beginning in August. Before this second visit took place, the church held 'a Solemn Day of Prayer'. In September, Booth received a unanimous call to the pastorate, which he accepted within two weeks. He was set apart for the pastorate by the imposition of hands on 16 February 1769, before a large congregation, which included the Countess of Huntingdon. William Nash Clarke, of Unicorn Yard, Southwark, presided and asked Booth for a confession of his faith; Benjamin Wallin, of Maze Pond, and Samuel Stennett, of Little Wild Street, both preached. A number of ministers offered prayer and joined in the laying on of hands.

The church in which Abraham Booth was installed as the new minister met in an elegant eighteenth-century meeting-house, erected in 1730. Prescot Street was in an area of Whitechapel known as Goodman's Fields, a fashionable area favoured by high-ranking naval officers and city merchants. At the time of Booth's arrival in this part of London, the description of the area as Goodman's Fields still had some meaning. Kenneth Dix has given the following description of this area, lying to the east of the historic 'Square Mile' of the City of London. 'Although Prescot Street Meeting House was only a few hundred yards from the Tower, it was less than half a mile from open fields.'[45] The countryman from the Midlands would not have been overwhelmed by such an urban landscape. The meetinghouse was tightly packed with pews, the congregation being seated around a carved octagonal pulpit situated on one of the long walls of the building, and there were galleries on three sides. In front of the pulpit was the oak communion table upon which rested two mahogany book stands for use in normal Sunday worship. From this 'table pew' the clerk announced the hymns and the precentor led the unaccompanied singing. Behind the sanctuary was a large vestry which could accommodate one hundred and twenty persons. This was used for smaller meetings. There was also a 'private vestry' for the minister and the deacons.

[45] Kenneth Dix, 'All Change: An East End of London Baptist Church in the Nineteenth Century', *Baptist Quarterly*, 33, 1989-90, p. 19.

Three Noteworthy Leaders

The move from an obscure provincial town to the historic Prescot Street Church must have been a daunting experience for Booth. He was called to follow a succession of able men, some of whom had made significant contributions to the wider life of the denomination. He had also come to London at a time when able men filled a number of the capital's pulpits. There was Samuel Stennett at Little Wild Street, John MacGowan at Devonshire Square, and the scholarly but isolated Andrew Gifford at Eagle Street. Dr John Gill, the outstandingly able theologian was now in the closing stages of his pastorate in Southwark, just south of the Thames. Booth was determined to equip himself for his new ministry as best he could. Since he had no training in the biblical languages, he now arranged for a tutor, a former Roman Catholic priest who regularly came to breakfast, to spend the first part of the morning teaching him Latin and Greek. Booth made considerable progress in both languages. Unlike Gill, he never became an accomplished Hebraist. However for the rest of his life he read daily from his Greek Testament, while Latin gave him access to the writings of the Continental theologians. As a result of his studies, he became well versed in the controversy with Rome and particularly well read in church history. Probably the greatest single theological influence upon him was John Owen, the great Puritan divine of the previous century.

Booth's pulpit style was plain. In February 1799, Nathan Smith of Barnoldswick, Lancashire, wrote a letter home in which he recorded his thoughts about the preacher of Prescot Street Church: 'Last Sabbath I heard Mr Booth. He appears to greater advantage in writing than in the pulpit. He is rather in danger of a decline. So plain was his appearance that I mistook him before he ascended the rostrum for a poor layman.'[46] Booth was not in good health at the time, and so these words do not portray the preacher at his best. William Newman who knew him over many years declared: 'His sermons were plain and textual, not systematic; highly instructive, always savoury and acceptable to persons of evangelical taste; for the glory, the government, and the grace of Christ were his favourite themes'. Although he was in demand as a preacher on special

---

[46] Quoted in Payne, 'Abraham Booth', p. 41.

occasions during the week, he made a point of being in his own pulpit regularly. He said to Joseph Ivimey: 'I have never left my people, since I first settled with them, more than two Lord's Days at a time. Had I left them so much as some pastors have left theirs, I have no doubt that my people would have left me as theirs have left them.'[47]

Whatever Booth's gifts as a preacher were, it was widely agreed that he was a man of prayer. Newman wrote: 'He had the gift of prayer in a very high degree, and whoever heard him was impressed with the idea that he was a man who prayed much in secret.'[48] After a visit to London, an American student vowed that 'when he returned home, he would have the pleasure of assuring the President and students of the College that while in England he had heard several ministers preach, but that he had heard *one minister pray*'.[49] In the light of this testimony, it is not surprising to discover that Booth was one of the ministers who responded to a call for prayer issued in 1784. Later, in March 1798, further meetings for prayer were arranged for the evangelization of London and the surrounding villages and, in February 1802, a monthly prayer meeting was established 'for the state of our nation and the spread of the gospel'.[50] Rippon reported that Booth 'visited many of us and prayed with us as if we had been his own charge. Some of his prayers which he offered to God, under my roof in seasons of affliction, can never be forgotten.'[51]

In 1800 Booth published a sermon entitled, *The Amen of Social Prayer, Illustrated and Improved*. The London Particular Baptist ministers had decided to arrange a series of studies in the Lord's Prayer. Booth was asked to take the last study, preaching on the Prayer's final word, 'Amen'. He was reluctant to respond to this invitation since he had always disapproved of novel texts and especially sermons based on single words of Scripture. After due consideration of the significance of the conclusion to the Lord's Prayer, he agreed to break his personal rule. Interestingly, John

---

[47] Ivimey, *HEB*, pp. 375 and 386. [48] Ibid, p. 375.
[49] Quoted in W. Jones, *Essay on the Life . . . of Abraham Booth*, p. 116.
[50] R. P. Roberts, *Continuity and Change, the London Calvinistics Baptists, 1760-1820*, Richard Owen Roberts, Illinois, 1989, p. 131.
[51] Quoted in Jones, *Essay on the Life . . . of Abraham Booth*, p. 121.

Three Noteworthy Leaders

Rippon opens a little window on how Booth responded to the prayers of others, and sheds some light on the practice of the churches at that time.

> When others concluded public prayer, where he was present, he was accustomed at the conclusion, softly, yet audibly to subjoin his AMEN – this practice he wished might prevail in all our congregations, and at our prayer meetings; but his example and influence, considerable as they were, have not rendered it general.[52]

Booth's pastorate at Prescot Street witnessed steady growth in the work. There were one hundred and twenty-two baptisms in the first decade and a total of four hundred and fifty-two during the whole of his pastorate. The pastor of this flock showed a deep concern for the lambs of the congregation. In 1775, Booth expressed his intention to catechize the children, and by 1801 Prescot Street Church had its own Sunday School. The school may have existed before that date, since a wealthy member, William Fox, was active in the establishment of a Sunday School Society in 1785. The Society aimed to promote the establishment of Sunday Schools among churches of all denominations.[53]

Booth's abilities soon gave him a position of leadership among the ministers of the Baptist Board, the influential ministers' fraternal in London. However, his wider influence was undoubtedly exercised through his writings, the best known being *The Reign of Grace*, which passed through nine English, one Scottish, and three American editions, before 1800.[54]

In 1770, he published a small work entitled, *The Death of Legal Hope, the Life of Evangelical Obedience*. This small work challenged tendencies toward doctrinal Antinomianism, which were beginning to appear in London. A further challenge emerged during the same decade in the form of a new interest in Socinianism.[55] A group of ministers, the most notable of whom was Theophilus Lindsey, left the Church of England because they could no longer subscribe to its Trinitarian formularies. A powerful

---

[52] Roberts, *Continuity and Change*, pp. 81 and 84.
[53] Ibid, pp. 232, 235.   [54] Ibid, p. 101.
[55] Socinianism took its name from two sixteenth-century members of the Italian Sozzini family, Laelio and Faustus, under whose influence some of the churches of the Reformation embraced a form of anti-Trinitarianism, denying the divinity of

advocate of Socinianism among the Dissenters was Joseph Priestley, who attracted interest as a result both of his unorthodox theology and his scientific researches. Booth's response was to edit and republish a work by the French Huguenot scholar Jacques Abbadie, *A Treatise on the Deity of Christ*, in 1777. The original French edition of this work had been published in 1689, and although an earlier English edition had appeared, Booth was not satisfied with it. He sought to improve the translation and edit the text. Booth's edition was published by subscription, and was well received by both Churchmen and orthodox Dissenters.

In the next year, Booth published *An Apology for the Baptists*, which was a defence of the practice of restricted or closed communion. Booth, a man who enjoyed good fraternal relationships with his paedobaptist brethren, was deeply concerned to answer the charge that 'Strict Baptists' were guilty of bigotry.[56]

In 1784, Booth went into print in an attempt to challenge the practice of infant baptism. *Paedobaptism Examined* proved popular and a second expanded edition in two volumes was brought out in 1787. It remains one of the most detailed treatments of the baptismal controversy from the Baptist perspective. A reply to Booth's work soon appeared from the pen of Edward Williams, entitled *Antipaedobaptism Examined*. According to Booth, Williams' response had failed to deal with his own arguments and so he initially felt he had no need to write a reply. However, he was goaded into doing so when Williams boasted that Booth's silence admitted he was incapable of replying. Booth's *A Defence of Paedobaptism Examined* appeared in 1792, and with this further publication the debate was brought to a close.

During this time Booth also wrote *An Essay on the Kingdom of Christ* (1788), in which he expounded the spiritual nature of the church of God, and demonstrated the inconsistency of a state church with the New Testament model.

Christ and rejecting the penal, substitutionary nature of his work. The new emphasis on the sufficiency of human reason which was a feature of the Enlightenment gave a fresh stimulus to Socinianism in the eighteenth century.

[56] Booth's *Apology* is discussed further in chapter 4.

Three Noteworthy Leaders

While wrestling with issues theological and ecclesiastical, Abraham Booth also found himself deeply involved in affairs outside his church. The 1790s were a turbulent decade. The French Revolution had exploded in 1789 and released powerful forces into Europe's political and social atmosphere. Initially, many Englishmen hoped that the Revolution would mark the end of tyranny, not only in France, but also in other European nations. Political reforms were needed in England, and fresh efforts were made at this time to lift the burden of the legislation that penalized the Dissenters. Booth seems to have been most deeply concerned about the evil of the ongoing trade in African slaves. In 1792, a number of petitions were presented to Parliament for its abolition; Booth supported the anti-slavery movement and published a strongly worded sermon on the issue.[57] Money from his congregation and friends was raised in support of the campaign. As it happened, however, the reported excesses of the French Revolution provoked a strong reaction in Great Britain, which ended the hopes of many for rapid reform.

The heightened political tensions of this period can be seen in a decision of the Baptist Board, in 1798, to expel one of its members, John Martin. He had asserted that in the event of a French invasion of Britain, the Dissenters should rise up in support of them.[58] However, the political uncertainty of these years did not hinder fruitful increase in the work of the gospel. The year 1792 saw the formation of the Particular Baptist Missionary Society at Kettering, under the leadership of William Carey, Andrew Fuller, John Ryland, Jr., and John Sutcliff. Generally speaking, the London churches were slow to support this new venture, but it was Abraham Booth who introduced John Thomas to the Society.[59]

---

[57] 'Commerce in the Human Species, and the Enslaving of Innocent Persons, Inimical to the Laws of Moses and the Gospel of Christ', *Works*, 3, pp. 185–218.

[58] Ivimey, *HEB*, 4, pp. 77–82. The relevant minutes of the Baptist Board are printed in the *Transactions of the Baptist Historical Society*, 6, 1918–19, pp. 93ff.

[59] Booth was absent through illness from the meeting to promote the Missionary Society in London and Samuel Stennett's extreme caution seems to have dominated the meeting in spite of the enthusiastic advocacy of John Rippon. Perhaps if Booth had been present there would have been stronger support; S. Pearce Carey, *William Carey*, Carey Press, London, 1934, p.113

Thomas was to become Carey's first colleague in India. Although Thomas was to cause Carey many problems on the mission field, Booth remained a valued friend of the Society. On 23 November 1796, William Carey wrote to Booth: 'Your very affectionate letters have been as cordials to my soul. Your counsels, your prayers, and good wishes excite my gratitude; may they be long continued.'[60]

In 1797, 'The Baptist Itinerant Society' was established in London. This Society's aim was to send 'such Calvinistic ministers of the Baptist persuasion as appear to them properly qualified for itinerant preaching'. This aim was further explained in an address to the churches drawn up by Booth.

> While we rejoice in the spiritual and laudable exertions of our Christian Brethren under different denominations to preach the gospel among the heathen in foreign climes, we should not forget the many myriads at home, who have scarcely anything pertaining to Christianity besides the name - who are profoundly ignorant, if not notoriously profligate and profane.[61]

This period, in which so many new societies were formed, was one of unprecedented expansion for English Nonconformity. This was to continue for the next forty years.

However, the nineteenth century began with a certain amount of uncertainty for the English Dissenters. Increased and widespread itinerant preaching by Dissenting ministers raised fears in some quarters of revolutionary activity in England, as well as provoking the ire of some sections of the Established Church. Various ways of curbing Dissenting activity in England were discussed in these years, although no new measures were introduced. More serious was the situation in many of the British colonies, where fears of slave risings heightened tensions. It was against this backdrop that the Assembly of Jamaica, in 1802, passed a law 'to prevent preaching by persons not qualified by law'. Anyone who addressed

---

[60] Quoted, E. F. Kevan, *London's Oldest Baptist Church*, London, 1933, p.123.

[61] The *Baptist Annual Register*, 2, 1794-7, pp. 465-70, gives the entire address with details of the committee and rules of the Society.

Three Noteworthy Leaders

assemblies 'of negroes or persons of colour' could be arrested as rogues or vagabonds, and if found guilty, were to be punished with hard labour and flogging. Those who allowed their premises to be used for such meetings were to be fined £100. The Dissenters of Jamaica appealed to their co-religionists in England. Led by Abraham Booth, Andrew Fuller, and Robert Hall, they also appealed to the Privy Council, which disallowed this law and one similar to it in the Island of St Vincent.[62]

In August 1804, Booth and two of his deacons, Joseph Gutteridge and William Taylor, were instrumental in the establishment of the London Baptist Educational Society. The purpose of the Society was to promote the training of ministerial candidates by supporting them for two years under the supervision of an experienced pastor. A few years after Booth's death, the Society promoted the establishment of the Stepney Academy, now Regent's Park College, Oxford.[63]

Abraham Booth and Andrew Fuller were the outstanding Particular Baptist theologians of the last years of the eighteenth century. Both men were self-taught and had reached their mature conclusions after a period of deep spiritual struggle. Booth came to his convictions from Arminianism, whereas Fuller had come to his from Hyper-Calvinism. Booth was a great admirer of the writings of John Owen, while Fuller owed a great debt to Jonathan Edwards and, to some extent, Edwards' New England successors. However, Booth was alarmed by the developments that took place in New England theology after the death of Edwards. Fuller and Booth seldom met; differences, and even misunderstandings, existed between the two men. These are of sufficient importance to merit separate consideration.[64]

For much of his life Abraham Booth enjoyed good health; he was well-built and seldom prevented by ill health from carrying out his pastoral responsibilities. In his last years of his life he was increasingly subject to attacks of asthma during the winter months. Whitechapel is a low-lying

---

[62] D. W. Lovegrove, *Established Church, Sectarian People*, Cambridge, 1988, pp. 134–5.

[63] R. P. Roberts, *Continuity and Change*, pp. 209–13.

[64] See chapter 7 below.

[55]

area of London and Booth lived near his meeting-house. His wife predeceased him by four years. Although the loss was severe, his friends noted his sense of calm resignation. There was a reason for this, as Booth explained:

> About three-and-twenty years ago my wife had a severe lying-in which so weakened her that we feared that she would never recover her strength. Her indisposition continued about two years, which was the occasion of our removing so near the meeting house. Shortly after the Lord was pleased to permit the family to be visited with the scarlet fever. My wife, and all except myself, were attacked with it. Her faculties were deranged, and the doctor said, 'I fear, Sir, your wife will never recover.' I attended all of them as well as I could. The Bible was then sweeter to me than ever it had been, even when I could only snatch from it a few verses at a time; and I well remember one solemn transaction. One evening I retired for the purpose of private prayer, and besought the Lord that I might find an entire resignation to his will. When I arose from my knees, I felt peculiar satisfaction in the perfection of God; and had such full persuasion of his righteousness, his justice, his mercy, and his love, that I lifted up my eyes to heaven, and said, 'O God, I give my wife, my children, my all to thee'; and if ever I prayed in my life, I prayed at that time. Seeing then, that he has given her to me for three-and-twenty years in answer to my prayer, dare I now to murmur? God forbid. All recovered but the nurse; she went away, had the fever, and died.[65]

He was, however, taken ill suddenly in September 1805. From then most of the services in Prescot Street were taken by his assistant, William Gray. Booth administered the Lord's Supper for the last time in January 1806, just a few days before his death on the 27th day of that month. In the Church Book, the devoted and grieving members of the church paid their tribute to their beloved pastor of almost thirty-seven years:

> He possessed a noble disinterestedness of spirit; he sought not ours but us; he was truly the servant of this church, for Jesus' sake. A pastor in the language of Jeremiah, according to God's heart; who fed his people with

---

[65] 'Memoir', *Works*, 1, p. lx.

knowledge and understanding. There are, perhaps, but few instances in the church of Christ, of one who has better exemplified the character of a Christian bishop, as drawn by the apostle Paul, *Titus* 1:7-9.[66]

He was buried in the burial ground of the Maze Pond Chapel in Southwark. The preacher on that occasion was John Rippon of Carter Lane. James Dore of Maze Pond preached at a memorial service held later at Prescot Street Church. The death of Abraham Booth took from the Particular Baptists one of their outstanding theologians and from the London churches one of their leading figures. Humble and unassuming, he stood steadfast in the classical Calvinistic theology the Particular Baptists had inherited from their Puritan forebears. A man of spiritual wisdom, his counsel was regularly sought and freely given, and although he disliked titles, he was well known before his death as 'the venerable Mr Booth'.

---

[66] *HEB*, 4, p. 372.

4

THE COMMUNION CONTROVERSY, 1772-81

From the seventeenth century onwards, Baptists had debated the question of whether communion should be closed or open, but it was not until the nineteenth century that differences over this issue led to distinct Strict Baptist groupings. Of the earlier debates the best known was the one between John Bunyan and William Kiffin. The publication of two pamphlets advocating open communion in 1772 reopened the whole debate among a new generation of Baptists.

The new challenge to strict communion may not be unconnected with the political climate of the 1770s. There were at that time many calls for greater religious and political freedom. A number of issues cast Parliament into a reactionary role. Significant among these was the John Wilkes affair. John Wilkes was four times elected MP for Middlesex and four times expelled by the House of Commons as an unsuitable member. The political details need not concern us in these pages except to note that Wilkes embarked on unprecedented political agitation. One writer comments, 'He did not propose simply to excite opinion out of doors. He organised, and gave it lasting shape; in so doing he turned the popular opinion which had been an episodic but normal feature of politics into a force capable of growth, which might alter the system.' Wilkes had a number of close acquaintances among the Dissenters.[1] Nonconformists, and even some Anglicans,[2] were pressing for the end of religious tests for

---

[1] J. Steven Watson, *The Reign of George III, 1760-1815*, Oxford, 1964, pp. 131-143; E. A. Payne, 'Nonconformists and the American Revolution', *Journal of the United Reformed Church History Society*, vol. 1, October 1976, p. 216.

[2] In 1772 a number of clergymen met in London to petition Parliament for relief

office in church and state.³ This unrest took place against the background of North American resistance to the government of George III, culminating in the Declaration of Independence of 1776 and the Revolutionary War. There was widespread support for the American cause among the Nonconformists.⁴ Some of the titles used by the open communionists included, *A Modest Plea for Free Communion*, 1772; *The House of God Opened*, 1777; and *The General Doctrine of Toleration Applied to the Particular Case of Free Communion*, 1781. These suggest that their authors saw themselves as pioneers of a wider freedom within the ranks of nonconformity.

While the atmosphere of social and political agitation cannot be discounted, it is more significant that the controversy was renewed as the impact of the Evangelical Revival began to be felt among the churches. Strengthened bonds of fellowship across denominational divisions sharpened the desire for wider terms of communion.⁵

1. JOHN COLLETT RYLAND AND DANIEL TURNER

The communion debate was reopened by tracts written by 'Candidus' and 'Pacificus'.⁶ Although published separately, these pamphlets are

---

from subscription to the Thirty-nine Articles. Parliament rejected this, Ivimey, *HEB*, 4, p. 27.

³ By the Toleration Act, 1689, Nonconformist ministers were required to subscribe to most of the Thirty-nine Articles of the Church of England. After a number of unsuccessful attempts to free themselves from this requirement in the 1770s, relief was granted in 1779. Ibid., pp. 27 ff.

⁴ Michael R. Watts, *The Dissenters*, vol. 1, p. 479; Payne, 'Nonconformists and the American Revolution', p. 210.

⁵ The breadth of Ryland's friendships has already been indicated in chapter 3.

⁶ Daniel Turner [Candidus], *A Modest Plea for Free Communion at the Lord's Table; Particularly between the Baptists and the Paedobaptists. In a Letter to a Friend*, London, 1772; John Collett Ryland [Pacificus], *A Modest Plea for Free Communion at the Lord's Table; Between True Believers of All Denominations: In a Letter to a Friend*, n.d. [1772]. For the establishment of the identity of these two pamphlets and the evidence of collaboration between Turner and Ryland and subsequently with Robinson, see R. W. Oliver, 'John Collett Ryland, Daniel Turner and Robert Robinson and the Communion Controversy, 1771-1781', *Baptist Quarterly*, 29 (April 1981), 77-79, reprinted as Appendix A below.

[59]

almost identical and the result of collaboration. They will therefore be considered here under the title *'The Candidus-Pacificus Tract'*. It was an open secret that 'Candidus' was Daniel Turner of Abingdon and 'Pacificus' was John Collett Ryland of Northampton.[7] When Abraham Booth replied to the pamphlets a few years later, he made it clear that he was answering Turner and Ryland.[8] This identification has never been challenged.

The breadth of John Collet Ryland's friendships and his passion for freedom must have promoted his collaboration with Daniel Turner (1710-98).[9] Turner was pastor of the Baptist Church at Abingdon, Berkshire, from 1748 to 1798. Prior to 1772, he had published hymns, poetry, and devotional literature. He shared Ryland's concern for education and produced works on rhetoric and English grammar. Common concern over the restriction of admission to the Lord's Table drew together two unlikely collaborators. Ryland's theology was close to that of Gill, whereas the speculations of Daniel Turner raised questions about his orthodoxy.

In the late 1750s a cloud of suspicion rested over Turner, which has never been properly explained. In 1752 he was accepted as the first student of the London Baptist Education Society, an institution set up to provide training for Particular Baptist ministers and students.[10] He received tuition in London under Thomas Llewellyn while at the same time continuing to serve the Abingdon church. For several years, until December 1756, reports of his good progress were given,[11] but the minutes for 4 January 1757 reported:

[7] Ivimey, *HEB*, 4, p. 35.

[8] Abraham Booth, *Works*, 3 vols. London, 1813 vol. 2: 'An Apology for the Baptists, in which they are Vindicated from the Imputation of laying an Unwarrantable Stress upon the Ordinance of Baptism and against the Charge of Bigotry in Refusing Communion at the Lord's Table to Paedobaptists', pp. 486, 489.

[9] There is no biography of Turner. Outline details have been drawn from E. A. Payne, *The Baptists of Berkshire*, London, l951, pp. 73-85.

[10] 'Minutes of a Society for the Support of Students for the Ministry', Angus Library, Regent's Park College, Oxford, Meeting of 7 Nov. 1752.

[11] Ibid.; see references to each half-yearly examination from 6 Nov. 1753 to 3 Dec. 1756.

The Communion Controversy, 1772–81

Mr Turner having also been examined, the question was moved, That it is the opinion of the Committee, that He is not a proper person to receive any further Assistance from the Society in his Education for the Ministry.[12]

There is no suggestion of any moral lapse. The first half of the 4 January minute refers to the satisfactory examination of two applicants 'with respect to their principles in religion'. This would suggest that Turner had disagreed with the Committee on some matter of doctrinal orthodoxy. There is no indication given as to what this was. In the following year, however, he made his first appeal for open communion in his *Compendium of Social Religion*.[13] After discussing church life in a practical way, Turner went on in the conclusion to 'add a few general observations in favour of a greater freedom in church communion than is generally practised'.[14] He accepted the need for discipline, but urged that Dissenters as lovers of liberty, should exercise the greater charity in inviting men to the communion table. Although he did not discuss the question of baptism as a term of communion, he insisted that

> in order to overbalance the strong presumptive evidence already produced, in favour of the more catholic as against the more limited communion; we ought to expect the clearest and most express direction for the prohibition of the former or the maintenance of the latter, or both.[15]

Turner's appeal for greater church freedom was consistent with a lifelong advocacy of liberty, which was to welcome the French Revolution, although deploring its later excesses.[16]

---

[12] Ibid., 4 Jan 1757. Although it was decided to report this decision to Turner's church, no reference to it appears in the relevant Abingdon Church Book, deposited in the Angus Library, Oxford.

[13] Daniel Turner, *A Compendium of Social Religion or the Nature and Constitution of Christian Churches*, London, 1758.

[14] Ibid., p. 118.

[15] Ibid., pp. 126–7.

[16] Daniel Turner, *An Exhortation to Peace, Loyalty and the Support of Government*, Abingdon, 1792, passim. Turner summarized his position, 'As Protestant Dissenters we are upon principle, sincere and warm FRIENDS to both Civil and Religious Liberty, yet as Christians utter ENEMIES to all licentious violence against the

Daniel Turner may have shared a love of liberty with John Ryland, but there were significant differences between the two men. In a letter written in 1782, Turner revealed that he did not subscribe to the doctrine of Particular Redemption. He wrote,

> I am one who with the good Mr Polhill, Mr How, Dr Watts and many others hold the doctrine of Particular Election and general Redemption as it may be called.[17]

These were unusual sentiments for a Particular Baptist minister in the 1780s. The same letter also refers to

> the puzzling nonsensical manner the orthodox people ... generally take in maintaining the Doctrine of the Deity of Christ & upon the stupid Athanasian plan – the language of A. C. [Athanasian Creed?] is as different from that of the Scriptures as Darkness from Light. Let us not attempt to explain the inexplicable.[18]

It is not known whether Turner held such views on Redemption or on the nature of Christ's deity, when he found himself in trouble with the London Committee fifteen years earlier. It is not clear to what extent he rejected the Athanasian Creed; but in both areas he was moving away from the orthodoxy both of the *1689 Confession* and of Gill's *Declaration of Faith and Practice*.[19] In matters of doctrine, as opposed to church practice, Turner's thinking shows greater affinities with that of his friend Robert Robinson of Cambridge than with that of John Ryland.

Government,' p. 8. Payne, *Baptists of Berkshire*, p. 83. It was a common love of freedom, which first drew together Turner and Robinson of Cambridge. In 1774 Robinson published his *Arcana* as a contribution to the campaign for freedom from compulsory subscription to religious creeds. Turner's reaction was 'When I was informed that the *Arcana* was written by a baptist minister, I replied, "No, it cannot be: we have not one amongst us who can write such a book as the *Arcana*"', George Dyer, *Memoirs of the Life and Writings of Robert Robinson*, London, 1796, p. 82.

[17] 'Daniel Turner to Mr Munn, Watford, 14 June 1782', Angus Library, Regent's Park College, Oxford.   [18] Ibid.

[19] Both the *1689 Confession* (VIII, 2) and Gill's *Declaration* (pp. 6, 7) reflected the teaching of the Athanasian Creed. Gill in fact strengthened his Declaration's statement on the person of Christ to counteract a current tendency to Sabellianism, Rippon, *Life of Gill*, p. 17.

THE CANDIDUS-PACIFICUS TRACT

The opening words of the *Candidus-Pacificus Tract* make it clear that Ryland and Turner were engaged in a domestic debate within the Particular Baptist community.

> I hear that I, and the church under my care, have been severely censured by several of our *stricter brethren of the Baptist denomination* for admitting Paedobaptists to commune with us at the Lord's Table.[20]

There is no suggestion of two denominations or indeed any desire to divide the Particular Baptists into two rival camps over this issue.

Compared to some of the later writings on the issue of the terms of communion, the Candidus-Pacificus Tract was a small contribution to the discussion. Its importance in re-opening the debate, however, necessitates a summary of its reasoning. Ryland and Turner argued that all true Christians 'must have an *equal right* to ALL the privileges of the Gospel', including access to the Lord's Table. Since all Christians derive such rights from Christ, no one has the right to deprive any who are 'as capable of enjoying, and improving those privileges, as effectually to all moral ends of their appointment as we ourselves are'. This overrides 'different sentiments or mistakes about the subject and mode of baptism'. Exclusion of true Christians from any means of grace is an invasion of Christ's prerogative as well as being an injury to the Christians concerned. Since Christ 'does accept of Paedobaptist Christians, when they remember Him at his table ... it therefore appears to us, a setting of our faces against the LORD JESUS CHRIST, and his conduct in the dispensations of his grace, to refuse admittance to his table to such of our Christian brethren as He himself admits there'.

We are commanded to receive the weak, allowing liberty of conscience to others as we claim it for ourselves. If we accept Paedobaptists as true Christians, we have to admit that the arguments about baptism, 'about which we differ, are not so clearly stated in the Bible (however clear to us) but that even *sincere Christians* may mistake them. A private opinion

---

[20] Pacificus, *Modest Plea*, p. 1.

therefore on the one side or the other, can never be justly made an *indispensable term of communion at the Lord's Table*.'[21]

There is no command or example in the Bible that makes baptism an essential term of communion.

Experience has shown that forbearance and charity are more likely to soften men's prejudices against baptism than rigidity is. To compel serious Christians to forego the Lord's Supper 'or to set up separate societies is opposed to the *uniting spirit*, which appears everywhere in the Gospel of Christ'. The authors concluded that exclusion is 'not a little contributing to the cause of infidelity'.[22]

Having made their plea for unity, Candidus and Pacificus went on to deal with objections. They considered first the obvious strict communionist objection that baptism is an initiating ordinance and logically precedes participation in the Lord's Supper. They agreed that order is of importance, but insisted that

> the edification of Christians, and their obedience to the acknowledged command of Christ to all his Disciples, Do this in remembrance of me, are points of infinitely greater importance; the least therefore ought to give way to the greatest.[23]

They also refused to attempt to force the conscience of a brother with reference to baptism.

The second objection was that open communion is the way 'to beget a cold indifference to the cause of truth and by degrees intirely [sic] ruin it'.[24] They replied that the opposite was their experience.

> The truth is great and will always prevail by fair and candid argument, managed according to the benevolent and forebearing spirit of the Gospel.[25]

The third objection was that of the person, whose conscience compelled him to exclude the unbaptized from the table. In reply, the writers stated that they respected such a conscience, but urged the objector to

[21] Ibid. [22] Ibid., p. 2. [23] Ibid.
[24] Ibid. [25] Ibid.

The Communion Controversy, 1772–81

make absolutely certain that his conscience was correctly informed in this serious matter.

The last objection, that some Paedobaptists revile Baptists and hardly acknowledge them as Christians, is dismissed as irrelevant, since such bigoted persons are unlikely to seek communion with Baptists.

The pamphlet concluded by appealing to New Testament arguments for unity and noted the way in which the Apostolic Church dealt with the division created by the problem of circumcision.

RESPONSE

For a full reply, Ryland and Turner had to wait until 1778, when Abraham Booth produced his *Apology for the Baptists*. In the meantime, there appeared a little pamphlet entitled *Candidus Examined with Candor* [sic] by Philalethes.[26] Its author was Dan Taylor, a leading General Baptist minister, who pointed out that most Christians insist on baptism as a prerequisite to church fellowship.[27] He appealed to the Baptist belief that only the immersion of adult believers is baptism and warned that to suggest that there were grounds for uncertainty about baptism 'would be a foul reflection on Jesus our great lawgiver'. This led Taylor to question the sincerity of those who could not accept his understanding of baptism. Candidus' position rested on a very dangerous premise:

> The whole of Candidus's reasoning seems to me to be built on this popish and unscriptural maxim that 'the church has authority to decree rites or to dispense with the ordinances and appointments of Christ, as the fancies, prejudices or interests of men may require'.[28]

---

[26] Dan Taylor [Philalethes], *Candidus Examined with Candor; [sic] or a Modest Inquiry into the Propriety and Force of What is Contained in a Late Pamphlet; intitled, a Modest Plea for Free Communion at the Lord's Table; Particularly between the Baptists and Paedobaptists by Candidus*, London, 1772. For identification of its author see Adam Taylor, *Memoirs of the Rev. Dan Taylor*, London, 1820, p. 86.

[27] Philalethes, *Candidus Examined*, p. 6. He appealed to 'most professors of Christianity ... whatever be their idea of baptism.'

[28] Ibid., p. 15.

Taylor's reply was a hurried production, not written for publication. It had originally been a letter to a friend, who published it without permission.[29]

2. *THE HOUSE OF GOD OPENED*, BY JOHN BROWN

Candidus' *Modest Plea* was followed by another pamphlet in favour of open communion, *The House of God Opened*, written by John Brown of Kettering in 1777.[30] Although this was a larger work than the *Candidus-Pacificus Tract*, it seems not to have attracted so much attention, possibly because its author was not as well known as Turner and Ryland.

John Brown (d. 1800)[31] had been ordained pastor of the Little Meeting, Kettering in 1752.[32] In 1765 he was one of the six men who founded the Northamptonshire Baptist Association,[33] acting as it moderator in 1767, when he also wrote its circular letter.[34]

When Brown was called to the pastorate of the Little Meeting, it was an open membership and open communion church, as it had been from its foundation in 1696.[35] However, after several years of church unrest – apparently unrelated to the communion question – it was decided in 1765 that all future members should be received by baptism and confession of faith.[36] This change was reflected in a new church covenant in 1768.[37]

What Brown thought of these changes at this time is unknown. However, in 1769 there was a division in the church over the administration of

---

[29] Taylor, *Memoir of Dan Taylor*, p. 86. Dan Taylor's own comment on the tract was that it was 'not in any way fit for the press as it was. However printed it is! May it do some service!'

[30] John Brown, *The House of God Opened and His Table Free for Baptists and Paedobaptists, Who are Saints and Faithful in Christ*, London, 1777.

[31] J. Ryland states that Brown died at Lymington, April 14, 1800: *The Work of Faith, The Labour of Love, and the Patience of Hope, Illustrated in the Life and Death of the Rev. Andrew Fuller* [1816], 2nd. ed. London, 1818, p. 347. So far no detailed biographical details have come to light.

[32] Gladys M. Barrett, *The Fuller Church, Kettering*, St Albans, 1946, p. 4.

[33] T. H. S. Elwyn, *The Northamptonshire Baptist Association*, London, 1964, p. 11.   [34] Ibid., p. 99.

[35] Barrett, *Fuller Church, Kettering*, p. 4.   [36] Ibid.   [37] Ibid.

The Communion Controversy, 1772–81

a society for poor relief.[38] In spite of an attempt by John Ryland, Jr. to mediate, John Brown and a group of members withdrew to form another church, which lasted until at least 1786.[39] This second church never joined the Northamptonshire Baptist Association. In 1782 Andrew Fuller moved to Kettering to become pastor of the Little Meeting[40] and so the pastorates of Brown and Fuller in Kettering overlapped. Fuller practised strict communion and was to write in its defence.[41]

By 1777 John Brown was ready to go into print to defend the practice he had followed for thirteen years at the Little Meeting, and which he was presumably doing at the second church. *The House of God Opened* followed a method similar to that of Turner and Ryland.

The preface is noteworthy for its usage of the expression 'strict Baptist'. Strict communionists are referred to as those who 'have adopted and go by the name of strict Baptists'.[42] This must be one of the earliest pieces of evidence that there were Baptists calling themselves strict Baptists.[43]

Many of John Brown's arguments had already been employed by Candidus and Pacificus, but there is evidence of some fresh thinking by Brown. He broke new ground, when he charged the strict communionists with inconsistency.

> Where will the strict Baptist find either precept or precedent to receive and retain persons in their Churches merely because they agree with them and submit to their mode of Baptism, and yet are unsound in the

---

[38] Ibid.   [39] Ibid.

[40] John Ryland, *The Life and Death of the Rev. Andrew Fuller*, 2nd ed. London, 1818, p. 59.

[41] *Complete Works of the Rev. Andrew Fuller*, ed. Andrew Gunton Fuller, London 1862. 'On Terms of Communion', pp. 852-3. 'Strictures on the Rev. John Carter's *Thoughts on Baptism and Mixed Communion*', pp. 853-4. 'Thoughts on Open Communion', pp. 854-5, 'Strict Communion in the Mission Church at Serampore,' p. 885, 'The Admission of Unbaptized Persons to the Lord's Supper Inconsistent with the New Testament: A Letter to a Friend', (in 1814), pp. 855-9.

[42] Brown, *House of God Opened*, p. 1.

[43] Peter Naylor has drawn attention to the use of this epithet in the Eastern Midlands as early as 1700, but there is no known evidence that the strict communionists had accepted it themselves (*Picking up a Pin for the Lord*, London: Grace Publications, 1992, pp. 69 ff.).

[67]

doctrine of the Trinity and the Sonship of Christ? Who embrace the absurd notion of the pre-existence of his human soul; who deny the Christian Sabbath and Christ's purchase of the blessings of grace and glory; that ministers should preach the law; and that it is the duty of unregenerate sinners to pray for spiritual blessings.[44]

The logic of this argument was later to prove counter-productive when some strict Baptists began to restrict admission to the Table even more rigidly. Brown also made a charge of inconsistency against those of his opponents who were prepared to ask Paedobaptist preachers to minister to them.[45]

John Brown openly argued for the admission of Paedobaptists into the membership of Baptist Churches. Whatever the practice of Turner and Ryland may have been, in their pamphlets they contented themselves with a plea for open communion. Brown believed that the admission of Paedobaptists was a right and not a concession. Replying to those who insisted that there were Paedobaptist churches for Paedobaptists, he declared:

> If there are, that will not justify you in barring them out of your churches, if they have a right of entrance and desire fellowship with you.[46]

John Brown went beyond the advocacy of open membership to question the wisdom of using one of the sacraments to label a religious party.

> Supposing the mode of immersion to be right, yet your adopting that unscriptural party-name and distinction of the baptised churches of Christ, and refusing fellowship with all who do not practice the same, is the ready way to let your good be evil spoken of; as it gives people great reason to think you lay too great stress on Baptism by immersion.[47]

Such a comment indicates that John Brown's thinking had changed in the thirteen years since he had helped to found the Northamptonshire Baptist Association. It must also explain why the second church in Kettering was never listed among the associated churches.

---

[44] Ibid., p. 11.
[45] Ibid., p. 23.
[46] Ibid., p. 16.
[47] Ibid., p. 8.

3. *Free Communion an Innovation* by William Buttfield

John Brown received a vigorous reply from William Buttfield, pastor of the Baptist Church at Thorn, near Dunstable.[48]

In 1773 Buttfield had been one of five signatories to a pamphlet which opposed the movement to free Dissenting ministers from the legal obligation to subscribe to the Thirty-nine Articles of the Church of England.[49] He and his associates declared themselves, 'well satisfied with the present mode of qualification prescribed in the Act of Toleration'. Any change would 'be going back to Popery', would encourage 'persons who deny the doctrine of the ever blessed Trinity and other important truths', and 'would give great offence to the Reverend clergy of the Church of England'.[50] Such sentiments were by no means typical of Baptists or even of strict communionists, some of whose London leaders were actively seeking freedom from subscription. They do, however, prepare us for the tone of William Buttfield's opposition to John Brown.

Buttfield was convinced that the Baptist doctrine of baptism could only be undermined by the practice of open communion. Before taking up Brown's arguments therefore, he defended the doctrine of baptism by immersion of believers only. The importance he attached to believer's baptism runs right through the work. He agreed that toleration in non-essentials should be exercised, but denied that this extended to baptism, 'which is the indispensable duty of all believers'.[51] Thus he rejected any suggestion that the Pauline arguments about things indifferent could ever be applied to baptism.

William Buttfield dismissed the hope that mixed communion would make Paedobaptists more ready to consider the Baptist teaching. Rather, he saw it as destructive of Baptist churches.

Throughout Buttfield's work, there runs a deep concern to uphold the Baptist doctrine of baptism. He shared a baptismal theology with Ryland,

---

[48] William Buttfield, *Free Communion an Innovation, or, An Answer to Mr John Brown's Pamphlet*, London, 1778.

[49] Ivimey, *HEB*, vol. 4, pp. 31–33 prints the pamphlet in full. The other signatories were W. Coles, N. Pike, T. Marshall, and E. Keach, all Bedfordshire ministers.

[50] Ibid., p. 33.   [51] Buttfield, *Free Communion an Innovation*, p. 16.

Turner, and Brown, but whereas the open communionists were confident that they could uphold their position by argument, Buttfield believed they could not, or would not, do so in mixed communion churches. To open communionists deeply concerned for the greater unity among Christians, Buttfield insisted that the demands of baptism overrode all considerations.

> One command of God cannot require the sacrifice of another, in order to a compliance with it.[52]

One is left with the impression that Buttfield considered that only a perversity of thought prevented Paedobaptists from submitting to Baptist teaching.

4. Abraham Booth's *Apology for the Baptists*, 1778.

William Buttfield's tract was soon eclipsed by Abraham Booth's *Apology for the Baptists*, which long remained the standard defence of strict communion.

Booth was not so outspoken on political matters as were Ryland and Turner. There is no evidence to reveal his feelings on the intensifying pressure for increased Nonconformist liberty in the 1770s. By far the greater number of the London Particular Baptist Ministers supported the American cause in the War of Independence. There are no grounds for supposing that Booth was not among the majority.[53] On one political matter he made his position very clear. In January 1792 he preached and published a powerful sermon against the slave trade, urging support for the Anti-Slavery Society.[54]

---

[52] Ibid., p. 23.

[53] In 1784 John Rippon wrote, 'I believe that all our ministers in town except two, and most of our brethren in the country were on the side of the Americans in the late dispute'; quoted in Payne, 'Nonconformists and the American Revolution', p. 210. Probably one of the two exceptions was John Martin of Grafton Street of whom Andrew Fuller wrote, 'he seems to have an antipathy to America in religion as well as in politics', Fuller, *Works*, 'Remarks on Mr Martin's Publication', p. 326.

[54] Booth, *Works*, vol. 1, p. xlix, and *Works*, vol. 3, 'Commerce in the Human Species and the Enslaving of Innocent Persons, Inimical to the Law of Moses and the Gospel of Christ', pp. 183–218.

The Communion Controversy, 1772–81

Theologically, Booth stood in the tradition of Evangelical Calvinism, which had been stimulated by the Evangelical Awakening. His rejection of the Hyper-Calvinism of Gill is evidenced by his *Glad Tidings to Perishing Sinners, or, the Genuine Gospel a Complete Warrant for Sinners to Believe in Jesus*.[55] He was clearly sympathetic towards the Evangelical Calvinism of men such as Henry Venn and other prominent figures in the Revival. He could not, however, allow this common agreement on the doctrine of salvation to weaken his ecclesiastical convictions. In this respect he displays an affinity with the Old Dissent, which had always laid great emphasis upon churchmanship.[56] One effect of the Revival was to play down ecclesiastical distinctions. Booth could not do this. As a young man he had left the General Baptists – to whom he owed so much – for conscientious reasons. In his farewell sermon to the General Baptists he had remarked that, 'fraud and concealment of various kinds may obtain the friendship of men – but when friendship is obtained by such means, he who gains it, and they who grant it are chargeable with injustice peculiarly execrable'.[57]

In middle life he felt obliged to resist the open communionists, because he believed that loyalty to Christ must forbid what seemed to him to be a tampering with the ordinances.

Booth's *Apology* was the most detailed work to appear on either side of the communion controversy since the seventeenth century. He took a broad view of the question, not limiting himself to answering contemporaries, but considered Bunyan's work as well. Although he did not allow any previous writer to mould his approach, he displayed a much greater sense of history than any previous eighteenth-century writer on this sub-

---

[55] Booth, *Works*, vol. 2, pp. 1–232.

[56] Bernard L. Manning, 'Some Characteristics of the Older Dissent', *Congregational Quarterly*, vol. 5, (1927), p. 289, 'Though the Evangelical Revival quickened and multiplied those pure in heart that see God, it weakened and diluted the older churchmanship of Dissent; because it brought into our Communion a mass of persons with no ecclesiastical connections or foundation or experience. And the essence of the Old Dissent was an ecclesiastical experience.' Cf. Wilson, *London Dissenting Churches*, vol. 4, Appendix, especially p. 557.

[57] Booth, *Works*, vol. 1, 'Memoir', p. xxiv.

ject. Much more irenic than Buttfield, he wrote with sympathy and respect for Paedobaptists, even though he could not receive them to the communion table. He was careful to explain that when strict communionists insisted that baptism was a prerequisite to communion, they were applying the same principle as the Paedobaptists.

> Our persuasion, therefore, concerning the necessity of baptism as a term of communion, having had the sanction of universal belief and universal practice for almost sixteen hundred years, it lies on our brethren to prove that it is false and unscriptural; and to show from the New Testament, that theirs has the stamp of divine authority.[58]

He went on to allege that

> that bold perverter of gospel truth, Socinus, introduced the custom of receiving unbaptized persons to communion.[59]

Booth insisted that his work was a piece of defensive writing, which would never have appeared but for attacks on 'those professors who are invidiously called STRICT BAPTISTS'.[60] He pointed out that he was not disputing with Paedobaptists, 'but with such as profess themselves Baptists, yet practice free communion'.[61] Indeed the *Apology* was an expansion of a series of letters written to a minister, who had sought advice, when he received a call to a mixed communion church.[62]

There are suggestions that the effects of the Evangelical Revival were causing tensions at this time.

> Our ministering brethren of the Tabernacle have sometimes taken the liberty of making reflections upon us, as if our opinion relating to baptism greatly intrenched on the honour and offices of Jesus Christ.[63]

The context makes it clear that Booth is referring to Whitefield's Tabernacle in Moorfields, less than a mile from Little Prescot Street. Later he quoted with approval an anonymous Paedobaptist who complained:

[58] Booth, *Apology for the Baptists*, p. 363
[59] Ibid., p. 417.
[60] Ibid., p. 332.
[61] Ibid., p. 354.
[62] Booth *Works*, vol. 1, 'Memoir', p. xliii.
[63] Booth, *Apology for the Baptists*, p. 338.

The Methodists have not, indeed, gone so far as their spiritual brethren (the Quakers) have done, in rejecting all external ceremonies; but they are taught to believe, that all concern about the ancient order and customs of the Christians is mere party spirit, and injurious to the devout exercises of the heart.[64]

George Whitefield died eight years before the appearance of the *Apology*, but with his catholic spirit and large following he did more to break down barriers among Christians than any other eighteenth-century figure. It was he who cried during a sermon, 'God help us all to forget party names and to be Christians in deed and truth!'[65]

Booth dismissed the charge that Baptists laid undue emphasis on the ordinance of baptism; he maintained that those who insisted on faith before baptism could not be accused of baptismal regeneration. Baptists therefore do not emphasize baptism as much as some paedobaptists do.

He also argued strongly that Christ alone has the authority to regulate the conditions of communion.

> A gospel church has no more power to fix the terms of communion, or to set aside those prescribed by Jesus Christ, than to make a rule of faith, or to settle ordinances of divine worship.[66]

The widespread belief of Christians is that there is a logical order for baptism and the Lord's Supper and the former precedes the latter. Open communion Baptists thus set themselves against the universal practice of the Christian church. Booth feared that such Baptists would become the only branch of the church which did not insist on baptism. A minister with such views 'does violence to his own distinguishing sentiment and is guilty of *Felo-de-se*'.[67]

He argued from the Great Commission, from the New Testament precedents, and from the nature of the two sacraments, that there is a natural

---

[64] Ibid., p. 458.
[65] Quoted in Arnold Dallimore, *Life of George Whitefield*, vol. 2, Edinburgh: Banner of Truth, 1980, p. 543.
[66] Booth, *Apology for the Baptists*, pp. 358-359.
[67] i.e., suicide; ibid., p. 367.

order to be observed, with baptism preceding the Lord's Supper. He concluded:

> Either Jesus Christ has informed us in the New Testament what baptism is and what is requisite to communion at his table or he has not. If the former, we cannot admit anything as baptism, which we believe is not so; nor receive anyone to communion, but those whom we consider qualified according to his directions without violating our allegiance to him as the King Messiah, and rebelling against his government. If the latter, there is no judge in Israel, and everyone may do that which is right in his own eyes, in regard to these institutions.[68]

Booth also argued that open communion presupposes a dispensing power in the church, which would allow a mutilation of either sacrament. He argued that obedience to God is displayed supremely in positive ordinances or commands, which can only be known because God has revealed them.

> Accursed then is the principle, and rebellious is the conduct of those professors, who think themselves warranted, by the grace of the Gospel to trifle with God's positive appointments, any more than the priests or the people were of old. For whether Jehovah lay his commandments on Gabriel in glory or on Adam in paradise, whether he enjoins the performance of anything on Patriarchs, or Jews, or Christians, they are all and equally bound to obey, or else his commands must stand for nothing.[69]

Booth's views on the New Testament order of the sacraments compelled him to argue that the only ground upon which a Baptist church could receive a Paedobaptist to the Communion was that the Paedobaptist believed himself to have been baptized. If this form of arguing were accepted, Booth suggested that baptism could be administered to anyone who desired it, without considering whether he were qualified or not. He insisted:

> It is not the measure of a believer's knowledge, nor the evidence of his integrity; nor is it the charitable opinion we form about his acceptance

[68] Ibid., pp. 417-418.   [69] Ibid., p. 399.

with God, that is the rule of his admission to the sacred supper; but the precepts of Jesus Christ, and the practice of apostolic churches.[70]

When Booth examined the New Testament passages used by the open communionists to support their case, he concluded that since they included no reference to baptism, they were irrelevant. He insisted that in Romans chapters 14 and 15, the Apostle Paul is concerned to maintain fellowship amongst those who were already baptized and in church fellowship. He appealed to a Paedobaptist writer, who stated:

> The Apostle is not here speaking of admission to church membership at all; – nor does he consider those to whom he writes in the precise light of members of the Church universal; but as members of a particular church or body; among whom there was some difference of opinion about meats etc., which was like to break their communion together, as is plain from the preceding chapter.[71]

Granted that these passages do not refer directly to differences about baptism, it surely may be asked whether the general principles employed by the apostle deal with sincerely held differences among Christians, and if such are not considered in Romans 14 and 15, where are such differences faced?

Booth had to face the charge that he lacked charity towards his Paedobaptist brother, but insisted that his supreme loyalty to Christ compelled him to require baptism before communion.

> Communion I have with you in affection; but fellowship at the Lord's Table is a very distinct act, a very different thing; and is to be regulated entirely by the revealed will of Him that appointed it.[72]

Already the open communionists had charged Booth and his friends with inconsistency because they welcomed Paedobaptist ministers into their pulpits, but refused to accept them as communicants. Booth replied:

---

[70] Ibid., p. 404.

[71] Ibid., p. 435, quoting Smith, *Compendium: An Account of the Form and Order of the Church*, pp. 109, 110.

[72] Booth, *Apology for the Baptists*, p. 463.

Public preaching is not confined to persons in a Church state, nor ever was; but the Lord's Supper is a Church ordinance, nor ought ever to be administered but to a particular church, as such. Now it is of a particular church, and of a positive ordinance peculiar to it, concerning which is all our dispute. There is not that strict mutual relation between bare hearers of the word and their preachers, as there is between members of a church and her pastor or between the members themselves.[73]

He pointed out that, when Paedobaptists minister to a Baptist congregation,

> it is in expectation that they will preach the gospel; that very gospel which we believe and love, and about which there is no difference between them and us. But when they receive Paedobaptists into communion, they openly connive at what they consider an error; an error both in judgment and in practice; an error of that kind which the scripture calls will-worship, and the traditions of men.[74]

Finally Booth considered the epithet, Strict Baptist, which was being used to describe his position. His opponents had invented the label, but Booth was prepared to accept it.

> If by the epithet strict, they mean exact, accurate, conscientiously nice; their candour deserves commendation. In that sense of the term we are not ashamed to be called Strict Baptists; we cheerfully adopt the character.[75]

After describing his critics as Latitudinarian Baptists,[76] Booth went on to make a passionate plea for consistency:

> If infant sprinkling be a human invention, disown it, renounce it, entirely reject it and no longer let it hold the place of a divine institution in any of our Churches. But if it be from heaven, embrace it, profess it, practise it in the face of the sun, and lay the other absolutely aside as destitute of a divine warrant ... Be either consistent Baptists or Paedobaptists; for according to your present practice, all thinking and impartial men must pronounce you an heterogeneous mixture of both.[77]

[73] Ibid., p. 473.   [74] Ibid., p. 474.   [75] Ibid., p. 499.
[76] Ibid., p. 503.   [77] Ibid., pp. 508, 509.

For the first time a leading Baptist minister had accepted the description, 'Strict Baptist'. This acceptance must not however be understood to suggest that Booth considered such a designation to be a distinct denominational title. He always considered himself to be a member of the Particular Baptist denomination, which included open and strict communionists. He was debating with colleagues with whom he had no desire to break fellowship. In 1798, Booth was visited by William Newman, a fellow strict communionist, who noted in his diary,

> Visited Mr Booth, who is but very poorly. He thinks Mr Hall of Cambridge, in parts and learning, the first man in our denomination.[78]

Although Booth maintained his support for strict communion,[79] he clearly accepted a prominent open communionist as a fellow member of the same denomination. Hall had not yet challenged Booth's teaching in print, but his church at Cambridge was a leading open-communion church and Hall's beliefs could have been no secret.

Like so many strict communionists Abraham Booth experienced a powerful tension. He felt very poignantly the differences that existed between brethren. He showed a real love for all his Christian brethren and a truly catholic spirit. He did not however feel free to challenge what he perceived to be a divinely-prescribed order in the administration of the sacraments.

5. Robert Robinson's *General Doctrine of Toleration*

After the appearance of Abraham Booth's *Apology*, nothing on the same scale appeared from either side for nearly forty years. There was, however, one small contribution which deserves to be noted, partly because of the fresh approach of its author, and partly because it was a direct reply to Booth. This was Robert Robinson's *The General Doctrine of Toleration Applied to the Particular Case of Free Communion*, a pamphlet of some

---

[78] George Pritchard, *Memoir of the Rev. William Newman, D.D.*, London, 1837, p. 168.

[79] Booth helped Newman to prepare his *Baptism, an Indispensable Pre-requisite of Communion* in 1804–5, Pritchard, *Memoir of Newman*, p. 179.

fifty pages, which appeared in 1781.[80] George Dyer, Robinson's friend and biographer, explained that it originated in a series of sermons on 'civil and religious liberty' first preached to the group in process of forming the New Road Baptist Church in Oxford.[81]

Robert Robinson (1735–90)[82] is one of the enigmas of Baptist history. Today he is best remembered for his hymn, 'Come, Thou Fount of Every Blessing'. Like John Collett Ryland and Daniel Turner, he was a passionate champion of liberty.[83] He delighted in debate and throughout his life showed a readiness to modify his opinions. Having professed conversion under the ministry of George Whitefield, he began his ministerial career as a Methodist; then for a short time he was an Independent, before finally becoming a Baptist.[84] During his Cambridge pastorate he associated with Rowland Hill, John Berridge, and several other Anglican

---

[80] I have shown that Ivimey, *HEB*, vol, 4, p. 35, mistakenly dated Robinson's pamphlet as 1771 and therefore suggested that Booth answered Robinson in his *Apology*. Ivimey's account has been followed by other historians, including, most recently, Robison, 'The Particular Baptists, 1760–1820'; and R. A. Coppenger 'Abraham Booth, 1734–1806'. In fact Robinson published his pamphlet in 1781 and replied to Booth; R. W. Oliver, 'John Collett Ryland, Daniel Turner and Robert Robinson and the Communion Controversy, 1771–81', *Baptist Quarterly*, 29, 1981–2, pp. 77–79.

[81] Dyer, *Memoir of the Life and Writings of Robert Robinson*, 1796, p. 197. It is not without significance that Turner was a witness to the New Road Church Covenant, Oxford, 1780. By this document, the church members, Baptists and Paedobaptists, pledged themselves to receive each other, 'because we can find no warrant in the Word of God to make such difference of sentiment any bar to communion at the Lord's Table in particular, or to Church fellowship in general; and because the Lord Jesus receiving and owning them on both sides of the question, we think we ought to do so too'.

[82] Biographies of Robinson include, Dyer, *Memoir*, William Robinson, 'Memoir' prefixed to *Select Works of the Rev. Robert Robinson of Cambridge*, The Bunyan Library, vol.2, London, 1861. Graham W. Hughes, *With Freedom Fired*. London, 1955, L. G. Schell, 'Robert Robinson (1735–90) with special reference to his Religious and Political Thought', Ph.D. thesis, University of Edinburgh, 1950.

[83] 'Others beside Robinson have been fired by freedom. What makes Robinson unusual is that his passion for freedom embraced the freedom of others as well as his own.' Geoffrey F. Nuttall, 'The First Seventy Years', *History of St Andrew's Street Baptist Church, Cambridge*, ed. K.A.C. Parsons, Cambridge, 1971, p. 11.

[84] Dyer, *Memoir of Robinson*, pp. 17–34.

Evangelicals.[85] He was also closely involved in the affairs of a number of neighbouring Congregational churches as well as with other Baptist congregations.[86]

The Cambridge church had wavered between open and strict communion before Robinson's time,[87] but he would not consider its call to him in 1758 until it declared itself firmly for open communion.[88] The church was Particular Baptist and at his ordination service, Robinson made a confession of his faith, which was Trinitarian and Calvinistic.[89] In the 1780s, however, he was to reveal himself increasingly impatient with Calvin and his teaching[90] and even with the orthodox doctrine of the Trinity.[91] His last sermon which was preached in Joseph Priestley's Unitarian Meeting House in Birmingham, included an attack on the doctrine of the Trinity.[92]

Robinson shared Ryland's and Turner's political views. He supported the American cause in the War of Independence,[93] and the French Revolution he was to describe as 'a truly wonderful work, and interesting in every view'.[94] His plea for open communion was part of a life-long crusade for freedom. He wrote against compulsory subscription to the Thirty-nine Articles by Anglicans and Nonconformists.[95] He fulminated against the managers of the Particular Baptist Fund, because they limited

---

[85] Ibid., p. 55.
[86] Nuttall, 'The First Seventy Years', p. 10.   [87] Ibid., p. 3.
[88] Ibid., p. 35. cf. W. Robinson, 'Memoir of Robinson', p. xxv.
[89] Dyer, *Memoir of Robinson,* prints the Confession in full, pp. 429–32.
[90] Select Works of Robinson, 'Letter to Dan Taylor', 1789, p. 261, 'What makes Baptists so fond of the name and creed of Calvin, seeing the barbarian burnt Servetus and denounced the vengeance of God and the civil magistrate against all Anabaptists?'
[91] Ibid., 'Letter to Mr Marsom of London', 1788, p. 248, 'As to personality in God, a trinity of persons, I think it the most absurd of all absurdities.'
[92] Dyer, *Memoir of Robinson,* p. 397. Dyer quotes Priestley's comment on Robinson's last sermon, 'His discourse was unconnected and desultory; and his manner of treating the trinity savoured rather of the burlesque, than serious reasoning. He attacked orthodoxy more pointedly and sarcastically than I ever did in my life.'
[93] Ibid., pp. 120 ff.   [94] Ibid., p. 427.
[95] See note 49 above, cf. Dyer, *Memoir of Robinson,* pp. 76 ff.

their grants to Calvinistic Baptists.[96] He insisted that truth needed no artificial defences: discussion would inevitably elucidate the truth. Freedom of discussion was the precious possession of the Dissenting churches.

> I am always edified by reading the controversies. I admire the constitution of our churches, because it admits of free debate. Happy community![97]

Robinson opened his pamphlet, *The General Doctrine of Toleration Applied to the Particular Case of Free Communion*, with a brief history of the communion controversy, but made no reference to the contribution of Turner and Ryland. His method was quite different from theirs. By insisting that terms of communion should be derived from the revealed will of Christ, he side-stepped Booth's appeal to the unanimous practice of the Christian church. He suggested that the idea of baptism as the entrance to the church was inherited from Rome and the Reformers, but not from Scripture.[98] For Robinson, baptism was

> An initiation into the profession of Christianity at large, not into the practice of it in any particular church.[99]

Robinson was prepared to accept that strict communion was a good thing, if there were no disputes about baptism.

> A church that tolerates is a good church, but a church that has no errors to tolerate is better. We do not therefore blame those churches, which were never required to admit unbaptized believers, for maintaining strict communion, we only say where the requisition is made, compliance with it is just and right.[100]

He proceeded by an interesting piece of natural theology to argue that it is in the nature of things to diminish difficulties we cannot wholly remove. A difference about baptism constitutes such a difficulty. It is

---

[96] *Select Works of Robinson*, pp. 260, 274.
[97] Quoted Hughes, *With Freedom Fired*, p. 51.
[98] Robinson, *General Doctrine of Toleration*, p. 45.
[99] Ibid., p. 32.   [100] Ibid., p. 16.

The Communion Controversy, 1772–81

wrong to punish for genuinely held differences. The church must therefore make provision for such differences.

> It would argue a great unfitness in any scheme of religion for this world, if it made no provision for human imperfections.[101]

Many of Robinson's arguments had been employed by others before him but he displayed great skill in their presentation. An interesting development was his analysis of New Testament teaching on private judgment. He argued for a biblical toleration. The problem is to decide how far to go. He stated that possible areas of toleration were errors of faith and irregularities of practice. In matters of faith, one distinguished between the facts and inferences from the facts. To deny the facts made a man an infidel and, as such, beyond the bounds of toleration in a Christian church. However, there was scope for toleration in the inferences men made from the facts. Considering irregularities of practice, he distinguished between those which proceeded from hatred of virtue and were therefore intolerable, and those which arose from infirmity and were to be tolerated. It was the latter, he argued that were tolerated by the apostle Paul in Romans 14.[102]

He faced the question of baptism. Robinson pointed out that baptism was administered for several years before there were any Christian churches and also that Jesus Christ was not baptized into any church, neither was the Ethiopian eunuch. Baptism was, therefore, an individual act and not a church ordinance.[103]

Robinson appealed to what he called the law of release and deprivation. To deprive a Christian of the Lord's Supper was to release him from the duty imposed by Christ.

> Now as we pretend to no authority to release from the duty, how is it we should claim authority to deprive of benefit?[104]

Robinson's rigorous intellectual arguments were followed by an appeal to the heart, in which he imagined a strict communion church considering an application for membership from ten eminent Paedobaptists

---

[101] Ibid., p. 21.   [102] Ibid., pp. 23ff.   [103] Ibid., pp. 30, 31.   [104] Ibid., p. 40.

[81]

including John Calvin, Isaac Watts, and Matthew Henry. An application from such outstanding and universally useful Christians, Robinson felt could not be rejected.

Robinson's pamphlet was the most able piece of writing on his side of the controversy at this time, but it does not seem to have gained the attention that it might otherwise have received. This was largely because Robinson's teaching was coming under suspicion in other more important respects. In the year of its publication, Robinson began a series of regular visits to London, combining preaching with research into Baptist history. George Dyer explained that his London preaching brought him into trouble.

> His hearers were rarely addressed on those points of doctrine from which they derived their comfort; and the orthodoxy of the preacher became suspected.[105]

By 1786 Robinson himself wrote:

> I have been seven weeks in London: my own party treated me with neglect, and even preached against me in my presence about mental error, which ... not a soul of them understands.[106]

Robinson's final doctrinal convictions are a matter of some uncertainty. He definitely rejected his earlier Calvinism and was in difficulties with the generally accepted statement of the doctrine of the Trinity. John Berridge of Everton, who knew him well, considered that he was ruined by pride. He 'was a modest, teachable and benevolent young man, but he possessed abilities and grew vain; I thought him a most gracious preacher, but he has forsaken the Lord.'[107]

At the end of his life he was deeply depressed and there is some evidence to suggest that he was suffering from a nervous disorder at the

[105] Dyer, *Memoir of Robinson*, p. 218.

[106] Ibid., p. 284. The reference to mental error arose from a statement made by Robinson in 1777: 'Mere mental errors if they be not entirely innocent in the account of the Supreme Governor of mankind, cannot be, however, objects of blame and punishment among men.' It led to a discussion as to whether men can be held responsible for believing the Gospel. Robinson, *Select Works*, pp. lxxx, lxxxi, 242, 247.

[107] Dyer, *Memoir of Robinson*, p. 55.

time of his final sermon in Birmingham.[108] Whatever his beliefs, he was increasingly ostracized by former friends, whom he in turn ridiculed. Dyer referred to a group, which included Samuel Stennett[109] and Abraham Booth, 'who preached against Robinson from their pulpits, and who were in return lampooned and be-sermonized by him'.[110]

6. The Significance of the Debate

The Controversialists

The controversy about the terms of communion was raised by open communionists. Initially Ryland and Turner were concerned to defend themselves, but the strict communionists quickly found themselves challenged, and Abraham Booth had to repel 'the charge of bigotry'.[111]

The suggestion of rigidity might imply that Hyper-Calvinists were of necessity strict Baptists. This was not always so. John Gill and John Collett Ryland were close friends and both were High Calvinists. Gill was, however, a strict communionist and Ryland an open communionist. Andrew Fuller described himself as a strict Calvinist as opposed to a High Calvinist like Gill, but Fuller was an advocate of strict communion. Fuller and John Ryland, Jr. took similar positions in their understanding of Calvinism, but differed on the communion question. Daniel Turner and Robert Robinson each fell into a category of his own. Both men showed an impatience with old creeds and a greater readiness to move in new directions than did most of their brethren. Men of such independence might be expected to demand greater liberty in their ecclesiastical connections.

These open communionists, who were prepared to defend their positions in writing, were men with a passion for freedom. Ryland, Turner, and Robinson all declared for the American colonists in the 1770s. This was also true of another open communionist, Caleb Evans, who wrote to

---

[108] Ibid., pp. lxxxiii–lxxxiv.
[109] Samuel Stennett (1727–95) was pastor of the Little Wild Street Baptist Church, London, 1758–95.
[110] Dyer, *Memoir of Robinson*, p. 295.
[111] See full title of Booth's *Apology*, note 8 above.

challenge John Wesley's criticism of the colonists.[112] The open communionists' support for the colonists was an expression of a deep and long-standing passion for freedom in English Dissent. It was a concern which the Revival was to challenge, many of whose leaders tended to be fearful of popular movements in politics.[113] The open communionists saw a freer admission to the communion table as an ecclesiastical application of a principle, which they already applied in politics. Robinson especially, considered it utterly inconsistent for Dissenters to press for freedom, while they engaged in what he regarded as acts of oppression themselves.[114]

Any description of the open communionists as champions of liberty should not lead to the conclusion that all strict communionists were political reactionaries like William Buttwell. Buttwell did not want to press for greater liberty for Nonconformists and he must have represented others, although it is impossible to say how many. On the other hand, there were strict communionists such as Samuel Stennett, who were active in the moves to secure abolition of Nonconformist subscription to the Thirty-nine Articles.[115] Booth does not seem to have involved himself in politics except in the anti-slavery movement. He seems to have considered his responsibilities to be theological and pastoral. It does seem, therefore, that open communionists were more ready to involve themselves in political discussion than were their strict communion brethren.

While the open communionists found themselves at variance with the political views of Methodism and the leaders of the Evangelical Revival, there can be no doubt that their cause was strengthened by the Revival. Ryland and Robinson had friends among the men of the Revival, and Robinson professed conversion under the preaching of Whitefield. New

[112] Payne, 'Nonconformists and the American Revolution' p. 220. Evans expounded his open communion views in a letter to William Richards in 1777: J. Evans, *Memoirs of the Life and Writings of the Rev. William Richards, LL.D.*, Chiswick, 1819. pp. 36–40.

[113] Payne, *Free Church Tradition in England*, p. 80; W. T. Owen, *Edward Williams, D.D., 1750–1813*, Cardiff, 1963, p. 2.

[114] *Select Works of Robinson*, 'Letter to Dan Taylor, 1790', p. 271.

[115] Ivimey, *HEB*, vol. 4, pp. 33 ff.

The Communion Controversy, 1772–81

friendships made men impatient with restrictions on their fellowship. Traditionally Dissent had laid considerable emphasis on churchmanship, whereas the men of the Revival emphasized Christian experience and were sometimes impatient of church organization.[116] The pressure Booth experienced from the Methodists has already been described.[117] Other Dissenters were concerned. In 1813 Walter Wilson, an Independent, wrote:

> But although the Independent interest has received large accessions in numbers, it has lost in quality. This has arisen chiefly from two causes: The introduction of uneducated and illiterate men into the ministry; and the prevalence of a spurious liberality.[118]

Wilson did not limit his criticisms to the Independents. He considered Dissent from the Church of England to be a matter of principle and not of expediency.[119] Too many Nonconformists were in danger of ignoring this.[120] He complained of the effect of Independent or Calvinistic Methodist Chapels. 'No people are more liberally minded than the Methodists. They consider all modes of discipline as indifferent, though most of them give a preference to the forms used in the established church.'[121] Baptists were not immune from the change of emphasis which was to result in an unprecedented degree of inter-denominational co-operation in the early nineteenth century.[122]

There is some evidence of this indifference to matters ecclesiological among Baptists in the late eighteenth century. Hugh Evans of Bristol, Principal of the Baptist Academy, was prepared to defend open communion by stating:

> I much question whether it [Adult Baptism] was ever made a term of communion, and whether the first Christian Church at Jerusalem were all baptized? Sure I am, there is no account of the baptizing of all the Apostles.[123]

---

[116] See comment of Bernard L. Manning, note 56 above.
[117] See pp. 72–3 above.
[118] Wilson, *London Dissenting Churches*, vol. 4, p. 557. [119] Ibid., p. 435.
[120] Ibid., pp. 550-551. [121] Ibid., p. 560. [122] Ibid., p. 550.
[123] *Memoir of Richards*, 'Hugh Evans to William Richards, 13 Feb. 1777', p. 35.

Continuing to consider the apostolic churches he wrote, 'It would be difficult to prove that all the saints, or saints in communion, were baptized then.'[124] These were extreme sentiments and were rejected by his son, Caleb Evans, who was, nevertheless, also an open communionist.[125] The Bristol Academy was the only Baptist theological college in existence in the late eighteenth century. Three successive principals, Hugh Evans, Caleb Evans, and John Ryland, Jr., were open communionists. Their influence on the Particular Baptist ministry at the time must have been important.

The Impact of the Controversy on the Particular Baptists
By 1781, the year in which Robinson's pamphlet appeared, the churches were turning away from the communion debate. Other issues pushed discussion of the terms of communion into the background. In 1784 Andrew Fuller's *Gospel Worthy of All Acceptation* appeared. This book asked how the gospel was to be preached and threw down a challenge to the old Hyper-Calvinism.[126] Fuller's work helped to provide a theological rationale for the establishment of the Particular Baptist Missionary Society in 1792 and thereby generated unprecedented activity among the Baptists and English Evangelicalism generally. New movements for evangelization at home and abroad followed. In addition there is evidence that in the 1780s and 1790s, Particular Baptist leaders were increasingly concerned about the development of Antinomian teaching among the Dissenters.[127] This fear of lawlessness in the churches should be seen against a growing fear of the excesses of the French Revolution, which in turn helped to generate an increasingly reactionary political climate in Britain.

Booth and Robinson brought the communion controversy to a hiatus which was to last for over thirty years. Each man had produced a work of undoubted significance. Minor tracts continued to appear, but it is not surprising that nothing of great importance was published until Robert

[124] Ibid.   [125] Ibid., 'Caleb Evans to William Richards, 14 Feb. 1777', p. 36.
[126] For a more detailed discussion of the issues raised by Fuller, see chapter 5 below.
[127] For a fuller discussion of Antinomianism see chapter 6 below.

The Communion Controversy, 1772–81

Hall and Joseph Kinghorn took up the debate again after 1815. Strict communion remained the practice of most of the churches until well into the nineteenth century.[128] It was not without significance that the leading Particular Baptist theologians at the turn of the century, Abraham Booth and Andrew Fuller, were both strict communionists.

The Particular Baptist denomination remained divided on the terms of communion but the two sides within the denomination agreed to differ. However, the debate on the terms of communion was not settled. Booth had produced a masterly defence of strict communion. The other side had nothing on the same scale. But there remained Baptists who wanted greater interdenominational fellowship and who had a deep desire for political and ecclesiastical liberty. These were the men, who were later to respond to Robert Hall's pleas. For the moment, however, debates on Hyper-Calvinism and Antinomianism were to occupy most men's thoughts.

There is no evidence whatsoever to suggest that when the issue of communion was discussed during the eighteenth century, those who participated in the debate envisaged two separate ecclesiastical groups. Abraham Booth had accepted the label 'strict Baptist', but only as a description of his practice, not as a denominational title. Although Robert Robinson was isolated from the main group, this was not because of his open communion views.

The various local associations' evangelistic enterprises did not insist on a particular practice in their doctrinal statements. When the Missionary Society was established in 1792, its committee included open communionists such as John Ryland, Jr. and strict communionists such as Andrew Fuller. These two men co-operated on terms of closest friendship, and it was Ryland who was to become Fuller's biographer. Booth's tribute to Hall has already been quoted.[129]

---

[128] Fuller's Works, 'Letter to the Editor of the Christian Instructor, 28th. Jan. 1814', p. 855; *The Works of the Rev. Robert Hall, A.M.*, ed. Olinthus Gregory, 6 vols., London, 1832-3. Vol. 2: *On Terms of Communion*, pp. 16, 17.

[129] See p. 77 above.

It seems clear, therefore, that although distinct Strict Baptist groups emerged in the nineteenth century, the men who discussed terms of communion in the 1770s envisaged no such developments. By 1800 the old Particular Baptist denomination still lived with its traditional division on these issues. The nineteenth century was to demonstrate that Antinomianism and Hyper-Calvinism were much more explosive subjects and played a much bigger role in reshaping the ecclesiastical landscape.

5

The Gospel Worthy of All Acceptation

I have preached and written much against the abuse of the doctrine of grace; but that doctrine is all my salvation and all my desire. I have no other hope than that from salvation by mere, sovereign and efficacious grace, through the atonement of my Lord and Saviour. With this hope I can go into eternity with composure.

Andrew Fuller, 1815

I preached what I felt, what I smartingly did feel, even that under which my poor soul did groan and tremble in astonishment.

John Bunyan

The second of the three great controversies to embroil the Particular Baptists during the reign of George III was occasioned by the publication of *The Gospel Worthy of All Acceptation* in 1785. The author was Andrew Fuller, pastor of the Baptist Church in Kettering.[1] This work, which was born out of a deep and painful spiritual experience, proved to be a powerful challenge to the prevalent Hyper-Calvinism in the Particular Baptist churches. Fuller, although a self-taught theologian, has been described by Dr Geoffrey Nuttall as one of the few men 'whose impact on

---

[1] *The Gospel Worthy of All Acceptation: or the Obligations of Men Fully to Credit, and Cordially to Approve, Whatever God Makes Known, Wherein Is Considered the Nature of Faith in Christ, and the Duty of Those Where the Gospel Comes in that Matter*, Northampton, 1785, hereinafter referred to as *The Gospel Worthy of All Acceptation*. Unless otherwise indicated references will be to the first edition.

[89]

theology has been sufficient to leave his name embedded in it'.[2] Admired by some and vilified by others, his writings proved to be a catalyst for major developments among the Particular Baptists. Ironically, he was charged with opening the door to Arminianism by critics whose own theology would have been regarded as a novelty by those stalwarts who did battle with Arminianism in the previous century.[3] Fuller himself, claimed to be an orthodox or 'strict' Calvinist, vigorously repudiating any suggestion that he had compromised with Arminianism.[4] Some modern writers, however, have argued that he paved the way for a union between Particular and General Baptists.[5] Certainly, early Strict Baptists considered that by attacking Hyper-Calvinism, Fuller betrayed the Particular Baptists and prepared the way for the theological deviations of the nineteenth century.[6] His teaching was opposed initially by men who revered John Gill, many of whom had known that theologian personally, but

[2] G. F. Nuttall, 'Northamptonshire and the Modern Question', *Journal of Theological Studies*, vol. 16, 1965, p. 101.

[3] 'Good Mr Brine had admitted the novelty of the opinion Mr Fuller opposed', J. Ryland, *Life of Fuller*, p. 132.

[4] Fuller declared that there were three forms of Calvinism among the Baptists, 'namely, the high, the moderate, and the strict Calvinists'. High Calvinists were 'more Calvinistic than Calvin himself; in other words, bordering on Antinomianism'. Moderate Calvinists were 'half Arminian, or as they are called with us, Baxterians'; a Strict Calvinist 'really holds the system of Calvin . . . I do not believe everything that Calvin taught, nor anything because he taught it; but I reckon strict Calvinism to be my own system', Ryland, *Life of Fuller*, 1818, p. 369. Fuller was always careful to repudiate Arminianism and Baxterianism, insisting that he was a Calvinist. See 'A. Fuller to B. Francis, 3 July 1788'; 'A. Fuller to J. Ryland 22nd Jan. 1803,' *Andrew Fuller's Letters*, Angus Library, Regent's Park College, Oxford.

[5] A. C. Underwood, *HEB*, p. 202; E. A. Payne, *The Baptist Union, A Short History*, London, 1958, p. 61.

[6] 'Mr G. [Gadsby] always considered and often stated publicly that Andrew Fuller was the greatest enemy the church of God ever had, as his sentiments were so much cloaked with the sheep's clothing', J. Gadsby, *A Memoir of the late Mr William Gadsby*, Manchester 1847, p. 33; cf. J. H. Philpot, *The Seceders*, vol. 2, London, 1932, p. 255, 'J. C. Philpot to J. Parry, 24 March, 1842'; W. J. Styles, *Guide to Church Fellowship*, London, 1902. p. 90. These charges have been revived recently by George Ella in his *William Huntington*, Darlington, 1994 and in *Law and Gospel in the Theology of Andrew Fuller*, Eggleston, 1996.

interestingly, the leaders of this group were to remain within the mainstream of the Particular Baptist denomination and even to co-operate with Fuller in some of his most important enterprises. The most enduring and determined opposition Fuller faced came from John Stevens and William Gadsby, men who had been subject to other influences, and who were pioneers of the emerging Strict Baptist groupings.

1. Andrew Fuller's Early Pilgrimage

Andrew Fuller was born in the Fenland village of Wicken in February 1754. His family attended the Baptist meeting in Soham, Cambridgeshire. The pastor, John Eve, was a godly man, but Fuller says that he, being 'tinged with false Calvinism, had little or nothing to say to the unconverted'.

Andrew Fuller mixed with the boys of the village and followed their ways but was often smitten by a guilty conscience. At about the age of fourteen, he came under conviction of sin. The preaching he heard could not help him. He longed to know what faith was and was painfully aware that he lacked it. His longings for salvation deepened as he read the writings of John Bunyan and Ralph Erskine. Some of his Christian friends believed that the forceful and unpremeditated recall of a passage of Scripture could be taken as a direct revelation from God.[7] Sometimes passages of Scripture would come powerfully to him, giving him hope that he was saved; but then sin would break out again in his life, plunging him into despair. Fuller knew that he needed Christ, but felt that he had no right to approach Christ. Later he was to write:

> I was not then aware that *any* poor sinner had a warrant to belief in Christ for the salvation of his soul; but supposed that there must be some qualification to entitle him to do it; yet I was aware that I had no qualifications. On a review of my resolution at that time, it seems to resemble that of Esther, who went into the king's presence, *contrary to law*, and at

---

[7] Such a view, which has been widely accepted among introspective Christians, was countered by Jonathan Edwards who showed that such experiences could be delusive; see 'Treatise concerning the Religious Affections', *Works*,1 [1834], repr. Edinburgh: Banner of Truth, 1974, pp, 249-50.

the hazard of her life. Like her I seemed reduced to extremities, even though I should perish in the attempt. Yet it was not altogether from a dread of wrath that I fled to this refuge; for I well remember, that I felt something attracting in the Saviour.[8]

As he ventured on Christ in this way, relief was granted, and Fuller found rest for his troubled soul in November 1769. At this time he received great help from conversation with a godly labourer employed on his father's farm. He was baptized in March 1770, and the following summer proved to be a time of great spiritual blessing for him. Joseph Diver, an older man baptized at the same time as Andrew, and described by him as 'a wise and good man', was another of his spiritual counsellors at this time.

The spiritual joy of these days was soon followed by a time of crisis. A member of the church was discovered to have been drunk. Andrew was one of the first to know and went to the man and reasoned with him. The man's reply was that he could not keep himself, and further no one could keep himself from sin. Andrew was indignant, telling him that as a Christian he should keep himself from open sin. The older man told his critic that he was young in the faith and did not yet know the plague of his own heart. The offender was summoned before the church and was disciplined, his excuse being considered an aggravation of his sin. Sadly, the whole affair plunged the Soham Church into a controversy about 'the power of sinful men to do the will of God, and to keep themselves from sin'. John Eve, the pastor, insisted that men had no power to do anything spiritually good, but they could keep themselves from open acts of sin. Most members were persuaded that men were not able to keep themselves. The debate became so heated that Eve left the church, and for a time it seemed that the church would be dissolved.

At this distance in time it is difficult to unravel exactly the positions of the two sides. The disputants themselves seemed to have been confused about responsibility in general and the radical change which takes place in regeneration. At first, Fuller supported the pastor whom he loved

---

[8] Ryland, *Life of Fuller*, London, 1818 [1816], pp. 18,19.

The Gospel Worthy of All Acceptation

dearly, but he later came round to the position of the majority, which included his friend Joseph Diver. He continued to struggle with the problem of understanding the purpose of scriptural exhortations against sin.

The small church at Soham was remote from other Particular Baptist causes. In its pastorless state much of the responsibility for the services fell on the members. Andrew was asked to take some part and eventually to preach. His evident gifts led to a call to the pastorate in 1775, and in the spring of that year he was ordained. The officiating ministers questioned the members closely about the causes of John Eve's departure, and Andrew Fuller was asked to speak for the church. The ministers said that they were satisfied, but one, Robert Hall of Arnesby, urged Fuller to study Jonathan Edwards on *The Freedom of the Will*. At this time Fuller's main reading was from the works of Bunyan, Gill, and Brine. Yet already these authors had presented Fuller with a problem:

> I perceived, however, that the system of Bunyan was not the same with his [Gill's]; for that, while he maintained the doctrine of election and predestination, he, nevertheless, held with the free offer of salvation to sinners, without distinction. These were things that I then could not reconcile, and, therefore, supposed that Bunyan, though a great and good man, was not so clear in his views of the doctrines of the gospel, as the writers that succeeded him. I found, indeed, the same things in all the old writers of the sixteenth and seventeenth centuries, that came in my way.[9]

Fuller continued to study this problem and was helped by a pamphlet by Abraham Taylor written some thirty years before. Taylor's demonstration that John the Baptist, Christ, and the apostles, had exhorted the ungodly to spiritual repentance and faith challenged him deeply. He was also challenged by a published sermon of John Martin who was later to be one of his sternest critics. He noted:

> I was equally unable to answer this reasoning as that of Dr Taylor, and, therefore, began more and more to suspect that my views had been antiscriptural. I was very unhappy. I read, thought, and prayed.

[9] Ibid., p. 36.

Sometimes, I conversed on these subjects with my friend Joseph Diver, and some others. He was nearly as much at a loss as myself. I made a point, however, of not introducing the question in the pulpit, till my judgement was fixed.[10]

There were however Christian friends who could give some help.

In 1776 I became acquainted with Mr Sutcliff who had lately come to Olney; and soon after with Mr John Ryland, jun. then of Northampton. In them I found familiar and faithful brethren; and who, partly by reflection, and partly by reading the writings of Edwards, Bellamy, Brainerd &c. had begun to doubt of the system of false Calvinism, to which they had been inclined when they first entered on the ministry, or, rather, to be decided against it. But as I lived sixty or seventy miles from them, I seldom saw them, and did not correspond upon the subject. I therefore, pursued my enquiries by myself, and wrote out the substance of what I afterwards published under the title of *The Gospel Worthy of All Acceptation*.[11]

Fuller came to the firm persuasion that gospel preaching must include exhortations to all hearers to repent and believe in Christ, and changed his mode of preaching accordingly. This was not acceptable to all the members of the Soham church, although it is clear he enjoyed the support of many. However, the church found it difficult to support him and his growing family. In the midst of these trials he received a call to the church at Kettering in Northamptonshire. After a long period of prayer and consultation with close friends, he accepted the call and moved to Kettering in 1782.

Fuller became aware that the issues that had been troubling him were perplexing others and so he passed his manuscript to friends who urged him to publish it. He hesitated about doing so for some time, knowing full well that heated debate would follow. Being eventually persuaded that it was his duty to publish, in November 1784 Fuller walked the fourteen miles to Northampton to take his manuscript to a printer, with the 'prayer that God would bless that about which I am going'.

[10] Ibid., pp. 37–8.
[11] Ibid., p. 35.

2. The Gospel Worthy of All Acceptation

The subtitle of Andrew Fuller's book indicates its thesis: he aimed to prove 'the obligations of men fully to credit and cordially to approve whatever God makes known'. He began by clearing the ground to show what was not in dispute. He was not disputing the Calvinistic doctrines of election and total depravity.[12] He foresaw and replied to the criticisms that he was undermining the doctrines of particular redemption[13] and human inability.[14] However, while adhering to these doctrines so tenaciously held by his denomination, Fuller developed a theme which had been long neglected and even opposed within his own circles. He marshalled and expounded a catena of texts, which led to the belief that 'faith in Christ is the duty of all men who hear or have opportunity to hear the Gospel'.[15] He buttressed his case with appeals to the Puritans (Stephen Charnock and John Owen), while also interacting with John Brine. Fuller was concerned to show that while he did not want controversy his argument was an important one.

> It appears to be the same controversy, for substance, as that which in all ages has subsisted between God and an apostate world. God has ever maintained these two principles: *All that is evil is of the creature, and to him belongs the blame of it;* and *all that is good is of himself, and to him belongs the praise of it.* To acquiesce in *both* these positions is too much for the carnal heart. The advocates for free-will would seem to yield the former acknowledging themselves blameworthy for the evil; but they cannot admit the latter. Whatever they may allow to the general grace of God, they are for ascribing the preponderance in favour of virtue and eternal life to their own good improvement of it. Others, who profess to be advocates for free grace, appear to be willing that God should have all the honour of their salvation, in case they should be saved; but they show the strongest aversion to take to themselves the blame of their destruction in case they should be lost. To yield both of these points to

---

[12] *Gospel Worthy of All Acceptation,* pp. vii, ix.

[13] Ibid., pp. 132–9 Fuller took care to gather support from such eminent Reformed writers as Elisha Coles, John Owen and Herman Witsius.

[14] Ibid., pp. 149–53.   [15] Ibid., pp. 37–49; 65–74.

God is to fall under in the grand controversy with him, and to acquiesce in his revealed will; which acquiescence includes *'repentance towards God, and faith towards our Lord Jesus Christ'*.[16]

Closely connected with his main argument was the nature of faith. The importance he attached to this doctrine is indicated by its inclusion in the subtitle, 'wherein is considered the nature of faith in Christ'. Fuller's painful early experience had forced him to consider the nature of faith, and he believed that the outcome had to be consistent with both the gospel call and the doctrines of grace. He rejected the definition of faith prevalent in Hyper-Calvinist circles, where it was held to be 'a believing [of] our personal interest in the Lord Jesus Christ'.[17] Fuller insisted that faith must instead rest upon an objective foundation:

> The Scriptures always represent faith as terminating on something without us; namely on Christ, and the truths concerning him; but this represents it as terminating principally on something within us, namely the work of grace in our hearts; for to believe myself interested in Christ, is the same thing as to believe myself a subject of special grace.[18]

Fuller thus taught that faith terminated on the gospel record of Christ's Person, atoning sacrifice, and willingness to save. It was popularly held that until a person believed that Christ had died for him he could not trust in Christ for salvation. The view he was opposing demanded this point of assurance before the exercising of faith. Of assurance of salvation he wrote: 'This consolation, no doubt, frequently accompanies faith.'[19]

Fuller's frequent appeals to seventeenth-century writers remind us that he was not teaching something new. There had been a discussion about man's obligation to believe the gospel in the 1730s–40s in the controversy over the so-called 'Modern Question'. This dispute had been occasioned by a pamphlet entitled *A Modern Question Modestly Answered*, written by

---

[16] A. Fuller, *Works*, London, 1862, 'The Gospel Worthy of All Acceptation', 2nd ed. [1801], p. 151

[17] *The Gospel Worthy of All Acceptation* (1st ed.), p. 5.   [18] Ibid., p. 6.

[19] Ibid., p. 6. In the second edition Fuller was to be more positive, 'Consolation will accompany the faith of the Gospel', Fuller, *Complete Works*, London, 1862, p. 153.

The Gospel Worthy of All Acceptation

a Congregationalist minister, Matthias Maurice of Rothwell. Maurice showed that the very questioning of the unbeliever's duty to believe was then a modern development. Amongst those who supported Maurice was Abraham Taylor, whose pamphlet was a source of help to Fuller as he faced this whole question. On the other hand, a number of Particular Baptists took the opposite view. Amongst these was John Brine, pastor of the Curriers' Hall Church, London, from 1729 to 1765. Brine wrote a small work entitled *A Refutation of Arminian Principles*. Gill and Brine were close friends and, although Gill did not take a prominent part in the controversy, his views were known. Not all Particular Baptists took the same position as Brine and Gill. Alvery Jackson of Barnoldswick, Yorkshire, wrote in opposition to Hyper-Calvinism. Nevertheless, it appears that the Hyper-Calvinist view received widespread support among the Particular Baptists.

By the year 1780, the time was ripe for further discussion and Fuller's book met a perceived need. In 1779 Robert Hall preached the sermon that was to be the basis of his *Help to Zion's Travellers*, published in 1781. As already noted, John Ryland, Jr. and John Sutcliff were discussing this subject. Although Fuller owed something of a debt to each of these men, it was the painful controversy at Soham, coupled with his reading of Edwards and his own vigorous thinking on the subject that helped him towards the conclusions he felt duty-bound to publish. His book was a timely piece of writing. His understanding of the gospel came with liberating power to others who felt trapped in the bondage of introspection. Gospel preaching received a new impetus, and in the words of Timothy George, 'the victory of Fullerism, as it came to be called, gave a solid doctrinal foundation to the modern missionary campaign.'[20]

3. Controversy

Although many accepted Fuller's convictions, such was the strength of Hyper-Calvinism that controversy was inevitable.[21]

---

[20] Timothy George, *Faithful Witness, The Life and Mission of William Carey*, Inter-Varsity Press, Leicester, 1992, p. 56.

[21] 'At the time Mr Fuller commenced a public profession of Christianity and

Ryland, who was in close contact with Fuller by the time *The Gospel Worthy of All Acceptation* appeared in 1785, wrote:

> Many ignorant people, who really knew nothing, before, of the controversy, began to raise an outcry against the book and its author; charging him and his friends with having forsaken the doctrine of grace, and left the good old way.[22]

Fuller was well aware of the suspicion which would develop and foresaw that some friendships would be severed. He wrote in his diary on 23 August 1784:

> The weight of publishing still lies upon me. I expect a great share of unhappiness through it. I had certainly much rather go through the world in peace, did I not consider this step as my duty.[23]

Much of the opposition took the form of petty criticism and ostracism,[24] but there were serious responses. They included the Arminian

---

entered on the work of the ministry, the state of the Baptist denomination [sic] in this country was truly deplorable. The writings of Hussey, Gill and Brine were all in vogue; and such was the veneration in which their names were generally held, that the system of doctrine which they contended for, almost universally prevailed; and their works not the scriptures, became in effect the standard of orthodoxy', J. W. Morris, *Memoirs of the Life and Writings of the Rev. Andrew Fuller*, London, 1816, p. 263. Cf. Ryland, *Life of Fuller*, p. 7.

[22] Ibid., p. 132. Preaching after Fuller's death, thirty years after the publication of *The Gospel Worthy of All Acceptation*, Joseph Ivimey declared of Fuller, 'He has been much blamed for this measure, as stirring up a controversy, fatal to the peace of our churches.' J. Ivimey, *A Sermon Preached at Eagle Street Meeting, London, May 21st 1815, as a tribute of affectionate respect to the Memory of the late Rev. Andrew Fuller of Kettering*, London, 1815, p. 12.

[23] Ryland, *Life of Fuller*, p. 131.

[24] 'I know the opposition made to "Andrew Fuller" in S——. And N——.' Andrew Fuller to Thomas Stevens of Colchester', Fuller's *Letters*, no date, but internal evidence suggests 1791 or 1792. N. and S. are probably Norfolk and Suffolk, 'A. Fuller to J. Williams, New York, 1st Aug. 1804' speaks of opposition to his teaching in Norfolk, Suffolk and Yorkshire. 'One of the churches in his neighbourhood refused for seven years to hold communion with him, or to allow any of their members to have fellowship with his church', J. W. Morris, op. cit, p. 271. Cf. 'A. Fuller to W. Carey 22nd Aug. 1798,' Fuller's *Letters*.

General Baptist Dan Taylor who deprecated Fuller's Calvinism. On the other side, William Button and John Martin, both Particular Baptists of some standing, opposed him.[25]

WILLIAM BUTTON (1754-1821)

William Button was a representative of those London churches which still revered the memory of John Gill. Although born in Sussex, his family moved to London during his childhood and there his father joined Gill's church, where he was appointed a deacon. When William's mother died in 1766, Gill preached and published a memorial sermon for her. William was sent as a boarder to John Collett Ryland's Academy in Northampton. There, at the age of thirteen, he was converted and baptized. Completing his general education, he returned to London and commenced ministerial studies under William Clarke of Unicorn Yard Church, Southwark. In 1773 at the age of nineteen he began to preach. By this time John Gill had died and opinion in his Carter Lane Church was divided over the choice of a successor. The majority called John Rippon, a student from the Bristol Academy, but a minority of members were sufficiently unhappy about the choice to withdraw and form a new church in Dean Street, Southwark. Relations between the Carter Lane Church and the seceders were clearly not acrimonious, since Rippon actually assisted the veteran pastors, Benjamin Wallin and Samuel Stennett, in the formation of the new church. This co-operation of Stennett, Wallin, and Rippon suggests that the new church was readily accepted by the London Particular Baptists. It was the new church in Dean Street which was to call Button as pastor in 1775.[26]

---

[25] W. Button, *Remarks on a Treatise entitled the Gospel Worthy of All Acceptation by Andrew Fuller*, London 1785; hereinafter, Button, *Remarks*; D. Taylor [Philanthropos], *Nine Letters on Mr A. Fuller's Scheme. A Reply to the Gospel Worthy of All Acceptation*, 1786; P. Withers, *Philanthropos, or a Letter to the Revd Fuller in Reply to his Treatise on Damnation*, n.d.[1786]; J. Martin, *Thoughts on the Duty of Man relative to Faith in Jesus Christ, In which Mr Andrew Fuller's leading Propositions on this subject are considered, Parts I to III*, London 1788-1791. Copies of Taylor's and Withers' works have not been traced, but both are listed by E. C. Starr, *A Baptist Bibliography*, Rochester, N.Y., 1976.

[26] Biographical details from Ivimey, *HEB*, 4, pp. 335-7; Ivimey, *The Preciousness*

Clearly Gill's influence had been strong in Button's family during his boyhood and he had been educated by John Collett Ryland, a close friend of Gill. It is not, therefore, surprising to find Button emerging as one of Andrew Fuller's first critics.

William Button was alarmed at the welcome *The Gospel Worthy of All Acceptation* received.[27] He made it clear that he was constrained to write a reply because he considered that Fuller's doctrine was tending towards Arminianism.[28] For his part, he stood unashamedly in the tradition of Gill and Brine and at the same time wisely protested against the abusive use of names, which frequently substitutes for serious thought.

> There are those, who warmly espousing Mr F.'s cause, have been pleased to say, they hope his book will cure some of their *Gillism* and *Brinism*. To such I beg leave to say, I am ashamed of their contemptuous manner of speaking of those great and good men, Gill and Brine, whose characters and works ought ever to be revered and esteemed by all, who call themselves Christians.[29]

As expected, Button offered a Hyper-Calvinistic interpretation of those passages used by Fuller to support his conviction that all should be exhorted to believe in Christ for salvation. However, the weight of his attack was launched against Fuller's definition of faith, which in his view failed to give sufficient emphasis to the element of trust. Button considered therefore, that Fuller could not distinguish between genuine and false faith. Referring to the citizens of Nazareth, described in Luke 4:16–20, he wrote:

> They were constrained to embrace his doctrine, yea and *cordially* to receive his testimony, which none can deny was truth. Yet, after all this,

---

of Faith in Times of Trial, A Sermon occasioned by the death of the Rev. William Button, preached in the Meeting House in Eagle Street, London, August 12, 1821. To which is appended An Address delivered at the Grave by William Newman, D.D., London, 1821, pp. 32-34. W. Wilson, London Dissenting Churches, 4, London, 1814, p. 227.

[27] 'I am sorry to find what is advanced in Mr F.'s treatise seems to gain so much ground, as it appears to me opposite to Scripture and experience', Button, *Remarks*, p. iv. [28] Ibid., pp. iii, 104, 105. [29] Ibid., p. v.

it seems they were strangers to true, special faith in Christ, as appears by their after conduct.[30]

He went on to argue that Scripture requires all men to believe the accuracy of whatever God reveals, but this does not imply that all men have a duty to trust Christ for salvation.

Is it unregenerate man's duty to impress the truth on his mind, and to make it abide there, so that it shall powerfully influence every faculty of his soul, and every action of his life? If so, is it his duty to do what God claims as his prerogative, and promises as a special blessing to his own people?[31]

Not surprisingly, William Button found himself in difficulties over the fact that Scripture does appear to exhort the unbeliever. Somewhat lamely he wrote:

That believing sometimes bears the appearance of a command is what I readily grant: but that it is always where it bears that appearance to be considered an *injunction* is what I cannot allow.[32]

Button insisted, however, that he did have a message for the unconverted. Even though the unbeliever could not believe unaided and so should not be exhorted to faith, he could be told to strive to enter the strait gate:

That is, use all the means, search the Scriptures, attend on the preaching of the word constantly and diligently; pray for a blessing on it, examine whether ye have entered in or not.[33]

Button believed that Fuller had not only weakened in his Calvinism but his teaching could only put the unbeliever in a position worse than he was before.

I believe the law to be *exceeding broad* . . . But don't let us make it broader than God has made it. Don't let us make it require that which

---

[30] Ibid., p. 18.
[31] Ibid., p. 21. Button speaks of the duty of the unbeliever who 'hears the solemn realities of religion to consider them as real', Ibid., pp. 20, 21.
[32] Ibid., p. 31.   [33] Ibid., p. 88.

the Lord never meant it to require, which man was never able to perform in innocence: and don't let us make it curse and condemn a poor sinner for the want of that which God never granted, and never meant to grant him; I mean special faith in Christ Jesus.[34]

Fuller had no doubt that Button was mistaken[35] and replied in a pamphlet which also responded to the remarks of the General Baptist, Dan Taylor.[36] Fuller maintained his position, but was careful to state:

> I speak with the greatest sincerity, when I say I have a high esteem for Mr B. and many others of his sentiments. I do not account them as adversaries, but as brethren in Christ, as fellow labourers in the gospel; and 'could rejoice (as was said before) to spend my days in cordial fellowship with them'.[37]

Both men had been educated in the same Hyper-Calvinist tradition. Fuller understood his critic's way of thinking, even though he differed from him in doctrine. The same fundamental respect existed between Fuller and John Martin, although there were times when relations between them were severely strained.

JOHN MARTIN, 1741–1820

John Martin,[38] an older man than Button and Fuller, was a widely esteemed Particular Baptist minister. Born at Spalding, Lincolnshire, he was converted at a Methodist meeting, which he had attended in order to mock the proceedings. While an apprentice watchmaker, he read whatever theological writings he could obtain. Gill became his favourite

[34] Ibid., p. 95.

[35] 'It is a matter beyond all doubt to me that Button's scheme is very antiscriptural', Fuller's *Letters*, 'A. Fuller to B. Francis, 3 July 1788.'

[36] A. Fuller, *A Defence of a Treatise, entitled the Gospel of Christ Worthy of All Acceptation, containing a Reply to Mr Button's Remarks and the Observations of Philanthropos*, Northampton, 1787.   [37] Ibid., pp. 11, 12.

[38] Biographical details from, J. Martin, *Some Account of the Life and Writings of the Rev. John Martin, Pastor of the Church, Meeting in Store Street, Bedford Square, London*, London 1797. Hereinafter referred to as Martin, *Autobiography*; Ivimey, *HEB*, vol. 4 pp. 42;77–82; 342–50; J. A. Jones, *Bunhill Memorials*, London 1849, pp. 164–71.

author; he eagerly seized an opportunity to visit London in connection with his trade in the hope 'of sitting at the feet of Dr Gill'. His experience of Gill's ministry did not disappoint him:

> Having found out his meeting, I kept closely by him while I staid in Town. Occasionally indeed, I heard Mr Whitefield, and some other popular preachers, but none of them pleased me so well as the Doctor. His discourses were more evangelical, better studied and argued, and I thought much more consistent than those which I heard at the Tabernacle, and in some other crowded places of worship; and they furnished me with more material for subsequent reflection than any services that I heard in London. I might indeed except a few I heard from the Rev. Mr Brine; but though his sermons were judicious, his delivery was not all that engaging.[39]

Having received such help from Gill and Brine, it is not perhaps surprising that Martin emerged as a champion of Hyper-Calvinism. He began to preach and was called to the pastorate of the Particular Baptist Church at Sheepshead, (now Shepshed), Leicestershire in 1766.

It is possible that Martin modified his High Calvinism for a time while at Sheepshead. Fuller heard him preach around the year 1774 and asserted:

> It is true we were so unhappy then, as well as now to differ in our sentiments. I, at that time, did NOT think as I do now, but Mr *Martin* DID. I own I disliked the violence with which he then maintained my present sentiments; and the supercilious language which he used of those who differed from him, whom I then understood to be GILL and BRINE, or writers of their stamp. Upon the whole, however, what he said set me a thinking, and I believe was of use to me.[40]

We have already seen that when Fuller was struggling with the question of Hyper-Calvinism, he claimed to have been helped by a published sermon of Martin's. Martin denied that he had ever attacked Gill or Brine, 'That I ever treated those worthies, whom I knew and loved while I was

---

[39] Martin, *Autobiography*, pp. 43, 44.
[40] A. Fuller, *Works*, p. 326.

yet young, as you are pleased to represent cannot be admitted.'[41] Martin admitted that he read Jonathan Edwards at this period of his life with a 'want of caution'.[42] Later, however, 'grown more cautious by reflection, Mr Edwards was read with greater care, the consequence was, my raptures were diminished, but real respect for his writings remained; nor is it yet destroyed.'[43]

W. T. Whitley claimed that when Martin wrote the Northamptonshire Association Circular Letter in 1770, he could not have been a Hyper-Calvinist. To support his assertion, he appealed to Martin's statement:

> Every soul that comes to Christ to be saved from Hell and sin by him is to be encouraged ... The coming soul need not fear he is not elected, for none but such will be willing to come and submit to Christ.[44]

Such a statement, however, could have been made by many a Hyper-Calvinist and does not prove Whitley's claim. Gill would have agreed that those who come are elected and need to be encouraged.[45] What was in dispute was whether it was the duty of all men to come to Christ for salvation, and whether the gospel exhortations are indiscriminate and universal. It seems, therefore, that if Martin did modify his Hyper-Calvinism, it could only have been a slight alteration and for a short period.

In 1774 Martin was called to the pastorate of a church in Grafton Street, London. On 20 September of that year he was admitted to membership of the Baptist Board, together with the young William Button,

---

[41] J. Martin, *Thoughts on the Duty of Man*, Part II, pp. 68, 69.
[42] Ibid., p. 73.   [43] Ibid.
[44] W. T. Whitley, *Calvinism and Evangelism, Especially among Baptists*, London n.d., p. 31. Of the letter on Election, 1770, Martin wrote in 1797, 'This letter was drawn up by me, and contains, Sir, those sentiments on personal election, which I yet approve', Martin, *Autobiography*, p. 67.
[45] J. Gill, *Exposition of the New Testament*, e.g. Acts 16:32; the Gospel 'encourages souls to believe in him; and faith comes by it and it contains things to be believed.' Cf. Acts 20:21, 'the order of the Gospel Ministry is very fitly here expressed, which is first to lay before sinners the evil, and their danger by it, in order to convince them of it; and then to direct and encourage them to faith in Christ Jesus.'

The Gospel Worthy of All Acceptation

then about to take up his responsibilities in Dean Street.[46] Martin was already well known in the Midlands, and for more than twenty years after his arrival in London he occupied a prominent place in the affairs of his denomination. Andrew Fuller seems to have hoped that he would be able to take some part in his induction at Kettering.[47]

When Fuller published his *Gospel Worthy of All Acceptation*, Martin was moved to reply. His motive, like Button's, was fear of Arminianism:

> In the year 1787, I was informed that several ministers of my acquaintance, were determined to propagate more Arminian tenets than they were once inclined to preach. Among these respectable ministers, the Rev. Mr Andrew Fuller, of Kettering, was much applauded for a Treatise which he published.[48]

Martin's reply appeared in three instalments and was larger than Button's, but the arguments were similar. He adopted, however, a much more haughty tone in dealing with his opponent. This he later regretted and also felt that he had not done justice to his beliefs. In 1797 he wrote:

> The plan of my performance does not now please me; nor is the temper of it, in some places to be vindicated; but I still think, I have said much in that Treatise, that cannot be refuted; and I believe, that those sentiments, however unpopular, are by no means unimportant.[49]

In Part I of his *Thoughts on the Duty of Man,* Martin argued that 'Mr Fuller's leading propositions' were '*obscure, inconsistent,* and *erroneous*'.[50] His thesis was that since spiritual life is '*supernatural, miraculous, of GOD, and not of man*',[51] no man can be obliged to produce it. To demand it is therefore unreasonable.

> *To* DO *anything beyond what is, or may be included in lawful endeavours, never* WAS, IS, *or* WILL *be required of them, as a matter of duty.*[52]

---

[46] 'Minutes of the Baptist Board, 20th. September 1774', *Transactions of the Baptist Historical Society,* vol. 7, 1918–19, p. 83.
[47] Ryland, *Life of Fuller*, p. 61.
[48] Martin, *Autobiography*, pp. 118, 119.   [49] Ibid., p. 120.
[50] J. Martin, *Thoughts on the Duty of Man*, Part I, p. 190.   [51] Ibid., p. 195.
[52] Ibid., p. 196.

Having devoted attention to Fuller's alleged inconsistencies and to what the unbeliever was not required to do, Martin turned to a more positive treatment of man's duty in Part II. Like Button, he considered this to consist mainly in the giving of attention to the Word of God[53] and prayer.[54] However, man should pray only for what he felt induced to ask, and if that inducement did not include salvation, he was not obliged to seek to be saved.[55]

Martin was no antinomian: he accepted the duty of all men to keep the Moral Law.[56] Fuller, he believed, had confused law and gospel and in so doing had devalued the gospel.

> The difference is *greater* than this good man has supposed and the tidings *better* than he has stated, for God in the gospel does not *offer*, but *bring* and *give* salvation to him that worketh not, and consequently *bestows* on the elect 'all things that pertain to life and godliness'.[57]

Like all Hyper-Calvinists, Martin had to face the charge that he preached a subjective warrant of faith.[58] In reply to Fuller he said: 'I am as averse to making inherent qualifications the *ground* of our confidence in Christ as yourself.'[59] Martin taught that when men were convicted of sin, they were compelled to seek Christ.

> If a man was not *compelled* to do this, by motives so urgent as to be to him invincible, we cannot be certain he would ever do it.[60]

He went on to question the validity of exhortations even to convicted sinners and believers.

> Sinners in my opinion are more frequently converted, and believers more commonly edified by a narrative of facts concerning Jesus Christ, and by a clear and connected statement of the doctrines of grace, and blessings of the gospel than by all the exhortations and expostulations that were ever invented.[61]

---

[53] Ibid., Part II, pp. 40–2.   [54] Ibid., pp. 42–5.   [55] Ibid., p. 51.
[56] Ibid., Part III, p. 6.   [57] Ibid., p. 7.
[58] For a fuller discussion of the debate on the warrant of faith, see pp. 151–7 below.
[59] J. Martin, *Thoughts on the Duty of Man*, Part III, p. 38.
[60] Ibid.   [61] Ibid., pp. 62, 3.

The Gospel Worthy of All Acceptation

Martin's *Thoughts on the Duty of Man* argued the case for Hyper-Calvinism from the premise of man's inability. Man could not respond to the gospel and so had no duty to do so. In all his pages of argument, Martin never gave serious attention to passages of Scripture which did exhort, or which suggested that man had a duty, to repent and believe. He presumably considered that his discussion of inability precluded any suggestion that such passages taught what Fuller considered they did.

PARTICULAR BAPTIST CO-OPERATION

To read the controversial tracts, written by Fuller on the one side and by Button and Martin on the other, might suggest a degree of bitterness and separation; but this is not borne out by the facts. Relations between Fuller and Button were to become closer than those between Fuller and Martin, but even in 1797 Martin could refer to 'Mr Fuller, whom after all I sincerely respect.'[62]

The developing societies provided a structure within which Fuller and his critics could co-operate. Fuller's prominent part in the formation and administration of the Particular Baptist Missionary Society for Propagating the Gospel among the Heathen is well known.[63] Equally important was Fuller's theology which provided the theological basis for the Baptist missionary. In spite of his theological difference with Fuller, Button was a prominent supporter of the Missionary Society from the early days. An appeal for Society funds in 1793 lists Button as the sole collector of subscriptions for the London area.[64]

This enthusiasm for foreign missions was soon paralleled by a concern for the spiritual needs of the United Kingdom. In 1797 there was established, The Baptist Society in London for the Encouragement and Support of Itinerant Preaching. It published an address to the Calvinist Baptist churches, which included the statement,

> While we rejoice in the spiritual and laudable exertions of our Christian Brethren under different denominations to preach the gospel among the

[62] Martin, *Autobiography*, p. 120.
[63] A. C. Underwood, *HEB*, pp. 165 ff., gives a useful summary. See also Ryland, *Life of Fuller*, pp. 147–212.
[64] *The Baptist Annual Register*, vol. 1, 1790–93, p. 531.

heathen in foreign climes, we should not forget the many myriads at home, who have scarcely anything pertaining to Christianity besides the name – who are profoundly ignorant, if not notoriously profligate and profane.[65]

The first committee of this Society included such 'Strict' Calvinists as Abraham Booth and John Rippon and Hyper-Calvinists such as John Martin and William Button.[66] This co-operation between London ministers with different interpretations of Calvinism appears to have been the norm in the 1790s. They took part in the activities of the Baptist Board and acted together in ordination services.[67]

Button and Fuller were even willing to distribute one another's books. Button combined a bookseller's business with his pastoral duties and as early as 1790 was listed in the *Baptist Register* as selling some of Fuller's titles, although *The Gospel Worthy of All Acceptation* was not apparently among those listed.[68] However, when, in 1801, Fuller compiled a list of theological works to be sent to the missionaries in India, alongside works by Edwards and Bellamy was included 'Button's Answer to Fuller on Faith'.[69]

From 1798 John Martin was estranged from his brethren, but politics, not theology, was the cause. He had long been known to hold views which differed from those of most of his associates. During the American War of Independence he had written against the colonists, at a time when many Dissenters supported the American cause.[70] His *Autobiography*

---

[65] *The Baptist Annual Register,* vol. 2, 1794-7, pp. 465-70, gives the address and rules of the Society and details of its committee.

[66] Booth's Calvinism is discussed below. Of Rippon, K. R. Manley writes, 'he was an ardent Fullerite', 'John Rippon D.D. (1751-1836) and the Particular Baptists', D. Phil. thesis, University of Oxford, 1967, p. 46.

[67] In 1792 Button was involved with Booth, Upton, Thomas, Rippon and Smith (Eagle Street) at the ordination of Joseph Swain at Walworth, *Baptist Register*, vol. 1, p. 522. In 1795 Stennett, Booth, Rippon, Swain, Button and Martin all took part in the ordination of Thomas Hutchings at Unicorn Yard, Southwark, *Baptist Register*, vol. 2, p. 348.

[68] *Baptist Register,* vol. 1, p. 122.

[69] Fuller's *Letters*, 'A. Fuller to J. Sutcliff, 18 Feb. 1801.'

[70] Martin, *Autobiography*, p. 98.

The Gospel Worthy of All Acceptation

showed that he had little sympathy with the Parliamentary side in the seventeenth-century conflict in England. He wrote of the 'usurpation of Oliver Cromwell' and 'the murder of Charles I'.[71] In December 1789, he opposed a move by the London Dissenting ministers to press for the repeal of the Test and Corporation Acts, which were designed to exclude Dissenters from Parliament, local government, and the English Universities.[72] Martin's arrogance on this occasion led to relationships being strained, but co-operation continued. His ministerial colleagues probably tolerated his idiosyncrasies and were unwilling to make his political views an occasion of division. Events, however, came to a crisis in 1798. In January, Martin preached a public lecture at Broad Street Chapel, London, in the course of which he declared:

> Should the French land, some, yea many of those different and differing people [the Dissenters] would unite to encourage the French, and to distress this country, provided they had a fair opportunity.[73]

Such remarks were inevitably inflammatory at a time when revolutionary France was victorious in Europe and when there was considerable social unrest in Britain.

Earlier some Baptist ministers had welcomed the French Revolution,[74] but by this time most had long been nervous of its excesses and fearful of a political and religious reaction in Britain.[75] Martin's statement could only give ammunition to the opponents of Dissent. The Baptist Board appointed Booth and Button to investigate Martin's assertion, but their report on 13 February 1798 said:

---

[71] Ibid., p. 50.
[72] Ibid., p. 122 Ivimey, *HEB*, vol. 4, pp. 346.
[73] Quoted Ivimey, *HEB*, vol. 4, p. 77.   [74] Ibid., p. 82.
[75] By the spring of 1794, Fuller was writing, 'At present I had rather be a subject in Russia than a citizen in France. I am persuaded there is the greatest tyranny there exercised by the few over the many', Fuller's *Letters*, 'A. Fuller to J. Thomas and W. Carey, 25th March to 25th May, 1794.' In the same letter he expressed his fears about reaction in England, deploring the fact that the Unitarian Joseph Priestley had felt it safer to go to America: 'It is to the disgrace of England to have driven him away. Such treatment is enough to make a bad cause appear a good one.'

Mr Martin could not be prevailed upon to make any concession, nor was in the least disposed to acknowledge he had done wrong.[76]

The Board waited a further month and then on 13 March 1798 resolved:

> That to the best of our knowledge and belief, the Representation Mr Martin has given of the Dissenters, does not apply to any individual in any of our Protestant Dissenting Churches, Resolved unanimously:
> That, Mr Martin's Representation, not appearing to be founded on fact, is considered by us as highly calumnious. Resolved *nem. con.* only one of the Brethren being neuter.
> That Mr Martin be therefore no longer a member of this Society. Resolved *nem. con.* only one of the brethren being neuter.[77]

The speed with which the Baptist Board acted is some indication of the strength of feeling against Martin's dangerous remarks. It is of interest to note that Button and Booth, whose views on faith were very different, were appointed to investigate the statement of Martin. While Martin had still more than twenty years of service ahead of him in his London pastorate, he remained an isolated figure among his London Baptist brethren.[78]

Martin's political views do not seem to have been supported widely by the Hyper-Calvinist Particular Baptists, many of whom continued to be drawn into closer co-operation with the promoters of Andrew Fuller's Evangelical Calvinism in the early years of the nineteenth century. There can be no doubt that a growing agreement concerning the duty of the Christian Church to preach the gospel to unbelievers at home and abroad was helping to bridge the gap, even though there was not complete agreement as to what constituted the gospel message. In 1813 Fuller wrote:

---

[76] 'Minutes of the Baptist Board, 13 Feb. 1798', *Transactions of the Baptist Historical Society*, vol. 6, 1918–19, p. 93. A Mr Burnside was appointed to act with Booth and Button, but he did not attend the meeting with Martin.

[77] Ibid., p. 94.

[78] When Martin died in 1820, the report in *The Baptist Magazine* read, 'Died, April 23, aged 79, the Rev. John Martin, late of Keppel Street. Particulars in our next', *Baptist Magazine*, vol. 12, 1820, p. 199. The announcement is in stark contrast to the usual notices of death. No further details were in fact given.

The Gospel Worthy of All Acceptation

Our High Calvinist Brethren are coming nearer: the mission attracts them, as well as the General Baptists; and we endeavour not to counteract its salutary influence by our behaviour, in either case.[79]

By this time both Button and Fuller were nearing the ends of their active service, but another important development involving both men had begun. The Particular Baptists felt the need of a national organization to link their independent churches. This was to come into existence as the Baptist Union.[80] Fuller was cautious,[81] but he attended the exploratory meeting held in June 1812 at Carter Lane Chapel, under the chairmanship of John Rippon.[82] On this occasion it was agreed 'that a more general union of the Particular (or Calvinistic) Baptist Churches in the United Kingdom is very desirable'.[83] It was also decided to meet a year later to form such a body. Two secretaries were appointed, William Button and Joseph Ivimey, both strict communionists, the former a Hyper-Calvinist and the latter a supporter of Fuller.[84] It was at the 1813 meeting that the decision was made to set up a General Union of Baptist Ministers and Churches.[85] Later that summer, Button resigned his pastorate apparently because of failing health and also the difficulties which had arisen in his publishing business. His activity in the initial stages had been important. Dr E. A. Payne pointed out that he had been 'active in the committee meetings which took place – in the early months of 1813 – in preparation for the first Assembly of the new Union.'[86]

---

[79] Fuller's *Letters*, 'A. Fuller to W. Ward, 7th. January 1813.'

[80] Ivimey, *HEB*, vol. 4, pp. 122ff; E.A. Payne, *History of the Baptist Union*, pp.15ff. The *Minutes of the Baptist Union, 1812-1817* are published in *The Baptist Quarterly*, vol. 4, 1928-9, pp. 56-60; 121-131; 171-74.

[81] Payne, *History of the Baptist Union*, p. 17.

[82] *Baptist Quarterly*, vol. 4, pp. 58-9, lists attendance.

[83] Ibid., p. 57.

[84] W. Button, A*n Answer to the Question, 'Why Are You a Strict Baptist?'*, London 1812. J. Ivimey's strong strict communion convictions are expressed in the preface to *HEB*, vol. 4, pp. iv, v. His admiration for Fuller is expressed in the Memorial Sermon he preached for him at Eagle Street.

[85] *Minutes of Baptist Union*, 24 June 1813, *The Baptist Quarterly*, vol. 4, p. 124.

[86] Payne. *History of the Baptist Union*, p. 22.

6

Antinomianism

[The Law] is of use to saints and true believers in Christ . . . to be a rule of life and conversation to them; not a rule to obtain life by; but to live according to; to guide their feet, to direct their steps, and to preserve them from going into bye and crooked paths.

JOHN GILL, 1770[1]

An erroneous conception of the function of law can be of such a character that it completely vitiates our view of the gospel; and an erroneous conception of the antithesis between law and grace can be of such a character that it demolishes both the substructure and the superstructure of grace.

JOHN MURRAY, 1957

1. Background

In the fifty years after 1770, the English Particular Baptists were deeply exercised about the relationship of the Christian to the moral law or Ten Commandments. The Antinomian controversy produced divisions among them that proved to be deeper than those caused by the debates about the terms of communion or the preaching of the gospel. When Abraham Booth published *The Death of Legal Hope, the Life of Evangelical Obedience* in 1770,[2] he explained that his volume contained the substance of a series of sermons previously preached to his church at Little Prescot Street, London.[3] Dedicating the book to the members of that

---

[1] *Body of Divinity*, p. 371.
[2] A. Booth, *Works*, vol. 1, 'The Death of Legal Hope, the Life of Evangelical Obedience', hereinafter referred to as 'The Death of Legal Hope'. [3] Ibid., p. 331.

[112]

congregation, he expressed the hope that 'while some professors of evangelical doctrine are verging towards Arminian legality, and others towards Antinomian licentiousness, it will be your happiness to be preserved from those wide and fatal extremes'.[4]

Booth argued that Christians are not under the Law as a Covenant of Works, that is, as a means of salvation; but once saved, the Law is 'a Rule of Moral Conduct to Believers'.[5] His *Death of Legal Hope* reflected the current sensitivity of Evangelical leaders to the charge of Antinomianism. Proper emphasis on the doctrine of justification by faith alone has often led to the accusation that, if good works are not a condition of salvation, Christianity gives saved sinners a licence to sin. Although the charge is mistaken, there have been those who have spoken of the law in disparaging terms and suggest that it has no part to play in the life of the believer. Such teaching has become known as Doctrinal Antinomianism. A few have gone further and condoned a complete freedom from any code of conduct. They are described as Practical Antinomians.[6]

Evangelical Christians have agreed that justification brings about a complete deliverance from the condemnation of the law and establishes a new relationship with God, which is not determined nor controlled by the moral law. The question that remains is whether the moral law continues to play any part in the Christian's life. Reformed teachers often refer

---

[4] Ibid., pp. 331, 2.

[5] Ibid., p. 419.

[6] W. Young, 'Antinomianism', *Encyclopedia of Christianity*, vol. 1., Wilmington, USA, 1964, gives a useful survey. Young discusses the difficulties of definition, pointing out that Luther coined the term, Antinomian, to describe those who opposed the Law, but subsequent debates, especially in the seventeenth century, widened the definition considerably. Young lists twenty Antinomian tenets, admitting that few Antinomians would have subscribed to them all. In this chapter the term is used in the sense current in the late eighteenth century, describing the position of those who insisted that the Moral Law is not the Christian's rule of life.

The seventeenth-century debates are reviewed in G. Huehns, *Antinomianism in English History with Special Reference to the Period, 1640-60*, London: Cresset Press, 1951. Cf. P. Toon *Hyper-Calvinism*. London: The Olive Tree, 1967, pp. 22, 49-66; Curt D. Daniel, 'Hyper-Calvinism and John Gill', Ph.D. Thesis, Edinburgh, 1983, pp. 608-82.

to the insistence that it does as 'the third use of the law'.[7] This third use of the law has proved to be a matter of controversy. Dr Jonathan Bayes has recently summarized the debate in this way:

> Both parties are at one in their rejection of practical antinomianism. However, whereas the doctrinal antinomians conclude that sanctification is achieved by the direct work of the Spirit alone, the advocates of the third use, while acknowledging that the Spirit is the enabling cause of sanctification, also give the law a role when employed by the Spirit.[8]

The apostle Paul was the first of many Christian teachers to face and answer the charge of antinomianism (*Rom.* 3:8; 6:1-2, 15). In the course of so doing, he insisted that the Christian is 'not under the law, but under grace' (*Rom.* 6:14); that he has 'become dead to the law by the body of Christ' (*Rom.* 7:4); and also that he is 'delivered from the law' (*Rom.* 7:6). The Antinomian controversy has revolved around the question of whether the law has anything to say to the believer.

In the years before Booth wrote, there had been isolated outbreaks of Antinomianism, both doctrinal and practical. In 1769 there was a stir in London over the views of James Relly.[9] Relly had at one time been an associate of George Whitefield, ministering frequently at both the Moorfields Tabernacle and the Tottenham Court Road Chapel. However, he adopted universalism and separated from Whitefield.

John Wesley charged him with Antinomianism and his popularity waned, although his views were to be vigorously promoted in New England.[10] Wesley was extremely sensitive to the danger of Antinomianism,

---

[7] The first use being the restraint of sin and promotion of righteousness in society generally, and the second, conviction of sin in the life of the elect sinner as he comes to Christ.

[8] Jonathan F. Bayes, *The Weakness of the Law*, Carlisle: Paternoster Press, 2000, p. 51.

[9] *Dictionary of National Biography*, 'James Relly'; W. Wilson, *Dissenting Churches*, vol. 1. p. 360.

[10] F. H. Foster, *A Genetic History of the New England Theology*, Chicago, 1907, p. 191. In New England Relly's views were promoted by Joseph Huntington, who had no connection with William Huntington discussed later in this chapter.

Antinomianism

especially after Roger Balls had taught practical Antinomianism in his Dublin Meeting; later, he was to cause more trouble for the Methodists in the Bristol Area.[11]

Over against antinomianism, Booth wrote of the moral law:

> It is a friend and guide, pointing to the way in which the Christian ought to walk, so as to express gratitude to God for his benefits, and glorify the Lord Redeemer. It shows him also, at the same time, how imperfect his own obedience is, and so is a happy means of keeping him humble at the foot of sovereign grace, and entirely dependent on the righteousness of his divine Sponsor.[12]

This statement reflected Particular Baptist thinking on this subject since the seventeenth century. The *1689 Confession* declared that, for believers, the Law of God is 'a rule of life, informing them of the will of God and their duty'.[13] Harmonizing the work of the law and the gospel, it insisted:

> ... neither are the aforementioned uses of the Law contrary to the grace of the Gospel, but do sweetly comply with it, the Spirit of Christ subduing and enabling the will of man to do that freely and cheerfully, which the will of God, revealed in the Law, requireth to be done.[14]

John Gill's teaching on the law is in harmony with that of the *Confession*. He wrote:

> ... it is of use to saints and true believers in Christ – (1) to point out the will of God unto them; what is to be done by them, and what is to be avoided.[15]

---

[11] *The Journals of the Rev. John Wesley, M.A.*, London 1837, p. 231 (23 March 1746), p. 306 (10, 11 April 1750), p. 426 (24th. Sept. 1758).

[12] A. Booth, *Death of Legal Hope*, p. 435.

[13] *1689 Confession*, XIX,6

[14] Ibid., XIX,7. This statement is taken directly from the *Westminster Confession*, as is that quoted above. The Westminster Divines assembled at a time when antinomianism was a matter of hot debate. See W. Young, op. cit., p. 276; K. M. Campbell, 'Antinomian Controversies of the Seventeenth Century', *Westminster Conference Papers*, London 1974, pp. 70 ff.

[15] J. Gill, *Body of Divinity*, p. 371.

Gill has been accused of doctrinal Antinomianism,[16] but it is evident that his teaching on the believer's duty to keep the moral law is in harmony with both the mainstream Puritanism of the seventeenth century and the evangelical Calvinism of men like Abraham Booth in the late eighteenth century. Recently, in his useful discussion of this issue, Jonathan Bayes has with some hesitation used John Brine as a representative doctrinal Antinomian. However, his quotations from Brine's writings do not establish his case, and the charge of Antinomianism never seems to have been made by Fuller and his associates, who were critical of Brine's Hyper-Calvinism. Bayes points out that Robert Hall, Sr. warned against Antinomianism in his *Help to Zion's Travellers* in 1781.[17] Certainly by the end of the century Particular Baptists were becoming increasingly concerned about this subject, but they did not see the problem of Antinomianism arising directly from the teaching of Gill and Brine.[18]

John Ryland suggested that the tendency towards Hyper-Calvinism and Antinomianism arose from another source:

> Some of the Calvinistic Methodists, especially in Lady Huntingdon's Connection, were becoming tinged with False Calvinism. These were not led into it like the admirers of Mr Brine and Dr Gill, by reading a great deal of controversial divinity, or by a polemical discussion of the five points disputed between us and the Arminians; but by a vague, crude idea of the term *power*, which led them to suppose, that nothing could be a bad man's duty, but what he *could* perform without any special influence from God. The same idea was spreading, faster than we

---

[16] W. T. Whitley, *Calvinism and Evangelism*, p. 27; W. Wilson, *Dissenting Churches*, vol. 4, p. 222. Such a view is tenable only with a definition of Antinomianism broader than 'against the Law'.

[17] Bayes, op. cit., pp. 27–29. Bayes refers to Whitley's suggestion that 'antinomianism was the dominant doctrine in eighteenth-century Particular Baptist circles'. Whitley however is not a reliable guide to eighteenth-century doctrinal issues.

[18] Of doctrinal antinomianism, John Ryland, Jr. wrote, 'The eminent divines, who verged to an extreme respecting the obligation of sinners to repent and believe the gospel, would have reprobated this doctrine, as tending to the greatest licentiousness. Dr Gill, Mr Brine, Mr Toplady etc. utterly condemned so vile a sentiment.' 'Preface' to Robert Hall, *Help to Zion's Travellers*, 4th edition, London, 1820.

Antinomianism

were aware, among our churches also: the ministers might distinguish between repentance and faith, and other internal duties; allowing the latter to be required, while they scrupled exhorting men to the former: but had things gone on a little longer in the same direction, we should have soon lost sight of the essence of duty, and of the spirituality of the divine law; and, consequently, men would have been treated as though, before conversion, they were fallen *below* all obligation to do anything spiritually good, and as though, after conversion, they were raised *above* all obligation to do anything more than they were actually inclined to perform. Thus, *inclination* would have been made the measure of *obligation*; duty would have been confined to the outward conduct; the turpitude of sin unspeakably lessened; and grace proportionably eclipsed, both as to the pardon of sin, and as to the application of salvation to the soul.[19]

By the 1780s it seems that Antinomianism was spreading among the Particular Baptist churches and possibly beyond. In 1787 John Ryland, Jr. decided to make it the subject of a sermon at the annual meeting of the Northamptonshire Association. This he subsequently published under the title *The Law Not Against the Promises of God*.[20] He pointed out that Christ had approved the summary of the law given in Matthew 22:37-40. Faith in Christ certainly delivers men from the penal effects of the broken law, but Christ

> ... hath confirmed instead of relaxing their obligations to devote themselves to the Lord – view the Law as expanded and unfolded in all the preceptive parts of the Word of God.[21]

Ryland insisted that the love which mankind had owed God since before the Fall, found its expression in obedience to the law.[22]

The law therefore should be preached, but he was aware that some ministers were being criticized for doing this. He spoke of 'some ignorant professors (though wise in their own eyes) who would revile

---

[19] J. Ryland, *Memoir of Andrew Fuller,* p, 7.
[20] J. Ryland, *The Law Not Against the Promises of God*, London 1787.
[21] Ibid., p. 35.
[22] Ibid., p. 41, 42.

such preachers, who think it their duty to explain the moral law, and insist upon its spirituality and excellence'.[23] Some years later he wrote:

> To me it appears a most marvellous instance of the deceitfulness of sin, if any man can think himself a friend to evangelical religion, who by sinking *unbelievers below* all obligation, and raising *believers above* all obligation, almost annihilates both duty and sin, and so leaves no room for the exercise of either pardoning mercy or sanctifying grace. The apostolic axiom, where there is no law, there is no transgression, justly leads us to conclude, that they who are below or above law have no guilt and need no Saviour; there is no room to show the riches of his grace, or the efficacy of his blood, in the pardon of those who never deserved punishment.[24]

Ryland's concern was shared by others. In 1789 Caleb Evans of Bristol wrote of the dangers of Socinianism and Antinomianism in the Western Association's *Letter to the Churches*.[25] Of the idea that the law is not the believer's rule of life, he wrote:

> A notion more corrupt, more false, more full of evil and dangerous consequences cannot possibly infect the human mind. The peace it brings is a false peace and will be found to be only the prelude of destruction.[26]

A year later Antinomianism was still troubling the Western churches, when Philip Gibbs wrote in the Association *Letter*, 'a second error of which we have too much cause to complain is the baneful and pernicious poison of Antinomianism.'[27]

From the late 1790s Andrew Fuller's correspondence makes frequent reference to the spread of Antinomianism. Of the churches in the Northamptonshire Association he wrote, 'Antinomianism, or as it is now called Huntingtonianism has made some inroads and required some exclusions.'[28] In 1804 he was complaining of its influence in Norfolk, Suffolk,

---

[23] Ibid., pp. 41, 42.

[24] Ryland, 'Preface' to Hall's *Help*, pp. x, xi.

[25] General Letter of the Elders, Ministers and Messengers of the Western Association, Bristol, June 1789.   [26] Ibid., p. 11.

[27] Western Association Letter, Plymouth 1790.

[28] Fuller's *Letters*, 'Fuller to Carey, 7 June 1799'.

Antinomianism

Yorkshire, and London.[29] He had also referred to it in Leicester,[30] from which town Robert Hall was to write, describing it as 'a monster'.[31]

2. WILLIAM HUNTINGTON

Fuller's use of the term 'Huntingtonianism' refers to the teaching of William Huntington. Huntington had a considerable impact on the Particular Baptists, even though he was never a member of their communion. It is strange therefore that modern historians have ignored the effects of his stormy career. Although Joseph Ivimey referred to his teaching and growing influence,[32] neither W. T. Whitley nor A. C. Underwood mentioned him. Possibly these later writers saw him simply as one of several opponents of Andrew Fuller, and just another Hyper-Calvinist, albeit a very controversial one. Contemporaries, however, made a clear distinction. Evangelical Calvinists such as Fuller would have fellowship with High Calvinists whenever possible, but not with Antinomians.[33]

Born William Hunt at Cranbrook, Kent, in 1745, Huntington was brought up in poverty and with minimal religious training. He eventually fled from his home district to escape the consequences of his youthful immorality. To help him break with his past, he changed his name from Hunt to Huntington.[34] During the 1770s he underwent a profound

[29] Ibid., 'Fuller to John Williams, 1 Aug 1804'; 'Fuller to Ward, 27 Oct 1804'.

[30] Ibid., 'Fuller to Ward, 31 Dec. 1803' – Fuller refers to W. W. Horne, one of the Leicester pastors, as a 'vile Antinomian & who for seditious words is likely in a little while to be led to prison, if not to Botany Bay'. The same letter refers to Antinomianism in Portsmouth and Plymouth.

[31] R. Hall, *Works*, vol. 6, London, 1833; 'Memoir' p. 146; cf. *Works*, vol. 2, 'Christian Baptism and that of John', 1816, p. 231, 'Antinomianism is making such rapid strides through the land, and has already convulsed and disorganised so many of our churches'.   [32] Ivimey, *HEB*, vol.4, p. 76.

[33] Ivimey states that the Particular Baptist Fund was willing to aid ministers who held the view of Gill and Brine, but not those who followed Huntington, *HEB*, vol.4, pp. 76–77. Fuller wrote, 'We distinguish between High Calvinists and Antinomians. With the former we do not refuse communion but with the latter we do'. *Works*, p. 844.

[34] Biographical details are taken from Thomas Wright, *The Life of William Huntington, S.S.*, London 1909. This is the standard life, well-researched and sympathetic, but weak on doctrinal issues. A more recent work, regrettably uncritical, is G. M. Ella, *William Huntington, Pastor of Providence*, Evangelical Press, Darlington, 1994.

conversion experience. Released from the bondage of his failure, he rose to heights of religious ecstasy.[35] Huntington considered this experience to have taken place without the involvement of anyone else, and this subsequently contributed to making him very independent of other Christians.[36]

Some time later Huntington came into contact with Torial Joss, a former associate of George Whitefield. With encouragement from Joss he began to preach in 1776, and later Joss ordained him as minister of an Independent church in Woking, Surrey. In connection with this pastorate, he engaged in a considerable itinerant ministry.[37] Huntington's popularity grew rapidly.

In 1782 he began to preach regularly at Margaret Street Chapel, London. In the following year his followers built Providence Chapel, Titchfield Street, which had to be enlarged to seat two thousand in 1798. When this chapel was burned down in 1810, a new one was built in Gray's Inn Road, and there Huntington preached right up until a few weeks before his death in July 1813.

Until the end of his ministry, Providence Chapel was crowded for every service.[38] His thirty-year ministry in the West End of London gave him a prominence which no other minister of similar views had ever enjoyed. At the same time, journeys to places as far apart as Plymouth, Bristol,

---

[35] Huntington recorded this in detail; see *The Works of the Reverend William Huntington, S.S.*, T. Bensley, London, 1811, vol. 1, 'The Kingdom of Heaven Taken by Prayer', pp. 69–72.

[36] 'This private method that the Saviour took in instructing me by His word and Spirit, without the ordinary use of published ordinances, led me to love private study and meditation, and even to this time I had rather spend one day alone with myself, in communion with Christ, than a whole week in company with all the gospel ministers in the kingdom' (Ibid., p. 117).

[37] Huntington described a typical week in 1780, 'From Ditton to Woking on Lord's day morning; to Worplesdon, in the afternoon; to Farnham in the evening; to Petworth, Sussex, Monday evening; to Horsham, Tuesday; to Margaret Street Chapel, London, Wednesday; and at Ditton on Thursday evening'. *The Bank of Faith*, quoted in E. Hooper, *The Celebrated Coalheaver*, London, 1871, p. 6.

[38] See the testimony of Samuel Adams, quoted in Hooper, *The Celebrated Coalheaver*, pp. 30–32.

Antinomianism

Birmingham, Leicester, and Helmsley in Yorkshire, helped to build up a considerable Huntingtonian following throughout the country.

Although he had a host of admirers, Huntington also made many enemies. He drew members from other Calvinistic churches; his supporters point to this fact and account for the criticism he received from fellow ministers on the grounds of envy and jealousy. However, the cause of the hostile feeling against William Huntington went deeper than that. While his isolation can be partly explained by some of the political views he held, a more serious explanation can be found in his attitude towards the moral law.

Huntington and Dissent

Before he became a minister in London, William Huntington had experienced the cruel depths of poverty. With such a background it is not surprising that he denounced oppression of the poor in scathing terms.[39] However, he later became a High Tory and greatly admired the younger William Pitt.[40] He was profoundly loyal to King George III and boasted of members of the royal household who attended his Chapel.[41] By the end of his life he was associating with people from a very different background than those of his earlier years. His second wife, whom he married in 1808, was Lady Elizabeth Sanderson, widow of a former Lord Mayor of London. A baronet and a knight were named as the executors of his will.[42]

Huntington's politics and associations were unusual for a Dissenter, but even stranger was his attitude to the Church of England. William Stevens, a member of his congregation, wrote:

> Although a dissenter in practice, he defended strenuously the doctrinal articles of the Church, and I have heard him declare in the pulpit, 'I would not, if I had the power, pull down our national church, for it is the great barrier between us and the Papists. They can never get at us until they pull down the Church.'[43]

[39] Huntington, *Works*, vol. 16, 'The Utility of the Books and the Excellency of the Parchments, preached on a Fast Day in March 1796,' pp. 367–406. Huntington especially denounced corn speculators.
[40] Hooper, *The Celebrated Coalheaver*, p. 15. [41] Ibid., p. 17. [42] Ibid., p. 112.
[43] W. Stevens, *Recollections of the Late William Huntington*, London, 1868, p. 38.

[121]

Ebenezer Hooper, whose parents were both children of Huntington's close friends, wrote:

> Strange to say for a Dissenter, he was a High Tory, an advocate for Church and State, consequently most of his followers were the same. Of the principles of Nonconformity, and the history of the Puritans, he does not appear to have read much. Compared with their persecutions and sufferings, his were light and of a different kind; his narratives show wherein he felt the errors of the Establishment, but in after life he was more hostile to the Dissenters.[44]

Huntington's views need to be seen against the background of Nonconformist resentment towards the injustices of the Test and Corporation Acts. Particular Baptists were active in the moves to gain relief from the rigours of these statutes. Their concern for liberty led some of them to support foreign revolutionary movements. As already noted, J. C. Ryland supported the American colonists during the War of Independence.[45] Daniel Turner[46] and Samuel Stennett[47] welcomed the French Revolution, although they deplored its later excesses. Even the heavenly-minded Samuel Pearce of Birmingham published a sermon against the Corporation and Test Acts,[48] while in 1793 Robert Hall published *An Apology for the Freedom of the Press and for General Liberty*.[49]

Huntington's passionate loyalty to the established order in Church and State was associated with his obsessive fear of revolution. While he was visiting Plymouth, he heard that a visiting preacher in his own pulpit at Providence Chapel had preached what he considered to be Jacobinism;[50] he rushed back to London immediately.[51] Discovering to his horror that

---

[44] *The Celebrated Coalheaver*, p. 15; cf. Anon, *The Voice of Years*, London, 1814, p. 31.

[45] A. C. Underwood, *HEB*, p. 143.

[46] E. A. Payne, *Baptists of Berkshire*, London, p. 83.

[47] Ivimey, *HEB*, vol. 4, p. 82.   [48] Ibid., p. 58.

[49] R. Hall, *Works*, vol. 3, London, 1833, p. 61.

[50] The Jacobins were members of a political club which promoted extremely revolutionary policies during the French Revolution. By the mid-1790s the term was being applied in England to any radical politician.

[51] T. Wright, *Life of Huntington*, pp. 105 ff.

Antinomianism

the visitor's statements were not unwelcome to some members of the congregation, Huntington proceeded to the extreme measure of dissolving and then re-forming his own church. William Stevens wrote:

> This caused Mr H. to reform his church, and several persons were not again admitted. Those who were, had new tickets given to them, but not before Mr H. had conversed with them.[52]

The storm was serious enough for Stevens to describe it as a 'great division and separation',[53] and 'the greatest ministerial trial he ever had'.[54]

Huntington's political extremism can also be seen in his readiness to describe Whigs as Jacobins. On the resignation of Lord Grenville's Whig administration in March 1807, he wrote to a friend:

> God reigns, George! Heaven and earth smile upon us! The king stands firm and God upholds him in standing. The Jacobins are dismissed with disgrace, contempt and scorn as enemies to God, the country, and all real religion.[55]

Such sentiments were doubtless pleasing to Tory governments, but could not fail to irritate those Dissenters who were chafing at their lack of political liberty.[56] It was galling to see a London minister with a large following supporting the privileged position of the Church of England and refusing to align himself with the political aspirations of the Dissenters.

HUNTINGTON AND THE MORAL LAW

Although politics must have played a part in alienating William Huntington from his fellow Dissenters, it was his doctrine of the law that proved to be the biggest scandal. He taught that the moral law was

---

[52] W. Stevens, *Recollections*, p. 8; *Voice of Years*, p. 30.
[53] W. Stevens, *Recollections*, p. 32.   [54] Ibid., p. 8.
[55] E. Hooper, *Facts, Letters and Documents*, London, 1872, p.116, 'William Huntington to George Landell, 2nd April 1807'.
[56] Another minister to isolate himself from his brethren by Tory politics was, of course, John Martin (see above, pp. 108–110). There is no suggestion of any co-operation between Martin and Huntington, but clearly both men were isolated from their brethren on political issues.

binding on the unbeliever, but was not a rule of life for the Christian. 'All the non-elect are under the law to Christ. But the believer is under grace to Christ.'[57] In reply to Rowland Hill, who had challenged his teaching, he wrote concerning the law:

> The master's commanding will is the bondservant's rule; it is the creditor's handwriting, and the debtor's account book; but the goodwill of the Father is the son's rule. These are the two covenants, and what the law requires, the gospel gives; and what Christ commands, he works in his saints by his Spirit to obey, and their obedience is the obedience of faith.[58]

His critics would have agreed the Holy Spirit's enabling is essential to obedience but Huntington insisted that the commandments of the Lord Jesus Christ had no connection with the law. When he was challenged with the words of Jesus, 'If you love me, keep my commandments', his response was:

> When Christ mentions those words *my commandments*, he never once means in all the four evangelists, the moral law; he never puts the word, *my*, to that.[59]

Summarizing his position in his sermon against Hill's teaching, he said:

> I conclude, the law is the saint's first husband and schoolmaster; and it is the bondservant's only rule, but 'they that are Christ's have crucified the flesh with the affections and lusts'; and 'against such there is no law'.[60]

Huntington expounded his doctrine of the law in many sermons and pamphlets. He never ceased to claim that the law of Moses had nothing to do with the believer. In *A Rule and a Riddle*, another popular presentation of his teaching, he wrote:

> This I do insist upon, that bondage, hardness of heart, revealed wrath, enmity against God, desperation, curses, hell and damnation, are the best things that men can fetch from the killing letter of the law of Moses: whether the man be a believer or an infidel it matters not. The law will

---

[57] Huntington, *Works*, vol. 11, 'The Broken Cistern and the Springing Well' [1791], p. 66.   [58] Ibid., p. 287.   [59] Ibid., p. 381.   [60] Ibid., p. 313.

Antinomianism

pursue the believer if he goes there. Christ alone is his refuge; it will entangle the believer, and yoke him again if he looks for help there.[61]

To the question of what the believer's rule of life is, Huntington replied: 'Faith is the rule of life according to the revealed will of God in Christ Jesus.'[62] After quoting many texts which speak of the Christian living and walking by faith, he appealed to Proverbs 13:14: 'The law of the wise is a fountain of life, to depart from the snares of death.' In his eyes the Mosaic law was only a ministration of death and a means of entanglement. 'If the law be a killing letter, and the law of death, it cannot be a fountain of life; by which the wise man departs from the snares of death.'[63] To sustain his arguments, Huntington had to draw a clear line of distinction between this law of the wise and the moral law:

> The law of the spirit of God produces more obedience to God in one hour, than ever hath been produced by all the living rules that have been drawn by human wisdom from killing snares.[64]

It is this law of the Spirit of God which produces 'the fruit of the Spirit, which is evangelical obedience'. The reader, however, is still left with uncertainty about what is the objective rule of life. In a published letter, Huntington wrote:

> Make the whole word of God your rule of faith and practice and lay your experience, your principles, yea, every sentiment, every impulse, every trial, every change, and every cross and every spiritual sensation to that, and so 'Cleanse your way by taking heed thereto, according to God's word.'[65]

This of course was sound advice, but in *A Rule and a Riddle* he left his reader in some confusion when, in a discussion of the rules of life, he declared:

> People who have no hope but in the written letter of Scripture, will find that the flood of wrath and final conflagration will leave them without an

---

[61] Huntington, *Works*, vol. 8, 'A Rule and a Riddle', p. 103   [62] Ibid., p. 57.
[63] Ibid., p. 65   [64] Ibid., p.68.
[65] Hooper, *Celebrated Coalheaver*, p. 88. 'Letter to Elizabeth Morton'.

anchor in that storm; and I am persuaded that the believer's rule of life must be found in his heart also, if ever he lives with God in heaven.[66]

That God should write his law on the believer's heart is a glorious promise of the New Covenant, but, as stated by Huntington (who did not believe that the moral law was the law written on the heart), this truth left many of his followers looking for some kind of experience, rather than looking to God's written revelation. Other statements from him, such as 'God's sovereign will is man's rule', intensified this confusion.[67] The danger inherent in his teaching was accentuated by Huntington's confident boast: 'I know that God the Saviour revealed this doctrine to my soul.' So convinced was he of God's revelation of this doctrine to him, that he suggested his critics were guilty of sinning against the Holy Spirit.[68] With an undaunted confidence he dismissed the teaching of 'St Basil, St Augustine, St Ambrose, Herman Witsius and saint nobody knows who'.[69]

Although he insisted that the law had nothing to do with a Christian's obedience, Huntington insisted that the Christian was not left free to sin. To Caleb Evans, he wrote:

> If you see an Antinomian making a flaming profession, when, at the same time, he is proud and haughty; a hater of, and a declaimer against those he knows in his conscience to be good; a lover of Mammon; aiming at wealth, following the antediluvian professors in making an affinity with the offspring of Cain, or the children of the devil, either to gratify the lusts of the flesh, the lust of the eye or the covetous spirit of Mammon ... you may well say that such men are in love with their own lusts; and that all their harangues about the law are nothing but their own whims and fancies, for they hold unscriptural notions and live in the practice of licentious principles.[70]

---

[66] ' A Rule and A Riddle', *Works*, vol. 8, p.62.   [67] Ibid., p. 133.

[68] Ibid., 'This, Sir, borders close upon the unpardonable sin, it is trifling with the folds of infinite wisdom, *Eph.* 3:10', p.120.

[69] Ibid., p. 499.

[70] Huntington, *Works*, vol. 10, p. 37.

Antinomianism

Huntington's teaching on the Christian life was however confused by a passive doctrine of sanctification. The eternal predestinating decree of God was declared to be the cause of a believer's obedience, to the exclusion of the Christian's responsibility to obey commandments.

> Good works do not spring from the will of God's commandments, but from his will of purpose: 'created in Christ Jesus unto good works, which God hath before ordained that we should walk in them'.[71]

Again he wrote, 'Nor is man the active agent of good works, but God, who works in him to will and to do.'[72] In a sermon he could say of sanctification, 'All this is willed and determined by the secret counsel of God; and as it is written, "For this is the will of God, even your sanctification".'[73]

Huntington stated his passive doctrine of sanctification so strongly that he had no room for the idea of progressive sanctification, as taught by Calvinists generally. In reply to Caleb Evans, he wrote:

> As to sanctification being a progressive work, it is best to consent to the wholesome words of our Lord Jesus Christ, lest we set poor weak believers to inquiring how long this progressive work is to be on the wheels, what part of it is wrought, what measure of it is required, and how much remains to be done: and like Sarah with her bondwoman, they begin to forward the business by the works of the flesh, instead of lying passive to be worked on. 'He that believeth shall not make haste', but he that hasteth with his feet sinneth.[74]

Confusion arose in part because Huntington implied that his critics suggested that the believer was left to obey the Ten Commandments apart from the enabling power of God. This led him to denounce the law, which he often personified as Moses:

---

[71] Ibid., p. 86.

[72] Ibid., p. 87.

[73] Huntington, *Works*, vol. 11, 'The Moral Law Not Injured by the Everlasting Gospel', p. 233.

[74] Huntington, *Works*, vol. 10, 'Letter to Evans', p. 3; cf. Joseph Cottle's Comment on Antinomianism, 'Imputed sanctification is the spring of all their errors', quoted James Bennett, *History of Dissenters*, London 1839, p. 345.

Make the law your only rule of life; read it, keep your eyes upon it, and live by it; and I will pray that I will be kept dead to the law, and alive unto God; that I may be crucified with Christ and yet live; yet not I but that Christ may live in me. If you make the law your rule of life, you are alive to the law and walk in the law. And if Christ lives in me, I shall be kept, alive unto God, and walk in newness of life.

Go on with the commandments, and I will go on with the promises. Make the law your rule of walk, and I will pray God to perform his promise in me.[75]

Gospel Preaching

With a doctrine of such complete passivity in the process of sanctification, it is not surprising to discover that Huntington's teaching on the law is linked to a Hyper-Calvinistic view of the gospel. While he admitted that apostles preached 'promiscuously unto all',[76] he appeared to deny any such right to his contemporaries:

> But what effect has it, or what power attends it [the gospel], from the mouth of Mr Ryland or Mr Fuller, when they make it the rule of a dead man's duty? Just as much as the adjurations of the sons of Sceva, the Jew, when they abused the name of the Lord Jesus in commanding the evil spirit, who left the man and mastered them.[77]

Huntington rounded on his critics, declaring,

> You set the law before the believer, as his only law of life and conduct; and the gospel is set before the unconverted as their only rule of duty. The carnal man has got an evangelical law and the heir of promise has got a legal one; the life-giving commandment is palmed upon the congregation of the dead, and the ministration of death is saddled upon the children of the resurrection; the believers are all sent to Moses, and the unconverted are all sent to Jesus Christ; Moses is to have the legitimate sons and Christ is to have the bastards.[78]

---

[75] Huntington, *Works*, vol. 8, 'A Rule and a Riddle', p.151.

[76] Huntington, *Works*, vol. 11, 'Excommunication, and the Duty of All Men to Believe, Weighed in the Balance', hereinafter referred to as 'Excommunication', p. 155.   [77] Ibid., p. 155.   [78] Ibid., p. 151.

Antinomianism

HUNTINGTON'S VIEW OF SCRIPTURE

Nearly ten years before Huntington wrote these words, he had published a small work, *The Arminian Skeleton*, which had alarmed the Calvinist Rowland Hill. The work is an attack on Arminianism, which he dubs 'universal charity'. Huntington's definition of Arminianism included any desire for the salvation of people in general. To sustain this thesis he had to accuse the apostle Paul of Arminianism:

> Paul himself, our great and blessed apostle, seemed to be caught in this web; but he soon finds the snare broken, and he is delivered; 'I could wish myself to be accursed from Christ for my brethren's sake, who are Israelites according to the flesh.' And this was fleshly affection with a witness, blown up to an amazing height; even to wish himself to be accursed from Christ for their sake (*Rom*. 9:3). Howbeit God sent him a few bonds, stripes and imprisonments, from his fleshly brethren, in order to wean him, and then he appears with a becoming zeal for his God: 'If any man love not our Lord Jesus Christ, let him be Anathema, Maranatha' (*1 Cor*. 16:22).[79]

Warming to his theme, he condemned Moses' intercession for Israel (*Exod*. 32:31–32): 'It appears to me that Moses was for a while taken in this snare.'[80] These statements come from one of Huntington's very early works, but there is no indication that he ever withdrew them. Such bizarre interpretations of Scripture gave orthodox Christians just grounds for alarm. Although Huntington professed a high regard for Scripture, he was prepared to do violence to it in order to accommodate his preconceived system of doctrine.

A critic who appealed to Romans 13:8–10 to question his teaching that the believer is not subject to the law as a rule of life was reminded that the church was a mixed body. He told his opponent that he was

> not considering that lilies and thorns, servants and sons, Israelites and hypocrites, wise virgins and foolish ones, are to go and grow together as tares and wheat until harvest. And on account of this mixture it is that

---

[79] Huntington, *Works*, vol. 2 , 'The Arminian Skeleton, or the Arminian Dissected and Anatomised' [1783], pp.23, 24.   [80] Ibid., p. 24.

the killing letter and the promise of life must go together; the promises are to the heirs of promise; and we know that what things soever the law saith, it saith to them that are under the law.[81]

Assurance

William Huntington's teachings on the law and the presentation of the gospel were not unconnected with his teaching on assurance. He had a very strong conviction of his own salvation and associated this with a number of very powerful and personal spiritual experiences. Huntington claimed that his assurance had been granted in a direct and immediate way.

Experimental preachers had long taught the prospect of an experience of God's love, and the saints of God have known such experiences down through the ages.[82] To preach such realities wisely, it is important that other truths should not be neglected or denied; it is also essential that experience should not be set over against doctrine. To go further, and to make experiences the basis of doctrine will only lead to fanaticism.

Huntington denied that gospel preaching includes a free and genuine offer of salvation to all men generally. His congregations were denied an objective warrant for approaching Christ by faith for salvation. Some hearers, who felt that they had no experience of the preliminary convicting work of the Holy Spirit, were left with the haunting fear that they had no entitlement to place their trust in Christ for salvation. Others could be tempted to seek spiritual experiences without coming to Christ as proclaimed in the gospel. This danger was undoubtedly complicated by Huntington's Antinomianism. He spoke of the law in terms which represented it as the enemy of the Christian and disparaged concern about 'marks of grace' as nothing more than legal bondage.

At the time Huntington became a Christian, many believers were experiencing the love of God in a remarkable way. Richness of spiritual

---

[81] 'A Rule and a Riddle', p. 52.

[82] Spurgeon could write, 'To feel [God's] love, to rejoice in the presence of the anointed Saviour, to survey the promises and feel the power of the Holy Ghost in applying precious truth to the soul, is a joy which worldlings cannot understand, but which true believers are ravished with', *Treasury of David*, on Psalm 84:10.

experience, and especially of the love of God, has often featured of times of revival. Whitefield's *Journals* provide fascinating examples of this phenomenon. Such accounts delight the Christian reader, but there is always the danger that these highly desirable experiences may be isolated from the necessity of Christian obedience. It was to guard against this very danger that Jonathan Edwards wrote his *Treatise concerning Religious Affections*. In it he wrote: 'It is the concurring voice of all orthodox divines, that there may be religious affections which are raised to a very high degree, and yet there be nothing of true religion.' In this connection he quoted Solomon Stoddard: ' Common affections are sometimes stronger than saving.' Yet Edwards was making an earnest plea for a religion which involved the heart; in fact he was expounding the words of 1 Peter 1:18: 'Whom having not seen ye love; in whom, though now ye see him not, yet believing, ye rejoice with joy unspeakable and full of glory.' Edwards proceeded to argue that true assurance is associated with sanctification. The appearance of the fruit of the Spirit in the life of a person confirms the reality of his faith. Unlike Huntington who disparaged the concept of progressive sanctification, Edwards taught that 'the progress of the work of grace in the hearts of the saints is represented in Scripture as a continued conversion and renovation of nature.' As a major argument in his work he set out to establish that 'truly gracious affections differ from those affections that are false and delusive in that they are attended by the lamb-like, dove-like spirit and temper of Jesus Christ'.[83]

Edwards felt the need to write as he did on religious feelings in 1746 because of the way in which some people were misinterpreting and misapplying extraordinary experiences of God's grace at the height of the Great Awakening. The evidence suggests that Edwards' teaching was urgently needed in the England of the late-eighteenth and early-nineteenth centuries.

---

[83] Jonathan Edwards, *Works*, vol. 1 [1834], repr. Edinburgh: Banner of Truth, 1974, 'Treatise concerning Religious Affections', pp. 246, 303.

7

WILLIAM HUNTINGTON'S CONTROVERSY WITH THE PARTICULAR BAPTISTS

> We do not reject the law and the works thereof, but, on the contrary, confirm them, and teach that we ought to do good works, and that the law is good and profitable, if we merely give it its right, and keep it to its own proper work and office.
>
> MARTIN LUTHER

> None have as yet attained to such a degree of wisdom, as that they may not, by the daily instruction of the Law, advance to a purer knowledge of the divine will. Then, because we need not doctrine merely, but exhortation also, the servant of God will derive this further advantage from the Law: by frequently meditating upon it, he will be excited to obedience, and confirmed in it, and so drawn away from the slippery paths of sin.
>
> JOHN CALVIN, *INSTITUTES*, II.7.12

Huntington's teaching on the believer's complete freedom from the law was something of a novel idea in the eyes of most Particular Baptists. However, his Hyper-Calvinism may have attracted some of their number who adhered to the theology of John Gill and who felt threatened by the spread of the evangelical Calvinism of Andrew Fuller and his friends. To such people Huntington's preaching and writings had a certain attraction. The concerns of John Ryland, Jr. and Caleb Evans about the spread of Antinomianism have already been noted. These concerns rapidly developed into a bitter controversy, involving John Ryland's father, John Collett Ryland.

William Huntington's Controversy with the Particular Baptists

In 1786 the senior Ryland resigned his pastorate in Northampton and moved (along with his boarding school) to Enfield.[1] Huntington had already expressed his disapproval of Ryland's *Body of Divinity*,[2] but was incensed by the appearance of a tract in 1871, entitled *Antinomianism Unmasked*, written by Maria de Fleury.[3] In spite of disclaimers[4] by Maria de Fleury, Huntington was convinced that the real author was John Collett Ryland.

Maria de Fleury had already had a sharp encounter with William Huntington. She was a member of a French Protestant refugee family and a member of an Independent Church which met at the Barbican, London.[5] She first met Huntington in April 1787, asking for a private interview, which Huntington promised for the following week. However, before this meeting took place, she wrote to him, explaining that she had been prejudiced against him, but hoped that the interview would clear up their differences.[6] Huntington did not keep the appointment, but sent a letter, reprimanding the enquirer for her temerity. In it he wrote:

> I defy the whole world to overthrow my testimony, or charge me with any gross crime since called by grace: this being the case your prejudice is ill-founded.[7]

Huntington considered it an impertinence for a woman to question his teaching and told Maria so. But he had not reckoned with the boldness of

---

[1] J. Culross, *The Three Rylands*, London 1897, p. 58. E. Hooper states that Huntington's second son, Ebenezer, was one of Ryland's pupils, 'but when the controversy with him commenced, he was removed, a step he ever deeply regretted', *Facts, Letters and Documents*, p. 55.

[2] Huntington, *Works*, vol. 11, 'The Broken Cistern and the Springing Well', hereinafter referred to as 'The Broken Cistern', p. 3.

[3] Maria de Fleury, *Antinomianism Unmasked*, London, 1791.

[4] See below pp. 135, 6.

[5] E. Hooper, *The Celebrated Coalheaver*, p. 64. M. de Fleury, *Divine Poems and Essays*, London, 1791, includes an Introduction by John Towers, who describes himself as Maria's pastor. Towers was minister of the Independent Church at the Barbican from 1771 to 1804. W. Wilson, *London Dissenting Churches*, vol. 3, pp. 223-7.

[6] M. de Fleury, *Serious Address to the Rev. Mr Huntington*, London, 1788, p. 8.

[7] Quoted, Ibid., p. 10.

his opponent: she wrote and printed an anonymous *Letter to Mr Huntington*[8] and had it sold outside the doors of his chapel.[9] Huntington countered with two sermons, which he published under the title *The Servant of the Lord Described and Vindicated*. It was not simply a rejoinder to Maria's arguments, but also a prophecy that 'the present prophetess that has made so free with my ministry shall sensibly meet with the visible disapprobation of God'.[10] He disapproved of a woman who presumed to correct a minister of the gospel:

> This venerable mother Jezebel is the only precedent that our present prophetess has got to countenance her in writing against the servants of God.[11]

Huntington also hinted that Maria de Fleury wrote on behalf of others, whom he described as 'the present combination'.[12]

Maria de Fleury replied to Huntington's sermons with *A Serious Address to the Rev. Mr Huntington*.[13] Accepting responsibility for the earlier *Letter to the Rev. Mr Huntington*, she reviewed the controversy, accusing Huntington of pride and an erroneous attitude to the law.[14]

1791 saw Maria de Fleury on the attack again with her pamphlet *Antinomianism Unmasked*. This closely printed tract of sixty-nine pages was more detailed than anything she had yet written, and reveals a fair grasp of the theological issues. This is probably the reason why Huntington considered Ryland the real author. Certainly Ryland was a friend of Maria de Fleury, and in the same year he wrote an introduction to a volume of her poems.[15] She, however, insisted that she was the author of *Antinomianism Unmasked*; what we know of Ryland leads us to believe it extremely unlikely that he would shelter behind anybody. John Towers,

---

[8] Anon. [Maria de Fleury], *A Letter to the Rev. Mr Huntington*, London, 1787. Elizabeth Morton, a supporter of Huntington, replied to it in *The Daughter's Defence of Her Father*, London, 1788, and Maria de Fleury admitted authorship in *An Answer to the Daughter's Defence of Her Father*, London, 1788, p. 5.

[9] Huntington, *Works*, vol. 7, 'The Servant of the Lord Described and Vindicated', 1788, pp. 197,198.   [10] Ibid., p. 174.   [11] Ibid., p. 207.   [12] Ibid., p,174.
[13] London, 1788.   [14] Ibid., p. 80.
[15] M. de Fleury, *Divine Poems and Essays*.

Maria's pastor, offered an interesting word of explanation concerning her writings:

> In many of her writings, her style is rather masculine, than otherwise, and therefore she has been suspected of publishing works under her name, which were not her own, but had some minister for their author: – Whoever thus judged, I am persuaded were altogether mistaken. Being frequently in the company of ministers, it is not to be wondered at, if she should imperceptibly speak or write, in some respects after their manner.[16]

Maria de Fleury did not refer to Huntington by name in *Antinomianism Unmasked*. She dealt with her subject quite broadly, criticizing some teachings, which were in fact foreign to Huntington's system. James Relly was the only contemporary she quoted, although his ideas developed into universalism, a tenet which Huntington abhorred. She wrote:

> The Antinomian thinks that the moral law is not to be considered as the rule of a believer's conduct; that sorrow for sin is unnecessary; that God never chastises his people on the account of sin, or hides from them the light of his countenance, that there is no spiritual warfare or conflict between the two natures in a Christian: 'that if the influence of the Spirit is now necessary to make men believe the gospel then God has not accommodated his gospel to mankind'. He denies the possibility of a believer's grieving the Holy Spirit of God; he speaks slightly of the means of grace and scoffs at all Christian experience and every idea of heart holiness, and humble walking with God: some have even gone so far as to say, they could not sin because there is no sin in a believer. These sentiments exist not only in the works of James Relly, but in the present day, they walk abroad in a public and triumphant manner in town and country: where they do not dare to appear in their full blown colours, they put forth their tender bud: he who would reject this dangerous and absurd system with horror and contempt were it laid before him in a full complex view, drinks it in little by little.[17]

---

[16] Ibid, p. lx.
[17] M. de Fleury, *Antinomianism Unmasked*, p. 13.

This was a direct challenge to the Antinomianism that was threatening the churches of that time in a number of different guises. Although Huntington was not named, he took up Maria de Fleury's challenge and replied later in the same year with a lengthy pamphlet, *The Broken Cistern and the Springing Well*.[18] In it he provided a powerful defence of his doctrine of the law, but of Maria de Fleury's tract he wrote:

> My doctrine, in this piece is jumbled in as a principal ingredient of a most dreadful composition; and like the poor man that fell among thieves I am ranked with a dreadful gang.[19]

Huntington was no universalist and declared: 'As to James Relly I know nothing of him; I never read anything of his.'[20] He then proceeded to denounce Maria and her friends, and made the suggestion that John Collett Ryland was the real author of *Antinomianism Unmasked*.[21]

Before the year ended, Maria de Fleury made a further reply with *A Farewell to Mr Huntington*, again insisting that Ryland played no part in her writings.[22] Huntington remained unconvinced, and in the following year replied with *An Answer to Fools; and a Word to the Wise; Addressed to the Reverend Maria de Fleury, John Ryland and Co*. The language of this pamphlet was abusive, describing Miss de Fleury as 'a parish girl; a hypocrite',[23] and accused her of intemperance.[24]

The controversy does not make edifying reading. Both William Huntington and Maria de Fleury lapsed into verbally abusing one another at times. While Huntington was the first offender, his opponent's prim lectures must have been irritating in the extreme and the sale of her

---

[18] Huntington, *Works*, vol. 11, 'The Broken Cistern and the Springing Well', 1791.
[19] Ibid., p. 5.   [20] Ibid., p. 6.   [21] Ibid., p. 3.
[22] M. de Fleury, *A Farewell to Mr Huntington, (Falsehood Examined at the Bar of Truth; or a Farewell to Mr Wm. Huntington and Mr Thos. Jones of Reading)*, London 1791. Here she declares, p. 5: 'I had no more assistance from Mr Ryland in writing it, than I had from Mr Huntington, neither did Mr Ryland so much as see a proof sheet; the Printer is a witness to this.'
[23] Huntington, *Works*, vol. 11, 'An Answer to Fools and a Word to the Wise. Addressed to the Reverend Maria de Fleury, John Ryland and Co', London, 1792, p. 323.
[24] Ibid., p. 346; pp. 354, 5.

William Huntington's Controversy with the Particular Baptists

pamphlets outside his chapel door lacked wisdom. The link with John Collett Ryland seems to have been suggested to William Huntington by London gossip;[25] but once Huntington was convinced, Maria's disclaimers were of no avail. This theological battle in London helps to explain Huntington's readiness to get involved in the affairs of the Baptists of Northampton, where John Ryland, Jr. was the pastor.

At some period before 1791, John Adams, a member of the College Lane Church, Northampton, became restive under the ministry of the younger Ryland. His dissatisfaction developed after he had accepted Huntington's teaching on the law.[26] At the same time, Huntington was invited to preach in Northampton by a Mr Hewet, who had earlier been excluded from membership in the College Lane Church for saying 'Mr Ryland did not preach the gospel.'[27] Surprisingly, Ryland was asked to loan College Lane Chapel for Huntington's visit. He refused.[28] A house was then licensed for worship in which Huntington preached; afterwards he received hospitality from Adams.[29] In the eyes of the members of the College Lane Church, Adams's offence was compounded by the fact that Huntington 'had himself just before he came down been writing against Mr Ryland snr. in defence of the pernicious notion that the law is not the rule of the believer's conduct'.[30]

Attempts to reconcile Adams to the Church failed and he was excommunicated from their membership. Huntington then published a pamphlet, which included the letter of excommunication together with his own comments. This tract entitled *Excommunication and the Duty of All Men to Believe, Weighed in the Balance*, ranged over issues connected with the preaching of the gospel and the believer's relationship to the law.

[25] W. Huntington, *Works*, vol. 11, 'Broken Cistern', p. 3.
[26] Huntington, *Works*, vol. 11, 'J. Ryland to J. Adams', quoted in 'Excommunication', p. 129.
[27] Ibid., p. 158.
[28] J. Ryland, *Serious Remarks on the Different Representations of Evangelical Doctrine by Professed Friends of the Gospel*, Part 2, Bristol, 1818, hereinafter referred to as *Serious Remarks*, p. 39.
[29] Huntington, *Works*, vol. 11, 'Excommunication', p. 130.
[30] Ibid., p. 130.

Huntington attacked Andrew Fuller and John Rippon, Gill's successor at Carter Lane, Southwark, as well as John Ryland, Jr.:

> Mr Ryland, Mr Fuller and Mr Rippon have made a decree that the gospel is the rule of an unconverted man's duty; and they have admitted Moses chief ruler in the synagogue, and the law is the saint's rule of the life of faith.[31]

Reference has already been made to the *Western Association Letter* of 1789 written by Caleb Evans. While Evans mentioned no names in his letter, Huntington felt that he was being attacked and so replied with *A Letter to the Rev. Caleb Evans*.[32] He defended his position on the law, but was careful to insist that a true believer cannot live in sin.

> I will defend no sort of Antinomians but such as are born again of the Holy Ghost, who live under the dominion of grace, and whose conduct and conversation are agreeable to the measure of faith received.[33]

Huntington refused to consider that his views could lead to practical Antinomianism. He considered Evans and his associates to be subverters of the gospel, whilst they clearly believed that his teaching must lead to licentiousness. 'If the Law be no rule of life to the believer, his breach of it can be no sin', wrote Evans.[34] Huntington's abusive language was not calculated to improve relations with those who differed from him. The law was described as 'a killing letter',[35] 'a bondservant's rule',[36] 'a ministration of death'.[37] Those who claimed it was their pattern for Christian obedience were described as 'pharisees',[38] and 'bastards',[39] and he was ready to denounce the judgment of God against them.

Thus by 1791, Huntington had engaged in acrimonious controversy with leading Particular Baptist ministers in London, Northampton, and

[31] Ibid., p. 187.
[32] Huntington, *Works*, vol. 10, 'A Letter to the Rev. Caleb Evans, M.A', 1789.
[33] Ibid., p. 117.
[34] C. Evans, *Western Association Letter*, 1789, p. 10.
[35] Huntington, *Works*, vol. 11, 'The Moral Law Not Injured by the Everlasting Gospel', 1792, p. 75.
[36] Ibid., p. 287, cf. p. 313.   [37] Ibid., p. 151.
[38] Ibid., p. 65.   [39] Ibid., p. 151.

William Huntington's Controversy with the Particular Baptists

Bristol. To make matters worse, he later ascribed the deaths of some of his opponents to the judgment of God upon them.

> Mr Evans went on till God struck him down and then went mad and at last [God] sent him to his grave; and Mr Gwynnep has toiled till he is so shut up that he cannot come forth either with a mouthful of truth or a grain of common sense, as a sermon of his now in my possession shows; and as for Maria and John Ryland, they are no more.[40]

Many years later John Ryland, Jr. commented:

> Had it pleased God to remove me from this world at any period between the year 1791 and the death of this man, no doubt he would have added my name to the list of those who were struck dead for not receiving him.[41]

Not surprisingly Ryland had grave doubts about Huntington's sincerity,

> His positivity, his volubility, with an abundance of low wit, and abuse of other ministers, acquired for him a considerable degree of popularity, though chiefly among the ignorant and illiterate; while he had a knack of so connecting detached sentences of scripture, without regard to their original import, as to make them appear to prove whatever he pleased. His profligacy before his supposed conversion, would have been no evidence that it was not genuine; but his effrontery in relating it afterwards in the most ludicrous and jocose expressions, must go far towards invalidating it; especially since after he had left off the indulgence of the lusts of the flesh no man seemed more completely under the domination of the lusts of the mind.[42]

THE SIGNIFICANCE OF THE CONTROVERSY

The controversy was bitter and at times lacked precision. On occasions the opponents seemed to be attacking each other in a fog of ideas. Each

---

[40] Huntington, *Works*, vol. 12, 'Letter to the Rev. Torial Joss', 1794, pp. 303-4. Joseph Gwennap (d. 1813) was pastor of a Baptist church in Piccadilly, 1783-98. His ministry apparently ended under a cloud, Wilson, *Dissenters*, vol. 4, p. 51.
[41] J. Ryland, *Serious Remarks*, p. 40.   [42] Ibid., pp. 38, 39.

side genuinely feared the effects of the teaching of the other. The Rylands were well aware of the fact that church history does supply examples of immorality sheltering under a religious cloak. Huntington, on the other hand, considered that the teaching of his antagonists reduced the Christian life to a slavish adherence to a code of rules. Such teaching, he believed, robbed Christianity of its distinctive joy and liberty.

There is no evidence to suggest that Huntington was immoral after his conversion. Rowland Hill repeated details of his profligate youth,[43] and there is no doubt that if evidence of later excesses existed, some opponent would have broadcast it. There may well have been scandals among his followers, but these were to be found in other religious groups as well.[44]

However, although Huntington must be cleared of any charge of practical Antinomianism, his failure in one area of his Christian witness did lay him open to criticism. His preaching failed to inculcate Christian duty. Ebenezer Hooper alleged that he preached on doctrinal and experiential themes to the exclusion of practical ones.[45] This allegation is supported by a study of his published sermons. His lack of balance in this matter may be explained in terms of his own life and character. His conversion had been a profoundly liberating experience and his sense of freedom from the penalties of a broken law filled his horizon until complementary aspects of Christian doctrine were excluded. He was an extremist in all

---

[43] To Hill, Huntington declared, 'Your digging into all the follies of my youth, and bringing them forth at your church meeting before an hundred people, concerning my name, child etc. etc., which I had published to the world at large, can never be called fulfilling the royal law.' Huntington, *Works*, vol. 11, 'The Moral Law Not Injured by the Everlasting Gospel', 1789, p. 208.

[44] An unhappy case was that of John Church, minister of a church in London, who was gaoled for homosexual practices in 1817. He claimed to have been converted under Huntington's ministry. After his release he was an isolated figure but supported by his own congregation of some 800. Anon, *The Infamous Life of John Church*, London 1817; Anon, *The Devil and Parson Church*, London, n.d.; J. Church, *The Gracious Designs of God Accomplished by the Malice of His Enemies*, London, 1819; J. Wells, *Funeral Sermon for John Church*, London, 1833.

[45] E. Hooper, *Celebrated Coalheaver*, p. 88 cf. p. 54; *The Voice of Years*, pp. 58–64.

his views, religious and political. He was a self-taught man, who, on his own admission shunned fellowship with other ministers.[46]

The battle was fought out in a series of fierce skirmishes. Unfortunately, no competent theologian published a complete and detailed analysis of the issues in question. Abraham Booth's *Death of Legal Hope* was the essay of a young man, published before Huntington appeared on the religious scene. The anonymous author of the Memoir, prefixed to Booth's *Works*, recalled a conversation with Booth towards the end of his life:

> Alluding to a notorious popular preacher of the independent class, who is well known to have done, perhaps more than any man of the age, to disseminate what are commonly called Antinomian principles, he added, 'Were I as young as I have been, one of the first things to which I would devote my time, should be a confutation of the system of that man. In order to do this effectually, I would read the whole of his numerous writings. I would collect from them as I proceeded, what are the sentiments that he holds on particular subjects, so as, if possible, to ascertain his whole system; and having once made myself master of that, I would, to the best of my ability confute it, by an appeal to the scriptures; and in doing this I should think I was rendering one of the best services in my power to the churches of Christ; but now I am too old to undertake it. I have mentioned the thing to several of my younger brethren in the ministry, but none of them seem disposed to engage in the labour of it.'[47]

Andrew Fuller suggested that Antinomianism had advanced 'While our best writers and preachers have been directing their whole force against Socinian, Arian and Arminian heterodoxy'.[48] Fuller wrote several short pieces on the subject and began a longer treatise, but this was never finished, although it was published as an incomplete work in 1816, after his death.[49]

---

[46] See above p. 120, footnote 36.
[47] A. Booth, *Works,* vol. 1, p. xli.
[48] A. Fuller, *Works*, p. 335.
[49] J. Ryland, *Life of Fuller*, p. 146.

William Huntington undoubtedly constituted a challenge to Evangelical Christianity in England. He quickly became popular as a writer and a preacher. Discerning readers soon realized that while there was a measure of orthodoxy in his writings, they did not stand in the mainstream of historic Calvinism, and that while he displayed a remarkable facility in quoting Scripture, he displayed an equally remarkable looseness when quoting from it. When such use of Scripture poured forth in his preaching, his sermons seemed almost oracular. He certainly gained a following among some Particular Baptists, but there is no evidence to suggest that they included those ministers who had been close to John Brine and John Gill.

John Ryland's comment that a form of Hyper-Calvinism began to emerge among some of the Calvinistic Methodists has been noted above. It is possible that a strong emphasis on Christian experience provided a link with the form of Independency Huntington represented. It was to the successors of Whitefield that Huntington was drawn at the outset of his ministry. He was ordained by Torial Joss and would have cultivated a friendship with Rowland Hill, but Hill resisted his overtures.[50] Later, Joss became worried about the development of Huntington's teaching on freedom from the law, although Huntington's discussion of this subject with Joss was much more good-natured than were his 'discussions' with many of his opponents.[51]

Connections with Antinomianism existed with other men influenced by the Great Awakening. The Anglican incumbent at Wallingford, Thomas Pentycross, for a time taught a doctrine similar to Huntington's. He gathered a considerable following, but becoming alarmed, drew back to a more moderate position. In doing so he lost many of his people and earned Huntington's stern rebuke.[52] In Birmingham, John Bradford, of

[50] T. Wright, *Life of Huntington*, pp. 192ff.
[51] Huntington, *Works*, vol. 12, 'Letter to Joss', pp. 293 ff.
[52] Pentycross was a Cambridge graduate and friend of William Romaine and Rowland Hill. For details of his ministry at Wallingford see J. W. Middleton, *An Ecclesiastical Memoir of the First Four Decades of the Reign of George III*, London, 1822, pp. 158ff. Of his early preaching Middleton wrote, 'He fed them with such doctrinal spicery as is sometimes used to conceal a tendency to corruption', p. 159. Huntington's criticism was entitled, 'Tidings from Wallingford', 1786 (*Works*, vol. 4).

the Countess of Huntingdon's Connexion and an Anglican minister, found himself in trouble with the Countess for preaching Antinomianism and withdrew to establish a new chapel, at the opening of which Huntington preached.[53] In Leicester, William Huntington gathered a following and established a work, which drew from the congregation of Thomas Robinson, vicar of St Mary's and a noted evangelical.[54]

In the Revival centre of Bristol, Huntington drew large crowds.[55] His ministry was also well received in Plymouth, where one of the Anglican vicars, Robert Hawker, accepted the description Antinomian and wrote in defence of the doctrine.[56] Hawker's teaching confirmed the link between doctrinal Antinomianism and a strong personal assurance. He wrote urging

> real followers of the Lord, to whose spirits the Holy Ghost bears witness that they are born of God; that while the Lord thus graciously witnesseth to them, they will openly and cheerfully bear their witness for God. No longer shrink from the charge of Antinomianism, because men who know not the Lord use it as a term of reproach to the Lord's people.[57]

Opponents of Antinomianism were ready to dismiss the doctrine as an aberration of the ignorant and uneducated, and certainly Huntington drew many hearers from such people; but that conclusion is not completely true. While Huntington himself had little formal education, his London congregation appears to have included many who benefited from greater educational opportunities. The adoption of such a creed by

---

[53] W. W. Horne, *Life of the Rev. John Bradford, A.B., late of Wadham College, Oxford; and Late Minister of the Gospel, City Chapel, Grub Street, London*, London 1806, pp. 107-8; 157.

[54] E. T. Vaughan, *Some Account of the Rev. Thomas Robinson, M.A.*, London, 1815. pp. 189 ff.; P. Hall, *A Memoir of the Rev. Thomas Robinson, M.A.*, London 1837, pp. 36, 37. J. Chamberlain, *Correspondence and Sermons*, vol. 1, Leicester, 1858, pp. 3, 9-13.

[55] T. Wright, op. cit., p. 80.

[56] Ibid., p. 105. R. Hawker, *Works*, vol. 9, London, 1831, 'True Portrait of Antinomianism,' pp. 515-52. For details of Robert Hawker, 1753-1827, see *Dictionary of National Biography*.

[57] R. Hawker, op. cit., pp. 549, 50.

Bradford, Hawker, and William J. Brook of Brighton[58] shows that educated men were also found among the Huntingtonians. When in the 1830s a group of Anglican clergymen were drawn to the Particular Baptists, they found their home with the associates of William Gadsby, the admirers of William Huntington. Therefore, it would be truer to say that Huntington's teaching, so powerfully moulded by his own experience, appealed to others who had a profound evangelical experience of conversion, and possibly also to men whose theology was governed by their experience rather than by the objective teaching of Scripture.

William Huntington was too much of an individualist to be contained, but he could not be ignored. In spite of opposition from denominational leaders, there is evidence to suggest that Antinomianism spread significantly after 1800. We have already noted Fuller's concern. A year after Fuller's death in 1815, Robert Hall wrote 'little penetration is requisite to perceive that antinomianism is the epidemic malady of the present, and that it is an evil of gigantic size and deadly malignity'.[59] There are also indications that Antinomianism may have developed into a more extreme form as the century progressed. Referring to Huntington, William Robertson Nicoll wrote to James Denney in 1913:

> Many declared that as Christians and as elect they were free from obligation to the moral law and might do as they pleased. I have investigated this subject rather carefully, and could tell you many astonishing things. We had nothing quite like it in Scotland. I remember Spurgeon telling me that this was the great difficulty of his early ministry, and in his sermons I see pretty frequent references to the fact.[60]

Huntington seems to have suffered because of his rejection of fellowship with his fellow ministers and because of his unwillingness to learn

---

[58] Brook, curate of St Nicholas Brighton, seceded and with Huntington's help opened an Independent Chapel in 1805. Wright, op. cit., pp. 129 ff.

[59] Robert Hall, *Works*, vol. 2, pp. 231, 2; cf. J. Bennett, *History of the Dissenters during the Last Thirty Years* [from 1808–38], London, 1839, pp 343–7. Bennett declared that the Particular Baptists were the denomination 'most troubled with this foul plague spot', p. 345.

[60] T. H. Darlow, *William Robertson Nicoll, Life and Letters,* London, 1925, pp. 366, 7.

William Huntington's Controversy with the Particular Baptists

from them. One of the ministers whom he attacked was Andrew Fuller. While there were ambiguities in Fuller's teaching, he nevertheless stood in the tradition of mainstream Calvinism.[61] Huntington, on the other hand, preached the five points of Calvinism, but combined these with so many eccentricities that he caused confusion and suspicion among brethren at a time when unity among Calvinists was a real necessity. Adherence to historic Calvinism was to weaken among the next generation of Particular Baptists. It is difficult to escape the conclusion that that process may have been encouraged by a reaction to some of the tensions raised by Huntington and his admirers.

---

[61] These ambiguities occasioned the debate between Andrew Fuller and Abraham Booth, see chapter 8.

PART TWO

WHEN GOOD MEN DIFFER

8

ANDREW FULLER AND ABRAHAM BOOTH

Yes, disconsolate sinner, you have no reason to hesitate, whether you have a right to receive it [salvation], and to call it your own. Believing the testimony which God has given of his Son, you receive it, and enjoy the comfort arising from it. Heaven proclaims your welcome to Christ, and eternal faithfulness insures acceptance to all that believe in him.

ABRAHAM BOOTH

Whether Christ laid down his life as a *substitute* for sinners was never a question with me. All my hope rests upon it; the sum of my preaching the gospel consists in it. If I know anything of myself I can say of Christ crucified for us, as was said of Jerusalem, 'If I forget thee, let my right hand forget; if I do not remember thee, let my tongue cleave to the roof of my mouth.' I have always considered the denial of this truth as being of the essence of Socinianism.

ANDREW FULLER

As the nineteenth century unfolded, differences among English Particular Baptists over the relationship between the doctrines of grace and the preaching of the gospel became more acute. The catalyst for this divergence was the teaching of Andrew Fuller. It was in the context of this division that a distinct Strict and Particular Baptist grouping emerged. In addition there were further repercussions in the wider Particular Baptist community. These developments can be better understood if we consider the theological differences between Andrew Fuller and Abraham Booth.

The publication of *The Gospel Worthy of All Acceptation* in 1785 involved Andrew Fuller in extended controversy with both Hyper-

Calvinists and Arminians. As he reflected on the issues raised in this debate he turned increasingly to the writings of Jonathan Edwards, and also his New England disciples, Joseph Bellamy, Samuel Hopkins, Jonathan Edwards, Jr., and Stephen West. These latter men did not themselves remain uncritical followers of the elder Edwards, and to some extent they influenced Fuller and some of his close associates.[1]

Joseph Bellamy is acknowledged as one of the most brilliant of Edwards' pupils. Like Edwards he had to defend Calvinistic orthodoxy against its North American critics. Just before the death of the elder Edwards, Bellamy published a work entitled *The Wisdom of God in the Permission of Sin Vindicated*. Its method has been described by Rousas J. Rushdoony as having 'a sound emphasis in part, but faulty in that it justified God's ways in terms of the current moral creeds'. Rushdoony went on to show that while Bellamy was arguing that Calvinistic Christianity did not destroy the basis of morality, 'he helped shift the theological emphasis to moral considerations'.[2] A further consequence of the ongoing debate in North America was that Bellamy, West, and the younger Edwards embraced a governmental theory of the atonement.[3]

Undoubtedly Andrew Fuller was impressed by the way in which these North American theologians sought to destroy rationalist critics with their own weapons. To some extent he tried to use the same methods to answer British Hyper-Calvinists and Arminians. I do not consider that the evidence justifies the assumption that he accepted the conclusions of his mentors in North America, where the debating issues were different, but some of his statements were sufficient to cause alarm among his associates and Fuller found himself at odds with Abraham Booth, a Particular Baptist leader who had long enjoyed widespread respect

---

[1] Joseph Bellamy (1719-90) who had been a pupil of the elder Edwards as had Samuel Hopkins (1721-1803), Stephen West (1735-1819) and Jonathan Edwards, Jr. (1745-1801). These men all ministered in New England and were prolific writers For biographical and theological details see F. H. Foster, *A Genetic History of the New England Theology*.

[2] Rousas J. Rushdoony, 'Joseph Bellamy', in Edward H. Palmer, ed., *The Encyclopedia of Christianity*, vol. 1, (Wilmington, Delaware: 1964), p. 624.

[3] This is discussed below, pp. 163-5.

Andrew Fuller and Abraham Booth

among the churches (see Chapter 3). Booth rejected the extremes of Arminianism and Hyper-Calvinism and his book, *The Reign of Grace*, published in 1768, had sealed his reputation as an exponent of historic Calvinism.[4]

By the end of the eighteenth century Booth and Fuller were regarded as the leading Particular Baptist theologians in England. Until the mid-1790s their relations were generally cordial and Booth gave warm support to the missionary society of which Fuller was the secretary.[5] Neither man had had the advantage of a formal theological education and both had reached their mature theological convictions only after a severe struggle. They owed much to theological giants of the past; Booth owed an especial debt to John Owen, and Fuller to Jonathan Edwards. The two men had come to their positions from widely differing starting points, Booth from Arminianism and Fuller from Hyper-Calvinism. They ministered to churches many miles apart and so seldom met each other. It is hardly surprising, bearing these factors in mind, that certain differences emerged between them, surfacing in discussions concerning the warrant of faith and the nature of the atonement. Sadly, the differences between them bred suspicion. This is all the more regrettable since there is some evidence that each misunderstood the other's position.

1. THE WARRANT OF FAITH

Tensions between Booth and Fuller were apparent following the 1796 publication of Booth's *Glad Tidings to Perishing Sinners, or, the Genuine Gospel a Complete Warrant for the Ungodly to Believe in Jesus*.[6] The

---

[4] A. Booth, *Works*, vol. 1, 'The Reign of Grace', London, 1813, pp. 59, 78, 96-8, 103-7.

[5] It was Booth who recommended John Thomas as a colleague for Carey; Fuller's *Letters*, 'A. Fuller to Thomas Steevens', n.d. c. 1793; cf 'A. Fuller to John Saffery, 30th May 1793'; 'A. Fuller to W. Carey, 9th Aug. 1769'. Booth also encouraged Fuller to write *The Calvinistic and Socinian Systems Examined*, 'A. Fuller to T. Steevens, n.d., c. 1791', *The Letters of Andrew Fuller*, Angus Library, Regents Park College, Oxford.

[6] A. Booth, *Glad Tidings to Perishing Sinners, or, the Genuine Gospel a Complete Warrant for the Ungodly to Believe in Jesus*, London, 1796, hereinafter referred to as *Glad Tidings*. Quotations are from the edition published in Booth's *Works*, vol. 2.

author was concerned to establish that the gospel itself warrants any sinner to believe in Christ. Although the way to faith may be through the experience of conviction of sin, conviction of sin in itself does not qualify the sinner to exercise faith in the Saviour. Booth propounded this thesis to counter the Hyper-Calvinist insistence that the inward work of the Holy Spirit constituted a warrant for the sinner to believe in Christ.

Booth's book, warmly recommended by an anonymous reviewer in the *Evangelical Magazine*,[7] was well received by evangelical Calvinists. It appeared to support the case which Fuller had argued eleven years earlier in *The Gospel Worthy of All Acceptation*.[8]

Although Fuller had taught that all men have a duty to believe the gospel, and so to be saved, he felt uneasy about Booth's work. In a letter to Samuel Hopkins he complained, 'Some of our monthly editions have bestowed indiscriminate praise without at all understanding the ground of the controversy.'[9] To Carey he was more explicit:

> Mr B's book is controversial, but very difficult to know who or what it opposes. What he aims to establish in the former part is denied by nobody that I know of, except the High Calvinists – yet he did not mean, I am persuaded, to oppose them.[10]

Booth did not refer to Fuller in his book; nevertheless, Fuller went on to say: 'I believe it was his intent to oppose our sentiments, and that he chose to attack us under Hopkins's name. The latter part I think is erroneous.'[11] In a later letter, he wrote: 'In fact it was written with a view to opposing me or of going between our views and those of High Calvinism.'[12]

---

[7] *The Evangelical Magazine*, vol. 4, 1796, pp. 348–9.

[8] 'People reckon, and so let them reckon, that his book is on the same side as my *Gospel of Xt* etc', Fuller's Letters, 'A. Fuller to W. Carey, 6 Sept. 1797' 'They think his first part savours of an agreement with me; and reckon therefore that the whole book was written in order to favour my sentiments on the duty of sinners to believe in Christ', Fuller's *Letters*, 'A. Fuller to S. Hopkins, 17 March 1798'.

[9] Fuller's *Letters*, 'A. Fuller to S. Hopkins, 17 March 1798'.

[10] Ibid., 'A. Fuller to W. Carey, 6 Sept 1797'.   [11] Ibid.

[12] Ibid., 'A. Fuller to W. Carey, 22 Aug. 1798'.

Andrew Fuller and Abraham Booth

Hopkins replied to Fuller with a response to Booth's *Glad Tidings*. Out of respect for Booth, Hopkins' manuscript was never published;[13] but Booth saw it and Fuller noted that 'he is since rigidly set against everything from America'.[14]

When Fuller's unease became known, the Anglican theologian Thomas Scott attempted to mediate between the positions of Hopkins and Booth in his *The Warrant and Nature of Faith in Christ*.[15] Scott did not refer to Booth by name but in a review in the *Evangelical Magazine*, Fuller wrote, 'The design of the treatise, if we rightly comprehend it, is to discuss various important points advanced in Mr Booth's "Glad Tidings to Perishing Sinners".'[16] Fuller returned to the discussion in a review of the second edition of Booth's *Glad Tidings*.[17] He also criticized Booth's position in an appendix to the second edition of *The Gospel Worthy of All Acceptation*, linking Booth's ideas with those of the Scottish Baptist, Archibald McLean, whose teaching was in some ways similar to that of Booth.

THE AREA OF DEBATE

Booth and Fuller agreed that the gospel itself provided sufficient warrant for sinners to believe in Christ. They differed however over the order of salvation (*ordo salutis*). Fuller taught that regeneration takes place in a sinner with a view to faith, although regeneration is an act of God of

---

[13] Ibid. Hopkins's opinion of Booth as a theologian is noted below, p. 165.

[14] Ibid.

[15] Thomas Scott, *The Warrant and Nature of Faith in Christ*, 1797. Quotations are given from the 2nd edition, Buckingham, 1801. In December 1796, Scott wrote, 'I am about to write a pamphlet on the sinner's *warrant* to believe in Christ, and the *nature* of justifying faith, by the desire of several of my brethren; as the American divines especially Hopkins, with those who hold the negative of the modern question have run into one extreme and many others into the contrary, particularly Mr Abraham Booth in a late pamphlet entitled, 'Glad Tidings', J. Scott, *The Life of the Rev. Thomas Scott*, London, 1823, p. 313.

[16] *Evangelical Magazine*, vol. 7, 1799, p. 199. The review is anonymous but included in A. Fuller's *Works*, p. 964.

[17] *Evangelical Magazine*, vol. 8, 1800, pp. 548–50. Again anonymous but see Fuller's *Works*, p. 965.

[153]

which the sinner is not immediately conscious.[18] Booth considered that such teaching compromised the fact that faith was the immediate duty of the ungodly. He feared the tendency that suggested that regeneration is temporally prior to faith and justification. He argued that regeneration, faith, and justification are simultaneous. He developed an analogy from the birth of a child:

> For the human nature, derived from his parents, and the relation of a son, being of completely the same date, there is no such thing as priority, or posteriority, respecting them, either as to the order of time, or the order of nature. They are inseparable; nor can the one exist without the other. – Thus it is I conceive, with regard to regeneration, faith in Christ, and justification before God.[19]

Booth was also unhappy with the way that some American theologians appeared to prescribe the way to faith. On this point Scott agreed with Booth that Scripture does not insist on sinners acquiescing in the justice of their own condemnation before they can believe.[20] For Booth, particularly obnoxious was the statement of Samuel Hopkins that

> A hearty submission to, and acquiescence and delight in, the law of God, rightly understood, and so a true hatred of sin, must take place IN ORDER to any degree of true approbation of the Gospel, and FAITH AND TRUST in Christ.[21]

Booth rounded on this and similar statements,[22] using them to accuse

---

[18] Fuller developed this argument particularly in controversy with the General Baptist, Dan Taylor, *Complete Works of Andrew Fuller*, London, 1862, 'Reply to Philanthropos', pp. 211-6.

[19] A. Booth, *Works*, vol. 2, 'Glad Tidings', p. 123.

[20] 'Perhaps they insist unduly on the necessity of a man's seeing the justice of God in his condemnation as a transgressor of the holy law, before he can believe in Christ to salvation,' T. Scott, *Warrant of Faith*, p. 3.

[21] Quoted in Booth, *Works*, vol. 2, 'Glad Tidings', p. 77.

[22] Ibid., p. 162, where he quotes Hopkins, 'The necessity of the sinner's exercising virtue, antecedent to his justification, and in order to it, is not because he needs any worthiness of his own, or can have any; but because by this ALONE can his heart be so united to the Mediator, as to be the proper ground of his being looked upon

Hopkins of incipient legalism,[23] Arminianism,[24] and even Romanism.[25] He argued that Hopkins's statements gave the impression that men had to be good before they could be saved and so were directly opposed to the preaching of the Apostles, who

> were commissioned to proclaim glad tidings to the profligate, impious and wicked world. Those, however, who are truly penitent and possessed of real holiness, are not *of the world*, but *of God*.[26]

In *The Warrant and Nature of Faith in Christ*, Thomas Scott showed that two different controversies had become confused in the current debate. In New England, the writings of Jonathan Edwards and his successors were aimed at countering careless evangelistic preaching by offering an analysis of the psychological preparation leading to a sound conversion; they were not insisting that such a preparation qualified the sinner for saving faith.[27] In England the controversy focused on whether sinners were duty-bound to believe in Christ.[28] That was not the issue being debated in New England. Scott agreed with Booth and Fuller that the gospel provided the sinner with all the warrant he needed to believe in Christ.[29] He pointed out that there was a difference between an objective warrant to believe and a subjective disposition to do so.[30] The sinner should never look within himself for a warrant to believe, but

> It can never discourage a trembling sinner, who honestly inquires, 'What he must do to be saved', to describe the nature of faith and explain the way of salvation; and then to invite, exhort and persuade him to believe in the Lord Jesus Christ, not doubting but in so doing he will certainly be saved.[31]

Over against Booth, Scott had no doubt that saving faith was the result of regeneration, and therefore faith was a holy exercise of the soul. At this point Scott and Fuller were agreed. Scott saw no danger of legalism in this

---

and treated so far one with him, as that his merit and righteousness may be properly imputed to him, or reckoned in his favour, so as to avail for his pardon and justification.' [23] Ibid., p. 162. [24] Ibid., p. 169. [25] Ibid., p. 171. [26] Ibid., p. 79. [27] T. Scott, *The Warrant of Faith*, p. 3. [28] Ibid., p. 3. [29] Ibid., p. 12. [30] Ibid., pp. 24-28. [31] Ibid., p. 27.

position because no man really understands the complex events of conversion until after he has believed. The unbelieving sinner has an immediate duty to believe and to do so in the consciousness that he is a sinner needing salvation. After he has believed, he may look back and see that, prior to faith, God had been working in him to bring him to salvation. Scott concluded his discussion of the issues by urging his readers to distinguish between such matters as

> A warrant to believe and a disposition to believe; between a man's being spiritually alive and in part sanctified, and his knowing himself to be so; between the holy nature of faith, and the sinner's perception of that holiness and taking courage from it in coming to Christ.[32]

The Significance of the Debate

Fuller resented Booth's criticism of Hopkins, with whose views he felt considerable sympathy. More seriously, he was being attacked at a very sensitive point: *The Gospel Worthy of All Acceptation* had challenged the concept of a subjective warrant of faith as it was taught by Hyper-Calvinists. Fuller had been through a very personal and painful struggle to see that Scripture itself provided an objective warrant for the sinner to believe in Christ. The insinuation, therefore, that his system implied the necessity of a subjective warrant of faith was deeply galling to him.

Fuller may have suspected that Booth's motive for writing was to mediate between Fuller's own position and that of the Hyper-Calvinists, but he soon came to see that some Hyper-Calvinists were in fact being drawn towards him. Writing of his and Booth's books in 1798, he declared:

> The High Calvinists, who will not read mine, read that, and some of them by that means are coming over to us.[33]

Booth's statement of man's duty was clear, as was his insistence on the free offer of the gospel.[34] The effect could only be to reinforce Fuller's

[32] Ibid., p. 122.

[33] Fuller's *Letters*, 'A. Fuller to W. Carey, 22 Aug. 1798'.

[34] 'For some, at least of the thirsting ones to whom the offer is there made, are spending money for that which is not bread, and their labour for that which satisfieth not,' Booth, *Works*, vol. 2, 'Glad Tidings', p. 190.

case. However, greater anxiety began to express itself when Fuller's Calvinism seemed to undergo a change. This change became apparent after 1800 and was a matter of further concern to Abraham Booth.

2. Controversy on the Atonement

When Andrew Fuller published the second edition of *The Gospel Worthy of All Acceptation* in 1801, he admitted that his views had changed somewhat in the fifteen years since the first edition appeared.[35] Some of these changes alarmed Booth, and Fuller, anxious for a better understanding, had several meetings with his fellow minister when the two of them were in London in May 1802. Although the two men enjoyed a measure of agreement, Booth charged Fuller with having changed his views on the doctrines of imputation and substitution.[36] The disagreement between the two men soon became common knowledge; the measure of the disagreement may have been exaggerated by report.[37] Fuller informed Ryland that 'About the middle of July, reports were circulated, both in town and country, that I had acknowledged myself to Mr Booth to be an Arminian.'[38]

Fuller was prepared to ascribe Booth's criticisms in part to old age. In November he wrote to Carey:

> Mr Booth gets old, and I think jealous and peevish. His memory also fails him. He has set strange reports of me this summer as if I had owned

[35] 'It would have been inexcusable for him to have lived all this time without gaining any additional light, by what he has seen and heard upon this subject,' A. Fuller, *The Gospel Worthy of All Acceptation: or the Duty of Sinners to Believe in Jesus Christ*, Second Edition, Clipstone, 1801, p. i.

[36] Fuller's account of the controversy is published in his *Works*, 'Six Letters to Dr Ryland respecting the Controversy with the Rev. A. Booth,' pp. 317-9, hereinafter referred to as' Six Letters to Dr Ryland'. These letters, written between 3rd and 22nd Jan. 1803, were first published in the first collected edition of Fuller's *Works* in 1831.

[37] It is interesting that the Eclectic Society, a London ministers' fraternal, discussed the question, 'In what sense is the sin of the believer imputed to Christ, and the righteousness of Christ imputed to the believer?' on January 17, 1803, J. H. Pratt, ed., *The Thought of the Evangelical Leaders* (1856), repr. Edinburgh: Banner of Truth, 1978, pp. 275-7.

[38] A. Fuller, *Works*, pp. 317-8.

it to him that I did not believe in the substitution of Xt. and the imputation of sin to him when it was merely a misunderstanding. But I am resolved to have no open dispute with him. He is jealous of our having written to you agst him: but I think I have never sd so much before as now. He is a good man and upright, tho' I think his views of imputation are too much like those of Dr Crisp, as tho' in the imputation of sin something more was transferred than the penal effect of it; and as tho' Xt was something more than treated as tho' he had been a sinner.[39]

Booth apparently wrote to John Ryland about Fuller's views, and so, in January 1803, Fuller wrote his *Six Letters to Dr Ryland* in defence of his teaching. Booth was clearly not satisfied with Fuller's explanations and decided to deal with the question publicly, but without mentioning Fuller by name. In September 1803 he preached a sermon at the monthly meeting of London Baptist ministers. This he entitled *Divine Justice Essential to the Divine Character*.[40] He expanded and published this with a lengthy *Appendix, Relative to the Doctrine of Atonement by Jesus Christ*. In the *Appendix* he also discussed Fuller's teaching on particular redemption. Fuller considered that he had been misrepresented, and replied with a series of dialogues entitled *Three Conversations on Imputation, Substitution and Particular Redemption*.[41] These were not published until 1806, the year of Booth's death, although they were probably composed soon after the appearance of Booth's *Divine Justice*. The issues raised in these publications now need to be considered.

IMPUTATION

Particular Baptist teaching on this subject reflected wider Protestant convictions. The *1689 Confession of Faith* states that God justifies sinners 'by imputing Christ's active obedience unto the whole law, and passive obedience in his death, for their whole and sole righteousness.'[42]

---

[39] Fuller's *Letters*, 'A. Fuller to W. Carey, 26 Nov. 1802'. On Crisp, see footnote 59.

[40] A. Booth, *Works*, vol. 3, 'Divine Justice Essential to the Divine Character', 1803. Hereinafter referred to as 'Divine Justice'.

[41] Fuller presented his case in the form of a dialogue between Peter (Booth), James (Fuller) and John (Ryland).

[42] *1689 Confession*, XI,1.

Although the term *impute* is not used to describe the reckoning of the sinner's sin to Christ, the *Confession* does refer to him 'undergoing in their stead, the penalty due unto them; [He] did make a proper, real and full satisfaction to God's justice in their behalf.'[43]

The debate between Booth and Fuller was over the way in which man's sin was imputed to Christ and Christ's righteousness imputed to man. Fuller described this imputation as figurative rather than proper. To grasp Fuller's meaning it is important to note the way in which he defined his terms. He considered proper imputation to be the reckoning of a person according to his true moral character; thus a wicked man's sin is properly imputed to him. Figurative imputation, on the other hand, takes place when guilt or righteousness is imputed to a person whose personal character does not accord with the imputed gift.[44] Thus he wrote:

> [Christ] was accounted in the Divine Administration AS IF HE WERE, OR HAD BEEN, the sinner; that those who believe on him might be accounted AS IF THEY WERE, OR HAD BEEN, righteous.[45]

As Fuller's letter to Carey of November 1802 indicates, he considered that Booth's teaching was too close to that of Tobias Crisp, who in the seventeenth century had written, 'God reckons Christ the very sinner'.[46] Fuller, however, complicated the issue by using the term *guilt* in a way which differed from Booth's usage and opposed any suggestion that actual guilt was imputed to Christ. He explained:

> Some have defined guilt as an obligation to punishment; but a voluntary obligation to endure the punishment of another is not guilt, any more than a consequent exemption of obligation in the offender is innocence. Both guilt and innocence, though transferable in their effects, are themselves untransferable.[47]

---

[43] Ibid., XI,3

[44] A. Fuller, *Works*, 'Six Letters to Dr Ryland', p. 319.   [45] Ibid., p. 319.

[46] Tobias Crisp, *Christ Alone Exalted*, vol. 1 (1690), repr. London, 1791, p.11. John Gill, Crisp's eighteenth-century editor considered Crisp's statement sufficiently unguarded to insert the footnote, 'that is, by imputation; not as the author and committer of sin'.

[47] 'Six Letters to Dr Ryland,' p. 320.

Since he refused to speak of a real imputation of sin to Christ or of righteousness to man, Fuller was cautious in his treatment of Christ's sufferings as punishment.

> As to Christ's being punished, I have no doubt, and I never had, of his sufferings being penal any more than I have of our salvation being a reward; but as the latter is not a reward to us, so I question whether the former can properly said to be a punishment to Him.[48]

In opposition to the views of Fuller, Booth insisted that imputation should be described as real. He wrote:

> If, therefore Jesus was made a curse, he was punished – in a real and proper sense PUNISHED: for scarcely any words can convey the idea of punishment more forcibly than those which are here used by the Apostle.[49]

To make his position absolutely clear, he went on to develop the idea of punishment.

> What is punishment but the infliction of natural evil, for the commission of moral evil? Punishment, necessarily supposes criminality, either personal or imputed; and here it must be understood of the latter.[50]

Booth also insisted that the imputation of Christ's righteousness to the believer must be real.

> It is not merely for the sake of Christ, or of what he has done, that believers are accepted of God, and treated as completely righteous; but it is IN him as their Head, Representative and Substitute: and by the imputation of that very obedience, which as such, he performed to the divine law, that they are justified. Hence they are said to be made, not barely righteous but righteousness; not even that only, but the righteousness of GOD.[51]

Regrettably, Booth and Fuller clearly were not using the terms 'real' and 'figurative' in the same sense. Earlier, Booth had written 'that justification,

---

[48] Ibid.
[49] Booth, *Works*, vol. 3, 'Divine Justice', p. 52.   [50] Ibid., p. 52.
[51] Ibid., pp. 47, 48.

therefore, about which the Scriptures principally treat ... is not by a *personal*, but by an *imputed* righteousness' [my italics].[52] What Fuller described as 'real', Booth called 'personal', and what Fuller labelled 'figurative', Booth called 'imputed'. Perhaps it is not surprising that confusion ensued.

However, Booth was not without grounds for supposing that Fuller might have opened the door to dangerous ideas from New England. In his sermon on *Divine Justice*, Booth again criticized Hopkins.[53] An appreciation of the New England theologian recurs through Fuller's correspondence,[54] and he expressed his views on imputation in terms very similar to those developed by Hopkins. Frank Hugh Foster, the historian of the New England theology, wrote of Hopkins's ideas, 'the definition of justification contains no real imputation'.[55] Booth and Fuller did not discuss the related question of the imputation of Adam's sin to his posterity, but Fuller seems to follow Hopkins, who taught that such imputation must rest on consent. Fuller wrote:

> Does it not belong to the nature of imputation that the party to whom the imputation is made, approves of the good or evil of what is imputed, ere it can benefit or injure him? And if so, is there anything to fear from Adam's sin with regard to dying infants?[56]

On this subject Hopkins wrote:

> It is not to be supposed that the offence of Adam is imputed to them [his posterity] to their condemnation while they are considered as in themselves, in their own persons innocent; or that they are guilty of the sin of their first father, antecedent to their own sinfulness. But all that is asserted as what the Scripture teaches on this head is, that, by a divine

---

[52] Ibid., vol.1, 'The Reign of Grace', p. 141.   [53] Ibid., vol. 3 p. 50.

[54] Declining a doctorate from the College of New Jersey, Fuller wrote, 'I should esteem it as coming from that quarter which beyond any other in the world, I most approve', Fuller's *Letters*, 'A. Fuller to S. Hopkins, 17 March 1789'; cf. 'A Fuller to J. Ryland, 21 April 1794'; 'A. Fuller to J. Sutcliff, 7 Jan. 1801.'

[55] Foster, *Genetic History of New England Theology*, p. 185.

[56] Fuller's *Letters*, 'A. Fuller to J. Ryland, 24 Dec, 1795'.

constitution, there is a certain connection between the first sin of Adam and the sinfulness of his posterity.[57]

According to Hopkins the 'certain connection' was consent:

It was made certain, and known, and declared to be so, that all mankind should sin as Adam had done, and fully consent to his transgression, and join in the rebellion he began; and by this bring upon themselves the guilt of their father's sin, by consenting to it, joining with him in it, and making it their own sin.[58]

Booth did not respond to Fuller's charge that he was advocating the teaching of Tobias Crisp, perhaps because he considered that his writings were free from the ambiguities of Crisp.[59] In the defence of his position he appealed to such accepted standards of orthodoxy as the *Homilies* of the Church of England and the writings of John Owen and Herman Witsius, indicating that he considered himself to be in the mainstream of Calvinistic thinking.[60] Nevertheless, confusion about the nature of imputation lies at the heart of the controversy between Booth and Fuller. From it arose their differences on substitution and particular redemption.

SUBSTITUTION

Particular Baptist theology, expressed in the *1689 Confession*, states that the sufferings of Christ were as a penal substitute for men's sins.[61] Andrew Fuller's acceptance of the penal character of Christ's substitutionary work has already been noted. He was, however, wary of any statement of this doctrine which made the atonement seem like a commercial transaction. He was concerned to guard against teaching which

---

[57] Samuel Hopkins, *Works*, vol. 1, Boston, 1852, 'System of Doctrines' [1793], p. 218.   [58] Ibid.

[59] Tobias Crisp (1600–43?), preacher and writer, was accused of Antinomianism by Samuel Rutherford. More recently, Dr William Young has argued that Crisp was not strictly an Antinomian, adding, 'There is a magnificence as well as a snare in the one-sidedness of Crisp's proclamation of sovereign grace', *Encylopedia of Christianity*, s.v. *Tobias Crisp*.

[60] A. Booth, *Works*, vol.3, 'Divine Justice', pp. 46–9.

[61] *1689 Confession*, VIII,4.

measured the degree of the sufferings of Christ by the number of the elect or the extent of their sins.

> The sufferings of Christ in our stead, therefore, are not a punishment inflicted in the ordinary course of distributive justice, but an extraordinary interposition of infinite wisdom and love; not contrary to, but rather above the law, deviating from the letter, but more than preserving the spirit of it.[62]

Once again Fuller's inspiration appears to have come from New England, where Joseph Bellamy and Jonathan Edwards, Jr. had embraced the governmental theory of the atonement. The Dutch jurist Hugo Grotius had originally developed this view in the early seventeenth century. It presented God, not as an offended judge to whom satisfaction must be made, but as the moral governor of the universe, who must do something to show his abhorrence of sin. The sufferings of Christ demonstrate God's hatred of sin, but must not be regarded as a strictly substitutionary penalty.[63] Stephen West, in his *The Scripture Doctrine of the Atonement Proposed to Careful Examination*, expounded the governmental theory of the atonement.[64] In 1795 Fuller described this to Sutcliff as a book 'for wh I wd not take 1/1 [one guinea]'.[65]

It has been alleged that by the time of the publication of the second edition of *The Gospel Worthy of All Acceptation* in 1801, Fuller had adopted the governmental theory of the atonement.[66] Certainly he admired the New England theologians who were propounding this theory and in a measure was influenced by them. Like them he had been profoundly influenced by the elder Edwards, and at times he used governmental language. At the same time, however, there is no evidence to suggest that he

---

[62] Fuller, *Works*, 'Three Conversations', p. 313.

[63] Foster, *New England Theology*, pp. 115, 116, 199–206.   [64] Ibid., p. 204.

[65] Fuller's *Letters*, 'A. Fuller to J. Sutcliffe, 22 Jan. 1795.' Cf. 'I have read Dr Edwards on Free Grace and Atonement with great pleasure. I suppose I read it some time ago; but I never relished it so well before', J. Ryland, *Life of Fuller*, p. 226; 'I very much longed for West on the Atonement', Ibid., p. 227.

[66] See for example, R. Philip Roberts, *Continuity and Change, London Calvinistic Baptists and the Evangelical Revival, 1760–1820,* Richard Owen Roberts Publishers, Wheaton, Illinois, 1989, p. 198.

rejected the substitutionary view of the atonement. As late as his controversy with Booth, he gave this assurance to Ryland:

> Whether Christ laid down his life as a *substitute* for sinners, was never a question with me. All my hope rests upon it; and the sum of my preaching the gospel consists in it. If I know anything of myself I can say of Christ crucified for us, as was said of Jerusalem, 'If I forget thee, let my right hand forget; if I do not remember thee, let my tongue cleave to the roof of my mouth.' I have always considered the denial of this truth as being of the essence of Socinianism.[67]

Fuller insisted on the absolute necessity of satisfaction to divine justice:

> If God required less than the real demerit of sin for an atonement, then there could be no *satisfaction* made to Divine justice by such an atonement. And though it would be improper to represent the great work of redemption as a kind of commercial transaction between a creditor and his debtor, yet the satisfaction of justice in all cases of offence requires *that there be an expression of the displeasure of the offended against the conduct of the offender, equal to what the nature of the offence is in reality.*[68]

In his survey of Particular Baptist theology Tom Nettles admits that Fuller used 'governmental language', but insists that the use of governmental concepts 'did not involve him in the errors of the governmentalists'.[69] In this respect Fuller's position appears to be similar to that of Jonathan Edwards, Sr., who has also been unjustly charged with governmentalism.[70]

---

[67] Fuller, *Works*, 'On Substitution', p. 320.
[68] Ibid., 'On the Deity of Christ, The Deity of Christ Essential to Atonement', p. 938.
[69] T. J. Nettles, *By His Grace and For His Glory*, Grand Rapids: Baker, 1986, p. 128.
[70] J. H. Gerstner defends Edwards against the charge of governmentalism. He writes of statements which it is alleged indicate this view in Edwards's writings, 'These are never at the expense of the satisfaction theory. Rather they are founded on it. True the manifestation of God's abhorrence of sin is as essential for Edwards as it is for Grotius. The difference is that for Grotius the manifestation is enough. For Edwards it is not only not enough, it is nothing apart from the satisfaction for sin on

Andrew Fuller and Abraham Booth

In fairness to Booth it has to be remembered that he was aware of and alarmed by moves towards governmentalism in New England, where Edwards' successors had moved beyond their teacher's position. Clearly he feared that this view was being promoted by the writings of Fuller.[71] It was in the light of his understanding of Fuller's teaching that Booth declared:

> No one can be pardoned and accepted of God, except on the ground of its [the Law's] righteous precepts being perfectly performed, and its equitable sanction completely satisfied by the vicarious obedience, and the substitutionary sufferings of our all sufficient sponsor.[72]

In 1798, Fuller had informed Hopkins that Booth was 'a great admirer of Owen, Vitringa, Venema etc; and seems to suppose that these have gone to the *ne plus ultra* of discovery'.[73] In his reply Hopkins was dismissive of Booth:

> I am far from wishing to say or do anything to alter your opinion of the honesty and holiness of Mr Booth; but from what I have seen of his writings, – which are only his *Reign of Grace* and *Glad Tidings*, – I cannot consider him a divine of a clear or orthodox head; and I think I have a divine warrant to say, that the religion which has its foundation on the principles he has asserted in both his *Glad Tidings* and *Reign of Grace* (see pp. 248, 270 of the latter edition of 1795) is altogether a selfish religion, and therefore abominable to God.[74]

These were strong words indeed, but it is significant that Fuller himself never employed such language, even though the two men found themselves in disagreement.

---

which the reality as a manifestation of divine abhorrence depends.' *The Rational Biblical Theology of Jonathan Edwards*, vol. 2, Orlando, Florida: Ligonier Ministries, p. 436.

[71] In *Divine Justice* Booth argued powerfully for substitution e.g. 'What adequate cause can be assigned for this amazing anguish; except that of his vicarious character – of his bearing imputed sin and of his undergoing the curse of the law, for those that were justly condemned?' p. 38.

[72] Booth, *Works*, vol. 3 'Divine Justice', pp. 17,18. cf. pp. 24–6.

[73] Fuller's *Letters*, 'A. Fuller to S. Hopkins, 17 March 1789.'

[74] Samuel Hopkins, *Works* (Boston, 1852), vol. 1, 'Memoir', p. 224.

[165]

Particular Redemption

This doctrine states that the saving purpose of Christ's sacrifice on the cross was the salvation of the elect alone. Since the Particular Baptists identified themselves by belief in this doctrine, it was widely regarded as a test of orthodoxy, and its discussion was a delicate issue. By the last quarter of the eighteenth century, Andrew Fuller's American friends had abandoned belief in Particular Redemption. In England, General Redemption was the distinguishing tenet of the General or Arminian Baptists. Joseph Bellamy, who continued to believe in the doctrine of election but rejected particular redemption on the ground that it choked the free offer of the gospel, had promoted the change in New England.[75] The doctrine of general redemption was popularized by Jonathan Edwards, Jr. in his *Three Sermons on the Atonement* and was expounded in greater detail by Stephen West in his *The Scripture Doctrine of the Atonement*, both published in 1785. The strictly substitutionary view of the atonement requires either that the sins of the elect were imputed to Christ, and he atoned for these alone, or that he died for all and saved all, which was universalism, long opposed by orthodox Christians. It was in controversy with the universalists that the New England men restated their teaching in governmental terms and linked it to the doctrine of general redemption, thus jettisoning strict substitution.[76]

As has already been demonstrated, the New England men influenced Fuller's thinking on imputation and substitution. He also admitted to Ryland in 1803 that since his controversy with Dan Taylor, he had modified his views on particular redemption.[77] This change can be seen by a comparison of Fuller's treatment of the objection that it is futile to exhort

---

[75] 'If Christ did not design by his death, to open a door for all to be saved conditionally, that is upon condition of faith, then there is no such door opened; the door is not opened wider than Christ designed it should be; there is nothing more purchased by his death than he intended; if this benefit was not intended, then it is not procured; if it be not procured, then the non-elect can not any of them be saved, consistently with divine justice,' quoted in Foster, *New England Theology*, pp. 116–7.

[76] Ibid., pp. 199–206. Fuller's appreciation of West's *Atonement* is noted above, p. 163.

[77] Fuller, *Works*, 'Six Letters to Dr Ryland', p. 322.

Andrew Fuller and Abraham Booth

those who do not as yet know that Christ has died for them to believe in Christ. His handling of this issue is not the same in the 1785 and 1801 editions of *The Gospel Worthy of All Acceptation*. In 1785 he wrote:

> Surely it cannot but be right for a man, whether he have a spiritual interest in Christ's death or not, to receive what God says in the love of it – to approve things that are excellent – to allow from his very heart of the Lord Jesus Christ in all his offices and excellencies – to desire an interest in him – and to resolve to no longer trust in his own sufficiency, which is but trusting in a lie, but to cast his soul upon Christ for mercy, determined either to be saved by him or perish at his feet.[78]

He also went on to say, 'There is no fear of Christ ever destroying any that venture upon him.'[79]

In the 1801 edition Fuller abandoned this method of answering the objection entirely. Instead, he rejected the idea of atonement as 'the literal payment of a debt', and proceeded on the assumption that

> Its [the atonement's] grand object [was] to express the Divine displeasure against sin, and so to render the exercise of mercy in all the ways wherein sovereign wisdom should determine to apply it, consistent with righteousness.[80]

Fuller's language at this point may appear to be governmental, but as has already been shown, he had not abandoned the concept of substitution. However, he went on to argue for a redemption which depended for its particularity upon God's decree and the execution of that decree by the Holy Spirit. From these effects he reasoned back to the purpose of the atonement:

> The application of redemption is solely directed by sovereign wisdom, so like every other event, it is the result of previous design. That which is actually done was intended to be done.[81]

---

[78] Fuller, *The Gospel Worthy of All Acceptation*, 1st ed., Northampton [1785], p. 132.
[79] Ibid., p. 133.
[80] Ibid., 2nd ed., 1801, p. 109.
[81] Ibid., p. 110.

The problem with this explication of the doctrine is that an important aspect of redemption is distanced from the cross. The limitation of Christ's sacrifice does not seem to relate to what actually happened at Calvary. Fuller appears not to face up to the question of whether the sins of the elect were specifically imputed to Christ. To Ryland, he wrote:

> If I speak of it irrespective of the purpose of the Father and the Son, as to the objects who should be saved by it, merely referring to what it is in itself sufficient for, and declared in the gospel to be adapted to, I should think that I answered the question in a Scriptural way by saying, It was for sinners as sinners; but if I have respect to the purpose of the Father in giving his Son to die and to the design of Christ in laying down his life, I should answer, It was for the elect only.[82]

Fuller was clearly stating a position long held by many Calvinists that 'the death of Christ was sufficient for all, but efficient for the elect'. He was concerned to safeguard an unfettered presentation of Christ to all, but at the same time to teach that the atoning sacrifice of Christ fulfilled the purpose of God in election.

Booth was unhappy with Fuller's arguments at this point. He admitted 'the sufficiency of Immanuel's death to have redeemed all mankind, had all the sins of the whole human species been equally imputed to him'.[83] However, this was a hypothetical point:

> We cannot perceive any solid reason to conclude that his propitiatory sufferings are sufficient for the expiation of the sins he did not bear or for the redemption of sinners whom he did not represent as a sponsor, when he expired on the cross.[84]

In the *Appendix* to *Divine Justice* Booth discussed Fuller's views on the atonement, although without naming him. He considered that Fuller was

---

[82] A. Fuller, *Works*, 'Six Letters to Dr Ryland', p. 321.

[83] A. Booth, *Works*, vol.3., 'Divine Justice', p. 61.

[84] Ibid., p. 61. R. A. Coppenger misinterprets Booth at this point when he says, 'Booth was in complete accord with Fuller on the limited atonement, which they both interpreted as limited in its application, but not in its sufficiency', 'Abraham Booth, 1734–1806', Ph.D. Thesis, Edinburgh 1953, p. 108.

Andrew Fuller and Abraham Booth

conflating the doctrine of particular redemption with related doctrines and in so doing isolating it from the doctrine of the atonement. Fuller wrote: 'I do not consider particular redemption as being so much a doctrine of itself as a branch of the great doctrine of election.'[85] Booth was concerned to sustain the particularity of Christ's atoning sacrifice:

> From the doctrine of Divine Justice, as it respects the atonement of Christ, we are led to infer, that redemption by his blood is not general but particular, and peculiar to the chosen of God. Redemption by Jesus Christ cannot, I conceive, be justly considered as either more or less extensive than his voluntary substitution; or than the number of persons for whom he performed that vicarious work which was finished on the cross. If, in his perfect obedience and penal death, he acted and suffered as the substitute of *all mankind*, they are all redeemed: but if, as the representative of *the elect only*, redemption must be considered as exclusively theirs. For, to imagine that the death of Christ, as the price of deliverance from the curse of the law, redeemed any for whom as a substitute, he did not suffer; and to suppose, that any of those for whom as a surety, he sustained the penalty of death are *not redeemed*, seem equally indefensible and absurd.[86]

For Booth, Fuller's explanation could only weaken the scriptural testimony that 'Christ died for our sins'. Booth considered that if particularity rested exclusively in God's decree, 'there is nothing in the atonement of Christ that infallibly ascertains its application to all those for whom it was made'.[87] The personal love of God would then be seen more clearly in God's election of a people than in Christ's love for them as individuals.

The concepts of sacrifice and propitiation were weakened by an emphasis that made election and effectual calling, to the exclusion of the historic event of Calvary, the means of making salvation a personal reality. Booth also rejected Fuller's suggestion that 'the principal design of our Lord's atonement was the manifestation of God's hatred to sin'. He accepted that God's hatred of sin was demonstrated in the atonement, but

---

[85] Fuller, *Works*, 'Three Conversations on Imputation, Substitution and Particular Redemption', p. 315.
[86] Booth, *Works*, vol.3, 'Divine Justice', pp. 59-61.   [87] Ibid., p. 84.

the grand idea suggested to the enlightened mind in the atonement of Christ, and to which the New Testament abundantly directs our attention, is, not God's hatred to sin, but his love to sinners . . . not his inclination to punish, but his determination to pardon.[88]

It was through the second edition of *The Gospel Worthy of All Acceptation* that Fuller's revised views became widely known. Fuller was concerned to extricate the free offer of the gospel from the objection of the man who was not sure that Christ had died for him. Booth did not see the resolution of this difficulty in 'universal sufficiency'. He insisted that Fuller's teaching represented 'a reconciling expedient or compromise'.

It is clear however that the two men held different positions on the doctrine of particular redemption. This theological difference can be traced back to their divergent understanding of the doctrine of imputation. Booth's greater emphasis on imputation and substitution led him to stress the particularity of the atonement in the events of Calvary itself.[89] He believed that Fuller had weakened his adherence to particular redemption. Fuller refused to concede this, and considered that Booth was old and stubborn. He believed that rather than weakening the doctrine of particular redemption by conceding that the atonement was sufficient for all mankind, he had in fact rescued it from neglect and confusion.[90]

Perhaps Booth did underestimate Fuller's commitment to the doctrine under discussion. Fuller did, however, admit a change of emphasis in his understanding of this doctrine. Nevertheless, to suggest that Fuller had become an Arminian is inaccurate. The 'sufficient for all, but efficient for some' formula had long been accepted within Reformed circles. Calvin appeared to allow the possibility, and it was explicitly stated in the Canons of Dordt.[91] Booth dismissed this as a hypothetical position, not germane to the issue, on the grounds that it was what God intended that was accomplished at Calvary. William Newman was to comment later:

[88] Ibid., pp. 89-90.
[89] Booth, *Works*, vol. 3 'Divine Justice', pp. 87-8.
[90] Fuller, *Works*, 'Six Letters to Dr Ryland', p. 322.
[91] Calvin, *Commentary on the Gospel according to St John, 11-21, and 1 John*, translated by T. H. L. Parker, Edinburgh, 1972, p. 244; *The Three Forms of Unity, Canons of Dordt*, Second Head, Article 3.

Andrew Fuller and Abraham Booth

Some appear to have imbibed a vague notion of atonement while redemption properly so-called is overlooked . . . Mr Booth thought Mr Fuller was verging to this extreme; in this however, I believe he misunderstood Mr Fuller.[92]

There was certainly misunderstanding, but it was not just on one side in this debate.

The death of Abraham Booth in 1806 removed Fuller's most able critic among the Particular Baptists. Fuller stood out as a theologian and a leader. Years earlier, he had courageously challenged the prevalent non-offer teaching and, although at first resisted by many, he saw a large number of his fellow Particular Baptists accepting his views, while a growing number of Hyper-Calvinists were ready to co-operate with him in the Missionary Society. The Presidents of the three Baptist Colleges, John Ryland, William Newman, and William Steadman,[93] were sympathetic to his teaching and undoubtedly influenced a growing number of ministerial students. His victory, however, was not quite complete. There were churches and individuals who remained loyal to the old Hyper-Calvinism, and yet others who felt that belief in particular redemption was in danger of being lost. No one seemed able to give the theological leadership that was needed. However, in John Stevens and William Gadsby there appeared two able preachers of considerable power who were to rally the Hyper-Calvinists and present their teaching in a new and popular manner. Unlike Button and Martin, they were able to build up a growing body of support beyond their own churches. They also revealed a readiness to follow their own way, outside the local Baptist Associations and the Baptist Union. Both Gadsby and Stevens attacked

---

[92] Newman's *Diary* quoted in G. Pritchard, *Memoir of the Rev. William Newman, D.D.*, London, 1837, p. 336.

[93] John Ryland at Bristol was, of course, Fuller's correspondent and biographer. William Newman of Stepney expressed his admiration in a memorial sermon, *A Sermon Occasioned by the Death of the Rev. Andrew Fuller*, London, 1815. Of William Steadman, principal of the Northern Academy, 1805–35, his son wrote, 'In digesting the system of religious truth, he was guided by the counsels and strictures of Fuller's herculean understanding', T. Steadman, *Memoir of the Rev. William Steadman, D.D.*, London, 1838.

Fuller's developed views (which became subjects of debate in the years after 1800), although neither could have been happy with the first edition of *The Gospel Worthy of All Acceptation*, or even with Booth's *Glad Tidings*.

It is regrettable that there was no theologian of Booth's calibre to continue the challenge to Fuller's thinking and to guide men who were deeply concerned by the issues he raised. In the years to come, much of the criticism of Andrew Fuller was unthinking and hostile to such a degree that his positive contribution to theology and the life of the churches was not given the consideration it deserved. In addition, the balanced teaching of Abraham Booth on gospel preaching, not to mention on the place of the moral law in the life of the believer, was forgotten.

9

WILLIAM GADSBY

He seemed a preacher made on purpose for the working classes. His popularity with the factory people of Manchester was extraordinary, as he was not a Lancashire man.

ROBERT HALEY, ON WILLIAM GADSBY

O brethren! Labour to feel the influences of religion upon your very hearts and reins! This will settle you more than all the arguments in the world can do; by this the ways of God are more endeared to men, than by any other way in the world. When your hearts have once felt it you will never forsake it.

JOHN FLAVEL

In the last thirty years of the eighteenth century, controversies over communion, Hyper-Calvinism, and Antinomianism exercised the Particular Baptists deeply, but by the time of Abraham Booth's death in 1806, a new zeal for gospel preaching at home and abroad was concentrating the minds of many. Andrew Fuller's teaching on the warrant of faith was widely accepted by English Particular Baptists by the time of his death in 1815.[1] Nevertheless, the extent of this acceptance must not be exaggerated. The old Hyper-Calvinism was not extinct, and this and other issues debated in the eighteenth-century controversies were to resurface in the ministries of William Gadsby and John Stevens. These

---

[1] 'Without doubt Fuller's first claim to recognition arises from the part he played in liberating his denomination from the tyranny of hyper-Calvinism', E. F. Clipsham, 'Andrew Fuller's Doctrine of Salvation', Oxford B.D. thesis, 1971, p. 277. 'With the publication of *The Gospel Worthy of All Acceptation*, the walls of High Calvinism fell flat', G. F. Nuttall, 'Northamptonshire and the Modern Question', *Journal of Theological Studies*, vol. 21, 1965, p. 123.

men were to provide dynamic leadership for the Hyper-Calvinists who had long been on the defensive; both were able to present their teachings in vivid and popular ways and were excellent communicators with the working classes from which they had emerged. Through their ministries groups of Strict and Particular Baptist churches were formed, which have continued to the present day; Gadsby and Stevens were the patriarchs of the new movement. Although the two men agreed on many issues, they differed significantly over the place of the moral law in the life of the Christian.

Today William Gadsby is the better remembered of the two.[2] Called to the Manchester Particular Baptist Church in 1805, he remained in that pastorate until his death in 1844. His boundless energy could not be contained within the confines of a local church; he carried his message into the growing industrial areas of South Lancashire, the West Riding of Yorkshire, Derbyshire, and Cheshire until, by the time of his death, nearly forty churches claimed him as their founder.[3] In addition to these churches, Gadsby visited London[4] for at least a month every year, and preached in centres as far from Manchester as Plymouth,[5] Bath,[6] and Ipswich.[7] Most of these preaching tours were, of course, conducted

---

[2] The chief source of biographical information for Gadsby is J. Gadsby, *A Memoir of the Late Mr William Gadsby*, Manchester, 1844. This is a badly compiled collection of anecdotes with little order. It was however written by his son and does contain frequent autobiographical references from Gadsby's sermons, as well as personal reminiscences. Except where otherwise indicated, quotations are from the 1844 edtion. Recently there has appeared, B. A. Ramsbottom, *William Gadsby*, Gospel Standard Publications, Harpenden, 2003. This is a fine work, although in places spoiled by an inadequate examination of the significance and teaching of Andrew Fuller. Another important contribution to this subject is Ian Shaw, *High Calvinists in Action*, Oxford University Press, 2002. Dr Shaw has made a careful study of Gadsby's work, setting it against a detailed treatment of early nineteenth-century Manchester and ministries exercised under similar conditions.

[3] *Memoir of W. Gadsby*, p. 77.

[4] Ibid., pp. 76, 121.

[5] W. Gadsby, *Sermons, Fragments and Letters,* London, 1884, p. 408.

[6] Ibid., p. 407.

[7] J. Foreman, *Funeral Sermon for the late Mr J. Stevens*, London, 1847, p. 22.

before the advent of rail travel. Gadsby proved to be a powerful controversialist, opposing the teachings of Andrew Fuller and promoting some of the views of William Huntington, but without the latter's bitterness. However, in the face of considerable opposition, he was able to secure a place for a modified Huntingtonian Antinomianism among the Particular Baptists.

1. Early Life

William Gadsby was born in January 1773, in the village of Attleborough near Nuneaton, Warwickshire. His father, John Gadsby, was married twice, and had seven children from each marriage. William was the second child of the second marriage. John Gadsby was a road mender and was therefore in no position to provide much of an education for his children. William received his minimal schooling at Nuneaton Church School; here he learned to read, but not to write.[8] The latter skill was to be acquired later.

William's limited opportunities were compensated in some measure by native wit and boundless energy. He proved to be a lively youth, not too careful with his language, and the acknowledged ringleader and entertainer of the local lads. Apprenticed to a ribbon weaver, he worked four years as a journeyman. He then served a second apprenticeship as a stocking weaver, later developing his own small business. He displayed considerable skill in this second trade, a fair degree of business acumen, and a readiness to exploit the new techniques that were being introduced as part of the industrial revolution.[9]

His parents took their children with them to a local Independent Chapel. As a youth William resented chapel, and made himself as much of a nuisance to the worshippers as he dared. However, after witnessing a particularly gruesome hanging at Coventry when he was seventeen, a change took place in him. Suffering the agonies of spiritual conviction, he began to attend the Independent Chapel at Bedworth, between Coventry and Nuneaton. Here he found a spiritual home, seizing every opportunity

---

[8] *Memoir of W. Gadsby*, p. 10.
[9] Ibid., pp. 11, 23–5.

of Christian fellowship and taking pleasure especially in the conversation of the older Christians, who delighted to discuss the issues of doctrine and experience.[10]

The Bedworth Independents were Calvinists,[11] but little is known of the nature of their Calvinism at this time. It may be significant that the teachings of William Huntington were spreading through the West Midlands at this time. Bedworth is less than twenty miles from Birmingham, where, in 1788, Huntington drew large crowds during a week's preaching.[12] As always, opinion concerning Huntington and his teaching was divided, but one result of his preaching in Birmingham was that John Bradford, minister in the Countess of Huntingdon's Connexion, left that group and formed a new Independent Church. Huntington returned in 1791 to open Bradford's new chapel in Bartholomew Street.[13] By that date, Huntington had been publishing popular books and pamphlets for more than a decade. These included autobiographical writings as well as polemics against Caleb Evans, Fuller, and the Rylands.[14] Whether Gadsby ever heard him is unknown, but he left his mark in Birmingham.

Gadsby's first contact with the Baptists came in 1793, when he met Paul Aston, assistant minister of the Cow Lane Baptist Church, Coventry. It was Aston who convinced Gadsby that he should be baptized by immersion. This took place at Coventry on 29 December 1793, after which Gadsby threw himself into the activities of the Cow Lane Church, even walking the eight miles to Coventry every Sunday to be in time

---

[10] Ibid., pp. 11-15.

[11] Aubry Mann, *The Old Meeting Church, Bedworth*, n.p., n.d.; R. G. Martin, *Zion Strict Baptist Chapel, Bedworth, 1796-1955*, Tunbridge Wells, n.d. p. 1.

[12] 'I am to preach here every night except Saturday . . . [I] have enough invitations to fill up my time for six months', W. Huntington, *Gleanings of the Vintage*, London, 1837, p. 75.

[13] W. W. Horne, *The Life of the Rev. John Bradford*, p. 157.

[14] Huntington published *The Bank of Faith* and *The Kingdom of Heaven Taken by Prayer* in 1784. Both were popular pieces of autobiography. Polemical works included *Letter to the Rev. Caleb Evans*, 1789, *The Broken Cistern and the Springing Well*, 1791 (against J. C. Ryland), *Excommunication*, 1791 (against J. Ryland, Jr. and Andrew Fuller).

William Gadsby

for the 7 a.m. prayer meeting.[15] The pastor at Coventry was John Butterworth, who had held the office since 1749.[16] A scholarly man who had seen prosperity in the work at Coventry, Butterworth was by now in his old age, and Gadsby seems to have been more closely associated with Aston. However, Gadsby's connection with Coventry did not last long. Marriage and new opportunities in business moved him to Hinckley, Leicestershire, some thirteen miles from Coventry in 1796.[17] A Particular Baptist work had been started in Hinckley in 1794 or 1795, and to this work he joined himself in September 1796.[18]

2. Early Ministry

When he baptized Gadsby, Paul Aston declared that he could 'see something in the young man, although so illiterate and uncouth, that seemed blessedly to prove that he would some time or other be made very useful to God's dear family'.[19] It was not until after his move to Hinckley in 1796 that Gadsby began to comment publicly on Scripture at cottage prayer meetings. Right from the beginning his hearers were impressed with him. His first sermon was preached to a small Particular Baptist Church at Bedworth in 1798.[20] In the nineteenth century, the Bedworth church was to stand firmly in the Gadsby tradition, but in February 1799 it welcomed Andrew Fuller as the preacher for the opening of its new chapel.[21]

By 1800 Gadsby's relations with his old church at Coventry were not good. Aston had moved to Chester, and the assistant pastor who succeeded him from 1798 was Francis Franklin, who came from the Bristol Baptist College with the warm recommendation of John Ryland.[22] Franklin, who was to succeed Butterworth as pastor, was a vigorous opponent of Gadsby's teaching on the law.[23]

---

[15] *Memoir of W. Gadsby*, p. 20.
[16] J. M. Gwynne Owen, ed., *Memorial Volume of the 250th Anniversary of the West Midland Baptist Association*, Birmingham, 1905, p. 153.
[17] *Memoir of W. Gadsby*, p.23.   [18] Ibid., p. 25.   [19] Ibid., p. 21.   [20] Ibid., p. 25.
[21] Fuller's *Letters*, 'A. Fuller to J. Sutcliff, 18 Feb. 1799 and 23 Feb. 1799'.
[22] J. M. Gwynne Owen, op. cit., p. 153. Ryland describes Franklin as 'a worthy young man, I think of no despicable gifts'.
[23] J. Gadsby, *Memoir of W. Gadsby*, pp. 21–22.

[177]

By this time, Gadsby was pursuing an active ministry in the towns and villages of Warwickshire and Leicestershire. As a result of his efforts a chapel was opened at Desford, Leicestershire, and there, on 24 July 1800, Paul Aston of Chester, Edward Vorley of Northampton, and William Hall of Irthlingborough ordained William Gadsby.[24] Gadsby combined the pastoral oversight of Desford with Hinckley, where a chapel was built in 1803.[25]

Gadsby was soon known as a convinced Particular Baptist who rejected the free offer of the gospel and taught that the gospel, not the law, was the believer's rule of conduct. Although called an Antinomian, he always repudiated any suggestion that a Christian was free to live in sin.[26] On the other hand, during his first visit to Manchester, he told his host, 'I am not a Fullerite.'[27]

At no stage in his life did Gadsby ever confine his efforts to his own pastorate. The conviction that he had a message for the people encouraged him to seize every opportunity to preach. Soon, however, other considerations entered into the motives behind his itinerant ministry. The Hinckley Church's first meeting place was an old dilapidated barn. In order to collect funds for the building of a new chapel, Gadsby 'went about the country preaching and begging'.[28] It was in this cause that he made his first visit to Manchester in 1803, having secured an invitation to preach at the Particular Baptist Chapel in St George's Road.[29] Further visits followed, before Gadsby accepted a call to the pastorate of this chapel in 1805.

3. The Manchester Pastorate

The Manchester church to which William Gadsby was called was a Particular Baptist cause founded by 1650.[30] It had passed through an unsettled period in the years before Gadsby's arrival. It was already divided

---

[24] Ibid., p. 28. [25] Ibid., p. 30.

[26] Ibid., p. 30, accused of teaching that the elect could live in sin, Gadsby replied, 'I know of no such people, and assure you I am not of that sort.'

[27] Ibid., p. 34. [28] Ibid., p. 30. [29] Ibid., p. 33.

[30] W. T. Whitley, *Baptists of North-West England, 1649-1913*, London, 1913, p. 49.

William Gadsby

over the issue of Fullerism, and Gadsby's early visits only intensified this controversy, as well as introducing the contentious issue of doctrinal Antinomianism.[31] Not only was the church divided, but also wild rumours about Gadsby himself swept across Manchester. He commented:

> The ministers were everywhere preaching to put down Antinomianism. Some of them told the people to keep their cupboards locked; for they must expect to find them emptied if they admitted me into their houses; and I believe I was for some time as great a dread to the professors as Bonaparte was to the combined forces.[32]

In spite of the divided church and the local hostility, Gadsby accepted the call. Feeling was, however, sufficiently strong for a group to secede and build a new chapel in York Street.[33] Gains at the old church more than compensated for losses. From 1807 to 1812 between five and ten new members were added to the church every month.[34] The continual increase made it necessary to build a new chapel in 1824 with double the seating capacity of the old building.[35] Ian Shaw has calculated that 'numerically Gadsby's chapel with a congregation of around 1000 in the later part of his life was the largest Dissenting cause in Manchester and one of the largest Protestant causes'.[36] He further draws attention to 'Gadsby's success in developing such a large cause in the extremely poor and deprived Angel Meadow area'.[37]

It became evident that Gadsby was blessed with preaching abilities that were remarkably suited to Manchester's growing population of industrial workers. A contemporary, Robert Halley, Principal of New College London, wrote of him:

---

[31] J. Gadsby, *Memoir of W. Gadsby*, pp. 33–4.   [32] Ibid., p. 35.
[33] Ibid., p. 36.
[34] Ibid., 1847 ed., p. 48. B. A. Ramsbottom, who has had access to the church records of Gadsby's church, concludes that this figure is an exaggeration and suggests about 25 to 30 a year (*William Gadsby*, p. 72).
[35] J. Gadsby, *Memoir of W. Gadsby*, pp. 39, 73; cf. E. Blackstock, *Autobiography*, London 1853, p. 110.
[36] I. Shaw, *High Calvinists*, p. 121.   [37] Ibid. p. 124.

He seemed a preacher made on purpose for the working classes. His popularity with the factory people of Manchester was extraordinary, as he was not a Lancashire man.[38]

Of his pulpit manner, Halley said:

> Illiterate as he was, he sometimes attracted men of learning and culture (I could mention remarkable instances), who heard him with great pleasure. His thoughts were natural, closely connected, logically arranged and lucidly expressed. Quietly earnest, never impassioned, never vehement, but always arresting attention, he is said to have presented in manner as well as in doctrine, a remarkable contrast to the popular Methodist preachers of his early days. His voice was wonderful and he knew well how to manage it.[39]

Preaching was Gadsby's main business. His son described him as 'indefatigable', and has left us a record of a typical month in the early days of his Manchester ministry.

> Besides preaching four times a week to his own people at Manchester, he for years preached four or five other sermons during the week and every week. After preaching at home three times on the Lord's Day, he would walk on the Monday morning to Rochdale, eleven miles from Manchester, to dinner. After dinner he would walk two or three miles farther, to preach in the afternoon; then return to Rochdale, and preach in the evening. On the Tuesday he would walk to Manchester, and preach to his own people at night. On the Wednesday he would walk to Oldham, Bury, Stockport, Pendlebury, or some other place, preach at night, and on the Thursday start off to another town, and preach and return home on the Friday. Another week he would procure a supply for his own place for Tuesday, and take a tour, almost always on foot, to Blackburn, Preston, Accrington, Rossendale, etc., etc. A third week he would go into Yorkshire; to Halifax, Bradford, Huddersfield etc., etc. And in a fourth week he would in like manner, visit Derbyshire, Cheshire, etc.[40]

---

[38] R. Halley, *Lancashire: Its Puritanism and Nonconformity, vol. 2*, Manchester, 1869, p. 484.
[39] Ibid., p. 485.
[40] *Memoir of W. Gadsby*, p. 99.

William Gadsby

This incessant round of preaching is similar to the early activities of William Huntington and the tours the early Methodists undertook. There was little time for study, but Gadsby knew that he had a message and knew how to communicate it. A greater contrast to the studious Hyper-Calvinists Gill and Brine can scarcely be imagined. Some Hyper-Calvinists may have preached to declining congregations, but Gadsby drew the crowds, wherever he went.

Although Gadsby's direct influence was greatest in the North, he built up a considerable body of support in London, where his first visit was to Redcross Street Chapel. This was the home of John Brine's old church, which, by the early years of the nineteenth century, had witnessed a serious decline. However, in 1807 the remnant there was joined by a group of Hyper-Calvinists who had seceded from Little Alie Street Chapel in Stepney under the leadership of Jonathan Franklin. It was Franklin who invited Gadsby to London, possibly because he felt the need of a theological ally. Gadsby soon packed the little chapel in Redcross Street and attracted the attention of some of Huntington's followers, although there is no evidence that Huntington and Gadsby ever met. This first visit of Gadsby to London in 1808 began a series of annual visits to the nation's capital.[41]

In 1820 William Gadsby preached at the opening of Gower Street Chapel, London. After Huntington's death in 1813, his chapel was controlled by a small group of trustees, who were unwilling to respond to pleas from some members of the congregation that Gadsby and his friends be invited to preach. A considerable minority left and opened a chapel in Conway Street, to which they called Edmund Robins of Bristol as pastor. The Conway Street venue was soon too small and a larger chapel in Gower Street was built. The former Huntingtonians who made

[41] Ibid., pp. 37, 38, 76. For details of Franklin's arrival at Redcross Street and its earlier history, see W. Wilson, *London Dissenting Churches, vol. 2*, p. 584 and *vol. 3*, p. 304. Of Franklin's followers, Wilson wrote, 'These persons are of the supralapsarian cast, and separated from Mr Shenston, because he did not preach the gospel; that is, was not sufficiently enlightened upon some of those high points, which they could digest as easily as common food. Having obtained a pastor to their own taste, he is very popular, has a large church, and the meeting is well filled' (Ibid.).

[181]

Gower Street their home were divided over the issue of baptism, and so an open communion and open membership church was formed. Interestingly Gadsby, a convinced strict communionist, was willing to open the chapel and to preach in it for many years to come. In the early years of its history it was to be an important West-End centre for both Baptists and Paedobaptists, drawn to the ministry of Gadsby and his associates.[42]

Some years later, Gadsby and his followers acquired an important base in the East End of London. In 1832, John Kershaw of Rochdale, one of Gadsby's faithful lieutenants, was asked to conduct an extended ministry at Zoar Chapel, Great Alie Street, Whitechapel. This Church had passed through an unsettled period too, but, as a result of the visits of Kershaw and other associates of Gadsby, by the late 1830s it had become another centre for Gadsby's distinctive teaching. Unlike Gower Street, the Great Alie Street Church practised strict communion throughout these years.[43]

4. Gadsby's Writings

William Gadsby was a prolific writer of tracts. These, of course, reached an even wider public than did his preaching tours. A few of them were evangelistic, some were didactic, but most were polemical in nature.[44] Together with the small selection of printed sermons which have survived, it is possible to gain an understanding of his theology.

---

[42] *Memoir of W. Gadsby*, p. 77; J. Gadsby, *Memoir of Hymn Writers and Compilers*, 5th ed., London, 1882, pp. 155-6; Richard Stonelake, *A City Not Forsaken*, Quinta Press, Oswestry, 2000. This is a fine modern history of the Gower Street church with information on related works in the West End of London.

[43] J. Kershaw, *Autobiography*, London, 1870, pp. 218 ff. Kershaw records that at the beginning of his first visit he was told, 'Before you have finished . . . you will see this chapel, which seats from seven to eight hundred people, filled from the pulpit door into the street. There is such a want of these great and precious truths being preached in this simple Bible style of language in this great city that there will be such a flocking to hear as will astonish you. . . . Before the four Lord's days were over numbers went away that could not get within the chapel doors' (pp. 223-4). For later details of Zoar Chapel, see A.T., *A Few Historical Links of Zoar Chapel*, London 1889.

[44] These were collected and published in *The Works of the Late William Gadsby, Manchester*, 2 vols., London, 1851, hereinafter referred to as *Gadsby's Works*.

William Gadsby

i. Antinomian Controversy

No sooner had he settled in Manchester than Gadsby found himself embroiled in controversy. His son explained: 'There was great opposition raised against him by certain influential persons in the Church, he having written against Mr Fuller.'[45] The trouble was caused by Gadsby's first pamphlet *The Gospel, the Believer's Rule of Conduct*.[46] This was a reply to a letter in the *Evangelical Magazine*, December 1804, entitled 'The Moral Law the Rule of Conduct to Believers' and signed by 'Gaius'.[47] 'Gaius' was a pseudonym used by Andrew Fuller. In opposition to the thesis that, the moral law or 'the commandments of God, whether we consider them as ten or two, are still *binding on Christians*',[48] Gadsby insisted that 'the glorious gospel is a revelation of Jehovah's will to Zion'.[49] He also insisted that the Old Testament law was inadequate for a Christian, pointing out that even Fuller (Gaius) admitted that it did not require baptism and the Lord's Supper.

> This rule is very deficient as a rule, and yet it is a perfect rule, for Gaius observes, 'Neither the ordinance of baptism, nor that of the Supper, is expressly required by them [the commandments].'[50]

He failed to note that Fuller had pointed out that the love to God required by the law would embrace the commands to be baptized and to celebrate the Lord's Supper.

Gadsby went on to state the view previously expressed by Huntington that the law was fulfilled *in* and not *by* the Christian.

> What he [Gaius] says upon love the Apostle fully answers, where he says, 'Love is the fulfilling of the law', and that the law is fulfilled in us, not by us, and believers are partakers of that love which fulfilled the law,

---

[45] *Memoir of W. Gadsby*, p. 50.
[46] W. Gadsby, *The Gospel, the Believer's Rule of Conduct, being a few remarks upon a letter written by Gaius and inserted in the Evangelical Magazine for December 1804*, 2nd ed., Liverpool, n.d. (published after J. Upton's *Addresses on Practical Subjects*, 1812, and before the death of Andrew Fuller, 1815). No copy of the first edition, c. 1805, has been traced.
[47] Andrew Fuller, *Collected Works*, p. 890. [48] Ibid., p. 890.
[49] W. Gadsby, *The Gospel, the Believer's Rule*, p. 9. [50] Ibid., p. 7.

[183]

yea, that is the end of the law for righteousness, for God is love, and God dwells in them, and they in him, so that Christ their righteousness dwells in them, the hope of glory. And thus 'the righteousness of the law is fulfilled in us, who walk not after the flesh, but after the Spirit' (*Rom.* 8:1-5). But can a scripture be found that speaks of the believer fulfilling the law by taking it as his rule of conduct?[51]

Over against this Fuller wrote: 'It is allowed that all true obedience is caused by the influence of the Holy Spirit; but that to which he influences the mind was antecedently required of us: He leadeth us "in the way that we should go".'[52]

Like Huntington, Gadsby had to rebut the charge that his teachings led to sin.

I do not contend for the believer's freedom from the law with a view to encourage sin, neither in myself nor any other person, but quite the reverse; for if I know anything of my own heart, I find nothing such a blow to sin as a sweet manifestation of the love of God to my soul, which makes me feel that I am dead to the law by the body of Christ; and if this does not cause the soul to love holiness, nothing will.[53]

Fuller on the other hand insisted:

If a believer be ruled by love in such a way as to exclude obligation, this is the same as if a son should say to his father, I have no objection to oblige you, sir; I will do your business from love; but I will not be commanded! That is, what he pleases he will do and no more. – No parent could bear such an answer from a child; and how can we suppose that God will bear it from us![54]

To make his position quite clear, in the second edition of this work, Gadsby disassociated himself from the statement of Tobias Crisp that 'sin can do a child of God no harm'.[55]

---

[51] Ibid., p. 8.
[52] Fuller, *Works*, p.891.
[53] Gadsby, *The Gospel, the Believer's Rule*, p. 30.
[54] Fuller, *Works*, p. 891.
[55] Gadsby, *The Gospel, the Believer's Rule*, p. 33.

William Gadsby

Gadsby adopted a very aggressive tone against Fuller in *The Gospel, the Believer's Rule*. Clearly, Fuller's description of Antinomian teachings as 'foul dogmas' and their preachers as 'pulpit libertines' stung him.[56] He claimed that his opponent's charity appeared to embrace all who claimed the name Christian, except the Antinomians.

> I know it is possible for men to deny the divinity of Christ, the work of the Spirit, the doctrines of election, particular redemption, justification by the righteousness of Christ imputed, and the final perseverance of the saints; and yet Gaius and his adherents hold such men in high reputation. Witness the Leicestershire Union meetings held every six months in Leicestershire in which Arians, Independents, and General and Particular Baptists unite; so that these, it appears, are his brethren, seeing they can unite together.[57]

It is not at all clear what meetings Gadsby is referring to, or indeed, whether they were religious or political. For social and political purposes Gadsby himself in later years was to share a platform with a Roman Catholic priest in Manchester.[58]

In 1808 Gadsby made a similar charge when his pamphlet *The Present State of Religion, or, What Are the People Miscalled Antinomians?* appeared.[59] He deplored the tendency of 'Arminians, Arians, Predestinarians and all classes (to) meet together, and preach and hear so as not to offend each other'.[60] This extended to all except Antinomians which 'is a kind of bugbear word to frighten people from the truth'.[61]

This criticism was unjust if it included Fuller, who had made it clear that those were not his sentiments: 'If I had reason to believe of any man that he did not call upon the name of the Lord Jesus, or rely upon his atoning sacrifice for acceptance with God, I could not acknowledge him as a Christian brother or pay him any respect in a religious way.'[62]

[56] Fuller, *Collected Works*, p. 890.
[57] W. Gadsby, *The Gospel, The Believer's Rule*, p. 6.
[58] Ian J. Shaw, *High Calvinists in Action*, p.139,
[59] W. Gadsby, *The Present State of Religion, or, What Are the People Miscalled Antinomians?*, Manchester, [1808], 2nd ed., 1809.   [60] Ibid., p. 10.   [61] Ibid., p. 13.
[62] Fuller, *Works*, 'Agreement in Sentiment the Bond of Christian Union', p. 848. The whole of this tract works out Fuller's position in detail.

By this time Gadsby seemed to be more anxious to avoid the term, *Antinomian*, and insisted that he and his friends 'maintain and preach most of the doctrines contained in the articles of the Church of England'.[63]

During this period Gadsby developed a more detailed exposition of his views. He preached a series of eleven sermons at Manchester from James 1:25 and published them under the title *The Perfect Law of Liberty*.[64]

In 1809, John Stevens, a fellow High Calvinist, entered the debate with his treatise *Doctrinal Antinomianism Refuted*.[65] Stevens, who was at this time pastor of a Particular Baptist Church in Boston, Lincolnshire, was anxious to counter the spread of Huntington's teachings in the eastern counties and was not immediately concerned with Gadsby. It was Gadsby, however, who replied with *'Doctrinal Antinomianism Refuted' Entangled in Its Own Maze*.[66]

Some time between 1812 and 1815 Gadsby brought out a second edition of *The Gospel, the Believer's Rule of Conduct*, which included an appendix replying to James Upton's *Addresses on Practical Subjects*.[67] There was little new in these later pamphlets, and there were soon indications that Gadsby was wearying of the controversy and more ready to adopt a charitable attitude to his opponents if they would reciprocate. In 1818 he was further criticized by J. Gawthorne in *The Coincidence of Antinomianism and Arminianism*.[68] Gawthorne challenged Gadsby per-

---

[63] Ibid., p. 14.

[64] W. Gadsby, 'The Perfect Law of Liberty. or, The Glory of God in the Gospel', n.d., *Gadsby's Works*, vol. 1, pp. 102-222.

[65] John Stevens, *Doctrinal Antinomianism Refuted*, London, 1809

[66] W. Gadsby, '*Doctrinal Antinomianism Refuted* Entangled in Its Own Maze', *Gadsby's Works*, vol. 1, pp. 223-43.

[67] J. Upton, *Addresses on Practical Subjects*, London, 1812. Upton was pastor of the Baptist Church, Church Street, Blackfriars, London from 1785 to 1834, W. T. Whitley, *London Baptists*, p. 136. Upton gave his account of the controversy in a letter to David Harris, published in D. Harris, *Real Facts Stated and Mis-Statements Corrected*, Kingston, 1832, p. 14.

[68] J. Gawthorne, *The Coincidence of Antinomianism and Arminianism*, Derby, 1818.

sonally and so the latter replied with *Gawthorne Brought to the Test*.[69] Gadsby made it clear that he had more important things to do than spend his days on this issue. He also insisted: 'I believe there are real men of God, and ministers of the adorable Redeemer, who cannot see eye to eye on this point.'[70] After nearly fifteen years, the energy of controversy seems to have been exhausted, and Gadsby showed a greater breadth of spirit, although he did bring out a third edition of *The Gospel, the Believer's Rule of Conduct*[71] in 1821, an indication that his convictions had not weakened.

ii. SANDEMANIAN CONTROVERSY

When Gadsby had been in Manchester for ten years, he found himself involved in another controversy concerning the nature of saving faith. This time he found himself taking the same side of the debate as Andrew Fuller had taken earlier. The controversy revolved around the teaching of the Scottish theologian Robert Sandeman; Archibald McLean of Edinburgh had introduced his teaching among the Baptists. Sandeman taught that bare assent to the work of Christ is alone necessary for salvation; his view of faith, therefore, was entirely cerebral and excluded the idea of trust.[72] McLean wrote:

> I have therefore noticed, that the great and fundamental truth contained in the Gospel testimony is this, 'That Jesus Christ is the Son of God.' Now salvation is always connected with the belief of that truth in its true and genuine sense.[73]

---

[69] W. Gadsby, *Gawthorne Brought to the Test: being a Reply to Mr Gawthorne's 'Coincidence of Antinomianism and Arminianism', to which is added a Hint to Messrs Bogue and Bennett*, Manchester, 1819.

[70] Ibid., p. 3.

[71] *The Gospel, the Believer's Rule of Conduct*, 3rd edition, Manchester, 1821.

[72] For Sandemanianism see J. Macleod, *Scottish Theology*, Edinburgh, 1943, pp. 185 ff.; *Profitable for Doctrine and Reproof, Puritan Conference Papers, 1967*: D. M. Lloyd-Jones, 'Sandemanianism', reprinted in *The Puritans: Their Origins and Successors,* Edinburgh: Banner of Truth, 1987, pp. 170–90.

[73] A. McLean, *Works*, vol. 4, Edinburgh, 1811, 'Belief of the Gospel [is] Saving Faith', p. 22; cf. his statement, 'Belief of the truth must be true and saving faith.'

McLean's views had been opposed by Fuller in an appendix to the second edition of *The Gospel Worthy of All Acceptation*. He developed his criticism further in his *Strictures on Sandemanianism* in 1810.[74] This was a complete review of the Sandemanian system and went far in settling the controversy among English and Welsh Baptists. However the debate rumbled on in South Lancashire.

Around the year 1816, William Leather, a member of Gadsby's church and an itinerant preacher, adopted Sandemanian views. He propounded this teaching at Hope Chapel, Rochdale, which had been established through Gadsby's preaching. The Rochdale church was unhappy and discontinued Leather's services. Later the Manchester church disciplined him.[75]

However, this was not the end of the controversy in Rochdale. In 1816 the church at Hope Chapel called, as pastor, John Kershaw, a close associate of Gadsby. Shortly afterwards the Old Particular Baptist Church in Town Meadows called William Stevens as pastor. Stevens, an actor before his conversion, served as a minister in Edinburgh prior to succeeding Abraham Booth at Little Prescot Street, London.[76] In London he added over seventy members in what turned out to be a three-year pastorate. The church became alarmed by his emphasis on 'points which they think of subordinate importance'.[77] On his arrival in Rochdale, Stevens proved popular and began to draw hearers from Kershaw, a local man and previous to his call to Hope Chapel, a poor weaver.[78] But after a few years this trend was reversed; apparently Stevens's doctrine alienated many of his

[74] A. Fuller, *Works*, pp 179 ff. 'On the Question whether a Holy Disposition of Heart be Necessary to Believing', Appendix to 2nd edition of *The Gospel Worthy of All Acceptation*, 1801; *Works*, pp. 256 ff, 'Strictures on Antinomianism in Twelve Letters to a Friend', 1810.

[75] J. Kershaw, *Autobiography*, pp. 152-5.

[76] Ibid., p. 177. Kershaw states that Stevens was in Manchester between leaving London and going to Rochdale. C. Stovel, *Preparations for Pulpit Exercises*, ed. by W. Willis, Q.C., London, 1888, p. xv. Of Stevens, Willis wrote, 'He was formerly on the stage. Many members were added by his ministry, and he removed to Rochdale in Lancashire.'

[77] *Little Prescot Street Church Minute Book*, 3 Oct 1810.

[78] J. Kershaw, *Autobiography*, p. 169 ff.

hearers. In 1821 he preached a sermon from 1 John 5:1 in which he expounded Sandemanian views.[79] This he published, causing considerable debate among the local Baptists. At this stage Gadsby intervened with an open letter entitled *Sandemanianism Weighed in the Balance and Found Wanting*.[80]

This is an important tract because as well as opposing Sandemanianism it summarizes Gadsby's own teaching on salvation. He objected to Sandemanianism because it reduced faith to mere assent, saying it 'is simply to believe that Jesus is the Christ'.[81] Gadsby insisted:

> Any natural man gives the same credit to God's word as he gives to other things which are true, so far it is well; but there must be a different belief of the truth than this, as a proof that man's faith stands in the power of God, for it is evident that this faith is but a natural, or as James terms it, 'a dead faith', similar to the faith of devils.[82]

In the light of his arguments, Gadsby went on to warn, 'Men may have a belief of the truth, which is not a fruit of the Spirit, and by this natural faith believe that Jesus is the Son of God.'[83]

Over against the Sandemanians, Gadsby taught that faith is the result of regeneration and not *vice versa*.[84] However, he went on to assert a Hyper-Calvinist position, denying the universal invitations of the gospel.[85]

Gadsby was a man who had personally received a very powerful assurance of the love of God and it is understandable that he was concerned that his hearers should enjoy this too. Such experiences became very important in the piety of Gadsby and his friends. As we have seen, earlier Particular Baptist ministers included a strong experimental emphasis in their preaching. Gadsby developed this in a distinctive manner. For example, in a published sermon he was reported as saying,

> If God's law does not stop your mouth, is not brought home to your conscience, does not destroy all your false projects, and bring you in guilty

---

[79] W. Stevens, *Faith in Christ and the New Birth Connected*, Rochdale, 1821.
[80] W. Gadsby, *Sandemanianism Weighed in the Balances and Found Wanting*, Manchester, 1823. Later republished as 'What is Faith?', *Works*, vol. 1, pp. 279 ff.
[81] W. Gadsby, *Works*, vol. 1, 'What is Faith?' p. 282.   [82] Ibid., p. 281.
[83] Ibid., p. 281.   [84] Ibid., pp. 288-90.   [85] Ibid., pp. 305-307.

and condemned at the feet of the Lord – if you never feel that, I believe you will be damned, as sure as God is in heaven.[86]

Similar statements to this can be found in his writings. The danger of course is that, while some Christians have found this to be their experience, not all have. Of more importance, Scripture nowhere prescribes such a dramatic route to faith as essential to salvation.

An additional element of concern is to be found in Gadsby's definition of faith. In the pamphlet, *What is Faith?*, he speaks of appropriating faith in these terms:

> A believing with the heart that he is my Christ, and that the blessed Father is my Father; and that the blessed Spirit witnesses to the truth in the heart; and thus, being enabled to claim relationship to the blessed Jehovah, we have fellowship with the Father and with his Son, the Lord Jesus Christ; and with holy pleasure can say, 'This God is my God for ever and ever, he shall be my guide even unto death.' This is not done by informing the judgment merely, but by the Spirit taking possession of our hearts, as a spirit of adoption. This is a blessed part of what I call heart religion; and those who ridicule it prove that all they know of religion is at best that knowledge, which puffeth up.[87]

Such a statement taken by itself is heart-warming, but is it an accurate description of faith? Earlier Particular Baptists would not have considered it to be so. Rather, they would have put it into the category of assurance and would have seen it as a beautiful description of assurance and communion with God.

Keach's Catechism provides us with an earlier Particular Baptist definition of faith: 'Faith in Jesus Christ is a saving grace, whereby we receive and rest upon Him alone for salvation, as he is offered to us in the gospel.'[88] Gadsby, of course, would have taken exception to the word 'offered'. Later, Spurgeon, perhaps aware of earlier controversies, was to modify the definition in his catechism to speak of Christ 'as he is set forth in the gospel'. Whether the words of Keach or Spurgeon are preferred,

---

[86] W. Gadsby, *Sermons*, London, 1884, pp. 6–7.   [87] Ibid., p. 308.
[88] *Keach's Catechism*, Question 94. This definition is borrowed from the Westminster *Shorter Catechism*.

the focus of faith is objective. Christ is the object of faith and not the believer's own relation to Christ primarily.

Confusing faith and assurance can lead to the dangerous tendency of defining faith exclusively in terms of our feelings. Few Christians enjoy constant elevated feelings and when these feelings are absent one is tempted to believe that faith is not present or has never been present, and therefore that one has been deceived with regard to one's standing in Christ. The compilers of the *1689 Confession* distinguished faith from assurance by saying:

> This infallible assurance doth not so belong to the essence of faith, but that a true believer may wait long, and conflict with many difficulties before he be a partaker of it; yet being enabled by the Spirit of God to know the things that are freely given him of God, he may by the right use of means, attain thereunto.[89]

Faith, therefore, has to be both exercised and cultivated. In words that Gadsby chose to include in his own hymn book, Christians were reminded:

> Faith is by knowledge fed,
> And with obedience mixed,
> Notion is empty, cold and dead,
> And fancy's never fixed.
>
> True faith's the life of God,
> Deep in the heart it lies;
> It lives and labours under load;
> Though damped it never dies.

These lines from Joseph Hart help us to a see that there was a counter-balancing factor in Gadsby's Hyper-Calvinism. To borrow a phrase crafted by J. I. Packer in a different context, it contained a great deal of its own antidote. While Gadsby rejected universal invitations, he could use remarkable freedom in presenting the gospel. This is especially clear in some of his own hymns:

---

[89] *1689 Confession*, XVIII, 3.

> Come, whosoever will,
> Nor vainly strive to mend;
> Sinners are freely welcome still
> To Christ, the sinner's Friend.
>
> His tender loving heart
> The vilest will embrace;
> And freely to them will impart
> The riches of his grace.

Further, one of the sublimest hymns he ever wrote includes the lines:

> Would we view his brightest glory,
> Here it shines in Jesus' face;
> Sing and tell the pleasing story,
> O ye sinners saved by grace;
> And with pleasure,
> Bid the guilty him embrace.

Gadsby's emphasis on the direct experience of God's love certainly stood out in stark contrast to the clinical approach of the Sandemanians. It was surely the warmth of this personal emphasis, preached with all the authority of his own experience, that made Gadsby's ministry so powerfully appealing, not only to the poverty-stricken workers of South Lancashire, but to whomever he preached throughout the country. It only became unbalanced when Christian living was seen exclusively in terms of fluctuating experience. As in the case of Huntington's followers, the Christian life could become a bewildering alternation of heights of delight followed by the depths of despair. In such vicissitudes the teaching of the *1689 Confession* would have provided a healthy corrective.

> True believers may have the assurance of their salvation divers ways shaken, diminished, and intermitted; ... yet they are never destitute of the seed of God and life of faith, that love of Christ and the brethren, that sincerity of heart and conscience of duty out of which, by the operation of the Spirit, this assurance may in due time be revived, and by the which, in the meantime, they are preserved from utter despair.[90]

[90] Ibid., XVIII, 4

William Gadsby

Reference to Gadsby's hymns is a reminder that he was a prolific hymn-writer and compiled a hymn book for his own congregation. This sold widely and, being considerably enlarged since its first publication, remains in print today; it is possibly the oldest hymn book amongst those still regularly used in England. Most of the hymns are drawn from other writers but the number of his own contributions is considerable. He did not have great talents as a hymn-writer; rhymes and metres are sometimes faulty, but at times he achieves something truly sublime as for example in the hymns, *O what matchless condescension*, and *Immortal honours rest on Jesus' head*.[91]

iii. COMMUNION CONTROVERSY

Although Gadsby did not write on the communion controversy, his attitude on the subject of communion requires some comment. He was a convinced strict communionist.[92] However, as already indicated, he preached at the opening of Gower Street Chapel, the home of an open communion and open membership church. He thereby made clear his willingness to co-operate with other Hyper-Calvinists, who did not share his views on baptism and communion. The men who closely associated with Gadsby shared this outlook.[93]

One incident, however, calls for further comment. In 1843 Gadsby refused to accept the annual invitation to preach at Gower Street Chapel, London. The reason for this decision was connected to Edward

---

[91] *Gadsby's Hymns*, 514, Gospel Standard Publications, Harpenden, Herts. *Gadsby's Hymns*, first published in 1814 and subsequently enlarged to include over 1100 hymns, continues in print and is almost exclusively used among the Gospel Standard churches. It is prized as a devotional work by many who would no longer use it in public worship.

[92] *Memoir of W. Gadsby*, p. 88.

[93] John Warburton of Trowbridge, one of Gadsby's closest friends was also a regular preacher at Gower Street, J. Gadsby, *Memoir of Hymn Writers,* p. 156. J. C. Philpot, John Gadsby's successor as editor of the *Gospel Standard* magazine, wrote in 1836, 'I am a decided Baptist, but I can stretch my hand across the water to God's Children, whose eyes are not open to see the ordinance, whilst there are thousands of Baptists to whom I would not willingly hand a chair', J. H. Philpot, ed., *The Seceders*, vol. 1, London, 1931, p. 316.

Blackstock, the new pastor at Gower Street, and a former member of Gadsby's Church in Manchester. For most of his ministerial career, Blackstock was a strict communionist. Late in the 1830s his views changed, and when called to the pastorate of Lakenheath Baptist Church, Suffolk, in 1838, he made an unsuccessful attempt to persuade that Church to adopt open communion. The following year he accepted a call to a Strict Baptist Church in Wolverhampton. When he accepted the call from the open-communion church at Gower Street in 1843, Gadsby 'positively refused to preach in Gower Street Chapel any more, as he could not countenance such an unstable man'.[94] Gadsby's action seems to have initiated the process by which Gower Street Chapel did become a strict-communion church after his death.[95] It did not alter the readiness of the Strict Baptists who associated with him to co-operate with fellow Calvinists with differing views on baptism and the communion.[96]

6. Political and Social Issues

The desperate poverty of the area around Gadsby's Chapel has already been noted. In a memorial tribute to William Gadsby, J. C. Philpot wrote:

> A great love of liberty, and hatred of real or supposed oppression, was another striking natural feature in his character. This we have thought, sometimes drew him into scenes, and brought him into contact with politics more than becomes a minister of the gospel. But he had this excuse, which we willingly offer, that he never interfered with political

---

[94] J. Gadsby, *Memoir of Hymn Writers*, p. 60, fn.; cf. J. Gadsby, *Memoir of W. Gadsby*, p. 77. For Blackstock's account see E. Blackstock, *Autobiography and Letters*, London, 1853, pp. 234 ff.

[95] A number of the Baptists left during Blackstock's pastorate and were formed into a strict-communion church by Kershaw of Rochdale. To these people Gadsby preached on his last visit to London. They subsequently increased and were able to return to Gower Street where the original congregation had dwindled in 1855: J. Kershaw, *Autobiography*, pp. 332, 335-6; J. Warburton, Jr., *Autobiography*, London, 1892, pp. 36-37.

[96] In 1861 Kershaw went on a visit to Edinburgh, where he preached for the Free Church of Scotland, J. Kershaw, *Autobiography*, pp. 343 ff. Philpot maintained close ties with John Grace, an Independent minister from Brighton, J. H. Philpot, ed., *The Seceders*, vol. 2, pp. 134-5.

William Gadsby

subjects where he did not see, or where he was not fully persuaded he saw, some oppression inflicted upon, or intended for, the poor and needy.[97]

From Philpot's comments it might be imagined that Gadsby's involvement in public affairs was exclusively occasioned by the sufferings of the poor: this was not strictly the case. He was a vigorous opponent of Catholic Emancipation and expressed himself so strongly that stones were hurled at him through his Chapel windows and for a time his friends had to escort him to his house.[98] His son suggested that his views were later modified:

> He subsequently, however, learned that the Church of England had been a greater persecutor of the Catholics and Dissenters than ever the Catholics, in this country at least, had of Protestants.[99]

Although Gadsby had friends who were Anglicans,[100] he was incensed against what he considered to be the unfair impositions of the Established Church. 'Church rates he opposed, and was almost sure to be present at any town's meeting called to oppose their being levied.'[101] He was equally opposed to the levying of tithes, writing that 'tithes and their appendages are rather a curse than a blessing to the religion of Christ'.[102]

In 1819 Gadsby took a risky stand against what he perceived as a grievous act of repression. On 16 August 1819 over 60,000 people assembled in St Peter's Fields, Manchester, to hear Henry Hunt a well-known orator, call for constitutional changes that would lead to the better representation of the northern manufacturing districts in Parliament. Although the

---

[97] *The Gospel Standard*, 1844, quoted J.H. Philpot, ed., *The Seceders*, vol. 2, p. 326.

[98] *Memoir of W. Gadsby*, p. 117.

[99] Ibid., p. 117. This statement was deleted from later editions.

[100] Gadsby was 'on very friendly terms' with the Rev. Mr Nunn of St Clement's Church, Manchester, J. H. Philpot, ed., *The Seceders*, vol. 2, p. 63; cf. quotation from *The Gospel Standard*, 1871, p. 427 in *The Seceders*, vol. 2, p. 65.

[101] *Memoir of W. Gadsby*, p. 118.

[102] W. Gadsby, *Works*, vol. 2, 'Musical Festivals and Their Patronizing Clergy', 1837, p. 128.

crowd was orderly, the magistrates took panic and ordered cavalry men to break up the meeting. Six people were killed and hundreds injured as a result. Local Anglican clergy supported the magistrates. Evangelical Christians were divided as to the propriety of this action. The Wesleyan Methodists removed four hundred people from their membership on account of radicalism at this time. Gadsby, on the other hand, signed a protest stating 'that we feel it our bounded duty to protest against and to express our utter disapprobation of the unexpected and unnecessary violence by which the meeting was dispersed'. He had come out very clearly on the side of Lancashire radicalism.[103]

Gadsby raised a furore in 1820 at the time that George IV was seeking a divorce from his wife, Queen Caroline. On 3 December 1820, he preached a sermon from Matthew 5:32 and published it under the title, 'The Nature and Design of the Marriage Union'.[104] Gadsby declared, 'Neither birth, title, nor station can authorise any man to violate the laws of God.'[105] He clearly rejected the charges made against the Queen:

> For a man to put away his wife, without a just cause, and spurn her from his bosom, his bed, and his table, and for years expose her to the snares and besetments of men, and then, upon the evidence of the vilest reptiles that ever reverenced the toe of a Pope, try her for adultery is indecency; and men who can with a good grace encourage such a proceeding must have a stomach capable of digesting anything that is nauseous.[106]

Gadsby broadened his comments to include criticism of the Cabinet:

> But let ministers say and do as they will, I sincerely believe that the Queen is an injured, persecuted woman, and if the truth were freely to come out, one of her greatest crimes in the eyes of her enemies is her attachment to the people.[107]

---

[103] Shaw, *High Calvinists*, pp. 136-7. This event became known as the 'Peterloo Massacre'.
[104] W. Gadsby, *The Nature and Design of the Marriage Union. A sermon preached at Manchester on 3rd December 1820, Occasioned by the Proceedings in the House of Lords against Queen Caroline*, Fourth Edition, Manchester 1836.
[105] Ibid., p. 19.   [106] Ibid., p. 19.   [107] Ibid., pp. 20, 21.

William Gadsby

Gadsby's stern rebukes were uttered at a time when the authorities were very nervous about public disorder. The 'Peterloo Massacre' in Manchester had taken place only a year before, while 1820 was the year of the Cato Street Conspiracy in London.[108] It was not surprising, therefore, that a deputy constable was sent to Gadsby's Chapel. Unabashed, Gadsby pointed out his presence to the congregation.[109] Gadsby was however no violent revolutionary. In his sermon, he cried, 'May tyranny, despotism and anarchy, sink in endless shame. Amen and Amen.'[110] In a revised edition of the *Memoir*, John Gadsby insisted that his father 'never encouraged anyone in opposing the laws of his country; but never hesitated to exert himself, publicly as well as privately, in endeavouring to get bad laws repealed'.[111]

As indicated in the sermon on the *Marriage Union*, Gadsby's sympathies were with the people. Faced with the effects of expensive food, he was active in the anti-Corn Law agitation. He was involved in this movement as early as 1819 and, according to his son, 'was the first Dissenting minister in Manchester who took an active part in the later successful agitation for a repeal of the Corn Laws. He was still addressing meetings on the subject in 1839.'[112]

While Gadsby would not co-operate in religious enterprises with those who rejected his Hyper-Calvinism, in matters of social justice and morality he adopted a different approach. Ian Shaw has shown that he was active in the movement for the disestablishment of the Church of England with the Presbyterian William McKerrow, and that he twice shared a platform with Peter Kaye, a Roman Catholic priest, in moves to promote better Sabbath observance.[113]

Gadsby was not content merely to address meetings. In 1826, a year of great distress in Manchester, Gadsby made an appeal from the pulpit of

---

[108] The Cato Street Conspiracy was a wild scheme to murder the whole of the Cabinet. It was discovered and the ringleaders were hanged.

[109] *Memoir of W. Gadsby*, 1847 ed., pp. 106–7.

[110] W. Gadsby, *The Marriage Union*, p. 21.

[111] *Memoir of W. Gadsby*, London, 1870, p. 125.

[112] Ibid., 1847 ed., pp. 106–7.

[113] Shaw, *High Calvinists*, pp. 138–9.

Gower Street Chapel, London.[114] The *Manchester Gazette* reported the occasion:

> We understand that the Rev. Mr Gadsby, who, by his praiseworthy exertions for the poor of this town, in canvassing among his friends in London, obtained 20 cwt of cast-off clothes, (the carriage and packaging of which cost him £18,) still continues to exert himself in acts of benevolence. We learn, from very good authority, that he has purchased and distributed, within the last week, ten pairs of blankets and four or five pieces of flannel; and that some of the members of his congregation have copied their pastor's laudable example. In recording the above, which does so much credit to Mr Gadsby's feelings, we cannot let pass the opportunity of hinting to other clergymen, and other influential persons, that it is their duty to 'go and do likewise'.[115]

* * * * *

In 1835 at the suggestion of his son, John, William Gadsby established the *Gospel Standard* magazine.[116] This was to form a bond of union amongst his followers. The development of this group will be considered in a subsequent chapter. It is sufficient to note here that by this time William Gadsby had established himself as a natural leader among the English Hyper-Calvinist Baptists and was leading them forward in a new advance. In spite of considerable opposition, he had secured a place for a modified Huntingtonian theology among English Baptists, although he was never a mere copier. He did not deny the authority of such passages as Exodus 32:31 and Romans 9:3, as Huntington had done earlier.[117]

Gadsby never modified his Baptist and strict-communion principles, although with the years he showed broadening sympathies. In contrast to Huntington's Toryism, he adopted a radical approach in politics. He proved to be a better leader than Huntington had been, and established a

---

[114] Ibid., p. 63.

[115] *Manchester Gazette*, 9th. Dec. 1826, quoted J. Gadsby, *Memoir of W. Gadsby*, p. 75.

[116] J. H. Philpot, ed., *The Seceders*, vol. 2, p. 60.

[117] See page 129 above.

faithful following, which was long to continue. He never lost touch with the people of his origins. He showed a ready sympathy in all cases of need and was able to present his Hyper-Calvinism in a way which was readily understood and attracted the support of a number of cultured adherents.

10

John Stevens

It is an indubitable fact that truth is evermore consistent with itself.

John Stevens

An eminently devout and holy man, as well as an able preacher.

The Baptist Magazine, 1847

Twentieth-century Baptist historians such as Whitley, Underwood, and Briggs include William Gadsby as a Strict and Particular Baptist pioneer, but strangely ignore the equally important contribution of John Stevens.[1] In part this may be because Gadsby's followers have kept in print various memoirs, collections of letters, and theological miscellanea, dating from the early nineteenth century, whereas Stevens's successors did not. Another cause of this neglect may be that John Stevens never involved himself in political lobbying in the way that Gadsby did. But whatever the causes, the failure to consider Stevens has led to a distorted view of Strict and Particular Baptist origins. Gadsby pioneered a group of churches, but it was not the only grouping of Strict and Particular Baptists. Stevens became the theological mentor and encourager of a group of churches whose base was in London and the Eastern Counties, but which had connections throughout England. This network of churches developed an ethos quite distinct from that of Gadsby's followers on the one hand, and from the largest group of Particular Baptists on the other. While Stevens and his friends opposed Fullerism as much as Gadsby did, they differed from Gadsby on the nature of the law and so aligned them-

---

[1] Ivimey, *HEB*, vol. 4, pp. 385–6, referred to the success of Stevens's pastorate in London, but makes no reference to his wider significance.

selves with mainstream Calvinist thinking on this issue. They also felt a strong sense of evangelistic responsibility, which was not found in the same measure among the followers of Gadsby.

1. Religious Development

John Stevens was born in 1776 into a humble home at Aldwinckle, Northamptonshire, where his father was the village shoemaker.[2] Although he was a bright boy, his parents could afford to give him only a very limited education. The village of Aldwinckle was divided into two parishes at this time. From 1764, the rector of All Saints was Thomas Haweis, a noted Evangelical. After 1774, the tremendously energetic Haweis combined his duties at Aldwinckle with itinerant preaching in his capacity as a chaplain to the Countess of Huntingdon. Later, he became one of the founders of the London Missionary Society.[3] At Aldwinckle he turned a neglected parish into an Evangelical stronghold, drawing hearers from a radius of twenty miles.[4] Haweis, the powerful evangelist, was a strict Calvinist and was also utterly opposed to any form of Antinomianism. He was a loyal Anglican and was sorely tried when the Countess of Huntingdon's Connexion broke with the Church of England in the 1780s. The strength of his evangelistic passion eventually overcame his Anglican scruples, and after a short break he continued to serve the Connexion while continuing in his parish duties at Aldwinckle.

At Aldwinckle, 'not only individuals, but whole families were converted under Haweis' ministry'.[5] It was under this preaching that John Stevens was converted as a teenager.[6] At first, Stevens quite naturally accepted the Evangelical Anglican Calvinism of Haweis.

[2] Anon, *Memoirs of Mr John Stevens*, London, 1848, p. 2. Hereinafter referred to as *Stevens's Memoirs*. These Memoirs were published by Stevens's church shortly after his death and, although unduly fulsome, contain important letters and diary extracts.

[3] For details of Haweis see A. Skevington Wood, *Thomas Haweis, 1734–1820*, London, 1957. See also Faith Cook, *Selina, Countess of Huntingdon*, Edinburgh: Banner of Truth, 2001.

[4] Skevington Wood, *Thomas Haweis*, p. 112.   [5] Ibid., p. 113.

[6] John Stevens, 'Birthday Observations on the Age of Man', *Gospel Herald*, vol .14, 1846, pp. 300–4. *Stevens's Memoirs*, p. 4.

This was soon challenged, however. As a young shoemaker he was sent to London to improve his trade, and there for the first time he came into contact with Dissenters. Always ready for a debate, Stevens 'imagined that it would be a perfectly easy matter to set these mistaken people right'.[7] In the event, it was the young Stevens who succumbed, and this was to be the first of his important theological adjustments. He began to attend the ministry of Richard Burnham at Edward Street (sometimes known as Berwick Street) Baptist Chapel, Soho, and it was in this Chapel that he was subsequently baptized. Burnham was a product of the Evangelical Revival. He had been converted through the preaching of Wesleyan Methodists but subsequently became a Particular Baptist. At this stage, Burnham was an Evangelical Calvinist, although he afterwards adopted Hyper-Calvinism. On account of an earlier moral lapse, the other London Particular Baptist pastors, most of whom enjoyed fellowship together in the Baptist Board, shunned him. Burnham nevertheless retained a considerable following.[8] Stevens thus began his life as a Baptist in an isolated church, and this may have been a factor in his readiness to work alone until he built up a group of sympathetic colleagues later.

Soon after his baptism, Stevens began to preach. After an initial failure in this exercise, Burnham encouraged him to try again, and in 1795 the Grafton Street Church formally approved his preaching. It was already clear that Stevens was an unusual character. According to Stevens's biographer, Burnham declared, 'He will prove a peculiar preacher to a peculiar people, but into my pulpit, he shall never enter while I live.'[9]

[7] *Stevens's Memoirs*, p. 6.

[8] For details of Burnham see T. Wright, *Richard Burnham,* London, n.d. and E. A. Payne, 'An Elegy on Andrew Gifford', *Baptist Quarterly*, vol 9, 1938-9. Payne mistakenly supposed that Burnham was a Hyper-Calvinist at this stage. Burnham's evangelical Calvinism is made clear in his pamphlet, *A Scriptural Address to Sinners,* London, n.d. Although the pamphlet is not dated, it must have been written before 1795 as Burnham is described as minister of Berwick Street Chapel, Soho, the address of his church from 1789 to 1795, when it moved to Grafton Street. Berwick Street Chapel is sometimes described as Edward Street. W. Wilson, *London Dissenting Churches*, vol.4, p. 27. For Burnham's change of views, see below, p. 218.

[9] *Stevens's Memoirs*, p. 7.

Burnham, it seems, was commenting on Stevens' personal eccentricities, for at this stage there is no suggestion of a doctrinal divergence between the two men.

Soon Stevens returned to Aldwinckle from London. After preaching in his grandfather's house, he embarked on a vigorous programme of village evangelism. He proved popular, and a number of people traced their conversions to his preaching. Thomas Haweis heard him preach and offered to secure him training for service in the Countess of Huntingdon's Connexion, on condition he would renounce his Baptist principles; but this he refused to do. Of this time in his life Stevens later declared:

> When I first began to speak, I was a sad blunderer, but I sometimes think that a greater blessing attended my blundering, than has since marked my more orderly attempts in the work of the ministry.[10]

Since a great change in his thinking was about to take place, it is likely that Stevens was referring to what he later considered to be his doctrinal blunders as well as his lack of experience in the pulpit.

2. Hyper-Calvinism

John Stevens's itinerant evangelism brought him into contact with a small group at Oundle, four miles north of Aldwinckle. He accepted an invitation to minister regularly to these believers. This he did for two years, from 1797 to 1799. He began his ministry accepting, in broad outline at least, the teaching of Andrew Fuller on the preaching of the gospel, indiscriminately calling upon all his hearers to repent and believe in Christ.[11] This policy would also have reflected the teaching of Thomas Haweis, and Richard Burnham at the time when Stevens had joined the latter's church. However, while at Oundle his views changed. Here Stevens made the acquaintance of John Whitmee, pastor of the neighbouring Particular Baptist Church at Great Gidding. Whitmee remained an obscure village pastor, but Stevens always acknowledged the debt he owed to him. It was Whitmee who introduced Stevens to the non-offer teaching of Gill and Brine.[12]

[10] Ibid., p. 8.   [11] Ibid., pp. ss10, 11.   [12] Ibid., p. 12.

John Whitmee had been pastor at Great Gidding since 1789. Earlier he had been a member of the Baptist Church at Steventon, Bedfordshire, where Joseph Clayton was the pastor from 1751 to 1790. Clayton had been a close friend and admirer of Gill, whom he had visited frequently.[13] Whitmee, who had been nurtured in the Gill tradition, was a resolute opponent of Andrew Fuller's growing influence in Northamptonshire and the surrounding counties. As a result of his reading, and under the influence of Whitmee, Stevens ceased to call upon unregenerate men to repent and believe the gospel. For the rest of his life he was to oppose Fuller's teaching vigorously. He published his new views in 1803 under the title, *A Help for the True Disciples of Immanuel*.[14] Stevens's work was a response to the second edition of Fuller's *The Gospel Worthy of All Acceptation*, which had appeared in 1801. Interestingly however, Stevens's Hyper-Calvinism had not dampened his enthusiasm for evangelism. In 1799 he left Oundle for St Neots, Huntingdonshire, where he pioneered a new work. A church was formed in 1800 and by 1805 this had grown from thirteen to seventy-three members.[15]

THEOLOGICAL DISTINCTIVES

Stevens's *Help* was his most significant work and arguably the most important nineteenth-century Baptist defence of Hyper-Calvinism. In 1814 he added a second part to the work, consisting of an examination of the texts used by Andrew Fuller in defence of his thesis. Stevens revised and enlarged the whole work in 1829.[16]

Stevens was conscious of his isolation. He explained that 'the author of the ensuing pages is neither a Calvinist, an Arminian, nor a Baxterian, yet

---

[13] J. Rippon, *Baptist Register*, vol.1. 1793, p. 494. Whitmee is mistakenly described as Whitnee. Corrected in index.

[14] J. Stevens, *Help for the True Disciple of Immanuel: being an answer to a book published by the Rev. Andrew Fuller, entitled The Gospel Worthy of All Acceptation; or the Duty of Sinners to Believe in Christ*, London, 1803. Hereinafter referred to as Stevens's *Help*. References are to the first edition, except where otherwise indicated.

[15] Stevens's *Memoirs*, pp. 12,13. W. Palmer, *A Brief Memoir of the late Mr George Murrell, for Fifty eight years Pastor of the Particular Baptist Church at St Neots, Huntingdonshire*, London, 1871, pp. 22, 23.

[16] Stevens's *Memoirs*, p. 14. *Help*, 2nd. ed., 1829, p. iv.

he believes many things in common with them all'.[17] It is difficult to imagine such a statement from Gill or Brine, who saw themselves as refiners and developers of Calvinism, and to whom Arminianism was anathema. Although he quoted with approval such eighteenth-century Hyper-Calvinists as Lewis Wayman,[18] John Brine,[19] and John Gill,[20] Stevens was not so anxious to identify himself with this or any other single tradition. In the first edition of his *Help*, he wrote: 'I have never read a page of Calvin's writings.'[21] Concerning the subject of gospel presentation, he was not afraid to disagree openly with such robust Puritan Calvinists as Elisha Coles[22] and John Owen.[23] He considered Fuller's teaching to be a dangerous concession to Arminianism. Of the period following the publication of *The Gospel Worthy of All Acceptation* he wrote:

> Arminianism has been making its unsuspected progress among the churches, both of the Independents and the Baptists; until the difference between them and the Methodists is now scarcely perceptible, as to the matter and scope of their ministrations.[24]

The structure of the *Help* was determined by its polemical and negative purpose. Stevens did not set out to produce a systematic theology or even a treatise on soteriology. Nevertheless it can be used to help establish the details of Stevens's position. He wanted to show the inconsistency of Fuller's system;[25] in marked contrast, he claimed that 'it is an indubitable fact, that truth is evermore consistent with itself'.[26] Arguing logically from the Calvinist doctrine of salvation he presented a robust theological system, which found acceptance with those Christians who were more concerned with clear-cut dogma than the detailed minutiae of scriptural exegesis.

---

[17] J. Stevens, *Help*, 2nd. ed., p. 1.
[18] Ibid., pp. 1-6. Lewis Wayman, an Independent minister from Kimbolton was the author of *An Inquiry after Truth*, 1735, a contribution to the 'Modern Controversy', opposing universal invitations. [19] Ibid., pp. 176. [20] Ibid., Part II, pp. 3, 28, 148.
[21] Ibid., p. 214. [22] Ibid., p. 190, 191. [23] Ibid., pp. 192-7.
[24] Ibid., 2nd. ed, p. v. [25] Ibid., p. viii.
[26] J. Stevens, *A New Selection of Hymns, including also Several Original Hymns Never Before Offered to the Public*, Boston, n.d., p. Iii.

OBLIGATION

John Stevens was careful to avoid any suggestion that the unbeliever was free from all sense of responsibility. He wrote of mankind in general being like Adam under the 'Law of Works'.[27] Adam, he insisted, had no need of a Saviour, and was not obliged, therefore, to believe in Christ as Saviour.[28] More cannot justly be demanded from fallen man than was required from unfallen man.[29] Fallen man would, therefore, be punished for breaking the law, not for failing to believe the gospel.[30] The law must be preached to him, although any suggestion that he could keep it must be avoided. It should be preached '*exegetically* for the maintenance of the rights of God his Maker, and to show forth the guiltiness of man; but to insist on this obligation *exhortatively*, would be *absurd*'.[31] He explained the absurdity of making general exhortations by stating his views on obligation.

> Man is so under an obligation to obey the law as to be liable to certain destruction for aught he can do to prevent it; but I do not believe that this supposes it to be right to exhort him to keep the law perfectly, and much less to be that which nothing but electing grace can make him. Nor do I believe that such an idea needs to be insisted on in preaching, in order to convince our hearers of sin. Such a preaching can neither be called Law nor Gospel with any propriety.[32]

THE WARRANT OF FAITH

Closely related to the question of obligation is that of the warrant of faith or sinful man's authority for believing in Christ as his Saviour. Both Andrew Fuller and Abraham Booth had argued that the gospel message itself provided an objective warrant for faith, and as such was sufficient to authorize any hearer to trust in Christ.[33] John Stevens, on the other hand,

---

[27] J. Stevens, *Help*, pp. 74, 75.   [28] Ibid., pp. 107, 8.
[29] 'It cannot be proved that men increase their guiltiness by not giving themselves special faith in Christ.' Ibid., Part 2, p. 125.
[30] Ibid., Part 2, p. 4.   [31] Ibid., Part 2, p. 4.
[32] Ibid., p. 74.
[33] For the views of Fuller, Booth, and Thomas Scott on this issue, see pp. 151-6 above.

insisted that only those who were conscious of spiritual need were entitled to believe in Christ as their Saviour. Consequently, faith was only operative as a response to the sinner's consciousness of the Holy Spirit at work within him. Stevens appealed to the fact that the gospel addresses itself to the weary, the hungry, and the thirsty; such descriptions he took to be references to conscious spiritual need.[34] Thus, the warrant of faith was in part subjective.

> Special faith in its actings doth not terminate on Christ as he is revealed in the Scriptures merely, but as he is shown to the mind by the Holy Ghost.[35]

This statement stands in stark contrast to that of Fuller:

> The Scriptures always represent faith as terminating on something without us; namely on Christ, and the truth concerning him.[36]

SAVING FAITH

Differences concerning the warrant of faith led to different understandings of the nature of faith itself. Fuller quoted with approval the statement of John Owen:

> When God calleth upon men to believe, he doth not in the first place, call upon them to believe that Christ died for them; but 'that there is none other name under heaven given among men, whereby we must be saved', but only of Jesus Christ through whom salvation is preached.[37]

Whereas Fuller taught that faith was the sinner believing on Christ *in order to be saved*, Stevens argued that faith was a matter of believing *that one had been saved*. In connection with the initial operation of saving faith he asked:

> Does not the weakest believer feel some degree of persuasion that Christ hath loved him and given himself for him? If not, how can he be said to have a good hope through grace.[38]

[34] J. Stevens, *Help*, p. 63.   [35] Ibid., p. 20.
[36] A. Fuller, *Works*, p. 153.
[37] Quoted, ibid., p. 171.
[38] J. Stevens, *Help*, p. 6.

He quoted with approval the definition of faith by Lewis Wayman:

> Faith as an act, is believing upon an inwrought persuasion, a persuasion upon an inwrought knowledge, being led by the Spirit into the truth.[39]

The Gospel

Stevens was aware that his conception of the gospel was not that of the strict Calvinism of Andrew Fuller, much less of the more moderate Calvinism which emerged after Fuller.[40] He defined the gospel as

> that form of inspired doctrine, by which God is revealed as strictly just, and sovereignly gracious, in saving the people of his choice for ever from sin and hell, to endless glory, through Jesus Christ.[41]

It will be noticed that he saw the gospel as being strictly doctrinal and that his definition includes no hint of exhortation or invitation. He went on to assert:

> We do not speak to the carnal of their ability, but of their weakness; we rather declare what they cannot do than what they can do.[42]

> We do not address sinners as though their eternal destiny were in their own hands, because we know it is in the hand of God.[43]

The Impact of Stevens's Help

Andrew Fuller made no response to Stevens's *Help*. He may well have felt that he had already written enough against Hyper-Calvinism. When the *Help* first appeared, Fuller was already involved in his dispute with Abraham Booth.[44] Although both Booth and Stevens were concerned because they considered that Fuller had compromised his Calvinism, their positions were by no means similar. Booth had championed the objective warrant of faith in his *Glad Tidings to Perishing Sinners*, whereas Stevens wrote against it. Both Booth and Stevens believed that

---

[39] Ibid., p. 2. For details of Wayman's theology see P. Toon, *Hyper-Calvinism*, pp 95, 96, 104ff., 119ff.
[40] J. Stevens, *Help*, 2nd. ed., p. 68.   [41] Ibid., 2nd. ed., pp. 68, 69.
[42] Ibid., 2nd. ed., p. 369.   [43] Ibid., 2nd. ed., p. 370, cf. pp. 175, 176.
[44] See chapter 8 above.

Fuller had weakened in his teaching on particular redemption and substitution. Stevens, however, went beyond Booth in his insistence that a literal debt had been paid in the atoning work of Christ.

> Therefore if we suppose anyone to stand in the place of one lost sinner, we are not in so doing, to imagine, that such a substitute must, on that account, suffer as much as though he represented all lost sinners. The greater the guilt, the greater the punishment: the greater the number of sinners, the greater the measure of guilt. It must therefore follow that, if more sinners had been saved, the sorrows of the Saviour must have been proportionally increased.[45]

Stevens's view of the atonement has been called the commercial view and has remained a part of the Hyper-Calvinist creed.[46] Like Stevens, Booth was unhappy with Fuller's argument that the atonement was limited by its application and not by its essential nature, but unlike Stevens, he was unwilling to push his logic to the point of alleging that the sufferings of Christ were proportionate to the number of the elect. In the years that were to follow, Booth's views on the nature of the atonement seem to have been increasingly disregarded by Particular Baptists, who polarized behind the positions of Fuller and Stevens.

Stevens's view did not go unnoticed in wider Evangelical Calvinistic circles. Fuller's one-time friend and biographer, J. W. Morris, wrote scathingly of Stevens, whom he described as the 'principal advocate' of Hyper-Calvinism. After suggesting that he was scarcely literate, he went on to assert that 'in hardiness of assertion, and in bold defiance of every principle of religion and morality, this man out-herods even Herod himself.' Speaking generally about Hyper-Calvinists, he declared them to be 'a set of illiterate Antinomians', and that 'the system itself is retiring into the back settlements, drawing with it the refuse of Christian society.'[47]

---

[45] J. Stevens, *Help*, 2nd. ed., p. 181.

[46] W. J. Styles, *A Manual of Faith and Practice*, 2nd ed., London, 1897, pp. 43–9. Styles, a leading High Calvinist at the end of the nineteenth century, appealed to W. Palmer (1799–1873) and John Hazelton (1822–88) as well as to Stevens as prominent teachers of the commercial view of the atonement.

[47] J. W. Morris, *Memoirs of the Life and Writings of the late Rev. Andrew Fuller*, London, 1816, pp. 305–8. Morris, successively pastor at Clipstone and Dunstable,

Morris's intemperate statements appeared after Fuller's death and thirteen years after the first appearance of Stevens' *Help*. By that time Stevens was pastor of a flourishing London church and was beginning to build up a considerable body of support in the country. His growing popularity contrasted with that of Fuller's earlier critics.[48] The strength of Morris's abuse may suggest some degree of alarm at the spread of Stevens's views.

3. The Antinomian Controversy

William Gadsby's pamphlet skirmish with John Stevens on the issue of the moral law has already been referred to in a previous chapter.[49] The issue of the place of the law in the life of a believer occupied a much greater place in Gadsby's thinking than in Stevens's. Stevens entered the controversy for pastoral reasons and without any initial intention of engaging with Gadsby on the matter.

From 1805 to 1811, John Stevens was pastor of the Walnut Tree Pastures Baptist Church, Boston, Lincolnshire, and was also exercising a wide itinerant ministry in the Eastern Counties of England. During this time, his biographer noted, 'the principles and tenets of the celebrated Mr Huntington were making considerable advance in some of the churches, and especially in those parts of Lincolnshire where Mr Stevens was called to labour in the gospel'.[50] Huntington had long been preaching at Grantham and more recently at Downham in the Isle of Ely; in both places he had loyal followers.[51] Although Stevens and Huntington were

---

was a friend of Fuller until around 1809 when they disagreed over Morris's extravagances, see Fuller's *Letters* for 1809 and Morris's Preface to Fuller's *Memoirs*, p. viii. Morris retained an admiration for Fuller although he was critical of his inflexibility. Morris's reference to Stevens and his associates as Antinomian was unjust as Stevens had already written against Antinomianism.

[48] William Button's church at Dean Street, Southwark, never was a prominent church. John Martin was an isolated figure for political reasons after 1798. Stevens on the other hand had outgrown Grafton Street Chapel by 1813 and moved to a large and prominent chapel in York Street, St James's. Details are given below.

[49] See above, p. 186.
[50] *Stevens's Memoirs*, p. 22.
[51] T. Wright, *Life of W. Huntington*, pp. 116, 7.

John Stevens

both Hyper-Calvinists, Stevens came from a tradition which rejected doctrinal Antinomianism. Both Thomas Haweis and Richard Burnham opposed it, and it was certainly alien to the teaching of Gill, which Stevens had embraced more recently.[52] He responded to Huntington's influence, therefore, by publishing *Doctrinal Antinomianism Refuted*[53] in 1809. An enlarged edition appeared in 1811, around the time he moved to his pastorate in London. At that time Huntington's Chapel was being rebuilt and a number of his hearers began to attend Stevens's Grafton Street Chapel, but Stevens' teaching on 'the obligatory nature of the irrepealable law of God soon induced them to quit'.[54]

Stevens defined his position clearly:

> By the Antinomians, it is asserted that the believer is under the authority of the law, 'in no sense whatever'. This I deny; this sentiment I detest, and deem it prudent and best not to cultivate needless intimacy with its abettors. The reader therefore will observe, that the debate is not about what produces holiness, but concerning the law that requires it; not about that influence which excites and enables a saint to obey, but about the law which makes certain acts of obedience to be his duty, and the omission of them to be sin.[55]

It was not Huntington, but Gadsby, who replied to Stevens in *'Doctrinal Antinomianism Refuted' Entangled in Its Own Maze*.[56] A element of confusion had arisen because, although Stevens had directed his fire against Huntington, Gadsby felt that he was being attacked, even though he had not been referred to by name. He also felt that he was being saddled with opinions he did not accept. He asked:

> Where is the man to be found, who denies the will of God in Christ Jesus, as being the Christian's rule and perfect rule too?[57]

---

[52] Skevington Wood, *Thomas Haweis*, p. 123; R. Burnham, *A Letter to a Friend on the Law of God,* London, 1800.

[53] J. Stevens, *Doctrinal Antinomianism Refuted* [Boston, 1809], 2nd ed., London, 1811.

[54] *Stevens's Memoirs*, p. 41.

[55] *Doctrinal Antinomianism Refuted*, 2nd ed., p. v.

[56] W. Gadsby, *Works*, vol. 1, London, 1851, pp. 223 ff. [57] Ibid., p. 241.

In reply, Stevens wrote:

> He professes to be 'ignorant that any man ever denied that the will of God in Christ was the Christian's rule'. I know that it has ever been part of the creed of Huntingtonians, that spiritual men are only under the law of inward love; and some have declared boldly that they did not do things because God commanded them, but because they felt the love of God in their hearts constraining them.[58]

It is likely that Stevens had encountered a form of Antinomianism in the Eastern Counties that had gone beyond Huntingtonianism.

In his second edition, Stevens seems to have made a distinction between Gadsby and Huntington. He also made it clear that he did not regard Gadsby as a very significant opponent:

> I kept in view the writings and followers of Mr Huntington. But they mostly pleaded for an inward law; and very rarely spoke of any commands, as being in any way binding on spiritual men. Mr G. in supposing that I chiefly levelled my observations at him, was very much misguided; my eye was fixed on the head officer, and my attention to Mr G. only a secondary consideration. My ambition, was, not to engage myself in the herring fishery; but if possible to take a whale.[59]

Like so many of his contemporaries, John Stevens saw the popularity of Huntington's teaching as a serious threat to morality. Although Gadsby considered his own views to be similar to Huntington's, they do not appear to have been so extreme. Stevens's reply to Gadsby gives the impression that the two men were differing about terms, since what Stevens called the 'law', Gadsby called the 'gospel'. Significantly, in a funeral sermon for Stevens, John Foreman recalled an occasion, when Stevens and Gadsby preached together at Ipswich:

> Mr Stevens said, 'All I contend for is the preceptive will as the rule of life.' Mr Gadsby declared. 'That is what I believe.' I said. 'There, if you chuse [sic] to call the same thing by different names, what is the use of your quarrelling about it?'[60]

---

[58] J. Stevens, *Doctrinal Antinomianism Refuted*, 2nd ed., p 112.   [59] Ibid.
[60] J. Foreman, *Funeral Sermon for Mr John Stevens*, London, 1847, p. 22.

Interestingly, Stevens's *Doctrinal Antinomianism Refuted* received a warm review in the *Baptist Magazine*, a monthly journal which represented the evangelical Calvinism more usually associated with Fuller and his friends.[61] A year later, when Stevens was defending his work against criticism in the *Gospel Magazine* (which was more sympathetic to Huntington), the *Baptist Magazine* sprang to the defence of Stevens, referring to his 'masterly performance'.[62] Huntington's controversies with the Particular Baptist leaders have already been considered, as has Fuller's anxiety over the spread of Antinomianism among the churches during the last decade of his life. Therefore, Stevens would seem to have been a welcome ally for the more moderate men in spite of his known opposition to Fuller's teaching. But Fullerism was too big an obstacle for close co-operation on Stevens's part and, unlike an older generation of Hyper-Calvinists, he remained separate from the mainstream. Stevens's attitude towards the law was to make co-operation with Gadsby and his associates difficult, and helps to explain why he and his followers emerged as a distinct party.

4. Christology

Soon after his arrival in London in 1811, John Stevens became involved in a controversy which was to reverberate throughout the rest of his life. He taught the doctrine of the Trinity, but denied that the second Person is eternally 'the Son of God'. Christ's sonship, he argued, related to his humanity and not to his divine nature. To this view he had added the doctrine known as pre-existarianism. This teaches that Christ's human soul was formed before the foundation of the world, so that references to Christ as Son before his incarnation refer to his humanity, or what Stevens called his 'complex person'. He declared:

> I hope I have made it appear, therefore, that I can resign the doctrine of eternal generation, and yet retain that of the eternal Trinity in essential unity; and that I also maintain the eternity of the Son of God, while I am likewise anxious to defend the doctrine of his pre-existence as the Man.[63]

[61] *The Baptist Magazine*, vol. 2, 1810, p. 618 f.
[62] Ibid., vol. 3, 1811, p. 119.
[63] J. Stevens, *A Scriptural Display of the Triune God*, London, 1813, p. 212.

There were two issues here. First, Stevens was teaching that the second Person in the Trinity, the Logos, is eternal and co-equal with the Father and the Holy Spirit, but that he assumed the office of Son of God in his incarnation to enable him to discharge his work as Mediator. He thereby denied the eternal Sonship of Christ or his eternal generation. Secondly, he argued that Christ's human soul predated his incarnation, a teaching known as *pre-existarianism*. The most famous proponent of pre-existarianism in the eighteenth century had been the Independent divine, Isaac Watts. Watts expounded the theory as a mediatory doctrine between Arianism and orthodoxy. It seems to have been introduced into Particular Baptist circles by John Allen, pastor of the Petticoat Lane Church, London, 1764-7. For Allen the doctrine provided a rational way of explaining the two natures of Christ. Allen was strongly opposed by Gill. Although pre-existarianism continued to be held in certain quarters, it was resisted by the leading ministers of the London Baptist Board, and by the end of the eighteenth century was no longer held by any members of that society.[64]

For some Hyper-Calvinists it seemed to offer a rational way of reconciling seeming contradictions in Christian doctrine. It was only after Stevens had embraced Hyper-Calvinism that he turned to pre-existarianism, and in so doing he further separated himself from orthodox Calvinists, as well as from Gadsby and his friends. It can be established that Stevens reached this position some time between 1808 and 1811. He informed W. H. Collyer, one of his critics, that he had not been a pre-existarian in 1808.[65] However, by the time he was considered for the pastorate at Grafton Street in 1811, it was apparent his views had changed.

> Some of the people, who on first hearing him, gave him a cordial reception, soon took alarm at the views he entertained of the person of Christ, as the anciently begotten Son of the Father; and suspecting the soundness of his faith in the great doctrine of the Trinity, henceforth erected a somewhat formidable opposition to his settlement.[66]

[64] P. Toon, 'The Growth of a Superlapsarian Christology', *Evangelical Quarterly*, vol. 29, 1967, pp. 24-9.
[65] *Stevens's Memoirs*, p. 80.   [66] Ibid., p. 26.

Stevens felt the need to expound and defend his beliefs. He knew that some pre-existarians denied the divinity of Christ. He was anxious to make it clear that he was a Trinitarian. Initially he produced a popular pamphlet in 1812, entitled *Verses on the Sonship and Pre-Existence of Jesus Christ*.[67] This was followed a year later by his major work on the subject, *A Scriptural Display of the Triune God and the Early Existence of Jesus's Human Soul*.[68] He argued that his teaching was more consistent with the divinity of Christ than the orthodox view, which he described as 'the scholastic doctrine of eternal generation'.[69] He wrote:

> The ideas of Christ, as a divine person, being begotten, brought forth, brought up, and the like are evidently at war with the doctrine of his self-existence, independence, and eternity.[70]

Discussing the names, Father, Son, and Holy Spirit, he wrote:

> Some good men have imagined them to have been founded in the very nature of God, and have spoken of paternity, filiation and spiration in divine nature. They speak of one divine person begetting another, and a third proceeding from the other two, and thus account for the names Father, Son and Spirit. But the ideas of begetting, or being begotten, and proceeding, are no way harmonious with the thoughts we are bound to entertain of the everlasting God. If Christ be in the highest existence a begotten Person, he cannot be personally self-existent and eternal. For if that which is produced or brought forth may nevertheless be as properly eternal as any other existence, then the distinction between self-existence and derived existence; infinite and finite; time and eternity, must be resigned. And as to the procession of the Holy Ghost, the scriptures are altogether silent about it; and what little is said conveys no information to the mind of the hearer or reader. Besides there is as much reason to speak of the person of Christ proceeding as there is to speak of the Holy Ghost.[71]

As earlier a desire to exalt the sovereignty of God had led Stevens to deny human responsibility, so now a concern to safeguard the equality

---

[67] J. Stevens, *Verses on the Sonship and Pre-existence of Jesus Christ*, London, 1812.
[68] J. Stevens, *A Scriptural Display of the Triune God and the Early Existence of Jesus's Human Soul*, London, 1813.
[69] Ibid., p. vii.   [70] Ibid.   [71] Ibid., p. 27.

and eternity of each member of the Trinity led him to adopt his pre-existarian views and deny the eternal sonship of Christ. Thus a large section of *A Scriptural Display* is devoted to the doctrine of the Trinity and to the self-existence of each Person. From this position he moved on to criticize the doctrine of the eternal sonship of Christ. His logical arguments seemed to carry him very close to Tritheism. The Persons of the Godhead are presented as self-existent and not related. To deal with the scriptural evidence for Christ's sonship he adopted pre-existarianism. Discussing John 1:1-30 and 1 John 1:1-3, he wrote:

> Such language is by no means applicable to a divine person abstractly considered, nor yet to a person merely human. Not the latter, because it is expressly said, the WORD was God, and made all things in the beginning: not the former, because the Word is spoken of as being begotten, manifested, heard, seen, looked upon and handled.[72]

Discussing Colossians 1:14-18, he declared, 'Jehovah cannot be, in his own nature, abstractly viewed, the first born of the creatures.'[73]

The leaders of the early church endeavoured to relate biblical teaching on the unity of God and the distinctions between the Father, the Son, and the Holy Spirit in the Godhead. They needed to steer between two extreme errors – Modalism and Tritheism. Modalists taught that the three Persons were separate roles assumed by the one God in carrying out his divine purposes. Such a notion clearly fails to do justice to the scriptural teaching on the distinctions and relationships between the three Persons. Over against Modalism, Tritheists emphasised the distinction between the Persons to the point that the unity of the Godhead was lost. The teachings of orthodox Christianity have been succinctly expressed in the Nicene and Athanasian Creeds. By denying that Christ's Sonship belongs to his divine nature and is therefore eternal, Stevens and his associates had distorted the biblical teaching on the Person of Christ. The *1689 Baptist Confession,* by contrast, reflects the teaching of the Council of Nicæa, AD 325, stating:

[72] Ibid., p. 122.
[73] Ibid., p. 150.

In this divine and infinite Being there are three subsistences, the Father, the Word or Son, and Holy Spirit, of one substance, power and eternity, each having the whole divine essence, yet the essence undivided: the Father is of none, neither begotten nor proceeding; the Son is eternally begotten of the Father; the Holy Spirit proceeding from the Father and the Son; all infinite, without beginning, therefore but one God, who is not to be divided in nature or being, but distinguished by several peculiar relative properties, and personal relations.[74]

It is to be regretted that Hyper-Calvinistic logic in this area was applied to this subject without any serious consideration of the teaching of early Particular Baptists. This is further evidence that many were no longer seriously considering the *Confession of Faith*.

5. The London Pastorate

In 1811 John Stevens was called to the pastorate of the Particular Baptist Church in Grafton Street, London. Amongst this people he had been baptized nearly twenty years previously. He returned to London with his theological opinions finally settled and to a sphere in which he could expound those opinions to audiences potentially larger than his earlier congregations.

The influence of Hyper-Calvinism was in decline among the ministers of the London Baptist Board. William Button and John Martin, its old leaders, did not have large followings. Button's church was small and Martin was ostracized because of his indiscreet political statements. Most London Baptists rejected pre-existarianism.[75] These were the areas of disagreement between Stevens and so many of his Particular Baptist colleagues. As indicated above (see p. 202), Grafton Street had long been an isolated church. Stevens was ready to embrace that isolation, but with the intention of making his new pastoral charge a focus for a new movement.

---

[74] *1689 Confession*, II, 3.
[75] *Stevens's Memoirs*, p. 33. Keeble of Blandford Street (1798–1824) was also a pre-existarian but was an isolated figure and never a member of the Baptist Board.

Stevens's predecessor, Richard Burnham, had become a Hyper-Calvinist by 1805.[76] His views on some of the finer points of theology, however, did not go far enough for at least one of the members of the church. William Foxwell and Burnham disagreed over the spiritual state of Adam before the Fall and, in 1807, Foxwell published *A Letter to Mr R. B. on the Primitive State of Adam*. In a somewhat galling paragraph, he made mention of John Stevens:

> John Stevens's answer to Andrew Fuller: and though he is younger than you, it will be no dishonour to you to receive instruction from him, for remember 'Great men are not always wise: neither do the aged (because they are aged) understand judgement'. Job xxxvii. 9. And observe it is our mercy to receive instruction from anyone God is pleased to make use of for that purpose.[77]

Three years later, after Burnham's death, Stevens was eventually called to the vacant Grafton Street Church. Foxwell, who subsequently quarrelled with Stevens, claimed that he was instrumental in securing Stevens's call to the church.[78] Certainly unease over Stevens's views made a powerful ally within the congregation desirable. Stevens defective views on the Trinity were criticized.[79] The church had over 200 members, but only one hundred and thirty-six voted in favour of Stevens', while forty-one voted against.[80] The minority felt so strongly opposed to Stevens's

---

[76] R. Burnham, *A Sermon Proving that Believers Are the Only Proper Subjects of Baptism, with a few short remarks on the Mode. Likewise a Sermon Preached at the Ordination of Mr John Bateman*, London 1805. He rejected general exhortations to sinners to believe, 'Tell not sinners, while going on in their wickedness, that they are immediately called upon to believe and trust that Jesus Christ will save them: this is an unguarded way of speaking' (p. 62).

[77] W. Foxwell, *A Letter to Mr R. B. on the Primitive State of Adam*, London, 1807, p. 26.

[78] W. Foxwell, *A Check for Lordly Pastors*, London n.d. [1812], pp. 3, 12, 13. The Angus Library copy has the date 1812 pencilled in it. This is confirmed by internal evidence. There is reference to a church meeting held in January 1812. It was however written while the church still met in Grafton Street, from which it moved in 1813.

[79] *Stevens's Memoirs*, p. 26.   [80] Ibid., pp. 26, 27.

arrival that his installation as pastor of the church 'was immediately followed by the withdrawal of about eighty of the members'.[81]

The appointment of so singular a pastor, the loss of eighty members, and an influx of new members, must have brought about a significant change in the character of the church. According to Foxwell, who soon accused Stevens of building a personal following,[82] fifty new members were added in just seven months.[83] The *Memoirs* state that one hundred and two new members were added between July 1811 and August 1812.[84] No extant records indicate an expansion approaching this figure in any other Particular Baptist Church in London at this time.[85] Further confirmation of the church's prosperity comes from Walter Wilson, who declared in 1813: 'The congregation is in a flourishing state.'[86] Within the first six months of his pastorate, Stevens suggested the church should dispose of the Grafton Street Chapel. Foxwell opposed the move, but nevertheless complained of 'the pressure of the place, as it was at that time crowded to excess'.[87] In 1813 the church did leave Grafton Street and leased York Street Chapel, St James's. Wilson described this as 'a large, handsome square building'.[88] The *Memoirs* state that it too was crowded, although no indication of the building's seating capacity was given. For nine years Stevens witnessed 'a continually increasing church'.[89]

However, in 1822 the church's prosperity was shattered by dissension. The *Memoirs* refer to 'a serious contention with some of his deacons, and

[81] Ibid., p. 27.
[82] W. Foxwell, *A Check for Lordly Pastors*, p. 5.   [83] Ibid., p. 21.
[84] *Stevens's Memoirs*, p. 31.
[85] I am indebted to the Rev. Philip Roberts for drawing my attention to the membership numbers of London churches. He has tabulated annual membership fluctuations for the following nine London churches. Their additions for 1812 are recorded in brackets: Devonshire Square (3), Eagle Street (59), Keppel Street (37), Little Wild Street (16), Maze Pond (25), Prescot Street (nil), Unicorn Yard (7), Mare Street, Hackney (11), Old Ford, Bow (24).
[86] W. Wilson, *London Dissenting Churches*, vol. 4, p. 25.
[87] W. Foxwell, *A Check for Lordly Pastors*, p. 4. cf. p. 20.
[88] W. Wilson, London Dissenting Churches, vol. 4. p. 54. Ivimey, *HEB*, vol. 4, p. 385 mistakenly dated the move to York Street as 1803.
[89] *Stevens's Memoirs*, p. 54.

a considerable portion of his people'.[90] John Gadsby, a critic of Stevens, later wrote, 'In Dec. 1822, the church was broken up, the causes of which it would be uncharitable to mention.'[91] It seems most likely that the cause was a clash of personalities. Foxwell's earlier criticism suggests that Stevens was over-bearing.[92] A doctrinal clash would almost certainly have developed into a pamphlet war, of which there is no evidence. Any serious moral lapse could hardly have gone unnoticed by the opponents of Stevens and his church. In dealing with the issue the *Memoirs* refer to 'the unhallowed tempers of good men'. The breach must have been eventually healed because in 1836 Stevens was one of the preachers at the opening of Soho Chapel, Oxford Street, which at that time became the home of the group which had left his church.[93]

Stevens, who had lost over one hundred and thirty members,[94] re-formed his church in January 1823 with one hundred and sixty-three members.[95] Within a year this number had increased to two hundred and forty-two, some of whom were returning seceders.[96] According to Ivimey, Stevens now wanted a smaller and cheaper building with vestries and a baptistry. He and his congregation then proceeded to build Salem Chapel, Meard's Court, Soho, which was opened in September 1824.[97] Numbers continued to increase and galleries were added in 1827, increasing the seating capacity to one thousand.[98]

At Meard's Court, John Stevens continued his ministry until his death in 1847. Numbers continued to increase. Ivimey reported three hundred and fifty members in 1827;[99] Stevens recorded a figure of four hundred

[90] Ibid., p. 55.
[91] J. Gadsby, *Memoirs of Hymn Writers*, London, 1882, p. 120.
[92] W. Foxwell, *A Check for Lordly Pastors*, pp. 4, 5.
[93] *Gospel Herald*, vol. 3, 1836, p. 52. The seceders had met in Lisle Street until Soho Chapel was built.
[94] *Gospel Herald*, vol. 9, 1841, p. 153.
[95] *Stevens's Memoirs*, p. 65.
[96] Ibid., p. 61. *Gospel Herald*, vol. 9, 1841, pp. 153, 4.
[97] J. Ivimey, *HEB*, vol. 4, p. 385.
[98] *Stevens's Memoirs*, pp. 61, 64.
[99] J. Ivimey, *HEB*, vol. 4, p. 35.

and eight in a letter dated December 1836, and wrote that these were 'many more than in any former period, and for a strict communion baptized church is comparatively large'.[100] When Stevens died in 1847 there were about four hundred members.[101] By this time, however, it would appear that the congregation was an ageing community. In one of the many funeral sermons preached after Stevens's death, the Rev. G. Bayfield declared: 'His congregation was made up, for the most part, of aged saints of God, fathers in the church, and mothers in Israel, who had been accustomed to hear his voice for many years.'[102]

When John Stevens died in 1847, the *Baptist Magazine* referred to him as 'an eminently devout and holy man, as well as an able preacher.' It also stated:

> Some peculiarities of sentiment prevented Mr Stevens from taking an active part in our public institutions, or associating very generally with his ministerial brethren in the metropolis.[103]

Stevens's Memoirs provide some explanation of this isolation; in connection with his early ministry in London, we are informed that 'he was wont to assail the strongholds of error existing in the churches of the Baptist denomination'.[104] It is not surprising therefore to read that, 'most of the ministers of London evinced an unwillingness to recognise Mr. Stevens, which doubtless arose from the decided stand he had made against the prevailing influence of those sentiments considered by himself so inimical to the gospel of free grace'.[105] Clearly Stevens' Hyper-Calvinism was a barrier to close co-operation with other Baptist ministers. Writing to a friend in 1819, he explained why he could not support the Baptist Missionary Society:

> The public is agitated, but the truth is not preached! I fear many who talk of converting the heathen are not converted themselves: nor do I

---

[100] *Stevens's Memoirs*, p. 86.   [101] Ibid., p. 112.
[102] G. Bayfield, *Funeral Sermon for Mr John Stevens, preached at Bloomsbury Chapel, Commercial Road East, October 24th 1847*, London, 1847, p. 127.
[103] *Baptist Magazine*, vol 39, 1847, p. 714.
[104] *Stevens's Memoirs*, p. 31.   [105] Ibid., p. 33.

apprehend, they half of them believe the doctrines of distinguishing grace to be scriptural. Can we imagine the Holy Ghost will attend the labours of such men? I feel I am unable to mingle with the good folks.[106]

The Introductory Observations to the 1829 edition of Stevens's *Help* indicate that his sentiments remained constant.[107]

However, there is some indication that Stevens later modified his views on separation, though not Hyper-Calvinism. In an address delivered at Meard's Court he said:

> Much has often been urged, that in those who advocate the cause of missions, there is much error and folly; but if we stand still till everything can be done exactly right, death will come to prevent us from doing anything, and here I am quite unhorsed! But now with the word of God, we have full directions: – success has attended their efforts – now what have we to do? I have been sluggish all my life – I have walked apart, and thought myself excused, and now I have come to this; that the principles of truth are to be maintained, but (let us ask) what can we do in the cause of Christ without sacrificing our sentiments?[108]

The address is undated, but it appears to have been delivered towards the end of his life. It may be significant that in 1844 William Denham, a former member at Meard's Court, sailed for Serampore as a missionary with the Baptist Missionary Society. In 1846 the *Gospel Herald*, the monthly magazine of Stevens' associates, published a letter from Denham to Stevens, reporting his activities and progress.[109]

6. EVANGELISM

The eighteenth-century Hyper-Calvinists had shown little interest in evangelism. Even among churches representing more moderate Calvinist Old Dissent there was more concern for an ordered and edifying church

---

[106] Ibid., p. 51.
[107] J. Stevens, *Help*, 2nd ed., 1829, p. v.
[108] *Stevens's Memoirs*, p. 89.
[109] *Missionary Herald*, vol. 59, 1844, p. 272. *Gospel Herald*, vol. 14, 1846, pp. 14-17.

life than with missionary expansion.[110] John Stevens, however, was ready to accept the Evangelical Awakening's new emphases on evangelism and itinerant preaching. As a boy he had witnessed Thomas Haweis' widespread evangelistic endeavours in both parish and country. When Stevens first went to London, the Evangelical Awakening's influence could be seen among the Particular Baptist churches. Richard Burnham owed his conversion to the Wesleyan Methodists.[111]

That these examples of evangelistic enterprise affected Stevens can be seen in his programme of village preaching near Aldwinckle in the early days of his ministry. Although this was undertaken before he embraced Hyper-Calvinism, his change of sentiments does not appear to have quenched his evangelistic zeal. In each successive sphere, Oundle, St Neots, Boston, and London, he tasted considerable success as a church builder. While some of his following may have been drawn from existing congregations, it would be unfair to suggest that all were. He never confined his efforts to his own congregation. While at Boston he preached regularly in other parts of Lincolnshire, and once a month in the area around St Ives in Huntingdonshire. In 1806 he wrote 'I sometimes ride fifty miles a day.'[112]

After moving to London he made frequent preaching tours in the counties of Lincoln, Huntingdon, and Cambridge, where he had a considerable following.[113] He was also able to inspire others to similar efforts. Men from Meard's Court were prominent in forming the Home Missionary Society in Suffolk in 1831[114] and a similar society in Cambridge and Huntingdon in 1835.[115] The Cambridge men were Hyper-Calvinists, but

---

[110] W. T. Whitley, *Calvinism and Evangelism*, p. 27; B. L. Manning, 'Some Characteristics of the Older Dissent', passim.

[111] Wilson, *London Dissenters*, vol. 4, p. 26.

[112] *Stevens's Memoirs*, p. 21.

[113] Ibid., p. 69.

[114] Samuel Collins, Pastor of Grundisburgh, who promoted the Suffolk Society was previously a member of Stevens's London church, *Gospel Herald*, vol. 49, 1881, p. 345.

[115] David Irish of Warboys, who was active in this venture, had previously been a member of Stevens's church. *Gospel Herald*, vol. 3, 1836, p. 27.

resolved 'that this meeting acknowledging the subsisting harmony between appointed means and determined ends, do hereby form a society for diffusing more generally the knowledge of divine truth'.[116]

John Stevens's church took up an annual collection for these two societies. In a published sermon on behalf of the Society in 1841, Stevens stated:

> The Society for which I now plead is of a like faith and hope with ourselves. Its ministers have been successful, and it has been instrumental in doing much good in the villages ... our brethren are not spreading principles hostile to our own faith and denomination.[117]

Gadsby was also a great itinerant preacher and travelled the country more widely than Stevens. His writings and statements however do not indicate the sense of obligation to preach the gospel to the unchurched that is to be found in Stevens's. It is surely significant that it was amongst men in the Stevens' tradition that a Strict Baptist Missionary Society was formed later in 1861.

7. The Significance of John Stevens

There is no evidence suggesting that John Stevens set out to form a separate body of churches. This is understandable since he considered that the Fullerites had compromised with Arminianism and so betrayed the true Particular Baptist position which he wanted to safeguard. He was too powerful to stand alone for long. By attracting men of similar outlook and by training a succession of preachers from his own church, he began to influence a growing group of churches and ministers. His teaching on the law, although important, did not occupy a great deal of his energy. It did preserve some link with the mainstream of Particular Baptist life but also created a difference between Stevens and Gadsby and their associates. His Christology was a more serious matter and was to fuel bitter controversy after his death. This legacy was a heavy burden, which his group took years to shake off. Of greatest immediate significance was his evangelistic Hyper-Calvinism. A modern writer has described his *Help* as 'the

---

[116] Ibid.   [117] *Stevens's Memoirs*, p. 91.

largest effort against Fuller', and also of 'special significance to the Hyper-Calvinist tradition'.[118] Tributes to his influence in the nineteenth century abound. In Suffolk, Samuel Collins of Grundisburgh was prominent in the formation of a new Association built on Hyper-Calvinistic lines. The writer of Collins' obituary in 1881 wrote: 'No small measure of the drift and spirit of his own ministry may be traced to the profound, masterly and energetic teaching of that great and good man' [John Stevens].[119] Later W. J. Styles, perhaps the last of the great systematic apologists for Hyper-Calvinism, wrote that John Stevens's *Help* was 'masterly'.[120]

The strength of Stevens' leadership lay in his ability to wed high doctrine to the evangelistic preaching inherited from the Evangelical Awakening. His message and approach to the unbeliever differed from that of the great preachers in the early days of the Revival, but the readiness to make use of every evangelistic opportunity and the tireless itinerant preaching was the same. The same enthusiasm may be seen in many of his associates. One of his closest friends and his successor at St Neots was George Murrell, who was converted in the Countess of Huntingdon's Connexion and began to preach as a member of the Zion Chapel Itinerant Society. Zion Chapel, Whitechapel, London, was one of Thomas Haweis's regular preaching stations.[121] In London, John Foreman of Hill Street, was also a close associate of Stevens. When Foreman died, the *Daily News* described him as 'one of the heads of the Strict Baptist Denomination' and 'a renowned roadside preacher'. Another journal stated 'we can well believe that multitudes ascribe their conversion to his

---

[118] Curt D. Daniel, 'Hyper-Calvinism and John Gill', (Ph.D. thesis, University of Edinburgh 1983), pp. 378 and 25. For reasons indicated below, I cannot concur with Curt Daniel's verdict about Stevens's group: 'Its influence was small', p. 25.

[119] *Gospel Herald*, vol. 48, 1881, p. 257.

[120] W. J. Styles, *John Hazelton*, London, 1888, p. 148.

Examples of other tributes include: George Murrell in *Gospel Herald,* vol. 41, 1874, p. 41; R. Hoddy, *Memoir of Israel Atkinson*, London 1882, 'a father in Israel, and a prince among preachers', p. 25; James Jones, who was associated with the *Gospel Standard* party and disapproved of Stevens's pre-existarianism, wrote highly of him, see Anon, *A Brief Memoir of James Jones* (Shovers Green). Wadhurst, 1889, p. 45.

[121] W. Palmer, *Memoir of George Murrell*, pp. 7–13; *Stevens's Memoirs*, p. 9.

means'.[122] Another pastor, less close to Stevens, but in the same tradition, was James Wells, who formed a church from open-air preaching and was eventually in 1864 to build the biggest Strict Baptist Chapel in England.[123]

The growth and prestige of Stevens's church in London was an inspiration to lesser men. Hyper-Calvinism was not extinct in London, when Stevens arrived, but it was in serious decline. During his ministry new churches came into being, and older ones associated with him. The twenty or so men sent into the ministry by the Meard's Court church pastored several of these churches.[124]

Norfolk and Suffolk had long been resistant to Fuller's teaching and in these Eastern counties of England, Stevens' teaching fell on receptive ground. His teaching and influence were important factors in the division of the Old Norfolk and Suffolk Association in 1830. With the backing of the new Association, Samuel Collins launched the *Gospel Herald* magazine to champion the views of Stevens's party.[125]

According to Styles, 'the principles and practices of the Strict Baptists were extending rapidly in the Fen district' during the 1840s. He ascribed this, in good measure, to the writings of John Stevens and to preachers who were influenced by him. He describes how 'agricultural labourers would discuss points like "Pre-existarianism", "The law or the Gospel our rule of life" or "Whether Job's wife was a godly woman", on their way to work.'[126]

Stevens did not write much on strict communion, although he made it clear that he believed this to be scriptural, and considered open

---

[122] Quoted. *Earthen Vessel*, 28, 1872, pp. 86, 87.

[123] *Earthen Vessel*, 21, 1865, p. 309. R. W. Oliver, 'The Dangers of a Successful Ministry: The Life, Teaching and Influence of James Wells', *Bulletin of the Strict Baptist Historical Society*, No. 8, 1971.

[124] *Stevens's Memoirs*, p. 97. The development of Stevens's party is considered in chapters 12 and 14.

[125] See Collins's first editorial for his resolve to oppose Fullerism and Antinomianism, *Gospel Herald*, vol 1, 1833, pp. 2, 3.

[126] W. J. Styles, *John Hazelton*, p. 61.

communion to be a serious deviation.[127] His practice was akin to what had been the majority position among the eighteenth-century Particular Baptists, and to this he held tenaciously at a time when opinion was moving in the opposite direction. Thus to the old dissenting emphasis on church order he added the new emphasis on evangelism characteristic of the eighteenth-century Revival, and thereby helped to create a distinct body of churches that formed a unique element within nineteenth-century Nonconformity.

---

[127] To admit unbaptized persons to communion would be to allow of known disobedience and error in the church, and that with respect to a public institution plainly commanded', J. Stevens, *Thoughts on Sanctification and a Glance at Strict Communion, Being an Extract from Several Discourses delivered in York Street, St James*, London, 1816, p. 59.

1. John Gill (1697-1771)

2. The Baptist Chapel, Bourton-on-the-Water. Benjamin Beddome ministered in Bourton from 1741 to 1795.

3. The manse built for Benjamin Beddome, now the Old Manse Hotel, Bourton-on-the-Water.

4. John Collett Ryland, Sr. (1723-1792)

5. Robert Hall, Sr. (1728-1791)

6. Abraham Booth (1734-1806)

7. Robert Robinson (1735-1790)

8. Caleb Evans (1737-1791)

9. Andrew Fuller (1754-1815)

10. William Huntington (1745-1813)

11. John Ryland, Jr. (1753-1825)

12. John Thomas, Andrew Fuller, William Carey, William Ward, and Joshua Marshman, key figures in the fledgling Particular Baptist Missionary Society.

13. William Gadsby (1773-1844)

14. John Stevens (1776-1847)

15. Robert Hall Jr. (1764-1831)

16. Joseph Kinghorn (1766-1832)

17. John Warburton (1776-1857)

18. John Kershaw (1792-1870)

19. John Charles Philpot (1802-1869)

20. Joseph Ivimey (1773-1834)

21. James Wells (1803-1872)

The Surrey Tabernacle, built during James Wells' long ministry in Southwark, London.

22. C. H. Spurgeon (1834-1892)

PART THREE

REALIGNMENT

11

MOVES TOWARDS OPEN COMMUNION

Satan knows that nothing is more fit to lay waste to the kingdom of Christ than discord and disagreements among the faithful.

JOHN CALVIN

It is not the actual differences of Christian men that are the mischief; but the mismanagement of those differences.

PHILIP HENRY

I. AN UNEASY TRUCE

Until well into the 1830s most English Particular Baptist churches continued to practise strict communion just as they had done since the seventeenth century.[1] The vigorous debate of the 1770s came to an end when Abraham Booth's magisterial work, *An Apology for the Baptists*, published in 1778, settled the issue for many.[2] In their understanding of the terms of communion, Abraham Booth and Andrew Fuller were in agreement.[3] When the two outstanding Particular Baptist theologians

---

[1] R. Hall, *Works*, vol. 2, London, 1833, 'On Terms of Communion' [1815], pp. 16,17; Ivimey, *HEB*, vol. 3, 1823, p. viii; A. H. Macleod, 'The Life and Teaching of Robert Hall, 1764–1831', M. Litt. Thesis, University of Durham, 1957, p. 399. This thesis is the best modern treatment of Hall's life and teaching.

[2] See pp. 63-79 above.

[3] A. Fuller, *Works*, pp 853-9, 'Strictures on the Rev. John Carter's "Thoughts on Baptism and Mixed Communion"', n.d., 'Thoughts on Open Communion in a Letter to the Rev. W. Ward,' 1800, 'Strict Communion in the Mission Church at Serampore', 1814, 'The Admission of Unbaptized Persons to the Lord's Supper Inconsistent with the New Testament', 1815.

concurred, not surprisingly most of their co-religionists followed their lead. On this issue Booth and Fuller were supported by the Principals of the newer Baptist theological colleges, William Steadman of the northern college at Horton near Bradford and William Newman of Stepney.[4]

Booth maintained that there are powerful theological arguments in favour of strict communion, once the Baptist claim that the immersion of responsible believers is the only Christian baptism is conceded. He had also shown that when Baptists insisted on baptism prior to admission into church membership and participation in the communion service, they were only applying a principle long held in common by most Christians. While these arguments carried impressive weight, there is evidence to suggest that some Baptists were finding it increasingly difficult to maintain a practice which turned the Lord's table into a place of separation from their fellow-believers.

Alongside this long-continued practice of closed communion by the majority, there had always been a strong open-communion tradition among the Particular Baptists. Particular Baptists of both closed- and open-communion convictions had always considered themselves to belong to one 'denomination'. A number of able writers had promoted open-communion teaching. It had also received the powerful support of successive Presidents of the Bristol Baptist College, the denomination's only ministerial seminary until 1806. Since 1758, when Hugh Evans took office, successive Presidents had been open communionists.[5] Bristol students must have been faced with the issue during their college courses. One such was Joseph Kinghorn, who later championed the cause of strict communion against Robert Hall. However, his letters indicate a considerable period of indecision before he came to his final conclusions on the matter.[6]

---

[4] For the views of Steadman see Thomas Steadman, *Memoir of the Rev. William Steadman, D.D.*, London 1838, p. 473. For Newman's view, see pp. 233, 271 below.

[5] Ivimey, HEB, vol. 4, p. 281. For the views of Hugh Evans and Caleb Evans, his successor, see pp. 97, 99 above.

[6] M. H. Wilkin, *Joseph Kinghorn of Norwich*, Norwich, 1855, pp. 165, 197, 237.

Moves towards Open Communion

One consequence of the Evangelical Awakening was to reveal the great measure of gospel agreement that existed between Christians who held varying convictions on matters of church order. In 1778 Abraham Booth considered that the communion practices of the London Baptist churches were already feeling a certain amount of pressure from the closer fellowship generated by the Awakening.[7] The years that followed saw an intensifying of united Christian activity through the creation of inter-denominational missionary and philanthropic societies.[8] In 1824 Joseph Ivimey, a warm supporter of the Bible Society, warned his fellow Baptists that co-operation at its meetings could pose a danger for the unwary.[9]

As early as 1805, William Newman felt that the Baptists were being misrepresented and 'must act upon the defensive'. He therefore wrote a pamphlet entitled, *Baptism An Indispensable Pre-Requisite to Communion at the Lord's Table*. His description of his critics is vague, but his reference to those 'who clamorously denounce the conduct of the Baptists as unkind and uncharitable',[10] suggests that the attack was coming from outside the denomination. He acknowledged his dependence upon Booth's *Apology*,[11] and also received help from Booth personally, who was at that time nearing the end of his life.[12] Newman's work was a popular restatement of the case for strict communion and particularly benefited those

[7] p. 72-3 above.

[8] C. Buck, *The Close of the Eighteenth Century Improved: A Sermon preached at Prince's Street Chapel, Finsbury Square, Dec. 28th, 1800; in which the Most Remarkable Religious Events of the Past Hundred Years are Considered*, 2nd ed. London, 1816, pp. 39-41, lists a number of these.

[9] J. Ivimey, *Baptism, the Scriptural and Indispensable Qualification for Communion at the Lord's Table: or Considerations Designed to Expose the Erroneous Practice of Departing from the Original Constitution of the Christian Church, by Founding Open Communion Baptist Churches, Especially in those Neighbourhoods where Evangelical Congregational Churches Already Exist, Including Animadversions on the Preface of the Rev. Robert Hall's 'Reply' to the Rev. Joseph Kinghorn*, 1824, hereinafter referred to as *Baptism, the Indispensable Qualification*, pp. 70, 71. For Ivimey's support of the Bible Society see G. Pritchard, *Memoir of the Life and Writings of the Rev. Joseph Ivimey*, London 1835, p. 185.

[10] W. Newman, *Baptism An Indispensable Pre-Requisite to Communion at the Lord's Table*, London, 1805, p. 3.   [11] Ibid., p. 4.

[12] G. Pritchard, *Memoir of the Rev. William Newman*, p. 179.

[233]

not able to read Booth's larger work. It offered no new light on the matter in debate. Like Booth, Newman was irenical in spirit, and urged a charitable attitude towards opponents, although he was clearly stung by the suggestion that those who practised strict communion were bigots. He appealed to the Puritan, Philip Henry, who had insisted, 'It is not so much our difference of opinion that doth us the mischief, as the mismanagement of that difference.'[13]

Andrew Fuller, as Secretary of the Baptist Missionary Society and an extensive traveller among the Baptist churches of England, was well qualified to assess the state of Baptist thinking on most issues in the early years of the nineteenth century. A year or so before his death in 1815, he wrote a tract entitled, *The Admission of Unbaptized Persons to the Lord's Supper Inconsistent with the New Testament*.[14] In January 1815, he sent the manuscript to William Newman, stating:

> I have sent you a manuscript of my own, and I wish none to see it but yourself, and that no mention be made of it. If anything be written on the other side, it may, if thought proper, be printed, but not else.[15]

Newman stated that this tract was written in anticipation of a 'long expected publication of Mr Hall'.[16] Although Fuller pledged Newman to secrecy, Joseph Kinghorn, at least, knew of the work. He and Fuller met on four occasions during the last twelve months of the latter's life. He wrote that on one of these occasions

> the subject of communion was brought forward, when Mr Fuller said he had written a pamphlet upon it, which lay by him in manuscript. He was asked if he would publish it. He replied, 'No; it would throw our churches into a flame' – he evidently seemed to think that while they were at peace, it was not right to disturb them.[17]

---

[13] W. Newman, *Baptism An Indispensable Pre-Requisite*, pp. 19,22.
[14] Fuller, *Works*, pp. 855–9.
[15] Pritchard, *Memoir of Newman*, p. 250.   [16] Ibid.; O. Gregory, 'Memoir of Robert Hall', *Works of Robert Hall*. vol. 6, p. 102. Gregory states that among his friends for three or four years before the publication of *Terms of Communion*, Hall often 'advocated a cautious revision of the practice of nearly all the churches'.
[17] J. Kinghorn, *Arguments Against the Practice of Mixed Communion and in*

Kinghorn was allowed to read the manuscript 'on condition that it should not be shown to other persons'.[18] Andrew Fuller died on 7 May 1815. Later that year Robert Hall, Jr.'s momentous work appeared, *On Terms of Communion, with a Particular View to the Case of the Baptists and Paedobaptists*.[19]

2. ROBERT HALL'S *TERMS OF COMMUNION*

ROBERT HALL[20]

In 1815 Robert Hall was the pastor of Harvey Lane Chapel, Leicester. He was fifty-one years of age, and at the height of his intellectual and oratorical powers. He was the son of Robert Hall of Arnesby, the friend and counsellor of Andrew Fuller. From his childhood the younger Hall had battled with ill health, but this had never impeded his intellectual development. Before he was nine years old he had read Edwards' *Religious Affections* and also *The Freedom of the Will*. During part of his education, he spent two years in John Collett Ryland's boarding school. The fiery veteran terrified him, but the boy came to appreciate the old man's passion for religious and political liberty.[21] In 1778 his father baptized him at Arnesby, and later that year he entered the Bristol Baptist College at the tender age of fourteen.

After three years at Bristol, he received a scholarship to Aberdeen University, where he spent four years earning his Master of Arts degree, graduating in 1785. He returned to Bristol to be the Assistant Pastor at Broadmead Chapel and the Classics tutor at the College. His wit and

---

Support of Communion on the Plan of the Apostolic Church with Preliminary Observations on the Rev. Robert Hall's Reasons for Christian in Opposition to Party Communion, London and Norwich 1827, p. 23.   [18] Ibid.

[19] R. Hall, *Works*, vol. 2, pp. 1–174.

[20] Contemporary lives of Hall included O. Gregory, *A Brief Memoir of the Rev. Robert Hall, A.M.*, London, 1833; J. W. Morris, *Biographical Recollections of the Rev. Robert Hall, A.M.*, London, 1833; J. Greene, *Reminiscences of the Rev. Robert Hall, Late of Bristol*, London, 1832. A.H. Macleod, 'The Life and Teaching of Robert Hall, 1764–1831', M.Litt. Thesis, University of Durham, 1957, is a good modern treatment. Unless otherwise indicated, biographical details in this chapter are drawn from Gregory.   [21] Greene, *Reminiscences of Hall*, p. 94.

lively mind enthralled the students, but relations with his superior, Caleb Evans, were not easy.

In 1791, therefore, he accepted a call to the Cambridge Baptist Church, where he succeeded the mercurial Robert Robinson. Under Robinson, Cambridge had long been an open-communion church. Hall gathered a large congregation, which included members of the University, a remarkable achievement, when all Oxford and Cambridge students had to be members of the Church of England. He gained a reputation for outstanding oratory, incisive thought, and radical politics. His Cambridge pastorate ended in 1805 following two nervous breakdowns. He later insisted that he was not converted until the first of these.[22] His penetrating mind and powers of oratory seem to have caused him to make a premature profession of faith and quickly precipitated him into the Christian ministry. In his diary for 7 May 1784, Andrew Fuller noted, 'heard Mr Robert Hall, jun., from "He that increaseth knowledge increaseth sorrow." Felt very solemn in hearing some parts! The Lord keep that young man!'[23] Hall was just twenty years old at that time. He certainly indulged in wild theological speculations in the earlier years of his ministry, which caused James Bennett to write, 'his ministry began with splendid faults, and closed with distinguished excellence'.[24] After recovering his health, he seems to have demonstrated a genuine faith. From 1808 until 1826, he pastored the Harvey Lane Church in Leicester, before returning to Bristol to serve the Broadmead Church for the last five years of his life.

Robert Hall was an outstanding figure among the Baptists. He was considered one of the greatest orators in an age which took public speaking very seriously. At Leicester he gathered a large congregation made up of many from the working classes, as well as many who would not normally have entered a Baptist chapel. 'It was impossible to sneer at a sect with

---

[22] Steadman, *Memoir of W. Steadman*, p. 423. Gregory, *Memoir of Hall*, p. 83.

[23] A. Fuller, *Works*, p. xxxix.

[24] David Bogue and James Bennett, *History of the Dissenters*, vol. 3 [1839], repr. Tentmaker Publications, Stoke on Trent, 2001, p. 328. Bennett adds, 'To his want of real religion may be traced the early faults of his ministry, which were calculated to do immense injury to the church of God', p. 329.

Moves towards Open Communion

which such a man had deliberately chosen to identify himself.'[25] Primarily a preacher, Hall was also 'a pioneer in the development of education, penal reform, trade unionism and parliamentary reform.'[26] He also wrote a powerful defence of the freedom of the press. At Leicester, he appealed on behalf of the Frame Work Knitter's Fund, an early trade union cause. Hall's impatience with anything that he considered was a restraint on Christian fellowship, led him to challenge the prevailing Particular Baptist practice of strict communion. Clearly, when a man of Hall's calibre spoke out on this issue, many were compelled to listen and even reconsider the whole matter.

TERMS OF COMMUNION

For a number of years before 1815, Robert Hall had argued the case for open communion in discussions with his friends. The widespread prevalence of strict communion among the churches grieved him, and he considered that the time was now ripe for him to challenge this practice. His work was written as a reply to Abraham Booth's *Apology for the Baptists*, which was 'generally considered by our opponents as the ablest defence of their hypothesis'.[27] A further reason for writing was that Hall considered Robert Robinson's defence of open communion, *The General Doctrine of Toleration*, was unsatisfactory, 'because it rests on principles more lax and latitudinarian, than it is in his [Hall's] power to adopt'.[28] Robinson had argued for the admission of persons of 'all the varieties of religious belief' to the Lord's Table.[29] By 1815, Hall was an orthodox evangelical, and argued that admission to the Lord's Table should be defined by the terms of salvation.[30]

---

[25] H. S. Skeats and A. Miall, *History of the Free Churches of England*, 1891, p. 436, quoted by Macleod, 'Life and Teaching of Hall', p. 395. Macleod, op. cit., pp. 1, 2, quotes a series of tributes to Hall's oratory, including those by Sir James Mackintosh, Hannah More, and the *Edinburgh Review;* Macleod, 'Life and Teaching of Hall', p. 397.

[26] Macleod, 'Life and Teaching of Hall', p. 397.

[27] Hall, *Terms of Communion*, p. 8   [28] Ibid., p. 7.   [29] Ibid., p. 8.

[30] 'No man, nor set of men, are entitled to prescribe, as an indispensable condition of communion, what the New Testament has not enjoined as a condition of salvation', ibid., p. 4.

[237]

Undoubtedly domestic considerations must have intensified Hall's passion for open communion. Unlike the Cambridge Baptist Church, the Church at Harvey Lane, Leicester, practised strict communion, and Hall knew he could never change their practice. He therefore adopted an expedient, already employed at Broadmead Chapel, Bristol. He formed a small church of paedobaptists, who joined in all the services of the main church, with the exception of the communion service. To the little church, Hall administered the Lord's Supper in the chapel, but on a separate occasion each month.[31]

Terms of Communion is divided into two parts. The first part considers the arguments adduced in favour of strict communion. In part two, Hall sets out 'the positive grounds on which we justify the practice of mixed communion'.[32] In both parts the various sections overlap with a fair degree of repetition, perhaps not surprising in a work intended to refute a well-argued position. Central to Hall's thinking was his doctrine of the church. This was better developed and argued than it had been by previous disputants and is the unifying principle in Hall's teaching.

Hall belonged to a denomination which laid great emphasis upon the local church. This emphasis he accepted, but contended that the existence of a multiplicity of small self-governing communities of Christians must never be allowed to obscure the church's fundamental unity.

> Whoever forms his ideas of the Church of Christ from an attentive perusal of the New Testament, will perceive that unity is one of its essential characteristics; and that, though it be branched out into many distinct societies, it is still but one.[33]

> Nothing more abhorrent from the principles and maxims of the sacred oracles can be conceived, than the idea of a plurality of true churches, neither in actual communion with each other, nor in a capacity for such communion.[34]

All true believers in Jesus Christ belong to his church, whether they are Baptists or Paedobaptists. Therefore the exclusion of such as are

---

[31] Gregory, *Memoir of Hall*, p. 108. Ivimey, *HEB*, vol. 4, p. 281, gives details of the practice at Bristol.

[32] *Terms of Communion*, p. 82.   [33] Ibid., p. 9.   [34] Ibid.

Paedobaptists is unlawful. He argued 'that paedobaptism is not an error of such magnitude, as to prevent the society, which maintains it from being deemed a true church'.[35] That being so, to reject the members of such a church from communion 'is the very essence of schism'.[36] Hall defined schism as the 'causeless and unnecessary separation from the Church of Christ or from any part of it'.[37] Hall felt so strongly on this that he wrote:

> This schism in the members of his mystical body, is by far the greatest calamity which has befallen the christian interest, and one of the most fatal effects of the great apostasy foretold by the sacred penman.[38]

Nowhere is schism more painful than at the Lord's Table. To separate from fellow Christians there, distorts the very nature of the service. The sacrament becomes a party symbol. Of the strict communionists he wrote:

> He who admits his fellow-christian to share in every other spiritual privilege, while he prohibits his approach to the Lord's table, entertains a view of that institution diametrically opposite to what has usually prevailed; he must consider it, not so much in the light of commemoration of his Saviour's death and passion, [but] as a religious test, designed to ascertain and establish an agreement in points not fundamental. According to this notion of it, it is no longer a symbol of our common christianity, it is the badge and criterion of a party, a mark of discrimination applied to distinguish the nicer shades of difference among christians.[39]

At this point Hall touched a raw nerve in the consciences of many of his readers. Nonconformists had long suffered at the hands of those who had used the Lord's Supper as a religious test. The Test Acts excluded Dissenters from many forms of public service because of their inability to receive the sacrament in the parishes of the Established Church.

Politics apart, Hall saw strict communion as a breach of the love that should exist within the Christian church.

---

[35] Ibid., p. 109.   [36] Ibid.   [37] Ibid.
[38] Ibid., pp. 9,10.   [39] Ibid., p. 14.

> It is to inflict a wound on the very heart of charity, for no fault, for none at least of which the offender is conscious, for none which such treatment is likely to correct.[40]

Hall strengthened his case by appealing to the sorrow expressed by many of his brethren when their position compelled them to exclude Paedobaptists from the Lord's Table.

> If the doctrine of our opponents be true, we shall be frequently summoned to the strange discipline of repressing the movements of Christian Charity; and the practice of quenching the Spirit, instead of being regarded with horror, will become on many occasions an indispensable duty.[41]

Hall considered that to deny the Lord's Supper to any believer was to inflict a serious deprivation upon him. He saw this sacrament as a means of grace.

> To consider the Lord's Supper, however, as a mere commemoration of that event [Christ's death], is to entertain a very inadequate view of it. If we credit St Paul, it is also a federal rite in which, in token of our reconciliation with God, we eat and drink in his presence: it is a feast upon a sacrifice, by which we become partakers at the altar, not less really, though in a manner more elevated and spiritual, than those who under the ancient economy presented their offerings in the temple. In this ordinance, the cup is a spiritual participation of the blood, the bread of the body of the crucified Saviour: and as our paedobaptist brethren are allowed to be in covenant with God, their title to every federal rite follows of course.[42]

To deprive a Christian of the Lord's Supper is excommunication and according to Hall was only justifiable on the ground of a man's 'embracing heretical sentiments or living a vicious life'.[43] Such an exclusion was a punishment, and so he believed that the strict communionist's attitude towards Paedobaptists was to 'deem those equally guilty in the sight of God, with those unjust persons, idolaters, revellers and extortioners, who are declared incapable of entering into the kingdom of heaven'.[44]

---

[40] Ibid., p. 86. [41] Ibid., p. 87. [42] Ibid., pp. 63-4. [43] Ibid., p. 118. [44] Ibid., p. 119.

Moves towards Open Communion

Stern facts compelled Hall to recognize that with the best of intentions on both sides, divisions do occur. He allowed for separation as opposed to schism, which was 'a causeless and unnecessary separation'.[45] Separation becomes valid, 'whenever it becomes impossible to continue in a religious community, without concurring in its practices, and sanctioning abuses which the Word of God condemns'.[46] However, by receiving Paedobaptists as Christian brethren, the Baptist is not required to participate in or to approve of paedobaptism.

Unnecessary division harms both sides; Hall was convinced that the Baptists had damaged their own cause by maintaining the practice of strict communion.

> By keeping themselves in a state of separation and seclusion from other christians, they have not only evinced an inattention to some of the most important injunctions of scripture, but have raised up an invincible barrier to the propagation of their sentiments beyond the precincts of their own party.[47]

Baptism had thus become the badge of a sect. This meant that far too often Paedobaptists refused to give the Baptist case a fair hearing:

> Nothing it will be acknowledged has a greater tendency to obstruct the exercise of free enquiry than the spirit and feeling of a party.[48]

Hall believed that strict communion discouraged Paedobaptists from even attending Baptist services where they would encounter the Baptist position.[49] He was convinced that Baptist teaching would ultimately triumph, but this would not be on account of strict communion.

> From a full conviction that our views as a denomination correspond with the dictates of scripture, it is impossible for me to doubt of their ultimate prevalence; but unless we retrace our steps, and cultivate a cordial union with our fellow-christians, I greatly question whether their success will, in any degree be ascribed to our own efforts.[50]

Robert Hall had to counter the argument that strict communion was a reflection of the New Testament practice and therefore should be

---

[45] Ibid., p. 109.   [46] Ibid., p. 110.   [47] Ibid., p. 4.
[48] Ibid., p. 150.   [49] Ibid., p. 161.   [50] Ibid., p. 165.

maintained. He side-stepped the argument that baptism was instituted before the Lord's Supper by arguing that there was no Christian baptism until after the resurrection of Jesus Christ, when he gave the Great Commission to his disciples. Thus Hall denied as Christian baptism, not only the baptism of John, but also the baptism Jesus' disciples administered before the crucifixion. Of the apostles and disciples up to the time of Pentecost, he wrote, 'My deliberate opinion is, that in the christian sense of the term, they were not baptized at all.'[51] From this conclusion he went on to assert:

> It now appears that the original communicants at the Lord's table, at the time they partook of it, were, with respect to Christian baptism precisely in the same situation with the persons they [strict communionists] exclude.[52]

This was a novel argument, designed to cut the Gordian knot, but it was to be challenged forcefully by his strict communion opponents.

When he turned his attention to the order of the commands in the Great Commission of Matthew 28:18-20, Hall confessed that he did not wish to overturn what seemed to be the natural order.[53] He acknowledged that the apostolic records suggested that baptism was normally prior to admission to the Lord's Table.[54] But to insist that this order is binding in every situation was unnecessary 'to evince such a *dependence* of the one upon the other, that a neglect of the first from an involuntary mistake, annuls the obligation of the second'.[55]

While precedents are important, they are not to be considered as binding laws.[56] There was no confusion in the apostolic period over the nature of baptism, and so the modern problem simply did not arise.

> While it is acknowledged that much deference is due to primitive example, there are certain usages in apostolic times, which few would attempt to revive. There is one general rule however, applicable to the subject, which is, that no matter of fact is entitled to be considered as an authoritative precedent, which necessarily arose out of existing circumstances,

[51] Ibid., p. 41. [52] Ibid., p. 43. [53] Ibid., pp. 46, 47.
[54] Ibid., p. 58. [55] Ibid., p. 47.

so that in the then present state of things, it could not fail to have occurred.[57]

In the New Testament period, Christians were baptized as believers in response to a divine command. Baptists make this claim, but 'our paedobaptist brethren, in declining the practice we adopt, regulate their practice by the same principle'.[58] It was not good enough, therefore, to charge Paedobaptists with disobedience. Paedobaptists are Christians, and as such can 'enter into the full import of the rites commemorative of our Lord's death and passion'.[59]

Hall had to face the objection that all Christians, Paedobaptists as well as Baptists, have required baptism prior to admission to communion. He was impatient with this argument, claiming that Baptists should be the last people to employ it, since they had not been afraid to part company with the rest of Christendom in their practice of baptism.[60] He argued that the practice arose from a long-standing confusion of baptism with regeneration.[61] He then went on to argue that the real innovators were the strict communionists, who were the only Christians who excluded from the Table, those whom they recognize to be spiritually qualified to participate.[62]

Having argued that there were insufficient scriptural grounds for the exclusion of Paedobaptists from fellowship at the Lord's Table, Hall insisted that Scripture provided for their inclusion. He appealed to the apostle Paul's argument in the Epistle to the Romans, chapters 14 and 15, that Christians who differed over matters of the observance of Jewish ritual requirements should nevertheless receive one another.[63] Open communionists had used this passage often in their arguments. Hall, however, further answered the strict communionist objection that this passage had nothing to do with baptism. He argued that 'to object to the application of a general principle to a particular case, that is not the identical one which first occasioned its enunciation is egregious trifling'.[64]

---

[56] Ibid., p. 57. [57] Ibid., p. 56. [58] Ibid., p. 61.
[59] Ibid., p. 63. [60] Ibid., p. 72. [61] Ibid., pp 74-78.
[62] Ibid., pp. 80-1. [63] Ibid., pp. 89-105. [64] Ibid., p. 97.

Hall's *Terms of Communion* was the ablest defence of open communion yet to appear in print. He rescued the case for open communion from the charge of expediency, establishing his position from arguments taken from Scripture. He also grounded his argument on the doctrine of the church. He put his strict communion opponents on the back foot by arguing that their position rested upon a semblance of scriptural support rather than upon a strong foundation.

> Where unbaptized christians are forbidden to participate; and all the answer we receive, consists merely of those inferences and arguments from analogy, against which they protest; so our opponents, unsupported by the letter of Scripture, are obliged to have recourse to general reasoning, not less than ourselves, however lame and defective that reasoning may be.[65]

3. The Debate

Robert Hall's prestige ensured a ready sale for *Terms of Communion* in both Britain and America.[66] The time was, however, ripe for a renewal of the debate. Although the majority of the Particular Baptist churches practised strict communion, there were those who felt an unease with the practice.[67] Such were eager to read Hall's thoughts on the subject. On the other hand, there were still influential figures ready to defend the majority practice, which had been championed by such respected leaders as Kiffin, Gill, Booth, and Fuller.

The first response to Hall appeared within a few weeks. It was an anonymous pamphlet entitled *A Plea for Primitive Communion*.[68] It was ascribed to George Pritchard,[69] joint secretary of the Baptist Irish Society

---

[65] Ibid., p. 115. [66] 'The first edition was quickly sold out and many other editions followed both in England and America', A. H. Macleod, 'Life and Teaching of Robert Hall', p. 290.

[67] See Kinghorn's comments, p. 246-7, and Ivimey's, p. 267, below.

[68] [G. Pritchard], *A Plea for Primitive Communion Occasioned by the Rev. Robert Hall's Recent Publication on 'Terms of Communion'*, London, 1815. Although the pamphlet was anonymous, the catalogue of the Angus Library, Regent's Park College ascribes it to Pritchard.

[69] G. Pritchard (1773-1852) was the friend and biographer of both Ivimey and

Moves towards Open Communion

with Joseph Ivimey. He wrote with a sense of great respect for Hall. He did not consider that Hall had shaken the strict-communion case as Booth had expounded it; although he did admit that Hall had produced one new argument, 'that the baptism administered by John and that appointed by Jesus Christ are two distinct and different institutions'.[70] This Pritchard sought to refute; otherwise his pamphlet was a restatement of earlier arguments and added little to the debate. The argument about John's baptism was shortly to be dealt with more ably by Joseph Kinghorn. Pritchard's pamphlet did, however, provoke Hall to elaborate his position on this issue in a tract entitled *The Essential Difference between Christian Baptism and the Baptism of John, More Fully Stated and Confirmed.*[71]

At this time Christmas Evans[72] and William Button[73] also produced small tracts in the defence of strict communion. Christmas Evans, a popular Welsh evangelist, warmed to the prospect of Christian unity, but then, in a remarkable piece of allegory, argued that there is no possibility of inter-communion without an agreement on baptism. Button, the champion of Hyper-Calvinism against Fuller and by this time joint-secretary of the Baptist Union with Joseph Ivimey, made no new contribution to the debate. He did, however, give a useful blow-by-blow account of the communion controversy from the seventeenth century onwards.

4. JOSEPH KINGHORN

The year 1816 witnessed the appearance of a much more substantial reply to Robert Hall. *Baptism, A Term of Communion at the Lord's*

Newman. He was later a founding editor of the *Primitive Communionist Magazine* in 1838.

[70] [G. Pritchard], *Plea for Primitive Communion*, p. 18.

[71] R. Hall, *Works*, vol. 2, 'The Essential Difference between Christian Baptism and the Baptism of John, More Fully Stated and Confirmed; in Reply to a Pamphlet, entitled, "A Plea for Primitive Communion"', 1816.

[72] C. Evans, *The Decision of a General Congress Convened to Agree on 'Terms of Communion', Occasioned by the Rev. Robert Hall's Pamphlet on that Subject*, London 1816.

[73] W. Button, *An Answer to the Question, Why Are You a Strict Baptist? A Dialogue between Thomas and John*, London, 1816 edition.

[245]

Supper[74] was the work of the scholarly Joseph Kinghorn, pastor of the Norwich Baptist Church, and a former pupil of Robert Hall at Bristol. He had come to his strict-communion convictions gradually and only after much heart searching.[75] When Hall was told that he should expect an answer from Kinghorn, 'He was pleased to say that he could not be replied to by a more respectable man than Mr Kinghorn; what he would write would be worth reading.'[76]

Kinghorn commenced his work by considering the religious climate in which the debate had re-opened. He welcomed the recent missionary spirit which 'has united together good men of different denominations in mutual attachment and exertions'.[77] Nevertheless he had to go on to warn that men's heads were in danger of being governed by their hearts:

> But with all this good feeling and Christian exertion, there has often been mixed a portion of bad reasoning; and it has appeared, as if some very excellent men were disposed to neglect the positive commands of the Lord, in their great zeal to unite all Christians in one body, and bury all party distinctions.[78]

Kinghorn claimed that there was a feeling abroad 'that the cause of mixed communion is popular among our young ministers; especially those who have enjoyed a liberal education'. But to this he replied:

> A general course, which may be of use in forming the taste and improving the mind, may accord with the sentiments of mixed communion; and if it extends no farther than to render those who pursue it agreeable to the best informed classes of society with which they mingle it is not at all unlikely to have that effect.[79]

A good general education might not lead a man to study this issue in depth. Kinghorn considered that ill grounded and inexperienced ministers were in danger of being put under pressure by the more voluble

---

[74] J. Kinghorn, *Baptism, a Term of Communion at the Lord's Supper* (1816), 2nd ed., Norwich, 1816.

[75] See above, p. 232.

[76] Wilkin, *Joseph Kinghorn*, p. 355, 'W. Button to J. Kinghorn.' Button wrote after staying twelve days with Hall, for whom he professed a great admiration.

[77] Kinghorn, *Baptism, a Term of Communion*, p. 19.   [78] Ibid.   [79] Ibid., p. 5.

members of their congregations. It was essential, therefore, that ministers should give themselves to a careful study of the debate. He was sure then that they would be convinced of strict communion by the sheer weight of the evidence.

> [If] after devoting the prime of their attention and study to the sacred oracles, they investigate the opinions and history of the ancient church, they will be convinced, that the maxims of antiquity would never lead them to adopt the plan of open communion.[80]

Clearly Kinghorn hoped that his book would contribute to the educative process.

Both Kinghorn and Hall were concerned to implement New Testament teaching, but each interpreted the evidence very differently. Kinghorn saw the movement towards open communion as an attempt to create Christian unity, albeit at too high a price. Hall considered it to be the expression of a unity, already in existence, but too long ignored or even denied. Because he saw unity as the outward expression of a common salvation, Hall wrote: 'No men or set of men are entitled to prescribe as an indispensable condition to communion, what the New Testament has not enjoined as a condition of salvation.'[81] To this Kinghorn rejoined:

> But the inquiry is 'what hath the LORD prescribed?' Now as he did require baptism as the evidence of faith in him, communion must *once* have required it also.[82]

Whereas the unity of the universal church was central to the thinking of Robert Hall, Joseph Kinghorn reasoned from the necessity of reproducing the features of the apostolic church in every age. He stated the principle behind his thinking as 'the obligation of taking the directions of the Lord, and fulfilling them in the order in which they are prescribed, and for the purpose for which they were designed'.[83] He wrote with confidence because he could see the pattern of the practice which he advocated clearly stated in the New Testament. The rising tide of

[80] Ibid., p. 6.
[81] Hall, *Terms of Communion*, p. 4.
[82] Kinghorn, *Baptism, a Term of Communion*, p. 19.   [83] Ibid., p. 74.

hostility to the practice of strict communion was seen as an expression of the opposition to biblical principles which their implementation has always encountered.

> Their great argument is, *the New Testament supports* our practice; and in all ages those who in other things pleaded for truths or practised duties only on this authority, have uniformly had a strong current of opinion to strive against.[84]

Hall and Kinghorn both agreed that baptism prior to participation in the Lord's Supper was the New Testament practice. For Hall this was a norm, which should not be made into a universal, perpetual law: for Kinghorn the precedent admitted of no variation. When faced with Hall's appeal to the Pauline argument about things indifferent in Romans, chapters 14 and 15, Kinghorn rejected this as simply irrelevant. The apostle, he claimed, deals with differences of opinion in areas upon which Christ had not pronounced. His argument could not justify 'our receiving such as oppose or neglect anything, that was in the days of the Apostle, a part of "the Kingdom of God" '.[85]

Kinghorn paid careful attention to Hall's argument about the baptism of John.[86] In contrast to Hall, he contended that the baptism of John and that of the apostles prior to the Great Commission was in essence the same as Christian baptism after the Great Commission. Both were baptisms of repentance and both required faith in what God had at the time revealed. John's baptism was accepted by Jesus Christ. If those who were baptized before the Great Commission were in ignorance of the full implications of the work of Christ, the same objection could be raised against the doctrinal understanding of the disciples at the time the Lord's Supper was instituted. Finally, the law promulgated by Jesus Christ just before his ascension was binding upon subsequent believers. If he required baptism and then communion, it was impossible to regard the apostles themselves as unbaptized, as Hall suggested.

Kinghorn indignantly repudiated the charge of illiberality against the strict communionists. While longing for the closest possible fellowship

[84] Ibid., p. 8.   [85] Ibid., p. 46.   [86] Ibid., pp. 132-142.

Moves towards Open Communion

with all other Christians, he argued that brotherly love 'should never induce us to act contrary to the will of Christ'.[87] He did not consider it to be a punishment to exclude from a church those who had never been members of it. Excommunication was the expulsion of an unrepentant church member who had sinned. To tell a person that he could not be received at the Lord's Table until he was baptized, was not a similar case.[88]

Unlike Hall, Kinghorn did not consider adherence to strict communion damaged the Baptist cause. He claimed that strict communionists

> persevere in the firm faith that by patient continuance in well doing, by holding up to view at proper times, the direct evidence of the subject and mode of primitive baptism, and of the primitive character of the Christian Church, they shall with the blessing and assistance of the Lord, see his cause gain the universal attention of all good men.[89]

The unpopularity of strict communion, he suggested, was in part the result of the success of the Baptists.

> The outcry now raised against them for bigotry and illiberality is, they believe, greatly owing to their exciting and increasing attention in the religious world.[90]

5. Continued Debate

Of Kinghorn's work, Hall was alleged to have said, 'It is probably the best defence of which the prevailing practice is capable.'[91] James Hinton, an open communionist, commended its liberal spirit, writing, 'My strict brethren will appear to the Christian world, as they always have to me, deserving the esteem and love from their fellow Christians, which they exercise towards them.'[92]

In spite of expressions of mutual esteem, the debate between Hall and Kinghorn rumbled on. In 1818, Hall produced *A Reply to the Rev. Joseph*

---

[87] Ibid., p. 39. [88] Ibid., p. 55 ff.
[89] Ibid., p. 69. [90] Ibid.
[91] Hall was quoted by James Hinton in 'J. Hinton to J. Kinghorn, 30th April 1816', Wilkins, *Joseph Kinghorn*, p. 356. [92] Ibid.

Kinghorn.[93] In 1820, Kinghorn responded with *A Defence of 'Baptism a Term of Communion', In Answer to the Rev. Robert Hall's Reply*.[94] There the debate between these two protagonists rested until 1826, when Hall published *A Short Statement of the Reasons for Christian in Opposition to Party Communion*.[95] This was intended to be a short and popular summary of the case Hall developed in his longer works. The title alone was provocative, and it is not surprising that Kinghorn replied with *Arguments Against the Practice of Mixed Communion and in Support of Communion on the Plan of the Apostolic Church*.[96]

These later contributions tended to re-work arguments already used. Hall complained of Kinghorn:

> The perpetual recurrence of the same matter, the paucity of distinct and intelligible topics of argument, together with the obvious want of coherence, and of dependence of one part on another, give to the whole the air of a series of skirmishes rather than regular combat.[97]

Of Hall's *Reply*, Kinghorn confided to a friend that he was 'astonished till wearied with astonishment'.[98] He was particularly grieved at Hall's 'endeavour to make us unchristianize the Paedobaptists'.[99]

Hall fought for his cause with all the fervour of a crusader and the ability of an orator. Kinghorn battled away at Hall's arguments in a more pedestrian manner, but not without considerable skill. Sympathizers with Hall's case were not always completely happy with his manner. For example, Olinthus Gregory, his friend and biographer, wrote of the debate:

---

[93] R. Hall, *Works*, vol. 2, pp. 233–495, 'A Reply to the Rev. Joseph Kinghorn: being a Further Vindication of the Practice of Free Communion' [1818].

[94] J. Kinghorn, *A Defence of 'Baptism a Term of Communion', in Answer to the Rev. Robert Hall's 'Reply'*, Norwich, 1820.

[95] R. Hall, *Works*, vol. 3, pp. 407–56, 'A Short Statement of the Reasons for Christian in Opposition to Party Communion' [1826].

[96] J. Kinghorn, *Arguments against Mixed Communion*, see footnote 17.

[97] R. Hall, *Reply to Joseph Kinghorn*, pp. 235–6.

[98] Wilkin, *Joseph Kinghorn*, p. 406.

[99] Ibid.

Moves towards Open Communion

I feel no inclination to deny, that in a few cases, he has suffered himself to indulge in terms of sarcasm, if not contempt, that added nothing to his argument, and had better been spared.[100]

Fifty years later Charles M. Birrell, an open communionist, wrote that the conflict 'spread in fairly courteous spirit over several years, and then ended with due admiration of the genius of the one combatant and the close logic of the other, but without visible change in popular practice'.[101]

Hall and Kinghorn's prominence in the controversy should not obscure those other men who entered the fray. In 1818, Francis A. Cox, pastor of the Mare Street Church, Hackney, issued *A Letter on Free Communion from a Pastor to the People of His Charge*.[102] Cox, like Hall, was a graduate of a Scottish University and had succeeded Hall at Cambridge before his arrival in London. When he wrote his pamphlet, Cox was a tutor at the Stepney Baptist College, where his relations with his President, William Newman, were strained at times.[103] His writing was also aimed at the Hackney Church, which he hoped to lead into the practice of open communion.[104] His pamphlet is a really brief summary of Hall's arguments. Joseph Ivimey entered the controversy with *A Reply to 'A Letter on Free Communion' by the Rev. F. A. Cox, M.A.*[105]

At this point William Newman issued his *Moral and Ritual Precepts Compared, in a Pastoral Letter to the Baptist Church at Bow, Middlesex*.[106] He associated the move towards open communion with Antinomianism,

---

[100] Gregory, *Memoir of R. Hall*, p. 105.

[101] C. M. Birrell, *The Life of William Brock, D.D.*, London, 1878, pp. 119, 120. Birrell's reference to 'visible change' refers to the 'popular practice – Eastern and Western together with nearly all Protestant Churches'.

[102] F. A. Cox, *A Letter on Free Communion from a Pastor to the People of His Charge*, London, 1818.

[103] R. E. Cooper, *From Stepney to St Giles, The Story of Regent's Park College 1810–1960*, London, 1960, pp 40 ff.

[104] J. Ivimey, *A Reply to 'A Letter on Free Communion' by the Rev. F. A. Cox, M.A., in Six Letters on Strict Communion, Addressed to a Young Minister,* London, 1818, p. 5.   [105] Ibid.

[106] W. Newman, *Moral and Ritual Precepts Compared, in a Pastoral Letter to the Baptist Church, at Bow, Middlesex, including Some Remarks on the Rev. Robert Hall's 'Terms of Communion'*, London, 1819.

[251]

the *bête noire* of most Particular Baptists of that period, including Robert Hall.[107] Hall had earlier criticized Newman for publishing Fuller's pamphlet on strict communion, regarding the move as being 'injurious to his fame' since 'his posthumous pamphlet on communion, will unquestionably be considered the feeblest of his productions'. He chided Newman for forgetting 'that we live in an age not remarkably disposed to implicit faith, even in the greatest names'.[108] In reply Newman wrote: 'Perhaps it will be sufficient for me to say when my learned and eloquent friend has proved damages, I shall be ready to make reparation.'[109] Of Hall's arguments, Newman wrote:

> He appeals in each of his treatises to moral principles for a directory in a ritual question – on such principles, we might receive from his pen a more specious defence of Paedobaptism than the world has yet seen.[110]

In 1824, Joseph Ivimey again joined the discussion with a substantial tract, *Baptism, the Scriptural and Indispensable Qualification for Communion*.[111] He argued that in areas where there was 'an evangelical congregational minister of acceptable talents and good reputation, those persons who are Baptists, who do not consider the error of Paedobaptists as a disqualification for communion with them at the Lord's Table, have no justifiable reason for founding a new church for the purpose of promoting either *mixed* or *open* communion'.[112] To do so could well promote schism among the Paedobaptists.

Ivimey was worried about ministerial students and younger ministers, many of whom were known to have adopted open-communion views,[113] although the conservatism of the churches continued to be a restraining influence.[114]

The pressure for open communion, he believed was the work of a vociferous minority.

---

[107] Hall's *Works*, vol. 4, pp. 441–55, Preface to 'Antinomianism Unmasked', by S. Chase.
[108] Hall, *Reply to Kinghorn*, p. 307.
[109] Newman, *Moral and Ritual Precepts Compared*, p. 30.   [110] Ibid., p. 16.
[111] J. Ivimey, *Baptism, the Indispensable Qualification*, see footnote 9.
[112] Ibid., p. lii.   [113] Ibid., pp. 65 ff.   [114] Ibid., pp 94–5.

Moves towards Open Communion

Since an importance has been given to those opinions by the popularity of Mr Hall as a writer, and especially as a preacher, the *strict* Baptists have been subjected in many instances to considerable reproach, the old cry of bigotry has been revived.[115]

The Independents read and appreciated Hall's arguments, and so Ivimey considered that part of the rising tide of criticism came from that quarter.[116] He also deplored the fact that by this time significant numbers of Baptists had become members of Independent churches. Ivimey urged them to return to their own denomination.[117] Two years later, he returned to this theme and made the claim that

> Mr H.[all] thinks that the principles of mixed communion increase the number of baptized believers. It is certain that many of our people have joined the Independent churches; and in all probability their rising families will be of that denomination, who would otherwise have been baptized persons.[118]

To support his contention that the demand for open communion was being exploited by a minority, Ivimey offered some interesting statistics. He stated that there were nearly seven hundred Particular Baptist churches in England and Wales, each consisting of around one hundred members. If the hearers in the congregations averaged twice as many as the members, the total number in Particular Baptist congregations was somewhere in excess of two hundred thousand. He estimated that there were perhaps fifty open-communion churches in this group and that in these there were probably not more than two hundred Paedobaptists coming to the Lord's Table.[119] The figures are of course estimates, but coming as they do from the Secretary of the Baptist Union and the author of a county-by-county history of the Baptists, they ought be treated with some respect.

---

[115] Ibid., p 55.   [116] Ibid., p. 56.   [117] Ibid., pp. 55 ff.

[118] J. Ivimey, *Communion at the Lord's Table Regulated by the Revealed Will of Christ, Not Party but Christian Communion: A Reply to the Rev. Robert Hall's Pamphlet, Entitled 'Reasons for Christian in Opposition to Party Communion'*, London, 1826, p. 47.

[119] Ivimey, *Baptism, the Indispensable Qualification*, p. 55.

6. Developments at Stepney Academy

Joseph Ivimey's concerns about the views of young ministers and 'students in our academies'[120] reflected a situation which did not bode well for the future of strict communion. The Bristol Academy had had a succession of open-communion Principals. In 1825 John Ryland died. Interestingly, he was the last man to combine the offices of pastor of the Broadmead Church and Principal of the Academy. Robert Hall, whose magnetic influence the Bristol students now experienced in a direct, personal way, succeeded him in the pastorate.[121] Ivimey had a closer knowledge of affairs at Stepney, where open-communion views were gaining considerable ground, to the distress of the College President, William Newman. Ivimey and Newman were close friends. Both had defended strict communion in print, and as fellow London pastors frequently met to discuss their concerns.

Although Stepney was not founded as a strict-communion institution, strict-communion men were prominent in its establishment; but so also was Robert Hall.[122] Its main benefactor was William Taylor, who had been a member of Abraham Booth's Church in Prescot Street for over sixty years.[123] Its first treasurer was Joseph Gutteridge, a member of the same church.[124] Before William Newman was appointed, the post was offered to Joseph Kinghorn, who declined.[125] It was Andrew Fuller, who then urged the appointment of Newman.[126] Francis A. Cox was also considered but rejected by the committee although he served as tutor of Mathematics from 1813 until 1822.[127]

---

[120] Ibid., p. 65.

[121] Hall took an active interest in the students and often invited groups to his home; Macleod, 'Life and Teaching of Robert Hall', pp. 332–3.

[122] Hall, *Works*, vol. 4, pp. 407–14, 'Address in behalf of the Baptist Academical Institution at Stepney.'

[123] Pritchard, *Memoir of Newman*, pp. 230, 345.

[124] Ibid., p. 329. E. Steane, *Memoir of the Life of Joseph Gutteridge, Esq.*, London 1850, pp. 5, 124.

[125] Wilkin, *Joseph Kinghorn*, pp. 328-30.

[126] Pritchard, *Memoir of Newman*, p. 231.

[127] Cooper, *From Stepney to St Giles*, pp. 34, 40.

Moves towards Open Communion

During the early 1820s the students proved restless, and William Newman's diary reflects his profound unease. There were several complaints by the students to the College Committee and on at least one occasion Newman suspected that Cox was encouraging the student discontent.[128] On three occasions – November 1820, November 1821, and from late 1825 to 1826, the Committee was compelled to investigate these complaints.[129] In 1821, three students were expelled after 'a paper called a "Remonstrance" was read, full of Radicalism'.[130]

From the 'Diaries', it is not always clear whether, by using the word 'Radicalism', Newman meant student discontent with the teaching and administration of the College or radical politics, which at that time was stirring in the country at large. If the latter were the case, the students would have approved of Hall's political tracts. Of more certainty is their interest in Hall's views on communion. Newman recorded two entries within three days of each other which are very interesting:

> 30th September 1820, The Students are anxious to debate the Question between Hall and Kinghorn.
>
> 3rd October 1820, The young men in several instances infected with a spirit of Radicalism.[131]

In December 1820, six out of the eleven students declared themselves for open communion. In November 1824, Newman noted that the students debated, '"Is it lawful to admit unbaptized Xtians to Church fellowship?" All in the affirmative except Whitewood and Pearce. The two youngest doubted.'[132]

A year later Newman was recording rumours of a new Baptist College in the London area in which Cox and others would be involved.[133] Unrest continued at Stepney where Kinghorn and Gutteridge supported

---

[128] W. Newman, 'Diaries', 7th July 1808–20th Aug. 1814; 15th July 1820–10th Oct. 1825; 10th Oct. 1825–10th Oct. 1833; 10th Oct. 1833–20th May 1834. These Diaries are deposited in the Angus Library, Regent's Park College, Oxford. 'Diary', 16th June 1826.
[129] Ibid., 14th and 15th Nov. 1820; 2nd Nov. 1821; 8th Dec. 1825.
[130] Ibid., 2nd Nov. 1821.   [131] Ibid., under dates indicated.
[132] Ibid., 1st Dec. 1820 and 27th Nov. 1824.   [133] Ibid., 20th Dec. 1825.

[255]

Newman at a meeting on 8 December 1825,[134] but on the following day Newman noted:

> Mileham told me what course was taken. He thinks that there is a party forming of young men against the old, the new school against the old – thinks the Treasurer secretly encourages it. (What could I do? Complaints have poured in against me from all sides.)[135]

Newman believed that what was happening at Stepney was part of a wider collapse of standards. After reading a prospectus for a new hymn book he wrote:

> Hymns on Baptism are to be omitted as sectarian! Everyone may see which way the wind blows – Baptists are ashamed of their baptism – Dissenters are ashamed of their Nonconformity – Protestants are crying after the Apocrypha – and if these things grow, Christians will be ashamed of Xt.[136]

On 13 December 1825 he wrote:

> I have committed two offences never to be forgiven – one – strict communion and the other is, I have not bowed sufficiently to the Treasurer![137]

Joseph Gutteridge, the College's Treasurer, had supported Newman in the early disputes. By now it seems that he was not so loyal. It is possible that his views on communion were changing and that Newman's firm line was an embarrassment. Although a long-standing member of Prescot Street, Gutteridge had bought and re-opened a run-down Baptist Chapel in Camberwell. He invited Edward Steane, an Edinburgh graduate, to work there. Here, in December 1824, 'a baptist church was organized on the principle of free communion'. Steane described Gutteridge as 'the principal supporter of the design', although he retained his membership at Prescot Street.[138]

The College Committee continued to discuss the troubles at Stepney in

---

[134] Ibid., 8th Dec. 1825.   [135] Ibid., 9th Dec. 1825.
[136] Ibid., 28th Dec. 1825.   [137] Ibid., 13th Dec. 1825.
[138] Steane, *Memoir of Gutteridge* pp. 123, 124.

Moves towards Open Communion

the early months of 1826. Newman's health was not good[139] and on 30 May he announced that he would resign at the end of the year. He stated:

> My opponents have withdrawn everything in the shape of an accusation, (and if they had not, no consideration on earth would have prevailed with me to resign). I need not add one in the shape of defence.[140]

At this point Solomon Young, the Classics tutor and Newman's successor, almost prevailed on the students to write an apology for their behaviour towards Newman. In the end they decided not to, for fear 'Mr Ivimey would get hold of it and print it'.[141]

Much of the cause of the unrest is now obscure. Personal rivalries entered in and make for sorry reading. Newman was suspicious of Cox who, according to R. E. Cooper, hoped to succeed him as Principal.[142] Newman felt isolated from a number of his younger brethren and the question of open or closed communion certainly entered into this. In view of all this, it is only fair to state that Hall and Newman remained friends, and that after Newman's resignation Hall wrote to say:

> With respect to the unhappy affairs at Stepney, I always thought you were very harshly treated, and still think so. I certainly felt for you as a gentleman, who merited a very different sort of usage from what you experienced.[143]

Newman must have welcomed Hall's kind words, but as he left the College to occupy himself with his pastorate at Bow, it must have been in the knowledge that many of the students, who had passed through Stepney Academy during the last seven years were supporters of Hall's views on communion rather than his own.

7. THE PROGRESS OF THE OPEN-COMMUNION MOVEMENT

In the first half of the 1830s most of the leading protagonists died: Robert Hall in 1831; Joseph Kinghorn in 1832; Joseph Ivimey in 1834; William

---

[139] Cooper, *From Stepney to St Giles*, p. 42.
[140] Pritchard, *Memoir of Newman*, p. 330.
[141] 'Diary', 16th June 1826.
[142] Cooper, *From Stepney to St Giles*, p. 43.
[143] Pritchard, *Memoir of Newman*, pp. 333–4

Newman in 1835. Francis Cox was to survive until 1853, and was elected on three occasions to the Chair of the Baptist Union.[144] In spite of their differences, these men regarded themselves as part of the same Particular Baptist denomination. Cox even took a prominent part in Ivimey's funeral service.[145]

When Hall died, strict communion was still practised by most Particular Baptist churches,[146] but a change was definitely in the air. One of Kinghorn's correspondents wrote in June 1830:

> Well my dear Sir! You see the practice of mixed communion is gaining ground among the English Baptist Churches, after all the labours you have bestowed upon them: and I do heartily wish that this were all; but I much fear that they are rapidly progressing into Arminianism.[147]

Joseph Ivimey expressed the same fear in 1833:

> Nor can I disguise the fact, that in my opinion the dignified tone and denominational zeal manifested by BOOTH, FULLER, and others are greatly lowered; and that a general spirit of laxity is introduced among us as to the *doctrines* of grace as well as to the discipline of the New Testament.[148]

After the Hall–Kinghorn debate, there were no new major works from either side, although smaller pieces continued to appear. The pressures to change to open communion remained, and an increasing large number of the leaders within the majority group of the Particular Baptist churches were of this persuasion.

The unfolding of events can be illustrated by the developments in Kinghorn's former church in Norwich. In 1833 the church invited William Brock, then a student at Stepney, to succeed Kinghorn. Brock made it clear that he was an open communionist, but was nevertheless

---

[144] K.A.C. Parsons, ed., *St Andrew's Street Baptist Church, Cambridge*, Cambridge, 1971, p. 55.
[145] Pritchard, *Memoir of Ivimey*, p. 297.
[146] Gregory, *Memoir of Hall*, p. 102.
[147] Wilkin, *Joseph Kinghorn*, p. 431.
[148] Pritchard, *Memoir of Ivimey*, p. 311.

invited on the condition that 'he should do and say nothing to effect an alteration in the existing order'.[149] Brock remained pastor until his call to Bloomsbury in 1848, but asked to be allowed to preach in favour of open communion in 1838 and to hold a separate communion service for Paedobaptists.[150] Under his successor, George Gould, open communion was introduced in 1857. This led to a lawsuit in which the Master of the Rolls gave judgment in 1860, stating that 'this congregation is at full liberty to alter its practice in respect of communion, if such should be the opinion of the majority of its members'.[151]

During the lawsuit, Gould's counsel submitted that details of the communion practice of two hundred and eight churches, formed before 1800, had been secured. Of these, one hundred and five practised strict communion and one hundred and three open communion, and of the latter group, thirty-one practised open membership as well. Details of another one hundred and thirty-seven churches formed before 1800 had not been secured, and of course the figures took no account of the considerable number of strict and open churches formed after 1800. What is significant is that of the pre-1800 group, eighty-two were known to have introduced open communion in the years 1800 to 1860, whereas only four open churches were known to have introduced strict communion during that same period.[152]

Strict communion remained the practice of the Hyper-Calvinist groups associated with Stevens and Gadsby. Hyper-Calvinism was to prove an insuperable barrier between these men and the followers of Kinghorn, Newman, and Ivimey, still remaining within the main group of Particular Baptist churches. This latter group was to find itself increasingly isolated within the denomination from the 1830s, as strict communion became more and more associated with Hyper-Calvinism – a fact which would have horrified Andrew Fuller!

---

[149] Birrell, Life of Brock, p.120.
[150] Ibid., p. 121. G. Gould, *Open Communion and the Baptists of Norwich*, Norwich, 1860, p. lvii.
[151] Quoted Underwood, *History of the English Baptists*, p. 207.
[152] Gould, *Open Communion*, pp 138 ff.

12

The Beginnings of the Strict Baptist Magazines

I have always thought that some knowledge of the Bible is necessary to an understanding of English history. Certainly the intensive private study of that book by many hundreds of persons otherwise unlearned, had more to do with the character, the mind and the imaginative power of our ancestors than we moderns can always understand.

G. M. Trevelyan

In the fifty years between the death of John Gill in 1771 and that of Robert Hall in 1831, momentous changes swept across Britain. The Herculean conflicts of the French Revolutionary and Napoleonic Wars had left their mark on the nation. New industrial towns were growing and the varied needs of town and country were reflected in the hated Corn Laws. Nonconformist and then Roman Catholic emancipation had been secured and the country was caught up in the political excitement which surrounded the passing of the Great Reform Bill. Religious changes were also apparent. The first thirty years of the nineteenth century witnessed a considerable advance in the strength of Protestant Nonconformity.

The Particular Baptist denomination had also changed considerably during these years. Fuller's teaching on faith was now widely accepted; the influence of the Missionary Society was powerful; and open communion was being advocated by several influential figures. Although strict communion was still the practice of the majority of the churches, its advocates were coming under increasing pressure to allow for change. From 1800 the Particular Baptist churches had 'steadily increased in

The Beginnings of the Strict Baptist Magazines

number and vitality'.[1] Commenting on a situation that existed among the Particular Baptists during this period of their history, the Congregationalist John Stoughton wrote: 'The hyper-calvinist controversy, the communion controversy and the Serampore controversy were so many family discussions.'[2]

Other changes within the Particular Baptist family also took place at this time. As the congregations increased and multiplied there seems to have been a decline in the doctrinal awareness of many churches. In 1832 the long moribund Baptist Union was reconstituted. The old Calvinistic basis of faith, adopted just nineteen years earlier in 1813, was replaced by a declaration of adherence to 'the sentiments usually denominated evangelical', and, as E. A. Payne pointed out,

> the way was opened for the adherence to the Union of Churches belonging to the [General Baptist] New Connexion. The process thus began which resulted sixty years later in the complete merging of the groups of Baptists.[3]

The way may have been open, but for many of the older leaders such implications, if foreseen, were not welcome. Until his death in 1834, Joseph Ivimey was still Secretary of the Union. In 1833, the aged John Rippon, pastor of the strict church in New Park Street, was the Union's chairman. Rippon was, however, to be succeeded by Francis Cox in 1834. During the 1830s the leaders of the Union were largely men who had been influenced by Fuller's teaching, while open and closed communionists still co-operated in Union organisations and activities. By contrast, it should be noted that in the year after the Baptist Union adopted its attenuated declaration of adherence, the Congregational Union accepted a Declaration which included twenty 'principles of religion'. This contained clear statements of Calvinistic doctrine.[4]

---

[1] E. A. Payne, *The Baptist Union, A Short History*, London, 1958, p. 56.

[2] Cited by Payne, op. cit., p. 44. The Serampore Controversy was a dispute over the administration of Mission funds and is not germane to this work.

[3] Ibid., p. 61.

[4] D. Bogue and J. Bennett, *History of the Dissenters*, vol. 3, pp. 396–402.

Closely associated with the Baptist Union was the monthly *Baptist Magazine*, which dated from 1809 and which, after an uncertain start, had gained the support of Andrew Fuller, John Ryland, and James Hinton. It was a safe denominational journal. 'In avoiding discord within the denomination, it was often rather tame and dull, but it faithfully reflected the Baptist consensus.'[5]

In the face of these changes the strict communionists did not present a united front. They represented an important tradition amongst the Particular Baptists, but the issue of Fullerism had left them divided. They had shared in the growth of the first three decades of the nineteenth century, but while some found fellowship in the ranks of the Baptist Union, others began to forge new links.

At first, many were drawn together by visits from preachers who had the encouragement of Baptist leaders like William Gadsby and John Stevens. Gadsby's faithful lieutenants included John Warburton of Trowbridge and John Kershaw of Rochdale. Some of Stevens's associates had been called to pastorates in the London area, the East Midlands, and East Anglia. From around 1830 another powerful influence among the churches was James Wells, pastor of the Surrey Tabernacle, Southwark, London. In the years before 1850, Wells maintained connections with both the Gadsby and Stevens groups.[6] Able preachers and leaders were to be found among both groups and many churches were either established or influenced by them. However, the lack of inter-church organization among these congregations and their dependence upon just a few strong personalities inevitably created a degree of instability.

Not surprisingly, a number of these churches were uneasy with the new trends of thought and practice advocated in the wider Particular Baptist denomination, and felt not a little threatened by the local Associations and the Baptist Union. Their initial response to these challenges was to establish magazines that reflected their Hyper-Calvinistic, strict-

---

[5] Rosemary Taylor, 'English Baptist Periodicals, 1790–1865, A Bibliography and Survey', M.Phil. thesis, London, 1974, pp. 18,19.

[6] R. W. Oliver, 'The Dangers of a Successful Ministry: The Life, Teaching and Influence of James Wells,' *Bulletin of the Strict Baptist Historical Society*, 8, 1971.

communionist ideas. A magazine could sustain morale and act as an instrument of propaganda; it could also become the focal point for a group of like-minded churches. The magazines that emerged during these years were the creation of strong-minded men who often disagreed with each other. They are of great importance for two reasons: they provide us with a record of the life of the various Strict Baptist groups; they also played a significant role in the development of these groups.

1. THE GOSPEL HERALD

The first of these magazines, *The Gospel Herald*,[7] was launched in Ipswich in January 1833. Suffolk had long been a stronghold of Hyper-Calvinism.[8] Tensions over Fullerism caused a division in the old Norfolk and Suffolk Association in 1830.[9] The leaders of the New Association, as the anti-Fullerite group was known, were George Wright of Beccles, Samuel Collins of Grundisburgh, and John Cooper of Wattisham.[10] Samuel Collins originated the *Gospel Herald* and edited it from 1833 to 1856, although no editors' names were supplied in the early issues and editorials were always signed by 'The Editors'. George Wright had some literary experience and may well have given some help, although his biography makes no reference to this. Before adopting Calvinism and Baptist principles, he had been a Methodist. A natural leader he played a major role in the affairs of the New Association.

---

[7] *The Gospel Herald, or Poor Christian's Magazine*, Ipswich, from vol 1, 1833. John Gadsby mistakenly believed that John Stevens originated the *Gospel Herald* (quoted in B. A. Ramsbottom, *The History of the Gospel Standard Magazine*, Carshalton, 1985, p. 6).

[8] 'I know the opposition made to "Andrew Fuller", in S[uffolk] and N[orfolk]', Andrew Fuller to Thomas Steevens, 1791, Fuller's *Letters*. 'Mr Fuller considered the Suffolk churches almost, "a perfect dunghill in society"', *Gospel Herald*, vol. 1, 1833, p. 132.

[9] The division of the Norfolk and Suffolk Association is discussed in chapter 13.

[10] For Wright see S. K. Bland, *Memorials of George Wright*, London, 1875. For Collins, see *Gospel Herald*, vol. 49, 1881, pp. 256 ff. Collins is described as 'the originator and for 25 years editor of this magazine'. See also A. J. Klaiber, *The Story of the Suffolk Baptists*, London, 1931, pp. 122 ff.

History of the English Calvinistic Baptists, 1771–1892

Samuel Collins was a Northamptonshire man who came under Hyper-Calvinist and Baptist teaching while he was employed in a draper's shop in London. Initially a member of John Keeble's Church in Blandford Street, he was drawn to John Stevens and became a member of his church by 1822. The influence of Stevens on Collins has already been noted.[11] Stevens's Church at Meard's Court recognized his preaching gifts and he was called to the Suffolk village church at Grundisburgh in 1826.

i. The Content of the Gospel Herald

The *Gospel Herald* consisted mainly of doctrinal articles. Included in its first issue was a Calvinistic basis of faith;[12] none of the distinctives of Hyper-Calvinism appeared in this statement. It was also baptistic, but did not specify a strict-communion position. From its inception the magazine included obituaries and news of the churches, under the heading, 'Religious Intelligence'. Not restricting its vision to East Anglia, the *Gospel Herald* welcomed news and contributions from other parts of the country.[13] The issue for January 1833 contained a piece by John Brine, as well as extracts from the Puritans: Christopher Love; Stephen Charnock; and Isaac Ambrose. As the months passed, there were more articles by contemporaries, but these were usually written under pseudonyms.

ii. The Calvinism of the Gospel Herald

The *Herald* laid much greater emphasis on the Calvinistic doctrines of grace than it did on believers' baptism. The first editorial made its position clear.

> The sentiments of ARMINIANISM (passing under different names) bid fair to inundate all the churches: against these we shall not fail to lift our voices, and by every possible means to caution our readers.[14]

It declared its opposition to Fullerism, which it dubbed a 'yea and nay gospel', because of its alleged contradictions.

---

[11] See pp. 223 n, 225–6 above.

[12] *Gospel Herald*, vol. 1, 1833, pp. 2,3.

[13] Addresses of signatories in volume 1 included, *inter alia*, Brighton, p. 67; Cheltenham, p. 77; Croydon, p. 83; Manchester, p. 131; and Poplar, p. 171.

[14] Ibid., vol.1, p. 2.

The Beginnings of the Strict Baptist Magazines

We promise our readers that the yea and nay gospel will find no sanction in our pages; such contradictions we deem derogatory to the glory of the Lord, and injurious to his family.[15]

The editors realized that the strength of their opposition to the Calvinism associated with Fuller could expose them to the charge of Antinomianism. This accusation they vigorously forestalled: 'Low sentiments and Antinomianism we equally detest.'[16] Throughout the period covered by this book, the *Herald* opposed Gadsby's teaching that the believer was free from the moral law. It suggested, however, that the accusation of Antinomianism 'is in general a mere bugbear to terrify the fearful and intimidate the enquirer'.[17]

According to the editors of the *Gospel Herald*, the ethos prevailing in the Baptist Colleges, together with the pressure for an academically-trained ministry, was a threat to the doctrinal integrity of the churches. They wrote in 1838:

> There is evidently a fixed determination on the part of men advocating Fuller's views to put down all ministers who have not passed through an academy, while they still strongly recommended any person, called educated for the ministry, even when there is [sic] neither natural or spiritual qualifications for the work.[18]

iii. CHURCHMANSHIP

The *Gospel Herald* also saw the Colleges as subversive of the practice of strict communion. In 1841 John Stock of Maidstone wrote:

> The sentiments of Andrew Fuller and Robert Hall have walked hand in hand over the length and breadth of many of our churches and are now the received sentiments in the various baptist colleges and academies; so much so that in one of our principal colleges, which contains about twenty-eight young men, who are studying for the ministry, there is not one strict communionist within the walls! Here are twenty-eight young

---

[15] Ibid., p. 3.

[16] Ibid., p. 2, 'low sentiments' here refers to Moderate Calvinism as opposed to High Calvinism.

[17] Ibid., p. 2; cf. vol. 2, p. 135.   [18] Ibid., vol. 6, 1838, p. Iv.

men who are to go forth and propagate these errors in our various churches.[19]

Although the *Herald* did not devote a great deal of space to the debate on the terms of communion, it made no secret of its position, deploring any move away from strict communion, which it considered to be 'New Testament order'.[20] It did not consider this practice to be in any way inimical to Baptist expansion. In 1841 a correspondent to the *Herald* reviewed the growth of the Baptist interest in Suffolk in the fifty years prior to 1835. During that period the number of churches grew from three to fifty-four. He pointed out that most of the preachers had been unlettered men and Hyper-Calvinists and he also noted that almost all of the churches practised strict communion during that half-century.[21] A later correspondent commented that Suffolk had sent four ministers of this type to London and 'they have become very useful and respectable ministers there, viz Messrs Keeble, Smith, Foreman and Dickerson'.[22]

The *Herald* was not opposed to education: 'We could wish that all our ministers were educated men.'[23] The content of the magazine was strongly doctrinal and it was clearly a venture in popular theological education. W. J. Styles' statement, quoted above,[24] indicates that biblical and theological topics were the subject of earnest debate in those communi-

---

[19] Ibid., vol. 9, 1841, p. 6. John Stock (1817–84) was himself an arts graduate of the new University College, London. Within eighteen months of writing this article, he had embraced the teaching of Fuller, but he never renounced his strict-communion views, *Gospel Herald*, vol. 10, 1842, p. 224; cf. Underwood, *HEB*, p. 209. A brief and inadequate life of Stock was published: A. M. Stalker, *Memorial Sketch of John Stock, LL.D*, London, 1885.

[20] *Gospel Herald*, vol. 4, 1836, p. 107.   [21] Ibid., vol. 9, 1841, p. 365.

[22] Ibid., vol 10, 1842, p. 38. John Keeble (c.1761–1824) was pastor at Blandford Street from 1798 to 1824, building up a flourishing congregation from a work almost extinct, R. Hoddy, *Memoir of Israel Atkinson*, London 1882, pp. 73–6. James Smith (1781–1839) pastor successively at Ilford, Essex, (1808-1833) and Providence, Shoreditch, 1834-9, C. Slim, *Memorials of Deceased Ministers*, Appendix, pp. 39–40. John Foreman (1791–1872), was pastor at Mount Zion, Hill Street, from 1827 to 1872, where he built up a church of nearly 500 members (Slim, *Memorials*, Appendix, pp. 15–17.

[23] *Gospel Herald*, vol. 9, 1841, p. 365.

[24] See above p. 226.

ties in which the *Herald* was welcomed. The anxieties of its editors arose from the fact that it regarded the Academies as hotbeds of Fullerism and open communion.

Within the *Herald*'s pages are frequent accounts of ordination services, at which the ordinand was expected to give a detailed statement of his faith. Those who considered they were called to preach were expected to submit themselves to their own church for the trial of their gifts, and to wait until these were approved before preaching more widely among the churches. If called to a pastorate, such a man should be ordained 'in fellowship with churches of the same faith and order'. Pastors alone should administer the Lord's Supper, and local preachers were expected to be among the communicants in the churches to which they belonged, when the communion service took place.[25] The concern about the practices of such preachers suggests that this procedure was not always followed. However, the concern itself reflects the exalted view of church order which had been characteristic of the old Dissent.

iv. CONTROVERSIES

Within the parameters of Hyper-Calvinism and strict communion, the *Gospel Herald* was prepared to allow some freedom of debate. Two issues were especially controversial among the emerging Strict Baptists in these years: the nature of Christ's sonship and the preaching of Christian experience.

The Sonship of Christ

John Stevens's pre-existarianism and denial that Christ was the Son of God by nature, have already been considered.[26] In 1835 these doctrines were criticized by W. H. Colyer, a Baptist minister from Foots Cray, Kent, and Frederick Silver, an Independent minister from London. A group of ministers met at St Neots to affirm their support for Stevens and his doctrine. Their *Friendly Address*[27] appeared in the *Herald*, which declared,

---

[25] *Gospel Herald*, vol. 2, 1834, pp. 257, 279-83; Ibid., vol. 3, 1835, p. 45.

[26] See pp. 213-7 above.

[27] George Murrell, et al., *The Friendly Address of Five Country Ministers to Mr John Stevens of London*, St Neots, 1835. This tract appears to have been distributed with the *Gospel Herald*, May 1835.

'The principles of justice dictated to us the course we have taken as the attempt has been made to fasten a falsehood on the character of one, whose moral and religious reputation ranks as high as any man we know.'[28] The views of Collins, the editor, on the controversial issues are unknown. He was, however, prepared to allow both sides to expound their views in the magazine. In 1843 William Fulton defended the orthodox view in the *Gospel Herald* and described pre-existarianism as 'a species of refined Arianism'.[29]

Experimental Preaching
It was not long before the editors of the *Gospel Herald* were facing another challenge. In 1836 the magazine reminded its readers that it had been the first cheap periodical to propagate the 'glorious doctrines of truth, believed, loved, preached, published, lived in and died in by Gill, Brine, Toplady and others'. It went on to refer to an abortive attempt 'to make a breach in our ranks during the year'.[30] This was probably a reference to the launch of *The Gospel Standard* magazine in 1835. This new publication advocated the Huntingtonian doctrine of the law, long preached by Gadsby but opposed by the *Herald*.

More seriously for future relationships, the *Standard* laid very heavy emphasis on what was termed 'experimental' preaching and which involved the analysis and exposition of Christian experience. This in itself should have caused the *Herald* little anxiety; Christian experience was an important theme in the preaching of Particular Baptists, as it had been in that of the Puritans. At its best this was to prove a valuable element in the preaching of men associated with the *Gospel Standard*. Christian experience is not, however, the only or even the primary theme of the Bible. What did not bode well for the future was a readiness in some circles to denounce doctrinal preaching as deficient and to dub those who expounded Christian doctrine as 'letter preachers'. A lack of balance at this point caused some experimental preachers to make experiences rather than the Word of God their rule. This has always proved a danger

---

[28] *Gospel Herald*, vol 3, 1835, p. lv.   [29] Ibid., vol 11, 1843, p. 43.
[30] Ibid., vol. 4, 1836, p. lii.

for men fascinated by this theme, but the danger was intensified in an age which delighted in all sorts of experiences. This was the age of Romanticism; the subordination of truth to feeling was widespread in the religious circles of the day, from Edward Irving and his associates to the Oxford Movement within the Church of England. The Baptists were not immune from the spirit of the age.

More detailed consideration of the contents of the *Gospel Standard* must be reserved for another section, but it seems that the editors of the *Gospel Herald* felt that they were under some pressure in 1836. They had gone on to the offensive against Arminianism and Fullerism, but were unprepared for the criticism from their fellow Hyper-Calvinists in the *Gospel Standard* on experimental preaching.

In 1841 an anonymous contributor to the *Herald*, after deploring the theology of J. H. Hinton, which he believed had gone beyond that of Andrew Fuller, proceeded to deal with another aberration.

> The device of the devil now seems to be to exclude doctrinal truth, by the substitution of an experience as the theme of the ministry; and so to set up a sort of anti-christ. We believe that an experience wrought by the Lord will come out – ought to come out in the pulpit labours – that it is right to tell what God has wrought in us and for us; but we know of no experience which is connected with salvation, apart from doctrinal truth. God has joined doctrine and experience together in the hearts of his elect.[31]

Further warnings appeared in the *Herald*. In 1847, a writer commented on the popularity of detailed accounts of spiritual experience:

> Hence of late years, we have had men writing their own biographies, relating many wonderful things in the true Huntingtonian fashion; either from a fear, it may be presumed, they should be forgotten, or from a desire to be known as great experimentalists.[32]

More specifically he noted:

> One of these periodicals (and which I have principally in view) is considered as the gauge or measure of Christian experience, and is modestly

[31] Ibid., vol. 9, 1841, p. 294.   [32] Ibid., vol, 15, 1847, p 94.

enough called the 'Gospel Standard', but which from its various sketches of character ... might be less inappropriately titled the Baptist Huntingtonian Portrait Gallery.[33]

In the same issue of the *Herald* further reference was made to admirers of the *Standard* as

Proud, boastful, heady and high-minded, the disciples of the Philpotonian school become a restless annoyance to the followers of peace in every church to which they belong. The ministry of the word, however faithfully and ably dispensed, is made the occasion of covert insinuation and open declamation against what is derisively termed 'dry doctrine' and 'legal duties'.[34]

v. THE READERSHIP OF THE GOSPEL HERALD

The subtitle of the *Gospel Herald* was *The Poor Christian's Magazine*. It sold at 2d per copy and was patently designed for the poor. The 'Address to Our Readers' in the first issue stated: 'We deeply regret that no cheap magazine upon gospel principles suited to the circumstances of the poor of the Redeemer's flock has found its way into existence.'[35] Presumably the more affluent could be expected to purchase larger works. The need to publish the magazine existed because 'the rapid increase and industrious circulation of books and tracts (containing the most fatal errors) among the poor, call with a loud voice to us, to exert ourselves in the use of all possible means, to check the pernicious influence of such publications.'[36]

Most of the articles were short, consisting of some two or three closely printed duodecimo pages, but in theological vocabulary and reasoning they made few concessions to the weak. Most of the ministers in the group associated with the *Herald* at this period seem to have been drawn from the agricultural working class or were tradesmen.[37] These sturdy rustic theologians showed a readiness to improve their own understand-

---

[33] Ibid. [34] Ibid., p. 99. [35] Ibid., vol. 1, 1833, p. 1. [36] Ibid., pp 1,2.
[37] Collins had been a draper's assistant; Foreman an agricultural labourer; William Palmer of Chatteris and London a brick maker; George Murrell of St Neots a shoemaker as had been John Stevens. James Wells had a succession of labouring jobs.

ing and presumably saw the pulpit as a means of educating their hearers. Such hearers, often of limited education, must have composed the bulk of the *Herald*'s readership.

Distribution figures are not available for the *Herald*. However, at the end of the first year the editors could write:

> Our magazine has succeeded beyond our most sanguine expectation; its voice is heard in nearly all the Counties of England. For this we are in part indebted to our esteemed Brethren in the Ministry, to whom we tender our warmest thanks; and earnestly invite their co-operation with us in this good cause.[38]

The title page of the first volume listed several agents in both East Anglia and London, as well as in Northampton, Banbury, Aylesbury, Tring, Coventry, and Birmingham. It also included an obituary and church news from as far afield as Manchester.[39]

Successive years indicate that the *Herald* had established itself among a body of faithful supporters. By the end of 1837, the editors noted: 'All suspicion is of course, by this time, removed from the minds of our Friends respecting the continuance of the *Gospel Herald* as a Monthly Publication.'[40] However, ten years later, the editor recorded:

> The *Gospel Herald* began its course under humble and discouraging circumstances. It has had a host of opponents, both professing and profane, who must have overcome it, but for divine aid. It has been deserted and betrayed by many, who once professed to admire its principles and to wish for its prosperity. It has seemed ready to give up all for lost; but has been saved to the present time from ruin and despair.[41]

In the absence of circulation figures, the reasons for the editor's note of discouragement are not completely clear. However, John Stevens had died in 1847. The year had also been one of some controversy for the Strict Baptist churches.[42] Nevertheless, the magazine continued to pay its way and had many years of circulation ahead. It was later merged with

---

[38] *Gospel Herald*, vol 1, 1833, p. lii.
[39] Ibid., pp 115, 128ff.
[40] Ibid., vol 5, 1837. p. Iv.
[41] Ibid., vol. 15, 1847, p. Iv.
[42] pp. 242, 264–6.

History of the English Calvinistic Baptists, 1771–1892

The Earthen Vessel and in the 1970s with *The Free Grace Record* to become *Grace Magazine*.

2. The Gospel Standard

The origins and early progress of *The Gospel Standard*[43] have been more clearly plotted than have those of the *Gospel Herald*. The *Standard* was the brainchild of William Gadsby's son, John, who with some difficulty overcame his father's fears that such a venture must fail. A preliminary prospectus was circulated among Gadsby's friends before the first issue appeared in August 1835 with a printing of five hundred copies. As orders poured into the Manchester office, it became clear that the supply was totally inadequate and a further five hundred copies were printed. With a steady demand from London and the south a further one thousand were printed, and by 1836 two thousand a month were being sold.[44]

i. John M'Kenzie and J. C. Philpot

William Gadsby's nation-wide peregrinations had created a reading public for the new magazine, but he never claimed great literary ability and almost certainly would not have had the time to produce a successful monthly. Quite soon, therefore, the Gadsbys called in the assistance of John M'Kenzie, a Scot of sound education who had views similar to their

---

[43] *The Gospel Standard, or Feeble Christian's Support*, vols. 1–13, 1835–46, Manchester; vols. 14– ,1847– , London.

[44] John Gadsby recounted his part in these events in an address reported in the *Gospel Standard*, 1885, p. 473 and reprinted in J. H. Philpot, *The Seceders*, vol. 2, London, 1932, pp. 60 ff. J. C. Philpot's account appeared in the *Gospel Standard*, 1864, and was reprinted in *The Seceders*, vol. 2, pp. 72 ff. There is also an account in S. F. Paul, *Historical Sketch of the Gospel Standard Baptists*, Hove, n.d., pp. 21, 22. Paul's account, which is superficial and without adequate documentation, suggests that one purpose in starting the *Standard* was to oppose Stevens's pre-existarian views, which were being broached in the *Gospel Herald*. The *Herald* did not promote Stevens's views on this subject and the early issues of the *Standard* make no reference to these. As indicated in the text, the doctrine of Law and the nature and importance of experience were more important areas of difference. B. A. Ramsbottom, *History of the Gospel Standard Magazine*, has recently given an account of these years, but unfortunately does not document his sources.

own. In 1835 M'Kenzie had left the Independents of Preston to form a small Particular Baptist church in that town.[45]

In March 1835 an event took place that was to prove to be of the greatest significance for the *Gospel Standard*. In that month Joseph Charles Philpot, fellow of Worcester College, Oxford, and perpetual curate of the parishes of Stadhampton and Chiselhampton, seceded from the Church of England and resigned his College Fellowship.[46]

Before his secession Philpot had proved himself an able preacher in a rural parish, packing his church with hearers drawn from miles around. During the 1830s, however, he completely lost sympathy with Anglicanism because of the inclusive nature of its formularies, which compelled him to assume the Christian character of all in the congregation and precluded effective discipline at the communion table. Gradually he moved to embrace Baptist convictions. Naturally cautious, Philpot hesitated for some time before turning his back on a situation of obvious usefulness. He finally broke with the Established Church and was also obliged to resign his Fellowship, which at that time was only open to members of the Established Church. His letter of resignation to the Provost of Worcester College, Oxford was published and passed through a number of editions. In it he declared:

---

[45] Philpot, *Seceders*, vol. 2, pp. 37–45. M'Kenzie's Calvinism seems to have been a bigger factor in his leaving the Independents than any convictions about baptism, ibid., p. 41; B. A. Ramsbottom, *History of the Gospel Standard Magazine*, p. 11.

[46] For details of J. C. Philpot (1802–69) see [Sarah L. Philpot], *Letters by the late Joseph Charles Philpot, M.A., with a Brief Memoir of His Life and Labours*, London 1871, hereinafter referred to as *Letters and Memoir*. The *Memoir* is brief but useful. Philpot's son, Joseph Henry, collected more letters together with those of William Tiptaft and these have been published in three volumes as *The Seceders (1829–69)*, vols. 1 and 2, ed. J. H. Philpot, London, 1931-2; vol. 3, ed. S. F. Paul, Brighton, 1960. Vols. 1 and 2 have excellent introductions with reminiscences by Philpot's son, who intended these volumes to be source material for a future historian (vol. 1, Preface to Second Impression). There is need for an adequate biography of J. C. Philpot. A comparison of the letters in *Letters and Memoir* and *The Seceders*, vol. 3, shows that Paul suppressed part of Philpot's correspondence and to some extent frustrated J. H. Philpot's design.

I secede from the Church of England because I can find in her scarce one mark of a true church. She tramples upon one ordinance of Christ by sprinkling infants, and calling it regeneration (the word of God allowing no other than the baptism of believers and that by immersion), and profanes the other by permitting the ungodly to participate. The true church is despised, but she is honoured. The true church is persecuted, but she is the persecutor. The true church is chosen out of the world, but she is part and parcel of it. The true church consists only of the regenerate, but she embraces in her universal arms all the drunkards, liars, thieves and immoral characters of the land. She christens them, she confirms them, she marries them, she buries them. And she pronounces of all for whom she executes these offices, that they are regenerate, that 'all their sins are forgiven them', that they are 'the servants of God'.[47]

Philpot's *Letter to the Provost of Worcester College, Oxford* was warmly reviewed in both the *Gospel Herald*[48] and the *Gospel Standard*.[49]

In September 1835, Philpot was baptized in the little village chapel at Allington, Wiltshire, by John Warburton of Trowbridge. Subsequently he became pastor of the Baptist Churches at Stamford and Oakham, in Lincolnshire and Rutland respectively. William Tiptaft of Abingdon, a close friend of his, who had seceded from the Anglican ministry nearly three and a half years earlier, had introduced Philpot to the Gadsby group.[50]

Tiptaft, a Cambridge graduate, was a powerful preacher, who had already fought his own battles with the ecclesiastical authorities. A man of action and generous to the point of self-impoverishment, he lacked Philpot's penetrating mind and literary abilities.[51]

---

[47] J. C. Philpot, *A Letter to the Provost of Worcester College, Oxford on Resigning His Fellowship, and Seceding from the Church of England*, 1835, pp. 16,17. The letter is also printed without its Preface in *The Seceders*, vol 1, pp. 267-88.

[48] *Gospel Herald*, vol. 3, 1835, p. 239 and vol. 4, 1836 p. 74, which notes that within less than a year 10,000 copies had been sold.

[49] *Gospel Standard*, vol. 1, 1835 pp. 94-5.

[50] *The Seceders*, vol. 1. pp 118-20.

[51] For details of William Tiptaft (1803-64) see J. C. Philpot, *Memoir of the Late William Tiptaft*, London, 1867, and *The Seceders*, vol. 1. Details of his secession are

Philpot was not the originator of the *Gospel Standard*; he was not baptized until after its first two issues appeared. Nevertheless, the Gadsbys had sufficient confidence in his sympathies and abilities to consult him. He was shown the proofs of the opening address of the first issue and later commented: 'I returned [it] without doing anything to it beyond suggesting one or two insignificant verbal alterations.'[52]

ii. THE EARLY GOSPEL STANDARD

J. C. Philpot's involvement with the *Gospel Standard* developed gradually. He contributed to the early issues, but had no editorial responsibility.[53] From 1838, he wrote the editorial 'Addresses', which appeared in each January issue, but even then, exercised no control.[54] He later explained:

> I was not one of the Editors till, I think, about the year 1840, when some circumstances unnecessary to mention convinced M'Kenzie and myself, for both of us somehow or other got into editorial harness, that it was desirable for us, as we had been for some time the real Editors of it, to assume the name and the office, and with it the whole control, he taking the part of reading and selecting the pieces for insertion, and I for the most part writing the Reviews and Addresses, etc.[55]

The powerful editorial control exercised by Philpot from 1840 until 1869, coupled with the subsequent posthumous influence of his writings, can easily obscure the character of the magazine in its first five years. It is important, therefore, to take a closer look at this early period of its history. The first issue made clear the *Standard*'s commitment to Calvinism and

---

given in W. Tiptaft, *A Letter Addressed to the Bishop of Salisbury*, Abingdon 1831. This is not published in *The Seceders*. Subsequently the Bishop threatened Tiptaft with legal action for preaching in unconsecrated buildings. The bishop argued that an Anglican clergyman could not resign his orders and was subject to episcopal control. Tiptaft's response was to publish the whole correspondence in *A Letter to the Bishop of Salisbury by William Tiptaft, to which are added Three Letters from the Bishop to Mr Tiptaft, Threatening Him with Legal Proceedings for Preaching in Unconsecrated Places and Mr Tiptaft's Answers*, Manchester, 1834. See also *The Seceders*, vol 1, pp. 61–3.

[52] *The Seceders*, vol. 2, p. 72.   [53] Ibid., p. 73.   [54] Ibid.   [55] Ibid.

strict communion.[56] In these respects its position was the same as that of the *Gospel Herald*. Its editors justified the new venture, however, on the grounds that they would uphold the Huntingtonian view of the believer's freedom from the moral law,[57] a view, which the *Herald*, of course, opposed. They also intended to be a Nonconformist journal, unlike *The Gospel Magazine*, which was an Anglican magazine that promoted Hyper-Calvinism at that time.[58] The editors of the *Standard* promised that 'our pages will not be altogether closed against fair and candid discussion'.[59] The first issue also stated that 'we shall be glad at all times, of information from all parts of the country, relative to Anniversaries, Change of Ministers, etc.'.[60] Unlike the *Herald*, however, very little information of that nature ever appeared in the body of the magazine, and Philpot later made it clear that while he was editor it never would.[61]

The *Gospel Herald* was promoted by the friends of John Stevens. It is not certain to what extent his pre-existarian views were accepted by his followers. The *Standard* would have nothing to do with such notions. In 1836, it reviewed a reprint of Joseph Hussey's *The Glory of Christ Vindicated*; the reviewer cautiously commended it, but considered that it was seriously marred by pre-existarianism, which he described as

> a doctrine or fabrication that we cannot receive; and we are much mistaken if it has not been a source of great uneasiness, contention and strife amongst God's people. Under these circumstances we cannot so heartily recommend the work as we otherwise should have done.[62]

Later in the same year the *Standard* briefly reviewed James Wells's *Protest Against the Pre-existence of the Human Soul of Christ*,[63] suggesting that the type of speculation discussed was unsuitable for its readers, although of Wells's tract it could write, 'We have reason to think the work will be found as good as most of the sort extant.'[64] Wells, already exercising an influential ministry in Southwark, was to become the most

---

[56] *Gospel Standard*, vol. 1, 1835, pp. 3, 4.   [57] Ibid., p. 1.   [58] Ibid., p. 2.
[59] Ibid., p. 4.   [60] Ibid., p. ii of cover.   [61] Ibid., vol. 15, 1849, p. 5.
[62] Ibid., vol. 2, 1836, pp. 140, 14.
[63] James Wells, *A Protest Against the Doctrine of the Pre-existence of the Human Soul of the Lord Jesus Christ*, London, 1836.   [64] *Gospel Standard*, vol. 2, 1836, p. 165.

The Beginnings of the Strict Baptist Magazines

popular of the London Strict Baptist preachers. At this time he was independent of the Gadsby and Stevens groups and was fairly well accepted by both.[65]

Differences of emphasis and even tensions between the *Herald* and the *Standard* did not preclude contact between the two constituencies. In 1836 and 1837 the *Standard* included extracts from John Foreman[66] and one even from John Stevens.[67] It recommended, albeit with certain reservations, the tracts of Charles Drawbridge of Rushden, another minister in this group, stating, 'They are the best tracts we see abroad and would make excellent supplanters of the rubbish generally circulated by Tract Societies.'[68]

The *Standard*'s heavy emphasis on the analysis and discussion of Christian experience was evident from the outset and represented a tradition that went back to the Evangelical Awakening, but which was modified by Huntington. The *Herald*'s more overtly doctrinal articles reflect more the traditions of the old Dissent, particularly as the school of John Gill had developed them. The difference should not, however be pressed too far. The *Herald* was interested in Christian experience, but as the application of Christian doctrine. Differences became more apparent after Philpot became the editor in 1840.

In the early years, William Gadsby and J. C. Philpot were not always in agreement. Tensions surfaced in 1837. Gadsby, although a robust Dissenter, had Anglican friends amongst whom was William Nunn of Manchester.[69] Gadsby asked Philpot to review a sermon by Nunn. Philpot

---

[65] Philpot wrote approvingly of the published experience of Wells, ibid., vol. 6, 1840, pp. 264–7, but was critical of George Wright for a lack of clear experience in his preaching, Ibid., vol. 9, 1843, pp. 589–62. Later he wrote of what he called Suffolk Divinity as 'very deficient in that power and unction, that vein of experience, that entrance into the very heart and conscience of God's people which are so sweet and profitable', Ibid., vol. 10, 1844, p. 63.

[66] Ibid., vol. 2, 1836 p.216; vol. 3, 1837, pp. 48, 96.

[67] Ibid., vol. 2, 1836 p. 192.

[68] Ibid., vol. 3, 1837, p. 262.

[69] There is an excellent discussion of the work of William Nunn (1786–1840) in Ian J. Shaw, *High Calvinists in Action*, Oxford University Press, 2002, pp. 69–110.

could not discover the right experimental note and wrote a blistering essay, stating:

> There is, indeed, abundance of dry doctrine to feed the dead Calvinists of Birmingham, with a head as keen, a tongue as smooth, and a heart as hard as their own cutlery. But where are the gracious operations of the Spirit entered into and experimentally traced out?[70]

He went on to question the genuineness of Nunn's Calvinism and his motives for remaining within the Church of England. Gadsby was shocked by Philpot's severity and would only allow the piece to be inserted as a letter, not as a review. According to John Gadsby, William exclaimed, 'Poor dear man! If Nunn had not been in the Church, this would never have been written.'[71]

Philpot's treatment of Nunn, not only expressed his impatience with Hyper-Calvinists, who remained within the Church of England, it also indicated his own pre-occupation with the more sombre aspects of Christian experience. This was to be characteristic of Philpot before about 1850. For this reason Gadsby took him to task, when he reviewed one of Philpot's most famous sermons, *The Heir of Heaven Walking in Darkness and the Heir of Hell Walking in Light*. Although he considered this to be 'well calculated for much good in this day of blasphemy and rebuke', Gadsby added by way of caution:

> Nevertheless we do frankly confess that we think a little more expression of the glory of Christ; of what God in his rich grace, has made his people in Christ and what they derive from Christ; and of the way in which the Holy Spirit draws them from self to Christ, would have been an additional glory to the discourse.[72]

William Gadsby did not hesitate to make political statements when he considered these to be necessary. He spoke on the platform of the Anti-Corn Law League and on occasions made political allusions in his sermons.[73] However, since the *Gospel Standard* was founded to cater for

---

[70] Ibid., p. 86. The sermon reviewed was preached in Birmingham.
[71] *The Seceders,* vol. 2, p. 65. [72] *Gospel Standard,* vol. 3, 1837, p. 118.
[73] See pp. 194–8 above.

the devotional and spiritual needs of Christians, its readers must have been astonished by the appearance of an article in December 1836, 'On the Horror of War'. This was a plea for pacifism submitted by a member of the Society of Friends. An editorial note expressed hesitation about its inclusion, as it was an 'evident digression', but associated itself with its argument by stating:

> The design of it is to carry conviction to the mind, of the horrors of war, and the awful responsibility attached to those who engage in it; and if it be made the means of accomplishing this, the end will be answered.[74]

The author of the article insisted that war could never be justified: 'No battle was ever fought, nor ever will be, without involving the guilt of murder.' Anticipating the Judgment Day, he portrays kings, statesmen, officers, and men before the last assize when 'every mortal wound at Waterloo will be held and adjudged as murder, the guilt of which will rest somewhere.'[75]

Gadsby's name had been enough to gather a readership large enough to make the *Standard* viable. However, by 1838 he was expressing doubts as to whether it could continue beyond the end of the year. It paid its way but there were not enough suitable articles forthcoming.[76] The need for suitable writing had presumably been the reason why Philpot had been asked to write the 1838 Annual Address.

The magazine did continue, but indicated some editorial confusion in 1839. In the February issue of that year, William Gadsby wrote a letter to the editors asking them to make it clear that a piece in the January issue bearing the initials W. G., was not written by him.[77] In the April issue, one of Gadsby's published sermons was very critically reviewed.

> We find from the preface, that the author very reluctantly consented to have this work published, and we hope that in future in a similar case, his objections will be too strong to be overcome. It was originally written for the amusement of Sunday-school scholars, and no doubt it has so far the desired effect, as the first part particularly is full of our friend's natural,

---

[74] *Gospel Standard*, vol. 2, 1836, p. 284.
[75] Ibid., pp. 287, 288.
[76] Ibid., vol. 4, 1838, pp. 235, 6.
[77] Ibid., vol. 5, 1839, pp. 41, 2.

good natured humour; but as it contains neither doctrine or experience, in other words as it is national and not spiritual starvation that is treated on, a spiritually hungry soul would look in vain for food.[78]

The style is Philpot's: he was writing reviews by this time.[79] In the same year he was also writing letters to the editors[80] and by his own statement was not an editor until 1840. The magazine was being run by an anonymous and possibly fluctuating collective leadership. The ageing William Gadsby was clearly not in control. His son, John, was an energetic businessman, but does not seem to have had the literary gifts of an editor. Lack of direction and uncertain editorial supervision may well be the circumstances hinted at by Philpot, which led him and M'Kenzie to assume control in 1840.

iii. THE READERSHIP OF THE GOSPEL STANDARD

Like the *Gospel Herald*, the *Standard* was intended for the poor. It was price at 2d a copy. In his first editorial, Philpot wrote:

> The children of God are mostly poor, and cannot buy books; and are usually much occupied in bodily labour, and have little time to read. Thus they can purchase a pamphlet, where they cannot buy a volume, and can read a magazine, where they cannot peruse a book.[81]

The first generation of preachers had emerged from poverty. William Gadsby, John Warburton, and John Kershaw had all been weavers. Many later preachers came from the labouring classes as obituaries and biographies testify. However, from the 1830s the *Gospel Standard* group attracted another type of preacher. Philpot, Tiptaft, John Kay, and Frederick Tryon had all been Anglican ministers and were University graduates. G. S. B. Isbell was reading for ordination before becoming an

---

[78] Ibid., pp 92,3.

[79] According to Mrs Philpot, the first review Philpot wrote for the *Standard* was of John Warburton's *Mercies of a Covenant God*, published in April 1838, *Letters and Memoir*, p. 97. In the previous year he had of course reviewed Nunn's sermon, but this was inserted as a signed letter.

[80] *Gospel Standard*, vol. 5, 1839, pp. 187, 8; 198–200.

[81] Ibid., vol. 4, 1838, p. 3.

The Beginnings of the Strict Baptist Magazines

Independent and then a Strict Baptist minister.[82] Grey Hazlerigg, of Leicester, was the son of a baronet and a former army officer.[83]

Published obituaries in the *Standard* show that many readers would not have had educational advantages, although Philpot's editorship would have also attracted another type of reader. Many deacons must have been poor men and of limited education, although Philpot's leading deacons at Oakham and Stamford were both physicians.[84] His correspondents and friends included Lady Hazlerigg and Lady Lucy Smith, grand-daughter of John Thornton of the Clapham Sect, but other correspondents included merchants at home and abroad as well as the poor.[85]

The magazine, which circulated about two thousand copies a month before Philpot became editor, rose to just under seven thousand by the beginning of 1841. Philpot indicated that it was being read throughout the land. By 1847 it circulated nine thousand copies a month.[86] In 1849, he said it was read, 'even in foreign lands where the truth is neither preached nor known, in the Australian hut or the Canadian loghouse, a piece from Rusk, or a letter from Huntington, not to mention living correspondents, may be a messenger of mercy'.[87]

John Gadsby was the proprietor and publisher of the magazine throughout Philpot's time and later. Although he exercised no control over its contents, he could have dismissed Philpot at any time, if the two had seriously disagreed. On his part,

> John Gadsby's keen commercial sense enabled him to make a small fortune from the success of the *Gospel Standard*. But there were few real money-spinners in the religious periodical trade as a whole, and the

---

[82] *The Seceders*, vol. 2, pp. 137–9.   [83] Ibid., pp 135–7.

[84] William Keal at Oakham was deacon throughout Philpot's pastorate. At Stamford J. G. de Merveilleux was a deacon until his death in 1843. He built the chapel at his own expense. Both men were doctors. *The Seceders,* vol. 2, pp. 81 ff.

[85] *The Seceders*, vol. 2, pp 122–32.

[86] *Gospel Standard*, vol. 7, 1841, p. 4; ibid., vol. 13, 1847 p. 7. In 1857, Philpot was to claim a circulation of nearly 10,000 copies a month, *Letters and Memoir*, p. 254. Rosemary Taylor quotes the figure 12,000 for 1865, 'English Baptist Periodicals', p. 177.

[87] *Gospel Standard*, vol. 15, 1859, p. 5.

Baptist market, though active, was too small to sustain more than a very few prosperous journals.[88]

3. THE PRIMITIVE COMMUNIONIST

In the years before 1850, there were no other Strict and Particular Baptist magazines, which could compare in influence with the *Gospel Herald* and the *Gospel Standard*. Nevertheless, two others, the *Primitive Communionist* and the *Earthen Vessel*, deserve some attention.

The Primitive Communionist[89] first appeared in 1838. From 1841 until its demise in 1857 it was known as *The Primitive Church Magazine*. It was never widely read; in 1851 the circulation was below one thousand five hundred copies a month.[90] Its importance lies in the fact that it was an attempt to retain the practice of strict communion among mainstream Baptist churches. Its editors, George Pritchard, William Norton, and Robert William Overbury, were all connected with the great strict-communion leaders of the past, and not one of them was a Hyper-Calvinist. Although strict communionists, they were therefore not close to those men who belonged to the Stevens and Gadsby schools.

The oldest member of this group was George Pritchard, who in 1838 had recently resigned from the pastorate of Keppel Street, London, where he had succeeded John Martin in 1817. He had known Booth and Rippon and had already defended strict communion in print. Joint-secretary of the Baptist Irish Society from 1823, Pritchard was also the biographer of Ivimey and Newman. His respect for these earlier leaders, together with his own convictions, helps to explain his involvement in the magazine at a time when the practice of open communion was spreading.[91]

---

[88] R. Taylor, 'English Baptist Periodicals', p. 177.

[89] *The Primitive Communionist*, London, vol. 1, 1838–40, *The Primitive Church Magazine* from vol. 2, 1841–57.

[90] R. Taylor, op. cit. p. 35.

[91] George Pritchard (1773–1852) had been a member of Keppel Street under Martin and at the recommendation of Martin, Booth and Rippon went to Eld Lane, Colchester, where he was pastor from 1804–12. (E. Spurrier, *Memorials of the*

William Norton's only pastorate was at Bow where he succeeded William Newman in 1836. He had been baptized in Norwich by Joseph Kinghorn and trained for the ministry at Stepney College. He resigned his pastorate following the breakdown of his health in 1841, and thereafter devoted himself to writing.[92] Together with R. W. Overbury, he set up the Baptist Tract Society in 1841. This existed to promote Baptist and especially strict-communion principles.[93]

Robert W. Overbury, the third editor, was Assistant to Joseph Ivimey at Eagle Street, London, and succeeded him in the pastorate there from 1834 to 1853.[94]

The editors of the *Primitive Communionist* considered that open communion was gaining ground, not for theological reasons, but 'because it seems to wear the lovely aspect of liberality'.[95] The open-communion men, it argued, were really out of step with Christian thinking generally, as well as with Baptists abroad.

> Most of our Paedobaptist brethren would, we believe, feel it their duty to refuse admission to the Lord's Table, to those whom they deem unbaptized. The Baptist Churches in America, who are much more numerous than those in England, with few exceptions walk by the same rule.[96]

Baptist Church Worshipping in Eld Lane Chapel, Colchester, Colchester, 1889. Pritchard was subsequently at Shouldham Street, London and Keppel Street, 1817–37, C. Slim, *Memorials of Deceased Ministers*, pp. 213-4).

[92] William Norton (1812–90) was the son of a Norfolk landed proprietor. He remained a powerful advocate of strict communion and was prominent in the lawsuit to prevent open communion at St Mary's, Norwich, in 1860 (G. Gould, *Open Communion and the Baptists of Norwich*, Norwich, 1860, passim). For obituary see *Baptist Handbook*, 1890.

[93] Titles included: *Strict Communion Defended by an Independent Minister, Questions and Answers on the Subject of Communion, The Practical Tendency of Mixed Communion*. Tract 10, p. 8, specifically stated that the society was formed to combat Robert Hall's views.

[94] R. W. Overbury (c.1811–68) pastor ar Eagle Street, 1834–53, and subsequently at Devonport until his death (C. Slim, *Memorials*, p. 199).

[95] *The Primitive Communionist*, vol. 1, 1838–40, p. 1.

[96] Ibid., p. 2.

In 1840 William Norton expressed the fear that 'if wishes, such as have been recently expressed', [for open communion and membership] 'gain prevalence, the Baptist denomination will soon cease to be.'[97]

No magazine devoted so much space to the communion controversy as did the *Primitive Communionist;* ironically, none had so little success. Robert Hall, Francis Cox, and their fellow open-communionists, had done their work well; their views advanced steadily. It is difficult to imagine a periodical sustaining interest for many years, when it simply existed to debate the communion controversy. The churches among which it circulated probably felt that on so many issues they had more in common with open-communion churches in the Baptist Union than with the strict-communion groups. The other Strict Baptist magazines were more concerned to expound their understanding of the gospel; for them strict communion was a secondary issue, practised in their churches, but seldom discussed in print.

4. *The Earthen Vessel*

The Earthen Vessel[98] was founded in 1843 by the pastor and publisher Charles Waters Banks; he was also its editor until 1881. During the years covered by this study, Banks was the pastor at Crosby Row Chapel, Southwark.[99] He was a curious mixture, a convinced strict communionist and High Calvinist, a Tory in politics, and an admirer of the Church of England.[100] In later years he wrote against the disestablishment of the Irish Church, and thereby incurred the wrath of C. H. Spurgeon and the commendation of the Bishop of Llandaff.[101]

Banks' aim was not to rival existing Strict Baptist journals, but to draw together groups which seemed to be moving further and further apart.

> The *Earthen Vessel* is not intended to oppose, or supersede, or take the place of any similar work previously in existence: its design is simply to

---

[97] Ibid., p. 205
[98] *The Earthen Vessel*, London, 1844 onwards.
[99] Adeline Mary Banks, *The Reverend Charles Waters Banks,* London, 1890, pp. 52-4.
[100] Ibid., pp. 169, 177.   [101] Ibid., p. 66.

carry the testimony of living souls to the power and fruitfulness, the value and savour, of vital godliness, not only among those who have already believed, but also into those dark parts of the earth, where the voice of the living ministry is seldom, or ever [sic] heard. The *Earthen Vessel* is the organ of NO PARTY: it is not under the influence or direction of any body of ministers: as far as man is concerned, it stands alone.[102]

Banks was a conciliator. He wrote warmly of William Gadsby[103] but also gave publicity to a group which broke away from Gadsby's old church in Manchester.[104] He admired John Stevens.[105] In the late 1840s, he was promoting James Osbourn's preaching tours[106] and sympathizing with J. C. Philpot, when the latter was being attacked on all sides.[107] He retained a close friendship with James Wells, who was not the easiest of associates.

All reconcilers are liable to be misunderstood and Banks was to find himself in an uncomfortable position in 1860, when controversy over the Eternal Sonship of Jesus Christ came to a head. He held the orthodox view[108] but was willing to allow both sides to expound their teaching in the *Earthen Vessel*.[109] As early as 1847 he published a somewhat confused article on 'The Sonship of Jesus Christ', in which the author argued against the terms 'eternally begotten' and 'eternal generation', but argued for the Athanasian Creed.[110] Banks, a man of action, was not as able in handling theological concepts as was either Philpot or Collins. The magazine was more popular in style than either the *Herald* or the *Standard* and included lots of gossipy news, much of it gathered by Banks on his frequent preaching tours and written up as articles in railway carriages.

[102] *Earthen Vessel*, vol. 5, 1849, January wrapper.   [103] Ibid., vol. 3, 1847, p. 124.
[104] Ibid., vol. 4, 1848, pp. 267–71.   [105] Ibid., vol. 3, 1847, pp. 245–51.
[106] Ibid., pp. 108-9; vol. 5, 1849, pp 161, 2. Osbourn is discussed further in chapter 13.
[107] Ibid., vol. 3, 1847, pp. 263,4; Ibid., vol. 5, 1849, p. 29.
[108] *Earthen Vessel*, 1860, p. 301, and 1874, p. 344, quoted in *Christian's Pathway*, vol. 36, 1931, p. 188.
[109] Ibid., p. 189.
[110] Ibid., vol. 3, 1847, pp. 145, 6.

The early years of the *Earthen Vessel* were a struggle. Its initial circulation was two hundred copies a month.[111] By the beginning of 1846 it was two thousand five hundred and by December 1848 it had risen to four thousand, selling at 2d per copy.[112] By the end of 1848 Banks met with financial difficulties. After the first two years of publication he had made a loss of ninety-six pounds. The magazine had no working capital, although Banks had purchased second-hand presses to do his own printing. These presses proved to be so unsatisfactory that he replaced them with new ones. By December 1848 he was facing bills of two hundred pounds without the prospect of being able to pay. Always resourceful, he transferred the ownership of the magazine to six trustees, who were members of the church at Crosby Row, issued an appeal signed by twelve ministers, and set off round the country to gather support.[113] By March 1849, he could report that he had collected one hundred and sixty pounds after a fund-raising journey of over two thousand miles.[114] Money continued to come in,[115] and the *Vessel* survived: over the next decade its circulation rose to over eight thousand.[116]

In spite of suspicion Banks pushed on. He considered all Strict Baptist Hyper-Calvinists as his associates and sought to unite them by his pen and his visits. Industrious to the end it was recorded that a few hours before his death, he had been sitting up in bed, 'surrounded with letters, pen, ink, and all the concomitants of an editor's room'.[117] When he died in March 1886, *The Times* wrote of him as 'long the most prominent representative of the Calvinistic Baptists'.[118]

* * * * *

The establishment and development of magazines in the two decades before 1850 reflects the growing self-consciousness of the Strict and

---

[111] R. Taylor, 'English Baptist Periodicals', p. 38.
[112] *Earthen Vessel*, vol. 5, 1849, January wrapper.   [113] Ibid.   [114] Ibid., p. 96.
[115] See acknowledgements on *Earthen Vessel* wrappers in 1849.
[116] R. Taylor, 'English Baptist Periodicals', p. 38.
[117] Quoted in Iain H. Murray, *Spurgeon v. Hyper-Calvinism*, Edinburgh: Banner of Truth, 1995, p. 45.
[118] Quoted in A. M. Banks, *Charles Waters Banks*, p. 177.

The Beginnings of the Strict Baptist Magazines

Particular Baptist groupings. They represent differences of emphasis and tradition, although the steady, if slow, progress of the *Earthen Vessel* suggests some overlap of the groups represented by the *Gospel Herald* and the *Gospel Standard*. The magazines not only promoted their own agenda, but they provided fellowship between churches and individuals that may previously have felt a sense of isolation. With the exception of the *Primitive Church Magazine*, they were busily promoting fellowship outside the ranks of the Baptist Union and showing that non-involvement with that body did not necessarily condemn a church to perpetual isolation. The failure of the *Primitive Church Magazine* indicates that strict communion was ceasing to be an issue in Baptist Union circles by the middle of the nineteenth century. The success of the *Gospel Herald* and the *Gospel Standard* indicates that Hyper-Calvinism was a more important factor in developing a distinct Strict and Particular Baptist identity than was strict communion.

13

Joseph Charles Philpot

I stand before Him, whose eyes are as flames of fire, to search out the secrets of my heart. And what is this poor vain world with all its gilded-clay, painted touch-wood honours and respectability, and soap-bubble charms? What is all the wealth of the Church piled up in one heap, compared to a smile of a loving Saviour's countenance?

J. C. Philpot

We are apt to get presumptuous. We, who have many comforts, get to think it is all right with us. May we, however, be kept awake! I would rather you should go to Heaven doubting your interest in Christ than that you should go to Hell presuming that you are safe when really you are not. It is a sad and sinful thing to be always doubting; but, still, it is infinitely better than to have a name to live while you are dead.

C. H. Spurgeon

Nineteenth-century Strict Baptist development cannot be understood apart from the life and work of Joseph Charles Philpot. Beloved by many, sternly criticized by others, his leadership was such that even those who resisted his influence could not escape its impact. His writings, composed with an easy elegance, have their own attraction and still circulate among groups of Calvinistic experientalists, of Paedobaptist as well as Baptist conviction.

Joseph Charles Philpot was the fourth child and third son of Charles Philpot, and his wife Maria, née Lafargue. Charles Philpot was rector of Ripple, a parish about two miles inland from Deal, on the coast of East Kent. There, on 13 September 1802, Joseph was born. His mother, although born in England, had an entirely French ancestry. His physician son, Joseph Henry Philpot, was to comment that this genetic heritage helped to explain his passionate temperament. Serious childhood illnesses also played a part in his development. Growing up near the Kent coast during the Napoleonic Wars, this intelligent boy cannot have been unaware of the national crisis. Military and naval activity surrounded him, and there was much talk of invasion. Throughout his life he was to display a shrewd appreciation of national issues and affairs of state even though he disdained any interest in party politics.

Quickly realizing that Joseph was the brightest of his sons, Charles Philpot laid the foundations of his education at home. After a good grounding in the classical languages, he entered Merchant Taylors' School at the age of nine. His schooling was soon interrupted by tuberculosis and, in the words of his son, 'He was sent home to recover or die.' He recovered, albeit slowly, but during the months of convalescence he spent hours in his father's library devouring histories, novels, and Restoration dramas, some of which, he later confessed, he wished he had never opened. He was, however, augmenting his formal education with a breadth of knowledge that would later undergird his writing and speaking. Classical tuition continued under the direction of his father until at the age of twelve he was sent back to London, this time to St Paul's School, where he excelled, and eventually won an open scholarship to Worcester College, Oxford.

Oxford in the autumn of 1821 was an exhilarating place for a bright young man, not least because of the galaxy of brilliant students who had been attracted to the University. During his undergraduate years Philpot's closest friend was Francis Newman, younger brother of John Henry, the future Cardinal. Of the brothers Philpot later wrote:

> I once well knew two brothers. I hardly like to mention their names, though none are better known through the length and breadth of the land. They were both men of most powerful intellect, refined and cultivated to the highest point by the most indefatigable study and were distinguished ornaments of the University to which they belonged.[1]

[1] J. H. Philpot, ed., *The Seceders*, vol. 1, 2nd Impression, London, C. J. Farncombe, 1931, p. 17. Joseph Henry Philpot identified these two friends of his father as John Henry and Francis William Newman.

His other friends included Frederick Oakley, who like J. H. Newman was to be a prominent figure in the Oxford Movement and later to join the Roman Catholic Church. Another was E. B. Pusey, who although slightly older than Philpot, was to be ordained by his side at the hands of Bishop Lloyd of Oxford in June 1828. He never knew John Keble well, but when as an exhausted undergraduate he fell asleep on the top of the London to Oxford coach, it was Keble whose protecting arm prevented him from falling on to the road.

Conversion

At Oxford, Philpot sustained his early academic promise, in spite of tubercular pneumonia, which caused another break in his studies and left him with a permanent serious weakness. Ill health did not however prevent him being awarded a First in Classics in 1824. After graduation he remained in Oxford, tutoring pupils for another twelve months and securing a Fellowship at his College. By now his father had died and his mother appears to have been partially dependent upon him for her support. It may well have been this family responsibility that led him to accept the offer of a generously-paid post as a tutor to the two sons of a wealthy Irish lawyer, Edward Pennefather, and his wife Susannah. Early in 1826 Philpot crossed the Irish Sea to begin his work at Rathsallagh, a beautiful country estate in the Wicklow mountains, south of Dublin. For over a year all went well, but in these idyllic surroundings Philpot fell in love with Anne, the eldest daughter of the family. Marriage to an impecunious don who had not yet made his way in the world was considered to be out of the question, and the young lady was sent away to stay with relations, while Philpot worked out the remaining three months of his contract.

Philpot was heartbroken. In his deep distress his formal Christianity had failed him, but now he began to pray as never before. Later he recalled the bitter spring of 1827: 'I have often wetted the pommel of my saddle with tears amid the lonely valleys of the Wicklow hills, or galloped half-distractedly along the sea-shore, where no eye could see, or ear hear me cry out and groan, sometimes from natural trouble and sometimes in

Joseph Charles Philpot

pouring out my soul before the Lord.' The seemingly unrelievable sorrow was not without fruit, for he was later to write: 'I have every reason to love Ireland, for there, in the early spring of 1827, the first beams of light and life visited my previously dead and benighted soul, and Irish valleys and mountains witnessed the first tears and prayers that went up out of the heart to the throne of grace.'

There was however one person at hand with some understanding of his needs. Edward Pennefather's wife, Susannah, was the elder sister of John Nelson Darby, later a dynamic leader among the Plymouth Brethren, although at this time still a curate in the Church of Ireland. Fifty years later, Darby was to claim that he had been instrumental in Philpot's conversion. This was probably an exaggeration, as Darby himself had not come to full assurance before Philpot left Ireland, while Philpot wrote of this time: 'Though not without a hope in God's mercy, I was not favoured until some years after with any special manifestation of Christ.' It would nevertheless appear that Darby was able to help Philpot, and interestingly, signed one of the testimonials required when Philpot presented himself for ordination in Oxford.[2]

STADHAMPTON AND CHISELHAMPTON

Leaving Ireland with its poignant memories, Philpot resumed his teaching in Oxford and also prepared for ordination, which took place in June 1828. By that time he was out of sympathy with the aspirations and interests of many of his colleagues and felt somewhat uneasy in the Senior Common Room of Worcester College. He fell foul of the Provost and Fellows when he and a group of friends held a meeting for prayer and Bible study in the Common Room. Outside the College he was playing a very active part in the affairs of the Oxford Evangelicals.

After ordination he accepted the charge of the twin parishes of Stadhampton and Chiselhampton as perpetual curate, caring for them in the absence of a superannuated rector. These parishes were about seven miles south of Oxford. 'I was raw indeed when I went there', he wrote,

---

[2] Timothy C. F. Stunt, *From Awakening to Secession*, Edinburgh, T. & T. Clark, 2000, p. 205; cf. Philpot, *The Seceders*, vol. 1.

'but had many trials and few friends or counsellors in them. I often acted very rashly and hastily, and frequently mistook my own spirit for the Spirit of the Lord.'

For seven years Philpot continued in this curacy. He threw himself into the work, preaching twice every Sunday, conducting a Sunday School and a catechism class, as well as an informal service every Sunday evening in his lodgings. No longer having to teach Latin and Greek in Oxford, his son noted that 'he set himself to study with all the greater diligence the languages in which the sacred writings have come down to us, and in this he persevered throughout the rest of his life. Seldom a day passed in which he did not devote a full hour every morning to the Hebrew Testament, and a like period every evening to the Greek.'[3] It is perhaps not surprising that there were times when his health broke down and he had to take long periods of rest.

The local squire did not appreciate his ministry and on occasions Philpot was very lonely; but gradually his preaching drew a large congregation, packing his village churches.[4] Some of these people travelled a considerable distance. News of his ministry reached Joseph Parry, a Wiltshire farmer and a deacon of the Baptist Chapel at Allington, near Devizes. Parry rode over to hear him in 1833 and later recorded: 'We found the church so thronged with hearers that there was hardly standing, much less sitting room.'[5] It was this occasion that laid the foundations of a life-long friendship between the two men.

Before this meeting Philpot had come to know William Tiptaft, the vicar of the neighbouring parish of Sutton Courtney. The two men met at a ministers' fraternal and became the closest of friends. As a result of their studies, both men gradually embraced the doctrines of grace by the early 1830s. Tiptaft was a forceful outgoing character, very different from the cautious and scholarly Philpot. While Philpot seems to have reached an understanding of the doctrines of grace before his friend, it was Tiptaft

---

[3] Philpot, *The Seceders*, vol. 1, p. 30.

[4] One of these, Chiselhampton, is an eighteenth-century architectural gem, celebrated in a poem by John Betjeman.

[5] Philpot, *The Seceders*, vol. 1, p. 100.

who first came to the conclusion that continuing in the ministry of the Church of England would prove impossible for them.

SECESSION

Tiptaft's initial concern arose from the formularies of the Church of England. Lack of discipline together with the over-inclusive nature of the Prayer Book services distressed him, convincing him that these were the cause of a worldliness that pervaded the whole Church. Never one to hesitate once his mind was made up, he wrote to the Bishop of Salisbury resigning his charge in November 1831. This letter was published.[6] In it he explained that his chief reasons for secession were objections to the liturgy. However, he also declared that he would be 'delighted to see many sound and faithful Ministers raised up within her walls, who may, through God's grace, be enabled to work such an *entire* change, as shall cause the hearts of *God's people* to rejoice.' For the present he maintained: 'I cannot hold my Living and a good conscience too.' It is interesting to note that he did not raise the question of believers' baptism in this letter, although he rejected the doctrine of baptismal regeneration, which he believed the Prayer Book implied.

Tiptaft's secession challenged Philpot, his close friend. Philpot's unease intensified but he was reluctant to leave his field of opportunity. 'No one knows what it is to give up a people who love you and a situation where the Lord has blessed you, but those who have the trial', he wrote at this time.[7] Tiptaft was baptized at Devizes some months after leaving the Church of England, and built a chapel at Abingdon, where he continued to minister until the end of his life in 1864. It was through Tiptaft that Philpot was introduced to John Warburton of Trowbridge, and perhaps even more significantly, to Joseph Parry.

For Philpot the break with the Established Church came in March 1835. He describes something of the struggle through which he passed:

> Oh! How the sacrament so-called used to gall me! At the head knelt my carnal Pharisaical squire, with his pleasure-loving, God-hating wife, who

[6] William Tiptaft, *A Letter Addressed to the Bishop of Salisbury*, Abingdon, 1831.
[7] Philpot, *The Seceders*, vol. 1, p. 103.

was so filled with enmity against me that she would never hear me preach. I was compelled to tell them individually and personally that Christ died for them and shed His blood for their sins (I believing all the while in particular redemption), of which I put the elements in their hands, saying 'Take, eat this,' etc. Lower down knelt a man generally suspected of having once committed a murder, and near him the most hardened Pharisee I ever knew in my life, whose constant reply to my constant warnings, etc., was 'I dare say it be as you says.' I was so cut up and condemned that at last I could not do it, and employed an assistant to do the whole, but then I had to kneel down with these characters, which was as bad; and so I found myself completely hedged in and driven from every refuge, till at last like an animal hunted down to a rock by the sea-side, I had only one escape, which was to leap into the water which bore me up and afforded me a sweet deliverance from my persecutors.[8]

To his amazed congregation he announced his immediate secession on 22 March 1835. Resignation of his College Fellowship followed. No Dissenter could be a Fellow of an Oxford College at that time. With very slender private means and no home, the future looked very bleak. Most of his library was packed up and sent to London where its auction took three days. Meanwhile, in Parry's hospitable home he found a refuge until his circumstances became clearer.

Philpot's Influence, 1840-50

The way in which Philpot became involved in the work of the *Gospel Standard* has already been outlined. From 1840 until his death in 1869 he exercised a powerful influence through the magazine, and this was augmented by a steady stream of pamphlets and published sermons. The years before 1850 were amongst the stormiest in his career, but from them he emerged a somewhat gentler and more mature person, although always ready to defend his views. His impact on the *Standard* was quickly seen. Although letters and extracts from Christian biography, as well as contributions from other writers continued to appear, it was apparent that a masterly hand was in control. Everything he wrote reflected the breadth

[8] Ibid., p. 97.

Joseph Charles Philpot

of his reading. He coupled outstanding classical scholarship with a lucid style that was readily understood by even his most uncultured readers. A superb teacher, he was aware of new religious developments and capable of commenting on movements from the Plymouth Brethren to the Oxford Movement.[9] Many of the leaders of the latter movement he knew personally from his days in Oxford. Closely associated with him was a small group of ex-Anglican clergymen who were also drawn into the Strict Baptist ministry[10] and who proved to be natural leaders; Philpot, however, was the dominant figure among them all.

Philpot and 'Experimental' Religion

Philpot's departure from the Church of England was not simply a matter of baptism. He wanted to associate with believers whose Christianity focused on a living experience of Christ. This vital concern at times made him appear to dismiss the doctrinal foundation upon which alone genuine Christian experience can be sustained. His fear of dead orthodoxy made him as critical of Particular Baptists as of Anglicans, and he clearly hoped to see the emergence of a group of churches that would be noted for the reality of their spiritual experience. This passion explains his frequent criticism of dead Calvinism. For example, in 1840 he wrote:

> I believe there are but two healthy states of soul; one hungering and the other feeding; one mourning and the other rejoicing; one sighing, groaning, and panting after testimonies, love favours, sprinkled blood, revealed righteousness, and eternal mercy, and the other banqueting on the same. But you find many towering professors who are neither in one

---

[9] *Gospel Standard*, vol. 8, 1842, pp. 77–84., vol. 7, 1841, pp. 319–23; cf. his statement in *Gospel Standard*, vol. 34, 1868, where he refers to the leaders of the Oxford Movement and refers to 'Mr Oakley, then a fellow of Balliol College, and a personal friend of our own', p. 153.

[10] These included Roger Hitchcock of Devizes, William Tiptaft and John Kay of Abingdon and Frederick Tryon of Deeping St James, whose relationship with Philpot was later to be difficult. According to Philpot 'between forty and fifty ordained clergymen in various parts of England quitted the Established Church in the years 1830–1835', *The Seceders,* vol. 1, p. 59. Of course not all of these became Strict Baptists.

state or the other. They neither spiritually mourn, nor spiritually rejoice; they neither grieve for Christ's absence nor are cheered by his presence. They are always the same.[11]

The preoccupation of the *Standard* men with Christian experience meant that their sermons tended to be descriptive and analytical rather than exhortatory. In one of his most famous sermons, after describing the rather theoretical preaching of some men, Philpot continued:

> We will leave, then, these speculators to their theories, and instead of speaking of things as they ought to be, will endeavour to describe things as they are.[12]

Philpot's type of experimental preaching led to accusations of 'corruption preaching'. Its proponents were accused of wallowing in descriptions of sin and an unhealthy pre-occupation with evil thoughts. Philpot indignantly repudiated this charge, but less able men may well have laid themselves open to such accusations.[13]

Philpot's emphasis on Christian experience was linked with a peculiarity in his teaching. With all Calvinists, he believed in the doctrine of total inability, that is, that unbelievers are incapable of pleasing God or doing anything in their own strength to secure salvation. Philpot, however, applied this doctrine to believers, and denied that a believer could respond to the commands of the Bible. In his teaching, therefore, the Christian appears like an automaton, totally unable to perform anything that is good, until God works the required ability in him. This doctrine of passivity separated him from the High Calvinists of the Stevens school and seemed to carry him beyond Gadsby, who sometimes exhorted

---

[11] *The Seceders*, vol. 2, p. 195, 'J. C. Philpot to a friend', 29th January 1840.

[12] From the sermon, 'Winter Afore Harvest', 1837, reprinted in J. C. Philpot, *New Years' Addresses, etc*, London, 1902, p. 558; cf. a report of a sermon by M'Kenzie in *Earthen Vessel*, vol. 4, 1848, p. 24, 'This is the way to raise up hope... by plentifully declaring the thing as it is, – and not by trying to flog them out of their doubts and fears with legal whips, as some attempt to do.' William Palmer's sarcastic use of the expression 'to describe "things as they are"' suggests this may have become a slogan with *Gospel Standard* men, W. Palmer, *A Plain Statement*, London, 1847, p. 24.

[13] *Gospel Standard*, vol. 7, 1841, pp. 84–92; ibid., vol. 11, 1845, p. 5.

believers.[14] In 1842 Philpot reviewed a sermon by Charles Drawbridge, sternly criticizing him for his use of exhortation:

> We should have thought that the preacher's judgment was too firmly convinced of the doctrine of man's helplessness to have laid such a load of exhortations upon his hearers . . . We think, after all these exhortations had fallen in such copious showers upon us, that we should have wanted to follow the preacher into the vestry, and from the vestry to his own house, and have watched him narrowly for the whole of the next week, whether he was all that he told us to be, and did all that he exhorted us to do. And if we found that inability was his theme in the parlour and exhortation his theme in the pulpit, we should be apt to say 'Pray, Mr Minister, let us have a little change. Preach the exhortation at home, and bring the inability abroad; and when you are all that you have told us to be in the parlour, we will allow you to come forward again with your exhortations in the pulpit. But till then our cry must be, "Physician, heal thyself."'[15]

Philpot admitted to a tendency to pessimism.[16] His health, never robust, may have played a part in his attitudes and when coupled with his doctrine of inability could produce a gloomy version of Christianity, which sometimes shocked fellow High Calvinists. One such with whom he came into conflict was James Osbourn. Osbourn was a Baptist preacher and an erstwhile hearer of Huntington, of whom he remained an admirer. After Huntington's death, he emigrated to the United States, but returned to England for an extended preaching tour from 1847 to 1849. Philpot, who was deeply interested in Huntington and those who had known him, recommended and used Osbourn's writings in the *Gospel Standard* from 1843 to 1845. He also warmly recommended Osbourn's autobiography.[17] When Osbourn returned to England, however, he was

---

[14] For example in 'The Perfect Law of Liberty', *Works,* vol. I, pp. 132, 188, 190.

[15] *Gospel Standard*, vol. 8, 1842, p. 24.

[16] *The Seceders,* vol. 1, p. 265. 'I think I observed that I knew more of the dark than of the bright side of religion, and I feel it to be so still', 'J. C. Philpot to Joseph Parry', 19 April 1834.

[17] James Osbourn, The Lawful Captive Delivered, Baltimore, 1835, reviewed in *Gospel Standard*, vol. 9, 1843, pp 316–20; 346–51; 370–6. Osbourn's writings in

dismayed at the state of the Hyper-Calvinist churches. He considered that Philpot had not arrived at a full understanding of the gospel and that many of the preachers associated with him were enthralled by their system.[18] Philpot declared himself to be shocked by Osbourn's freedom of expression in the pulpit.[19] Before he returned to the United States, Osbourn published a criticism of the paralysis which he saw creeping over the High Calvinist churches. In particular he denounced Philpot's doctrine of inability, arguing that it was a novelty and a travesty of the teaching of Huntington.[20]

In one area Philpot's doctrine of inability led him to a surprising departure from traditional Hyper-Calvinism. In his *Help*, Stevens had argued that the many biblical exhortations to repentance and faith were not indiscriminate and so unbelievers should not be called upon to believe. In 1840 James Wells developed this argument in *The Moral Government of God*.[21] Wells recognized that unbelievers were exhorted, but insisted that such exhortations were to moral duties, not spiritual. Man had a duty to be good even if he did not have a duty to be Christian. Philpot treated Wells' work to an extended review in the *Gospel Standard*.[22] Much of it he accepted. He welcomed Wells's acceptance of man's responsibility, which was denied by some High Calvinists. As for the reality of exhortations, Philpot insisted: 'If we take the Scriptures as a divine revelation we must

---

Gospel Standard, include vol. 9, 1843, pp. 257–61; pp. 289–93; vol. 10, 1844, pp. 193–7; vol. 11, 1845, pp. 65–70.

[18] 'For the first three or four months after my arrival in England, I was perfectly amazed to see the enthralled state of mind the preachers were in with whom I mingled, and in whom I expected to find a superior state of things', J. Osbourn, *Earthen Vessel*, vol. 4, 1848, pp. 91, 92. For Osbourn's encounter with Philpot see J. Osbourn, *Liberty Taken Without Grant; or an Experimental, Faithful and Discriminating Letter to the Rev. Joseph. C. Philpot of Stamford in Lincolnshire*, London, 1849, pp. 11–14.

[19] *Gospel Standard*, vol. 13, 1847, pp. 348–51.

[20] J. Osbourn, *Liberty Taken Without Grant*, pp. 23, 32.

[21] J. Wells, *The Moral Government of God; Wherein it is Shown that The General Exhortations of the Bible are not Founded in The Principle of Man Being in a Salvable State, But in the Principle of Moral and Individual Responsibility*, London, 1840.

[22] *Gospel Standard*, vol. 7, 1841, pp. 52–7; 76–84.

receive them implicitly without questioning or cavilling.'[23] Dealing with the connection between predestination and man's responsibility, Philpot sounds almost like Andrew Fuller. He wrote of

> An intermediate link between divine predestination and human responsibility, which God has not seen fit to reveal, either for the exercise of our faith, or because it surpasses our present comprehension.[24]

Wells insisted that all general exhortations to unbelievers were to a natural obedience, which brought rewards in this life or a mitigation of eternal punishment. Philpot was too astute to follow Wells through the exegetical distortions demanded by this theory. He declared: 'Our conviction is, that there are many exhortations to spiritual actions used generally in both Old and New Testament.'[25] Philpot had then to explain why he did not use such exhortations. He wrote:

> We look upon these exhortations, invitations, calls and so on, to be lodged in the Scriptures, as in a vast reservoir and magazine of truth, out of which the Blessed Spirit, from time to time, takes such portions as he sees fit to quicken, convince, teach, rebuke or comfort the spiritual seed.[26]

The exhortations were thus written in Scripture to be applied by the Holy Spirit to the elect. Andrew Fuller would have agreed, but would have insisted that the preacher use such passages as he exhorted his congregation from the pulpit. It was at this point that Philpot's doctrine of inability took over:

> It may be objected, that spiritual exhortations to natural men must be absurd, because they have no power to perform spiritual actions. This seems to be so convincing an argument to Mr W[ells] that he considers all such exhortations, if such were their drift, to be 'useless'; (p.85) and that it would be to 'mock men, and trifle with them, tauntingly, and with apparent sincerity, tell them to do impossibilities'. (p.87) But surely we may reply; Are there any spiritual exhortations in the Epistles to regenerate characters to perform spiritual actions, such as 'Put on, therefore,

---

[23] Ibid., p. 55. [24] Ibid. [25] Ibid., p. 81. [26] Ibid., pp. 81, 82.

as the elect of God, holy and beloved, bowels of mercies'? (*Col.* iii.12) Now, are spiritual men one whit more able to perform spiritual actions than natural men, unless the Lord work in them to will and to do of his good pleasure?[27]

Believers and unbelievers alike were unable to respond. This still left the question as to whether ministers should exhort them as the apostles had clearly done. Philpot replied:

> No. If they were to use them they would do so, conscious of their impotency, and might as well imitate Peter in bidding the lame beggar, rise up and walk, as imitate the apostles in exhortation to repent and believe the gospel. We look, then, upon exhortations both general and special as a part, and a very necessary and blessed part, of the sacred volume, and to be used by the Spirit, just in the same manner as promises, doctrine, and so on, for the edification of the church of God.[28]

In practice Wells and Philpot were in agreement that unbelievers should not be exhorted to respond to the gospel, but Wells considered that Philpot was 'coming very near to general Calvinism'[29] or Fullerism. Wells' Hyper-Calvinism, which passed to an extreme beyond that of Philpot, seems to have prevented him from praying specifically for the conversion of any unconverted person because they might be reprobate.[30] Philpot refused to modify his position although he acknowledged in the following year that he was being accused of Fullerism.[31]

Philpot made clear his opposition to Fullerism in a review of William Rushton's *Defence of Particular Redemption* in 1842. Rushton criticized Fuller in the same way as Abraham Booth had done earlier. He considered that Fuller had undermined the doctrine of particular redemption. Philpot considered that Rushton had 'disentangled Fuller's knotted web',[32] and in a letter he wrote: 'I think that my daily and almost hourly sense of my miserable helplessness . . . would keep me from assenting to

---

[27] Ibid., p. 82.　[28] Ibid.　[29] Ibid., p. 172.
[30] See Ian Shaw's discussion of this point, *High Calvinists in Action*, p. 260.
[31] *Gospel Standard*, vol. 8, 1842, p. 321; *The Seceders*, vol. 2, p. 255.
[32] *Gospel Standard*, vol. 8, 1842, p. 316.

Andrew Fuller's lies.'[33] Yet the review gives the impression that he had never read Fuller![34]

Foreign Missions

The influence of Andrew Fuller's theology upon the missionary movement is widely recognized. As has already been shown, there were many Hyper-Calvinists who had also come to accept their responsibility to send missionaries, even though they did not accept Fuller's theology. The Gadsby group, however, remained unconvinced. In 1837 an anonymous writer in the *Standard* deplored the pressure to support missionary societies, stating: 'We have no command to form societies for such purposes.'[35] He did not discount the possibility of sending missionaries, but contented himself with the sentiment, 'When the Lord pleases it shall be done.'[36]

In 1841, Philpot referred scathingly to missionary societies as 'joint-stock companies to convert the world'.[37] He felt that the sovereignty of God was being usurped by carnal activism. However, he went on to say: 'We believe God may be using these societies, not to convert savingly any individuals, but to prepare a way for a gospel ministry hereafter, and that perhaps out of the people themselves, when the societies shall have ceased to exist.'[38] He compared the societies to Augustine and his monks in Saxon England. The real work, he believed, began later, 'as in his own time God raised up gospel ministers, as Wickliffe, Tyndall, and others and has ever since maintained the candlestick then set up'.[39]

Philpot returned to this theme in October 1841. A tract entitled *Foreign Missions* had been written by William Palmer of Chatteris on behalf of an *ad hoc* committee which had been set up to promote a Hyper-Calvinistic missionary society. Philpot was concerned: the tract had been 'very widely diffused through the Particular Baptist churches in the counties of Huntingdon, Cambridge, Bedford etc.'[40] Most of the review was an

---

[33] 'J. C. Philpot to Joseph Parry', 24th March 1842, *The Seceders*, vol. 2, p. 255.
[34] Philpot speaks of his understanding of Fuller, 'as far as we can gather his views from Mr Rushton's extracts from his works'. *Gospel Standard*, vol. 8, 1842, p. 317.
[35] Ibid., vol. 3, 1837, p. 54. [36] Ibid., p. 53. [37] Ibid., vol. 7, 1841, p.145.
[38] Ibid., p. 147. [39] Ibid., p. 146. [40] Ibid., p. 295.

attack on religious societies in general and the promoters of this venture in particular. He claimed that he did not object to the gospel being preached to the heathen, 'but to the instruments employed – the men who send them and the men who are sent. Are the senders men who know and love the truth?' He replied:

> Let their opposition and enmity to men of the truth furnish the answer. Let their expressed or generally understood determination to keep out of their pulpits such men as Gadsby, Warburton, etc., testify what is their real spirit, and what their professed love of the gospel.[41]

Sadly, Philpot did not ask why men whom he considered did know the truth were doing nothing to promote foreign missions. His friend William Gadsby had founded new churches, but many of these appear to have been established out of division from existing congregations. It is difficult to escape the conclusion that Philpot's emphasis was seriously dampening evangelistic concern. Palmer waited six years before replying to Philpot, but when he did, he subjected Philpot's position to a broad criticism, involving much more than foreign missions.[42] Before this reply appeared, Philpot had to face serious charges against himself.

ANTINOMIANISM

The teaching of Huntington and Gadsby on the believer's freedom from the moral law made it clear that both men deplored any suggestion that the Christian was free to sin.[43] Some of Huntington's followers seem to have been willing to accept the description 'antinomian'.[44] Philpot strongly deprecated this. 'We neither call ourselves "Antinomians"', he wrote, 'nor ever allow ourselves to be so called without protesting against the title.' He believed that the law was used by God to convict sinners of

[41] Ibid., p. 298.
[42] W. Palmer, *A Plain Statement; Followed by a Few Reflections upon Mr Philpot of Stamford, as a Christian, a Preacher and a Reviewer*, London, 1847.
[43] See pp. 126, 184 above.
[44] For example Washington Wilkes, *A Fearless Defence of the Leading Doctrines Preached and Received by Modern Antinomians*, London, 1830. Warburton seems to have accepted the title, J. Warburton, *Mercies of a Covenant God*, London, 1859, pp. 24, 27.

their guilt, but that as a standard of Christian obedience it was inadequate. He pointed out that the name 'Antinomian' was normally used to describe 'a loose and careless liver, one who continues in sin that grace may abound'.[45]

Philpot, however, was to face a personal charge of Antinomianism. On 16 February 1845, he was criticized from the pulpit of Zoar Chapel, London, on the ground that he married Sarah Louisa Keal of Oakham in 1838 in the knowledge that she was not converted.[46] His critic, Frederick Tryon, was another ex-Anglican minister and pastor of the Strict Baptist Chapel in Deeping St James, Lincolnshire. Subsequently, Tryon alleged, Philpot had condoned mixed marriages by a piece in the *Gospel Standard*.[47] Tryon's procedure was, to say the least, odd. It was his first visit to Zoar, a church to which Philpot preached annually and where he had many friends. Tryon lived only seven miles from Philpot, had often visited him, but had only raised the matter of his marriage on one occasion.[48] Tryon justified his action in a pamphlet, while Philpot was defended by a Mr H. W. Shakespear, who only succeeded in making matters worse. After eighteen months of controversy, Philpot issued a five-page statement in the *Gospel Standard*, acknowledging many of the charges.

> The first evil, then, and by far the most prominent, which I wish to confess is, my marriage in 1838 with a person of whom I was not persuaded that she was at that time a partaker of grace.[49]

Philpot paid high tribute to his wife and said that he believed 'the Lord has since touched her heart with his grace'.[50] He did not, however, consider that this justified his action in marrying her. He also

---

[45] *Gospel Standard*, vol. 9, 1843, p. 76.

[46] H. W. Shakespear, A *Refutation of the Falsehoods Contained in Mr Tryon's 'Letter to Mr. J. C. Philpot'*, London, 1847; F. Tryon, *A Reply to a Letter entitled 'A Refutation of the Falsehoods contained in Mr Tryon's Letter to Mr. J. C. Philpot'*, by H. W. Shakespear, Peterborough, 1847.

[47] An obituary of a woman who believed she was told by God to marry an unconverted man. This was published without editorial comment, *Gospel Standard*, vol. 8, 1842, p. 59.

[48] Philpot's claim, quoted by Shakespear, op. cit., p. 18.

[49] *Gospel Standard*, vol. 13, 1847, p. 318.   [50] Ibid.

acknowledged the lack of wisdom in publishing an obituary in 1842 that seemed to justify mixed marriages.[51] He also apologized for some sweeping remarks in the January 1847 issue of the magazine, which had been taken generally to apply to Tryon.[52] His long statement concluded with these words:

> In what ever instance, publicly or privately, by pen or tongue, I have said, written or done, since these unhappy divisions arose, anything in my own spirit, or unbecoming to the gospel, I desire publicly to acknowledge my sorrow for it, being well convinced of this, that it becomes those who profess the Gospel of Jesus Christ, when accused rightly to confess it humbly, when accused wrongfully to bear it patiently and in all things to seek to know and to do the revealed will of God and follow the example of the Lord Jesus.[53]

Meanwhile Tryon had issued two more pamphlets attacking Philpot's published sermons.[54] In both he charged Philpot with Antinomianism. The burden of his accusation was that Philpot made awareness of sin an evidence of grace. Philpot had tried to comfort those who confessed that they could not see that they had done the will of God, with the words:

> No, you cannot see it; because your eye is single to the glory of God; and your body full of light, the light of your body shows the sins of your path.[55]

Tryon commented acidly:

Poor Zion, what will she be told next? To what depths of delusion will professors sink before they feel danger?[56]

Tryon was convinced that an over-emphasis on experimental preaching was producing a dangerous state of affairs. He called attention to

---

[51] Ibid., p. 319.   [52] Ibid.   [53] Ibid., p. 320.
[54] F. Tryon, *The Single Eye, or Remarks on Number 118 of the 'Zoar Pulpit'*, London, 1847; F. Tryon, *Old Paths and New*, London, 1847. The Sermons criticized were republished in the *Gospel Pulpit*, vol. 9, London, 1899, 'Peace, Tribulation and Victory', 13th July 1847, and 'Doing the Will of God', 25th July 1847.
[55] Tryon, *The Single Eye*, p. 6; Philpot, *Gospel Pulpit*, vol. 9, p. 354.
[56] Tryon, *The Single Eye*, p. 7.

Joseph Charles Philpot

the very great lack of reproof, rebukes and exhortations in the ministry most popular among us. The precepts of the Bible are greatly neglected through mock humility.[57]

Tryon was persuaded that men were trusting to the subjective evidence of their fluctuating feelings instead of to the Bible. He contrasted his associates with the Bereans in the Acts of the Apostles:

> They dare not trust to their own feelings under the word till the pure scriptures confirmed the truth of what they heard; it is a common thing in this day for people to be positive all is right, because it is just what they feel, and their heartfelt experience is the bar to which everything is brought to trial.[58]

Palmer's *Plain Statement*

Tryon's criticisms were from the ranks of Philpot's associates. At the same time William Palmer chose to reply to Philpot's earlier onslaught with a tract entitled *A Plain Statement*.[59] Palmer claimed that the Particular Baptist churches were facing a crisis which had recently confronted him directly. Since Philpot's riposte to the *Foreign Missions* tract, there had been an attempt to persuade Palmer to loan his chapel at Chatteris for a service at which Philpot would preach. When Palmer refused, he was subjected to verbal abuse.[60] He refused because of Philpot's attitude to 'Stevens, Foreman, Murrell, Wright, Collins, Cooper, etc.'[61] as well as to himself. He considered that the churches were under threat:

> The 'old leaven' of Huntingtonianism has, for the last few years, been silently diffusing itself in many places; and if not arrested in its progress ere many years have passed away will effect dissension, separation and divisions.[62]

Like Osbourn, Palmer considered the weakness of Philpot's system to lie in his doctrine of inability: 'The exhortations of God's word find no

---

[57] Tryon, *Old Paths and New*, p. 16   [58] Ibid., p. 23.
[59] See note 42 above.
[60] W. Palmer, *A Plain Statement*, pp. 1, 2.
[61] Ibid., p. 14. The names are all of prominent ministers in the Stevens group.
[62] Ibid., p. 3.

cordial welcome in his soul for Mr Philpot is not one who 'exercises himself unto godliness'.[63] Philpot, he claimed, failed to understand the nature of Christianity:

> 'Are you then going to affirm that the believer is able to obey Jesus Christ?' Undoubtedly I am. 'But wherein consists his ability?' Not in his creatureship, but in his christianity; all arguments, therefore founded upon man as a sinful creature, are inapplicable to man as a regenerate being.[64]

Like Tryon, he concluded that Philpot's teaching was confused:

> By making no distinction between christian experience and the experience of a Christian, he preaches experience in a loose general way, and here lies the charm of his ministry. People find comfort in sin, sloth and selfishness; and travel miles to hear him. Worldly minded, self-opinionated, disorderly and spiteful souls look up and are fed.[65]

Palmer eventually reached the question of missionary societies, the subject of his original pamphlet. He argued that 'to diffuse gospel light is as much a moral duty as to obey God, or to love mankind'.[66] He accused Philpot of blindness to the facts, asking:

> Have all the labours of the Moravians, Wesleyans, Independents, Presbyterians, Baptists, Episcopalians, etc. been in vain in the Lord? Is it to be believed that none of the heathen who have hitherto heard the gospel from the lips of missionaries, have 'believed through grace', 'died in faith' and been 'received up into glory'?[67]

Philpot did not reply to Palmer. For much of the second half of 1847 he was ill.[68] He had made many enemies by his cutting writings and was now reaping what he had sown. Over the next two years the controversy with James Osbourn rumbled on. The events of these years, however, made a lasting impression on Philpot and his sermons and writings began to

[63] Ibid., p. 21. [64] Ibid., p. 26. [65] Ibid., p. 33.
[66] Ibid., p. 57. [67] Ibid., p. 59.
[68] From his undergraduate days Philpot had suffered from a weakness of the lungs. His health broke down in August 1847 and he was unable to preach again until April 1848, although he continued his literary work; *Letters and Memoir*, p. 99.

reveal a gentler spirit. Always incisive, and an able controversialist when necessary, his later years witnessed the employment of his considerable abilities in a more positive way.

Churchmanship

Philpot made no secret of his admiration for such Independents as Joseph Hart and William Huntington, neither of whom were Baptists.[69] He was, however, convinced of strict communion, and in 1840 contributed two articles to the *Gospel Standard* on this subject. These were later published as a tract entitled *Strict Communion Vindicated*.[70]

Philpot's attitude to the Christian ministry reflects both his emphasis on divine guidance and his reaction against Anglican clericalism. He regarded the ministry as a high calling, teaching that 'the call to the ministry is as sovereign as the call by grace.'[71] He rejected the professionalism of both the Established Church and of Nonconformity, refusing the title Reverend, pulpit robes, and ordination by the imposition of hands.[72] He even considered that any church member could baptize or administer the Lord's Supper, so long as the local church gave him permission to do so.[73]

He considered that ministerial training was superfluous and often dangerous, as human learning could usurp the place of divine teaching.[74] It is interesting to note, however, that he kept up his linguistic studies and daily read the Bible in its original languages. He was also prepared in his writings to settle disputed points by appeals to Hebrew and Greek. In addition, he was competent in French, German, and Dutch.[75]

---

[69] 'J. C. Philpot to John Grace', 2 Jan. 1861, *The Seceders*, vol. 3, p. 147; 'J. C. Philpot to Mr. S.', 24 Nov. 1869, *The Seceders*, vol. 3, p. 309.

[70] *Gospel Standard*, vol. 6, 1840 'Strict Communion', pp. 97–103, and 'Were Christ's Disciples Baptized?', pp. 157–62.

[71] J. C. Philpot, *Letter to the Provost of Worcester College, Oxford*, p. 13. He continued: 'Jehovah will take the tinker from his barrow, and the cobbler from his stall and send them to preach his word, as he took Elisha from the plough, and Amos from gathering sycamore fruit.'

[72] *Gospel Standard*, vol. 8, 1842, p. 350.   [73] Ibid.   [74] Ibid., p. 319.

[75] *Letters and Memoir*, p. 97.

Philpot had a high view of the powers of the local church, resisting any attempt to vest too much power in pastors or deacons. He was aware that church meetings could be difficult, but insisted that the remedy was 'the fear of the Lord in spiritual exercise', not an increase in the power of church officers. If the leaders became too powerful, then

> All the power now inherent in the church would fall into the hands of the pastor, or the pastor and deacons, in other words, the present republican constitution of the churches would merge either into a monarchy or an oligarchy.[76]

He deplored the tendency, commonly found among ministers, that concentrated the powers of the church in their hands:

> Ministers professing truth, and perpetually railing against popery, had openly avowed a desire and determination to concentrate all the power which properly belongs to the church in the person of the pastor; and thus are re-introducing that priestly domination which was the first origin of Antichrist.[77]

Philpot always considered himself to be a Particular Baptist, but considered that the bulk of the Particular Baptist churches had been led astray by Fuller's teaching.

> We are Particular Baptists, and our Periodical defends those principles; but neither privately or publicly have we any more communion with the great mass of Particular Baptist churches than we have with the Wesleyans.[78]

On another occasion, however, he wrote:

> The Strict Baptist churches have hitherto been not only almost the sole bulwarks of Gospel truth in the land (we admit that there are signal exceptions) but the only bulwarks of Gospel discipline.[79]

He appeared to consider that strict communion was essential to a proper maintenance of Particular Baptist principles. In 1857 he wrote to a Dutch friend, explaining that he belonged to the denomination of

[76] *Gospel Standard*, vol. 10, 1844, p. 85.　[77] Ibid., p. 84.
[78] Ibid., vol. 8, 1842, p. 321.　[79] Ibid., vol. 10, 1844, p. 120.

Joseph Charles Philpot

Particular Baptists and that such held that the Lord's Supper is, by Apostolic practice, restricted to baptized believers, holding those particular doctrines which are generally termed the doctrines of grace and which were so clearly laid down at the Synod of Dort.[80]

Philpot's views of the local church would probably have commended themselves to most of his fellow Particular Baptists. His rejection of ordination was, however, a new development: the older churches had insisted on the practice, as is seen in an article in the *Gospel Standard* in 1838 that advocated the laying on of hands for this purpose.[81] Interestingly, in the 1850s, C. H. Spurgeon was to take a similar line to that of Philpot on the issue of ordination.[82] This thinking within Nonconformist ranks may have been a reaction against the sacerdotalism of the Oxford Movement.

Politics

Unlike Gadsby, Philpot disapproved of any political references in the *Standard*. He made his position clear in 1842 when he reviewed a sermon by Gadsby, much of which he approved. But

> We must say that one thing did alloy our satisfaction; we mean the political allusions under the first head. Our objection is to politics of every kind in the pulpit. Whatever be our feelings on these exciting subjects, let us leave them outside our chapel doors. They shall never enter into the pages of the *Standard*, at least with our present feelings, and we have determined to resign all connection with it sooner than suffer them to be introduced in any shape or form.[83]

Much later, he was even more forthright. In an issue of the magazine, he replied to a reader who had asked for advice on casting his vote:

> We could not, however, comply with your request without getting on political ground, which we have always endeavoured, as much as we can, to avoid. As we have ourselves a profound distrust of both parties, and a

---

[80] 'J. C. Philpot to G. Tips', 30th. Oct. 1857, *The Seceders*, vol. 3, p. 82.
[81] *Gospel Standard*, vol. 4, 1838, p. 40.
[82] A. Dallimore, *Spurgeon: a New Biography*, Edinburgh: Banner of Truth, 1985, p. 47.
[83] *Gospel Standard*, vol. 8, 1842, p. 177.

desire to be mixed up with neither, the line which we have prescribed for ourselves is, to observe strict neutrality by not voting at all.[84]

Philanthropy

Although Gadsby's political remarks met with Philpot's disapproval in 1842, he explained that his friend's concern arose out of the intense distress in the industrial areas of the North of England: 'Surrounded as he is with such a mass of suffering, we can hardly wonder that his sympathising heart overflows.'[85] Two months later, a letter was printed in the *Standard*, urging that chapel collections be made to relieve the poverty in the North and that the proceeds be sent to Gadsby for distribution. The editors heartily endorsed this suggestion.[86]

Appeals to the charity of *Standard* readers were not restricted to the needs of Gadsby's associates in the North, nor even to England. Philpot always retained a keen interest in Ireland, where he had been a tutor from 1826-7. He still had contacts there. When the Irish Famine of 1846-7 occurred, the *Gospel Standard* appealed for help. Following a generous response, Philpot sent funds to 'trustworthy individuals, known to us personally or through friends, who distribute what is sent to them without respect to creed, sect or party'.[87] The magazine carried graphic accounts of the distress in the south and west of the island, with further appeals to the readers: 'Surely every human, not to say gracious heart will cry, "Let me do what I can to relieve such appalling misery. It may be little that I can do, but let me do what I can."'[88]

No similar magazine showed the same degree of concern for the plight of the distressed at this time as the *Standard*. Much of this concern must have arisen from Gadsby's and Philpot's knowledge of the areas involved. The bulk of support for the *Gospel Herald* lay in the relatively prosperous areas of London, the south east, and East Anglia, where church leaders do not seem to have shared an awareness of the need to a similar degree.

---

[84] Ibid., vol. 34, 1868, October Supplement, p. 1.
[85] Ibid., vol. 4, 1842, p. 177.   [86] Ibid., pp. 237-8.
[87] Ibid., vol. 13, 1847, p. 122.   [88] Ibid.

Both groups of Strict Baptists supported the Aged Pilgrims' Friend Society, an inter-denominational society, which had been formed in 1807 at Whitefield's Tabernacle.[89] Preaching on behalf of the Society in 1840, Philpot said: 'This is the only religious society that I belong to; the only society that I can conscientiously support; the only society I ever feel inclined to preach for.'[90] The needs of the poor always touched him deeply.[91]

After the controversies of the 1840s Philpot had approximately another twenty years of ministry before him. He continued his pastorate in Stamford and Oakham until ill health compelled him to retire in 1864. Thereafter he continued to preach when able, but his literary work, which centred on the editorship of the *Gospel Standard,* went on until his death in December 1869. One further major controversy erupted in 1859 when he launched a powerful defence of the Nicene doctrine of Christ's eternal sonship. Generally, however, these later years were more peaceful and bore fruit in a lasting spiritual legacy. There was on the other hand a serious negative legacy, which was soon to produce disastrous consequences. While Philpot exercised his considerable gifts to promote and encourage a high standard of Christian piety, weaknesses in his doctrine promoted the establishment of a group of churches which shelved their responsibilities under the Great Commission. Undoubtedly many members of these churches maintained high standards of personal godliness, but they succeeded in establishing a cloistered society which, like the monastic communities of the early church, rejected an ungodly world, but did very little to challenge or change it.

---

[89] J. E. Hazelton, *'Inasmuch', A History of the Aged Pilgrims' Friend Society, 1807–1922*, London, 1922, pp. 55–76. Hazelton indicates the breadth of evangelical support, which included Anglicans and various groups of Dissenters.

[90] J. C. Philpot, *Early Sermons*, vol. 1, London, 1906, p. 35.

[91] Perhaps an even more remarkable example of philanthropy was William Tiptaft, who built his chapel at Abingdon at his own expense rather than burden his needy people, and steadily gave away his capital to the poor until, at the end of his life, he was dependent upon the charity of his friends.

14

ORGANIZATIONS

A holy unity exists amongst us when, consenting in pure doctrine, we are united in Christ alone.

JOHN CALVIN

The bond of holy union is the simple truth. As soon as we depart from that, nothing remains, but dreadful discord.

JOHN CALVIN

Notwithstanding all the sad divisions in our churches, the saints among us, so far as they are sanctified, are already one. The things in which they are agreed are . . . far more considerable, than are the things wherein they differ. They are of one mind concerning sin, that it is the worst thing in the world; concerning the favour of God, that it is better than life; concerning the world that it is vanity; and concerning the Word of God, that it is above rubies.

MATTHEW HENRY

Although the establishment of magazines after 1830 helped to foster fellowship among the Strict and Particular Baptists, some churches wanted the links between the churches to be more structured. They considered that there were occasions when inter-church co-operation was required and collective viewpoints needed to be published. As Particular Baptists they were heirs to a tradition of local associations of churches, which could be traced back to the seventeenth century. Not surprisingly, as new bonds of fellowship were forged in the first half of the nineteenth century, there were a number of attempts to set up new associations. Such efforts, though, were never easy. Some churches were reluctant to break

Organizations

connections already established. A bigger difficulty lay in discussion about the doctrinal bases of the new associations. Groups of churches had to decide whether to insist on both strict communion and Hyper-Calvinism or only on one of these. Those who adhered to one of these distinctives did not necessarily hold to the other. In London especially, this dilemma proved a stumbling block to the formation of new associations for many years. In addition, there was resistance to the very idea of associations; this may have been a legacy of Huntingtonian Independency; it expressed itself most strongly among the *Gospel Standard* churches.

1. East Anglia

It was in East Anglia that the most successful Strict and Particular Baptist Association was established in this period. There had been a Norfolk and Suffolk Particular Baptist Association in existence since 1769. Its declaration of faith was similar to that of most other Particular Baptist Associations and was couched in terms broad enough to be acceptable to both Fullerites and Hyper-Calvinists.[1] On the terms of communion, it was neutral, although strict communion appears to have been the practice of most East Anglian churches.[2]

After slow progress in the early years, the Association increased from five churches with a total membership of four hundred and ninety members in 1795, to twenty-eight churches with 2,967 members in 1825.[3] Much of this growth took place through the establishment of village churches.

[1] The founding churches were Worstead, Claxton, Shelfanger and Yarmouth in Norfolk; and Woolverstone and Wattisham in Suffolk (Klaiber, *The Story of the Suffolk Baptists,* p. 108). The *Declaration of Faith* read, 'The important doctrine of three equal persons in the Godhead; eternal and personal election; original sin; particular redemption; free justification by the imputed righteousness of Christ alone; efficacious grace in regeneration; the final perseverance of real believers; the resurrection of the dead; the future judgement; the eternal happiness of the righteous; and the everlasting misery of such as die impenitent; with the congregational order of the churches inviolable', Ibid., p. 109.

[2] Ibid., p. 112.

[3] Rippon, *Baptist Register,* vol. 2, 1794–7, p. 188; Klaiber, *Suffolk Baptists,* p. 113.

Job Hupton, pastor at Claxton, Norfolk, from 1794 to 1849, was one of the more important leading figures during this period. Hupton, formerly a Staffordshire blacksmith, had been converted through the ministry of John Bradford.[4] He was introduced to the Countess of Huntingdon and spent a short time at Trevecca College in Wales. A very able preacher, he joined the Countess of Huntingdon's Connexion, but while serving at Ipswich, adopted Baptist views and was recommended to the Particular Baptist Church at Claxton in 1794.[5] His ministry was immediately fruitful: he baptized ninety-two believers between June 1796 and June 1799.[6]

Whatever his earlier views may have been, Hupton emerged as a vigorous opponent of Fuller, publishing *A Blow Struck at the Root of Fullerism* in 1804.[7] He also contributed a number of articles on High Calvinism to *The Gospel Magazine*, between 1803 and 1809.[8] He was soon a man to be reckoned with in the Norfolk and Suffolk Association. As early as 1795 he was elected the Association's Moderator, an office he was to hold on three further occasions. He also wrote a number of the Association Letters, including that of 1811 on 'Eternal Justification'.[9]

As early as 1791, Andrew Fuller realized that his teaching was viewed with suspicion in Norfolk and Suffolk.[10] Hupton's arrival must have provided leadership for that resistance. Given this theological climate within the Association, it is not surprising to read that the 1806 Annual Meeting called for a statement to be issued against Fullerism. This was drawn up

---

[4] See pp. 142-3 above.

[5] For biographical details see J. Stocker & J. Hupton, *Hymns and Spiritual Poems*, London, 1861, pp. i-iv; J. J. Julian, *Dictionary of Hymnology* (1907), New York, 1957, s.v.; John Bradford through whom Hupton was converted was later a friend and associate of William Huntington, see pp. 142-3.

[6] Stocker & Hupton, op. cit., p. iv. 'Many flocking to hear the word, in 1796', Rippon, *Baptist Register*, vol. 2, 1794-7, p. 490.

[7] J. Hupton, *A Blow Struck at the Root of Fullerism*, London [1804]

[8] Collected and reprinted as J. Hupton, *The Truth as It Is in Jesus*, London, 1843. Subjects include Eternal Justification and a series of essays entitled 'Ministerial Offers of Spiritual Blessings not Warranted by Scripture'.

[9] Hupton was moderator in 1795, 1799, 1809 and 1812. He wrote the circular letters for 1811, 1814, 1816, 1817 and 1821; Klaiber, *Suffolk Baptists*, pp. 208-11.

[10] See p. 98, fn. 24 above.

Organizations

and accepted as the 1807 circular letter. Its author is now unknown, but it certainly reflected Hupton's published views.[11]

In the 1820s the Hyper-Calvinist party in Suffolk was further strengthened by the arrival of two younger ministers, George Wright of Beccles and Samuel Collins of Grundisburgh. George Wright was a diligent student, gifted writer and preacher; a natural leader, he could disagree with his critics, yet without rancour. He had been a Wesleyan preacher before adopting Hyper-Calvinist and Baptist convictions. He also developed views on the law akin to those of Huntington and Gadsby, but he never allowed these to divide him from Hyper-Calvinist colleagues who thought otherwise. From 1823 until 1870 he was pastor of Beccles Baptist Church, which had come into being as the fruit of Hupton's preaching in the area.[12] Samuel Collins was pastor at Grundisburgh from 1826 to 1876. He was one of several men sent into the ministry from Stevens's church in London.[13]

The neutrality of the Norfolk and Suffolk Association on the issue of the terms of communion was enshrined in its foundation documents and appears to have reflected an attitude widespread among the eighteenth-century associations.[14] Churches whose communion practice differed

---

[11] Klaiber, *Suffolk Baptists*, p. 117. Klaiber located a copy of this *Testimony Against Fullerism* in the archives of the Suffolk and Norfolk Association. A recent search has failed to find this.

[12] For biographical details see S. K. Bland, *Memorials of George Wright*, London, 1875 Wright's views on the Law are expounded in a letter, 'The Law and the Gospel', ibid., pp. 228–42.

[13] For biographical details see *Gospel Herald*, vol. 49, 1881, pp. 256–60; 321–5; 353–6. Grundisburgh was the largest church in the Association in 1828 with 262 members, *Suffolk and Norfolk Association Circular Letter 1828*, p. 21. Hereinafter Association Letters will be referred to as follows:-

    N. & S. Letters, until 1827.
    S. & N. Letters, 1828 and 1829.
    S. & N. (Old), for Old Association Letters from 1830.
    S. & N. (New), for New Association Letters from 1830.

[14] The 5th Article read, 'That the Association Churches agree, that in those things wherein one Church may differ from another in what is not Essential to Salvation, or Strict Communion [they], Shall not impose upon particular Churches any Sentiments peculiar to themselves, but leave every Church to their own Liberty, to walk

from one another maintained a healthy mutual respect. However, by 1822 this neutrality had disappeared, as can be seen by the publication of the Association Letter on 'Church Discipline'. Written by T. Hoddy of Clare, it strongly argued in favour of the closed-communion position.[15]

The conservatism of the East Anglian leaders could not completely shelter their churches from the winds of change which were blowing through the English Baptist churches in the first half of the nineteenth century. The Hyper-Calvinism which had become entrenched in East Anglia was challenged by Cornelius Elven, pastor at Bury St Edmunds from 1823 to 1873. A native of Bury, Elven was brought up as an Independent, but adopted Baptist views. Within two years of his baptism, he was called to the pastorate of the Bury church. Possessed of a 'deep passion for evangelism', his church increased from fifty-two members in 1822 to one hundred and fifty-six in 1828.[16] In 1827 he was unanimously appointed Secretary of the Association.[17]

The year 1827 proved to be a significant one in the affairs of the Association. The Association Letter, written by George Wright, was on 'The Sin of Apostasy'. His warnings against the perennial dangers of declension resulting from indolence must have been appreciated by all. More difficult to accept was his statement 'that we are surrounded by the darkness of an awful defection from the truth'.[18] He explained that, since the Reformation, the greatest threat had come from 'the overspreading influence of Socinian, Arian and Arminian errors and delusions'.[19] He was in no doubt that the Association was facing a challenge:

---

together as they have received from the Lord'. This should be compared with the 4th which included the Statement, 'we have no authority or Power to Prescribe or Impose anything upon the Faith and Practice of any of the Churches of Christ in this Association', quoted Klaiber, op. cit., p. 110.

[15] *N. & S. Letter, 1822*, p. 7.

[16] Klaiber, op. cit., pp. 70, 71, 81–3. Church membership statistics.

[17] *N. & S. Letter, 1827*, p. 2. This is the last use of the title 'Norfolk and Suffolk'. From this time the Association was described as 'Suffolk and Norfolk', reflecting the fact that the majority of the churches were now in Suffolk.

[18] Ibid., p. 3.   [19] Ibid., p. 22.

Organizations

We hasten to close by cautioning against one symptom of defection and tendency to apostasy, the most threatening to the welfare of the church, because the most prevailing, specious and insinuating: we mean the concealment of the discriminating doctrines of the gospel in the public ministry. We point you to no party, but we enjoin you to watch all.[20]

To make his meaning quite clear, Wright identified the concealed doctrines as the Calvinistic doctrines of grace.[21] The letter was approved and published, but one pastor, Daniel Wilson of Tunstall, noted:

Some disputes and clashings about the doctrine called Fullerism, which some of the churches have begun to embrace, and it seems likely to make disputes, if not a division of the Association.[22]

After the 1828 meetings, Wilson observed, 'The subject of duty faith seems spreading, which causes a deal of demur among us.'[23] That year's letter on 'Prayer', written by Philip Dickerson, can have caused no controversy. However, for the 1829 letter, Wright was the author again, and his theme this time was 'The Power of Godliness'. Much of his treatment was unexceptional. However, he took the opportunity to say that the unbeliever had no natural ability to respond to the gospel,[24] arguing that God did not intend that it should be

the duty of man to have a spiritual life by the indwelling of the Holy Spirit, nor that he should exercise those evangelical graces, and bring forth the fruits of the Spirit.[25]

The debates generated by Wright's letter took up so much time that other Association business suffered. It survived attempts at amendment and was passed by the Association, but it was resolved that no further letters should be issued.[26] It was at this point that Wright and his friends decided to take further action.

[20] Ibid.
[21] 'The concealment of the peculiar doctrines of grace is studied as a means of conciliating men, where prejudice should be resisted, not accommodated', Ibid.
[22] Quoted Klaiber, *Suffolk Baptists*, p. 122.   [23] Ibid., p. 123.
[24] *S. & N. Letter, 1829*, p. 7.   [25] Ibid., p. 8.
[26] Klaiber, op. cit., pp. 123-4 The report on the proceedings published with the letter does not record this decision.

The Suffolk and Norfolk New Association

On 22 September 1829, ten ministers and deacons, representing six churches, met at Grundisburgh and 'resolved to withdraw and form ourselves into a Separate Association'. The reason they explained was because of 'a departure . . . from the original PRINCIPLES of the Association'. These principles

> have ever been held, to the exclusion of the sentiment that it is the duty of all men to believe with the faith of God's elect; and in opposition to the practice of general and indiscriminate offers and exhortations in the ministry.[27]

They further alleged that

> a defection had taken place in several Churches, and as some of our brethren appear more disposed to countenance than oppose that defection, we know of no means of securing our own comfort, and uniting our efforts, to advance the true glory of our Lord's kingdom, other than that of adopting the measures we have taken.[28]

They agreed that those whom they opposed claimed still to believe 'the doctrines which head the Circular Letter', but considered that 'sentiments are blended with them, which in their direct and legitimate consequences, negative those doctrines'. They also believed that the doctrine of particular redemption was being redefined:

> The peculiarity of redemption, we are informed, is not to be found in the blood-shedding of Jesus, but in the hand of the Spirit. Thus while they hold the doctrine of particular redemption in words, they give a turn to the expression, which denies intrinsic and essential peculiarity, and set up a redemption limited by power, not by price – a redemption indefinite in itself, that warrants the faith and confidence of every man, and particular only when applied.[29]

[27] W. Reynolds et al., *Circular Letter to the Baptist Churches of Suffolk and Norfolk*, Grundisburgh, 1829, p.1 The signatories were William Reynolds and George Pearson of Wattisham; George Wright of Beccles; John Gowring and John Lay of Halesworth; Philip Dickerson and Thomas Blundell of Rattlesden; Samuel Nunn of Hadleigh; and Jonathan Wright and Samuel Plowman of Stonham, Ibid., p. 3.

[28] Ibid., p. 1.   [29] Ibid.

Organizations

It is not surprising that a rider was added to the doctrinal basis, the Calvinism of which had been stated in the same terms as in the 1769 *Statement*. It read:

> The doctrines expressed in the previous Article are held by this Association to be wholly incompatible with the doctrine, that asserts that saving faith is the duty of all men, and are therefore maintained by the respective churches to the exclusion of that doctrine.[30]

There could be no doubting the Hyper-Calvinistic stance of the New Association.

The only other addition to the doctrinal basis of the original Association declared:

> together with the necessity of baptism on a profession of faith and as a pre-requisite to the Lord's Supper, the obligation of believers to practical obedience to the declared will of Christ as King in Zion.[31]

The new Association was thus formed on a closed communion basis. There is little evidence that the question of the terms of communion caused much concern to the churches of the pre-1829 Association, but as previously indicated, the debate between Robert Hall and Joseph Kinghorn made this a live issue among Particular Baptist churches across the counties of England.[32]

The statement about believers' obligations was clearly designed to safeguard the Association against any charges of Antinomianism. Wright's views have been noted. These aroused some discussion at the first Association Meetings when he was accused of holding sentiments 'repugnant to practical godliness'. In reply he maintained that 'he uniformly and earnestly insists upon the obligation of believers to obey the preceptive will of the Redeemer, as the Sovereign and Lawgiver of his people'.[33]

---

[30] Ibid., p. 2.   [31] Ibid.

[32] Kinghorn's church in Norwich never joined the Norfolk and Suffolk Association, probably an indication of his lack of sympathy with its Hyper-Calvinism. Six years after his death, his church joined the Norfolk and Norwich Association, which was formed as the East Norfolk Association and affiliated to the Baptist Union in 1836, C. B. Jewson, *The Baptists in Norfolk*, London, 1957, pp. 89-90.

[33] *S. & N. (New) Letter, 1830*, p. 24.

[319]

George Wright was Secretary of the Association from 1829 to 1865.[34] Its first Treasurer was George Pearson, a deacon at Wattisham. He held office from 1829 until his death in 1837. Before moving to Suffolk, Pearson had been a member of Stevens's church in Boston and he remained a close friend and admirer of Stevens after the latter's removal to London. When Pearson died, his pastor, John Cooper, wrote:

> The doctrinal sentiments of our friend were in general accordance with those of Gill, Brine etc., which he maintained inviolate, but never suffered zeal for the truth to betray him into a bitter and acrimonious spirit.[35]

The New Association grew steadily. In 1829 twenty-four churches had met in the original Association. By the time of the 1830 Association Meetings, eleven of these had withdrawn, although only seven committed themselves to the New Association in that year.[36] Growth, however, continued and in 1832, there were twelve churches representing 1,225 members in the New Association.[37] By 1850 there were twenty-nine churches with 2,416 members.[38] In 1848 the word 'New' was dropped, since the 'Old' Association, which had been reduced to just eight churches, went out of existence; its place was taken by the Suffolk Baptist Union.[39]

[34] Bland, op. cit., pp. 72, 73.
[35] *Gospel Herald*, vol. 7, 1839, p. 33; biographical details, ibid, pp. 29-35; *S. & N. (New) Letter 1830*, p. 24.
[36] The Churches were Wattisham, Beccles, Halesworth, Rattlesden, Hadleigh, Little Stoneham and Bardwell with a total of 604 members. 'Minute Book of Suffolk and Norfolk New Association', (hereinafter referred to as *S. & N. (New) Minutes*, 11th and 12th May 1830.
[37] Ibid., 8th and 9th May 1832.
[38] Ibid., 4th and 5th June 1850.
[39] Ibid., 20th and 21st June 1848; *Gospel Herald*, vol 16, 1848, p. 170. The Old Association had been weakened in 1846, when eight churches, including Elven's at Bury St Edmunds broke away to form the Suffolk Baptist Union, which produced no doctrinal statement, but welcomed any evangelical Baptist church in the county, *Gospel Herald*, vol. 14, 1846, p. 143; Klaiber, *Suffolk Baptists*, p. 144. The Suffolk Baptist Union thus adopted the basis of the reconstituted Baptist Union of Great Britain and Ireland, see below, p. 329.

Organizations

The Suffolk Hyper-Calvinists soon demonstrated that their doctrine did not inhibit evangelism. At the 1831 Association Meeting it was agreed to ask the churches to establish a Home Missionary Society for Suffolk and Norfolk.[40] Collins of Grundisburgh proposed

> that village Preaching might be more extensively encouraged. This was urged on the grounds that our Ministers have been too much neglected by the London Society, and their applications too much disregarded: and from a conviction that the interest of the Redeemer's Cause would be more efficiently served by the formation of a local Society.[41]

A committee to promote the aims of the Society was made up of Wright, Collins, Cooper of Wattisham, Nunn of Ipswich, and Dickerson of Rattlesden.[42] Wright wanted the Society to be an auxiliary of the London Home Missionary Society, but was overruled.[43] In September 1831 the Suffolk and Norfolk Home Missionary Society came into existence at a public meeting in Ipswich, adopting the doctrinal basis of the New Association.[44] Collins held office as Secretary from 1831 to 1876, and was assisted by Cooper for much of that time.[45] In 1835 churches in Cambridge and Huntingdon asked for help, and Collins facilitated the establishment of a similar society for those counties.[46] The two societies combined in 1842 to form the Baptist Home Missionary Society for the Counties of Suffolk, Norfolk, Cambridgeshire, and Huntingdon.[47]

[40] 'S. & N. (New) Minutes', 10th and 11th May 1831.

[41] 'S. & N. Home Missionary Society Minutes', May 1831.

[42] 'S. & N. (New) Minutes' 10th and 11th May 1831.

[43] 'S. & N. Home Missionary Society Minutes', 26th July 1831.

[44] Ibid., 13th Sept. 1831.

[45] Cooper was pastor at Wattisham from 1831 to 1879. With Wright and Collins he gave impressive leadership to the Association. Klaiber, *Suffolk Baptists*, p. 127, mistakenly suggests that Cooper came from Stevens's church in London. This was not so: he was a Suffolk man and had been in membership at Rattlesden before going to Wattisham. He did receive a call to succeed Stevens in London, but declined, *Gospel Herald*, vol. 49, 1881, pp. 97–103; 129–137; 161–167.

[46] 'S. & N. Home Missionary Society Minutes', 6th Oct. 1835; *Gospel Herald*, vol. 3, 1835, p. 239.

[47] 'S. & N. Home Missionary Society Minutes', 2nd Nov. 1841; 19th Oct. 1842; *Gospel Herald*, vol. 10, 1842, pp. 354, 5.

The demands of evangelism abroad were powerful enough to constrain the Old and New Associations to establish a joint auxiliary committee for the Baptist Missionary Society.[48] In 1846 the New Association withdrew and urged support for Home Mission Funds.[49] Two years later, however, the Association Meeting resolved to correct any misapprehension about the Society, and 'to recommend the claims of the "Baptist Foreign Missionary Society" to the consideration and support of the churches'.[50] In 1849 the Association declined to set up an auxiliary but renewed its recommendation of the Society to the churches.[51] By this time the desire for a Strict Baptist Missionary Society was growing.[52]

The Suffolk and Norfolk New Association was the first Baptist Association to be established on the twin foundation of Hyper-Calvinism and strict communion. This example was imitated elsewhere but not with the same degree of success. The East Anglian association's progress must have owed much to good leadership and the kind of expansionist attitude that lay behind the formation of the Home Missionary Society. Before the division of 1829, the Suffolk Baptist churches had enjoyed many years of prosperity under ministry that was predominantly Hyper-Calvinist. When the division came, the leaders on both sides held their differences without bitterness.[53] It is perhaps also significant that the Strict Baptists of Suffolk were able to agree to differ on the significance of the moral law. This factor may explain why the *Gospel Standard* gained a relatively small following in this county.

2. London

Until the second half of the nineteenth century, Baptist Associations of every shade of opinion had a precarious existence in London. During the

---

[48] 'S. & N. (New) Minutes', 14th and 15th June 1842.

[49] Ibid., 9th and 10th June 1846. The Old Association was by this time in serious decline.

[50] Ibid., 20th and 21st June 1848.   [51] Ibid., 5th and 6th June 1849.

[52] See Palmer's tract, *Foreign Missions*, referred to p. 301 above.

[53] See W. Reynold et al., *Circular Letter to the Baptist Churches of Suffolk and Norfolk*, Klaiber, op. cit., p. 125. Dickerson and Elven appear to have been on good terms, *Gospel Herald*, vol. 48, 1880, p. 250.

Organizations

eighteenth century, and for much of the nineteenth, the Baptist Board, a ministers' fraternal, provided the most effective means of co-operation.[54] Attempts to link churches together led to the widely-scattered Berks and West London Association in 1825, and the London Baptist Association in 1834.[55] Outside of these two groups a Hyper-Calvinistic group was to emerge. Their first attempt at organization was a ministers' fraternal.

THE UNION OF BAPTIST MINISTERS

The Union of Baptist Ministers was established on 31 December 1833 at Soho Chapel, Oxford Street.[56] Its constitution described its members 'as ministers . . . of the Particular Baptist Denomination', but its statement of faith was so strongly Hyper-Calvinistic that it is difficult to imagine anyone who had a concern for evangelism wishing to join.[57] It required a disciplined approach to communion although it did not specify closed communion. Its leaders included George Comb of Soho, J. A. Jones of Brick Lane, and John Foreman of Marylebone. The ministers met quarterly for discussion, after which one of their number preached a public sermon.[58] The Union lasted just five years, coming to grief over the communion controversy. The strict communionists formed the majority of the members, but the open communionists had an able leader in James Castledon, the popular preacher of Hampstead. George Comb wavered on the issue, before finally deciding in favour of strict communion.[59]

---

[54] See page 12 above.

[55] W. T. Whitley, *The Baptists of London*, pp. 61-4. W. C. Johnson, *Encounter in London, The Story of the London Baptist Association, 1865-1965*, London, 1965, p. 18.

[56] *Gospel Herald*, vol. 2, 1834, pp. 69, 70.

[57] Article 4 included the statement, 'The system or doctrine of an universal sufficiency, that warrants and calls for the faith of every man, the valid redemption of Jesus to be more or less as man shall perform his duty of believing, we discard and disavow; as founded on general and not on particular redemption.' Article 5 stated 'we do not hold with or believe in, the doctrine which maketh it the duty of all men to believe in Christ to the salvation of the soul'. Article 6 taught eternal justification, Ibid., p. 70.

[58] *Gospel Herald*, vol. 9, 1841, pp. 155, 6.

[59] Ibid., pp. 156, 173.

History of the English Calvinistic Baptists, 1771–1892

The London Association of Strict Baptist Ministers and Churches
Despite the failure of the London Union, the desire for association remained strong.[60] At a meeting on 31 March 1846, it was agreed to form 'an Association of Strict Baptist Ministers and Churches in and around London'. The meeting was called by J. Oliver, a deacon at Trinity Chapel, Borough. Of the eighteen ministers invited to attend, thirteen came to the meeting. The chairman was Philip Dickerson of Little Alie Street, who had been the first moderator of the New Suffolk and Norfolk Association, back in 1830. Those present included the Hyper-Calvinist George Wyard of Soho, and William Norton, editor of the *Primitive Church Magazine* and an advocate of Fullerism. Amongst those invited but who did not attend were R. W. Overbury, another editor of the *Primitive Church Magazine*, Daniel Curtis of Homerton, and W. B. Bowes of Blandford Street.[61] Overbury's church at Eagle Street had been a founder member of the London Baptist Association in 1834, and he may well have been unwilling to break fellowship.[62] Curtis and Bowes pastored High Calvinist churches and may have been suspicious of the new venture. John Foreman made it clear in an open letter to William Norton in 1845 that he could join no Strict Baptist Association which did not repudiate duty-faith.[63] Significantly, Foreman, Stevens, and Wells, the

---

[60] In 1843 an itinerant preacher urged the establishment of a London Association like that in Suffolk and Norfolk. He stated that he had asked J. A. Jones, J. Foreman and J. Stevens to act. Ibid., vol. 11, 1843, pp. 313, 4.

[61] '*Minute Book of the London Association of Strict Baptist Ministers and Churches*', 31st March, 1846, Angus Library, Regent's Park College, Oxford.

[62] Whitley, *London Baptists*, p. 63.

[63] Curtis was a founder and deacon at Hill Street and played a prominent part in Foreman's settlement there before going as pastor to Homerton Row in 1837, Earthen Vessel, vol. 9, 1853, pp. 217, 220. Bowes was pastor at Blandford Street, long a High Calvinist stronghold. When invited to the pastorate he was told the church admitted to communion only 'persons professing the same faith and order as ourselves', 'CMB Blandford Street', December 1834. 'Open Letter to William Norton', published as a series of articles in *Gospel Herald*, vols. 13 and 14, 1845-6. Re-published as J. Foreman, *Remarks on Duty Faith*. London, 1860. To the latter Norton replied, W. Norton, *Responsibility: An Answer to Mr John Foreman's 'Remarks on Duty Faith'*, London, 1868.

Organizations

Hyper-Calvinist leaders among the London Baptists, did not receive invitations to the inaugural meeting.

Seven churches representing 961 members formed the Association in April 1846.[64] By 1850 the total membership of the Association's churches rose to 1,059, but after some losses and gains, still only seven churches were involved.[65] The ministers met quarterly for edification and consideration of the needs and opportunities among their respective churches. They held an annual public meeting. Visitors attending the fraternal meetings from abroad during 1846 included a New York pastor[66] and J. G. Oncken, the German Baptist pioneer.[67] The Association received a visit of encouragement in the same year from the Secretary of the Kent and Sussex New Association.[68] As part of its concern for the wider Baptist community, the Association petitioned the King of Sweden in 1850 to grant religious liberty to Baptists in his kingdom.[69]

However, the Association ran into difficulties over the issue of Fullerism. Some leading Hyper-Calvinists did not join the Association, possibly because of its neutral stance on this doctrinal issue. William Norton seems to have played no further part in its proceedings after the initial meeting, although in February 1848 the Association passed a resolution defending the editor of the *Primitive Church Magazine* against criticism in the *Baptist Magazine*.[70] In 1850 John Box of Woolwich resigned from the Association, stating that,

> he believed it to be our duty to preach the Gospel to every creature – to warn the ungodly, but he did not believe it was the duty of every creature to believe with the faith of God's elect – but most of the brethren he said did so believe and did so say.[71]

---

[64] The Churches were Trinity Street, Borough; Little Alie Street; Grafton Street, Soho; Stratford; Westminster; Wild Street and Cumberland Street, Shoreditch, *'Minutes London S.B. Churches and Ministers'*, 17th April 1846 and 20th Oct. 1846.

[65] Grafton Street and Westminster had closed and Cumberland Street left. Wandsworth, Phillip Street and Romney Street, Westminster joined. Ibid., 15th Oct. 1850.

[66] Ibid., 18th Aug. 1846. [67] Ibid., 20th Oct. 1846. [68] Ibid., 16th June 1846.
[69] Ibid., 18th June 1850. [70] Ibid., 15th Feb. 1848. [71] Ibid., 15th Jan. 1848.

Box also indicated his intention of joining another association. The assembled ministers repudiated Box's accusation of duty-faith and asked for names. Box apologized for saying that many believed in 'duty-faith', but insisted that some of the ministers did.[72] Discussions within the Association had often revealed a greater concern to maintain strict-communion practice than to establish the correctness of Hyper-Calvinism. However, given the strength of feeling displayed by some strict communionists on the latter issue, it is not surprising to learn from Box's comments that a new Association had come into existence; for while the London Association of Strict Baptists did not repudiate duty-faith formally, many of its members did. The lack of clarity on this issue led to its weakness as an organization.

The New Association of Particular Baptists in London and Its Vicinity

Even before the demise of the London Association, Box was one of eleven ministers who set up a New Association in February 1849. Other founding ministers included Daniel Curtis, and also George Wyard who had attended the first meeting of the earlier Association, but whose church had not joined.[73] However, Foreman and Wells, pastors of large Strict and Particular Baptist churches still stood aloof: they were preachers and individualists rather than committee men. They would, however, have had no difficulty with the aim of the Association:

> to unite those ministers and churches who beside practising strict communion, are opposed to the popular usage of 'offering' Christ and gospel grace and of inviting men indiscriminately to believe unto salvation; and opposed also to the sentiments by which this inconsistent practice is attempted to be vindicated.[74]

A manifesto published by this new Association made it clear that its members were concerned about certain developments in Baptist theology that went far beyond the teaching of Fuller.

---

[72] Ibid., 19th Feb. 1850.
[73] *Gospel Herald*, vol. 17, 1859, p. 100.   [74] Ibid.

Organizations

Many of them affirming that there is an inherent efficacy in the religious means, and some of them boldly asserting that man is able to turn to God and do his whole duty without the Holy Spirit.[75]

This appears to be a reference to the teaching of John Howard Hinton, pastor of Devonshire Square Church from 1837 to 1863 and a Secretary of the Baptist Union from 1841 to 1866.[76] Originally written in 1830, Hinton revised and re-issued *The Work of the Holy Spirit in Conversion*,[77] in 1841. His statements about the work of the Holy Spirit indicate that he had moved far from the teaching of the older Particular Baptists:

> He [the Holy Spirit] imparts no power, but merely sets in motion existing powers by an extraordinary impulse; so that on this ground also, the power of turning to God must be admitted to exist without his influence.[78]

Although persuaded of their strong Calvinism, the men of the New Association were keen to emphasise their goodwill to other orthodox Christians:

> We do not thus come together in the spirit of antagonism to any other Association. We wish well to all others, in so far as they hold and advocate the truth and discipline established by God and by his holy apostles.[79]

Such protestations of goodwill, however, could not conceal the disarray that existed among the Baptists of London.[80] It clearly made sense for the two Strict Baptist Associations to unite. In 1852 negotiations began which lead to a union of the two groups in January 1853 at Cumberland

---

[75] Ibid., p. 239.

[76] Dictionary of National Biography, s.v.

[77] J. H. Hinton, *The Work of the Holy Spirit in Conversion*, London [1830], revised 1841.

[78] Ibid., p. 62 Hinton's theology was frequently discussed in the *Gospel Herald* in the early 1840s – vol 9, 1841, pp. 31, 32; 160-2; 279-81; vol. 10, 1842, pp. 288-92; vol. 11, 1843, pp. 90-5.   [79] *Gospel Herald*, vol. 17, 1849, p. 239.

[80] 'Thus in 1851 there was the Great Exhibition of London Baptists in three groups of Particulars, two groups of Generals, and most outside every group', Whitley. *London Baptists*, p. 63.

Street, Shoreditch, a church which had left the first Association for the second.[81] To unite the differing emphases of the two Associations, they avowed

> That while the gospel is to be preached to every creature, irrespective of class and condition, spiritual and saving faith is the gift of God.[82]

The united Association disappeared within a year or so. Like its two component parts, it did not enjoy the support of the influential Wells and Foreman, men who seemed to divide their time equally between their large churches and preaching tours. Whereas the East Anglia Association had able leadership from the outset, the London Associations did not have men who could rally others. In addition, uncertainty about the doctrinal basis probably only increased the sense of doctrinal confusion. It was not until the formation of the Metropolitan Association of Strict Baptist Churches in 1871, by a new generation of Baptist leaders, that the capital gained an Association that was to endure.

3. THE KENT AND SUSSEX NEW ASSOCIATION

By the 1840s debates on Fullerism and the terms of communion were agitating churches in the West Kent and Sussex Association. The 1841 Association Meetings, held in Tunbridge Wells, witnessed a discussion on particular redemption.[83] Two years later a Kentish farmer wrote to the *Gospel Herald*, complaining of 'several ministers and churches who advocate general redemption etc. and practice open communion.' He referred to discussions about the establishment of a new Association 'on the principles of sound orthodoxy and strict communion'.[84] The Kent churches of Borough Green, Hadlow, Meopham, and Tunbridge Wells, and the Sussex churches of Wadhurst and Wivelsfield formed such an Association in 1844.[85] By 1847 there were fifteen churches in the Association,

---

[81] *'Minutes London S.B. Churches and Ministers'*, 19th Oct. 1852, 9th Nov. 1852, 9th Feb. 1853.

[82] Ibid., Article 12 of 1853 Association.

[83] F. J. Buffard, *History of the Kent and Sussex Baptist Associations*, Faversham, 1963, p. 83.

[84] *Gospel Herald*, vol. 11, 1843, p. 263.   [85] Buffard, op. cit., p. 83.

although the reports of the Association meetings in the *Gospel Herald* spoke of the 'mournful nature' of its statements, which arose from a prevailing mood of 'indifference and lethargy'.[86] The following year's reports were more cheerful.[87] Nevertheless, the Association appears not to have continued long. Both Kent and Sussex were to prove fertile grounds for Strict Baptists, but their churches were not inclined to work together in formal Associations. Many Sussex churches began as Huntingtonian communities, which later changed their views on baptism.[88] They naturally gravitated to the *Gospel Standard* group with its tendency of opposition to Associations. An older Baptist tradition existed in Kent, but as the nineteenth century progressed, a powerful *Gospel Standard* influence developed among the Strict Baptists of this county.

4. National Organizations

The Baptist Union was established in 1812 by a group of men closely associated with Andrew Fuller, but it also included Hyper-Calvinists of the John Gill school, as well as both open and closed communionists. Its basis of faith was decidedly Calvinist and very similar to those of the various local Associations.[89] Early hopes of national cooperation were not realized, and for years the Baptist Union had an insubstantial existence. Its leaders were busy pastors and the demands of the Missionary Society, the Itinerant Preachers Society, the Baptist Irish Society, and the local Associations, must have weighed heavy on them, in days when travel was not easy.

When the Baptist Union was re-constituted in 1832, the climate of thought had changed. The old basis of faith was replaced by a pledge of adherence to 'the sentiments usually denominated evangelical'.[90] E. A. Payne observed that 'though at the time many felt this to be too vague, it

[86] *Gospel Herald*, vol. 15, 1847, p. 195.

[87] Ibid., vol. 16, 1848, p. 218.

[88] R. F. Chambers, *The Strict Baptist Chapels of England, 2, 'Sussex'*, Thornton Heath, n.d., pp. 2, 3.

[89] E. A. Payne, *History of the Baptist Union*, p. 24. The statement is almost identical to that of the Norfolk and Suffolk statement of 1769, p. 313, 1, footnote 1, above.

[90] Ibid., p. 3.

had the advantage of opening the door to closer association with the churches of the New Connexion of General Baptists.[91] It was sixty years before a formal union between the General and Particular Baptists came about, but as early as 1842, the Union was to have its first General Baptist chairman.[92] Payne ascribed the change in attitude to the influence of Andrew Fuller's theology, as had J. C. Philpot earlier.[93] Given Fuller's expressed views, this seems unfair.[94] It might be better to claim that the catalyst for change was the younger Robert Hall. He rejected particular redemption, and according to A. H. Macleod, his close relationship with the General Baptists in Leicester suggested that he hoped for a union between the two denominations.[95]

It was, however, after Hall's death that the changes became more apparent. A number of prominent leaders passed from the scene during the 1830s. Looking back on these years, a later observer wrote:

> Amongst Baptist ministers of moderate Calvinistic views who died, may be named Rippon, Ivimey and Upton, all of whom adhered to the primitive order of communion at the Lord's Table. After, however, these men, who had been leaders of the people in their day, had been laid in their graves, the low sentiment churches began to adopt 'mixed communion' at the table of the Lord.[96]

New leaders emerged. Francis Cox was chairman of the Union in 1834 and John Howard Hinton in 1837: both were prominent open communionists. Another open communionist, Edward Steane, was appointed Secretary of the Union in 1835, an office he was to hold until 1882. From 1841 until 1866, he shared the office with Hinton, whose theology had moved far from that of Andrew Fuller.[97]

---

[91] Ibid., p. 4.   [92] J. G. Pike of Derby, Ibid., p. 65.
[93] Ibid., p. 61. *Gospel Standard*, vol. 8, 1842, pp. 319, 320.
[94] 'If, on account of what I have here and elsewhere avowed, I were disowned by my present connexions, I should rather choose to go through the world alone than be connected with them (the Arminians), A. Fuller, *Works*, 'Six Letters to Dr Ryland', 1803, p. 324.
[95] A. H. Macleod, 'Life and Teaching of Robert Hall', p. 377.
[96] *Gospel Herald*, vol. 49, 1881, p. 43.
[97] E. A. Payne, *History of the Baptist Union*, pp. 257–62, lists office holders.

Organizations

There were of course still strict communionists in the Union, but they felt their position to be under pressure. To meet the challenge and 'to confer respecting the state and prospect of the churches as affected by the spread of OPEN COMMUNION', twenty-one ministers and eighteen 'brethren' met at Eagle Street, London, on 27th and 28th April 1841. Most of the participants were from London, but Wright and Collins came from Suffolk, John Stock from Maidstone, David Wassell from Bath, and T. Winter from Bristol. J. A. Jones attended, but most of the other London Hyper-Calvinists did not. Overbury and Norton, editors of the *Primitive Church Magazine* were appointed secretaries and Overbury presided. Amongst the resolutions passed was the determination

> to endeavour by all Scriptural means to arrest the progress of open communion and bring back the churches in this respect to the model of the New Testament.[98]

This resolution indicated that the meeting was to act as a pressure group and that there was no intention at this stage to set up a rival organization to the Baptist Union. Another resolution stated that the proceedings of the meeting should be published in the *Primitive Church Magazine* and the *Baptist Magazine*, but the latter chose to ignore the meetings completely.[99]

Annual meetings continued to be held. At the 1842 meetings, the closed-communion churches were warned against 'the choice of pastors favourable to mixed communion'.[100] By 1843, a scheme for training younger men under the supervision of experienced pastors was under discussion. In the same year, the meeting approved a doctrinal basis almost identical to that later adopted by the first London Strict Baptist Association.[101]

The 1844 meeting sought wider support in the form of a Convention of Strict Baptist Churches; this would be 'a general association of all Baptist churches in the kingdom holding strict communion, and the great principles of truth'.[102] However, cracks in the Association were beginning to

[98] *Gospel Herald*, vol. 9, 1841, pp. 192, 3.   [99] Ibid.
[100] Ibid., vol. 10, 1842, pp. 190, 1.   [101] Ibid., vol. 11, 1843. pp. 225, 6.
[102] Ibid., vol. 13, 1845, p. 236 fn, 'S. & N. (New) Minutes', 11th & 12th June 1844.

appear. It was at this time that Foreman made the announcement that he would not support a Strict Baptist Society that did not repudiate duty faith.[103] J. A. Jones, who had given his support in the 1841 meeting, had grave reservations about the future ministerial training of the proposed Convention. He wrote:

> As the three secretaries are avowedly of the late Mr Fuller's sentiments on duty faith, we may fairly suppose the features of the theological training etc. etc. If this convention receives the approbation of the Suffolk ministers, they will do more to open the Suffolk Churches to the reception of Fuller's sentiments than Fuller himself could ever accomplish.[104]

Overbury, Norton, and Stock, the promoters of the Convention, found themselves increasingly isolated. The vigorous strict-communion group in London, led by Stevens, Wells, and Foreman, refused to have fellowship with them because of their alleged 'Fullerism'. On the other hand, their promotion of strict communion gained little support among the men who were increasingly prominent in the Baptist Union. John Stock was able to rally some support for his position in the north of England, but in terms of the country as a whole, it was not significant.[105]

5. THE *GOSPEL STANDARD* AND ASSOCIATIONS

The isolation of William Huntington has already been noted. He had been ordained to the Christian ministry by the followers of George Whitefield. Whitefield had been extremely reluctant to organize his converts into a new denomination for fear of promoting a personal following.[106] Out of the Calvinist wing of the eighteenth-century Revival sprang a host of independent churches, many of which had no formal ties.[107] A man of Huntington's temperament readily accepted an extreme form of

---

[103] See above, p. 324.
[104] *Gospel Herald*, vol. 13, 1845, pp. 236, 7.
[105] Underwood, *HEB*, pp. 208, 209.
[106] From 1749, Whitefield relinquished the leadership of the Calvinist Methodist movement to assist the Revival in all its branches, A. Dallimore, *George Whitefield*, vol. 2, Edinburgh: Banner of Truth, 1980, pp. 256–9.
[107] W. Wilson, *London Dissenting Churches*, vol. 4, 1814, pp. 556, 7; 560–3.

independency. His doctrine of the law, which was so frequently condemned at Baptist Association meetings, virtually sealed his isolation. However, those Baptists who did admire him felt that they were occupying an embattled outpost.

William Gadsby was a more gregarious man than William Huntington, but he did not favour Associations either: in his view, they too often promoted co-operation among churches at the expense of faithfulness to the gospel.[108] A statement in an 1836 issue of the *Gospel Standard* read:

> We are by no means friendly to Associations of Ministers, as, however fair may be their show, however positive and scriptural their declarations, however good their intentions, at the outset, they invariably, sooner or later lead to the lifting up with pride, to the lust of ambition, or to the gagging of its members. Little by little [corruption] creeps in, till the whole becomes corrupt.[109]

J. C. Philpot's opposition was just as strong. He countered the suggestion that Associations were a source of strength:

> All strength gained by such means is a departure from that weakness in which alone divine strength is made perfect. All such strength is therefore carnal strength, and as such involves a departure from Gospel principles.[110]

He urged his readers to 'resist where you can, and where you cannot, flee out of Associations'.[111] The dangers were inevitable, since Scripture offered no precedent for such groupings.

In spite of his opposition to Associations, Philpot saw the need for some form of union among the churches in which he served. This union, he believed, could be promoted by the *Gospel Standard* magazine. In 1838 he wrote:

---

[108] J. Gadsby, *Memoir of W. Gadsby*, p. 26. 'Witness the Leicestershire Union meetings, held every six months in Leicestershire, in which the Arians, Independents and General and Particular Baptists, unite, so that those, it appears, are his brethren, seeing they can unite together', W. Gadsby, *Works*, vol. 1, 'The Gospel the Believer's Rule of Conduct', p. 6.

[109] *Gospel Standard*, vol. 2, 1836, p. 69.   [110] Ibid., vol. 7, 1841, p. 296.
[111] Ibid.

All the living members of Christ's body have a secret union and sympathy with one another as fellow-sufferers and fellow-heirs. But they must be brought together, and come into contact before this secret union can be openly manifested, and their hearts sweetly knit together. Should our publication effect this, it would indeed be highly favoured of God; and we trust in some instances it has been thus blessed.[112]

It was ironic that Gadsby should reject the idea of a union of separate and equal churches in an Association for the reason that it would lead to 'the gagging of its members', whereas Philpot advocated an informal union orchestrated by a privately-owned magazine edited by a strong-minded man.

It was not until after Philpot's death that the full dangers of this arrangement manifested themselves. During the 1870s, charitable societies were established in connection with the *Gospel Standard* magazine. These societies were formed with the worthy aim of helping aged and infirm ministers, their widows, and later poor members of suitable congregations. The committee responsible for the administration of the societies' funds soon came to exercise considerable powers of patronage. Until the end of 1877 the *Gospel Standard* magazine was the private property of John Gadsby, but during that year he announced his intention of donating it with its profits to the committee of the charitable societies, who would appoint the magazine's editor. The committee appointed Grey Hazlerigg, pastor of Zion Chapel, Leicester, as editor. Hazlerigg had been a friend and associate of Philpot, but was soon accused of error by Gadsby, a charge later withdrawn; but in the ensuing controversy, Gadsby resumed control of the magazine and forced through the acceptance of four additional articles of faith. These included the following statements:

> We believe that it would be unsafe, from the brief records we have of the way in which the apostles, under the direction of the Lord, addressed their hearers in certain cases and circumstances, to derive absolute and universal rules for ministerial addresses in the present day under widely different circumstances.

[112] Ibid, vol. 4, 1838, p. 3; cf. vol. 6, 1840, p. 5.

Therefore, that for ministers in the present day to address unconverted persons, or indiscriminately all in a mixed congregation, calling upon them to savingly repent, believe, and receive Christ, or perform any other acts dependent upon the new creative power of the Holy Ghost, is on the one hand to imply creature power, and, on the other to deny the doctrine of special redemption.

According to the written testimony of William Wileman, who was present as a secretary at the meeting which approved these statements, they were a compromise and an attempt to ward off something more extreme.[113] They were drawn up in a single afternoon in the course of a heated debate. Hazlerigg, who tried to ward off a greater danger by promoting the compromise, later deplored his action, writing:

> I confess to having held, as is well known by some, strong objections to the addition of Articles 32, 33, and 34 to the original ones. The multiplication of highly elaborated Articles seemed, and still seems, to me dangerous. It may be a source not of safety but of division.[114]

The whole episode is a sorry example of how a wealthy businessman exerted pressure in a situation where there was no proper representation of churches or ministers, and where the apparatus of a magazine and charitable societies were able to exert moral pressure upon a group of churches. They found themselves under a Hyper-Calvinistic yoke more rigorous than anything ever seen among the Particular Baptist churches of England.

* * * * *

The nineteenth century saw many attempts to draw the Calvinistic Baptist churches together. Sadly the overall result was to fragment the witness of those Baptist churches which loved the doctrines of grace. While the largest organization, the Baptist Union, was drifting towards Arminianism, churches with a real commitment to the sovereignty of God in

---

[113] *The Christian's Pathway*, 26, 1921, William Wileman, 'The Secret History of the Four Added Articles', pp. 206–10.

[114] Quoted, Kenneth Dix, *Strict and Particular*, The Baptist Historical Society, Didcot, 2001, p. 263.

salvation were dividing over church order and, in their grasp of the doctrines of grace, were moving away from the theological position of their seventeenth-century predecessors.

In all of the attempts to promote union among the churches from the 1830s onwards, no attempt was made to bring the churches back to the original basis of Particular Baptist unity as expressed in the *1689 Confession of Faith*. The various discussions took place as though that *Confession* had never existed. Several Baptist leaders had recovered much of its theology at the end of the eighteenth century. Even though Fuller and Booth had their disagreements, they were conscious of being within a Particular Baptist consensus and both men could have expressed their agreement within the terms of the historic Confession. When the Baptist Union was established in 1813 it was on a Calvinistic basis. Tragically, within twenty years that particular doctrinal basis was jettisoned. As the generation represented by Ryland, Kinghorn, and Ivimey passed away in the 1820s and 1830s, a generation of men followed who seem not to have appreciated the old theology. At the same time, the more conservative churches were fossilizing in Hyper-Calvinism, and the historic, evangelical, and experimental Calvinism of an earlier age seems to have all but disappeared from the English Particular Baptist churches. By the time C. H. Spurgeon attempted to restore historic Calvinism among those Particular Baptists churches, too many of their ministers and members had lost sight of the teachings of their fathers.

15

Charles Haddon Spurgeon

The old truth that Calvin preached, that Augustine preached, is the truth that I must preach today, or else be false to my conscience and my God. I cannot shape the truth; I know of no such thing as paring off the rough edges of a doctrine. John Knox's gospel is my gospel. That which thundered through Scotland must thunder through England again.

C. H. Spurgeon

I would warn our young members especially against that form of faith which holds only half the Bible; against those who proclaim the Divine election but ignore human responsibility, and who preach up high doctrine, but have little or nothing to say about Christian practice. I am persuaded that this is another net of the Flatterer, and many have I seen taken in it. They have ceased to care about the souls of others, have become indifferent as to whether children were perishing, or being saved, have settled on their lees to eat the fat, and drink the sweet, and have come to think that this is all for which they were redeemed. Their compassions have failed; they have had no weeping eyes over perishing sinners; in fact they have thought it unsound to care about saving sinners at all.

C. H. Spurgeon

In 1854 the Particular Baptist Church meeting in New Park Street, Southwark, London, called Charles Haddon Spurgeon to be its pastor. The decision was surprising since Spurgeon, not quite twenty years old, was being called to a church whose previous pastors included such outstanding Baptist leaders as Benjamin Keach, John Gill, and John Rippon. Although relatively unknown to the Baptists of London,

History of the English Calvinistic Baptists, 1771-1892

Spurgeon's short ministry in the remote Cambridgeshire village of Waterbeach had been remarkably blessed. By contrast the New Park Street Church had fallen on hard times. Although it had a fine building capable of seating some 1,200 people, the congregation was in serious decline by the 1850s. The church was unfavourably located and already Nonconformist families were moving out of this rather unpleasant part of the city to more salubrious suburbs. The church was however blessed with a group of godly deacons and in contrast to many Nonconformist communities, was unashamedly loyal to the Calvinism of earlier years. Under the long ministry of John Rippon from 1773 to 1836, it had been delivered from the Hyper-Calvinism previously in vogue. At the time of his call to London, Spurgeon wrote: 'The people are Calvinistic, and they would not get on with anything else. They raised £100 last week for a city missionary, so they have the sinews of war.'[1]

The story of the remarkable blessing that followed upon Spurgeon's settlement is well known. Twice the commodious chapel was enlarged, but such was the scale of the increase in the crowds that wanted to hear the new preacher, that a much larger building was required; and so another site was found at Newington Butts, Southwark, and the Metropolitan Tabernacle was built. The new building's cavernous sanctuary with its twin galleries could seat five thousand people, and was opened in 1861.

1. A Calvinistic Ministry

It has not always been appreciated that this growth took place under a ministry committed to historic Calvinism. Charles Spurgeon came from a family whose roots lay deep within the Calvinistic Independency of Essex and Suffolk. Young Charles grew up under powerful Christian influences: in his family home the Word of God was loved, family worship was practised daily, and chapel attendance was a regular feature of family life. From early childhood he delighted in books. He was the oldest in a family of seventeen children. Since there were so many children to

---

[1] *Letters of Charles Haddon Spurgeon*, ed., Iain H. Murray (Edinburgh: Banner of Truth, 1992), p. 47.

nurture, Charles spent long spells at the home of his grandfather, James Spurgeon, who was pastor of the Independent Church at Stambourne, Essex, for over fifty years. There in his grandfather's old manse, he discovered and read Bunyan's *Pilgrim's Progress* and Foxe's *Book of Martyrs*, and other spiritual classics. It was there that his grandmother paid him a penny for every one of Isaac Watts' hymns that he learned by heart. He progressed at such speed that the rate of payment had to be reduced, but the spiritual benefits of this memory work paid handsome dividends for the rest of his life. Although converted in a Primitive Methodist Chapel, a foundation of Calvinistic teaching about God, man, and sin, had already been laid in his soul. Later, while occupied as a young school-teacher in Newmarket, his Christian mentor was an old cook who was an avid reader of the *Gospel Standard* and with whom he discussed subjects such as the covenant of grace, election, the final perseverance of the saints, and the meaning of personal godliness. He later wrote: 'I do believe that I learned more from her than I should have learned from any six doctors of divinity of the sort we have nowadays.' The *Gospel Standard* was still being edited by J. C. Philpot at this time; after his death in 1869, Spurgeon wrote of him: 'We have read Mr Philpot's sermons with much profit; he was incomparable on his one theme.'[2]

It soon became clear that the theology of Spurgeon's spiritual youth was to provide the basis for his preaching in London. Within a year of his settlement he republished the *1689 Confession of Faith*. He wrote:

> I have thought it right to reprint in a cheap form this excellent list of doctrines, which were subscribed to by Baptist ministers in 1689. We need a banner because of the truth; it may be that this small volume may aid the cause of the glorious gospel by testifying to its leading doctrines . . . May the Lord soon restore unto his Zion a pure language, and may her watchmen see eye to eye.[3]

When he penned these words, Spurgeon was clearly aiming at a wider constituency than the New Park Street congregation, but turning his

[2] C. H. Spurgeon, *The Early Years* (London: Banner of Truth, 1962), pp. 38–9.
[3] *Things Surely Believed Among Us, 1689 Confession* (Tunbridge Wells: E. J. Harmer, n.d.), p. 5.

attention to his own flock, he reminded them that their church was a witness to apostolic Christianity, as proclaimed by 'martyrs, confessors, reformers and saints'. The *Confession* he explained

> is not issued as an authoritative rule, or code of faith, whereby you are to be fettered, but as an assistance to you in controversy, a confirmation in faith, and a means of edification in righteousness. Here the younger members of our church will have a body of divinity in small compass, and by means of Scriptural proofs, will be ready to give a reason for the hope that is in them.[4]

At the time Spurgeon reprinted the *Confession* there were probably many in attendance at the New Park Street services who had little understanding of the teaching that had sustained the life of the church before Spurgeon's arrival. Spurgeon's direct manner of preaching and lively illustrations were of course new in the experience of old and young alike, but his doctrine was no novelty for the older members of his congregation. In September 1855 he preached a sermon on election and felt it necessary to appeal to the ever-increasing number of hearers to lay aside their prejudices and give him a fair hearing. As he developed his theme he appealed to the seventeenth article of the Church of England, an old Waldensian Confession, and the Baptist *1689 Confession*. He continued:

> I have only used them as a confirmation of your faith, to show you that whilst I may be railed upon as a heretic, and as a hyper-Calvinist, after all I am backed up by antiquity. All the past stands by me. I do not care for the present. Give me the past and I will hope for the future. Let the present rise up in my teeth I do not care. What though a host of the churches of London may have forsaken the great cardinal doctrines of God, it matters not. If a handful of us stand alone in an unflinching maintenance of the sovereignty of our God, if we are beset by enemies, ay, and even by our own brethren, who ought to be our friends and helpers, it matters not, if we can but count upon the past; the noble army of martyrs, the glorious host of confessors, are our friends; the witnesses of the truth stand by us . . . But the best of all is, *God is with us*.[5]

[4] Ibid., p. 6. [5] C. H. Spurgeon, *The New Park Street Pulpit*, Vol. 1 (London: Banner of Truth, 1963), p. 313.

Charles Haddon Spurgeon

The volumes of the *New Park Street Pulpit* include sermons entitled 'The Sin of Unbelief', 'Free-Will a Slave', 'Particular Redemption', and 'Human Inability', as well as many others expounding the doctrines of historic Calvinism. It was probably because considerable time had passed since such subjects had been brought to the attention of the wider religious public that the accusations of Hyper-Calvinism were levelled against Spurgeon. Whatever the cause, it soon became apparent that there was strong resentment that Calvinistic doctrine was once again being preached. In 1858 one of Spurgeon's critics wrote:

> By many, the Calvinistic controversy has been considered as long since settled, and comparatively few in these times, amid such enlightened views of Christianity, dare to proclaim, openly and without disguise, the peculiar tenets of John Calvin. Even in many professedly Calvinistic pulpits, the doctrines are greatly modified, and genuine Calvinism is kept back. But there are some who hold it forth in all its length and breadth, and among these, the Rev. C. H. Spurgeon, the notorious preacher at the Music Hall, Royal Surrey Gardens, is the most prominent.[6]

Spurgeon continued his ministry in the same vein as he had begun. The services arranged to mark the opening of the Metropolitan Tabernacle included expositions of the Five Points of Calvinism and Baptist principles. The growing church was exposed to the same doctrines that had established the church under the ministry of Benjamin Keach some two hundred years previously. Further, the religious world of London could not ignore London's most popular preacher.

In 1864 Spurgeon took another step that deliberately linked his church with the Puritanism of an earlier generation. He published a *Catechism*, in the introduction of which he wrote:

> I am persuaded that the use of a good Catechism in all our families will be a great safeguard against the increasing errors of the times, and therefore I have compiled this little manual from the Westminster Assembly's

---

[6] Silas Henn, quoted in Iain H. Murray, *The Forgotten Spurgeon* (London: Banner of Truth, 1966), p. 52.

and Baptist Catechisms, for the use of my own church and congregation.[7]

The *Baptist Catechism* to which Spurgeon referred, had been drawn up in the 1690s at the request of the General Assembly of Particular Baptist Churches.[8] It drew extensively from the Westminster *Shorter Catechism*. The language of Spurgeon's revision however is even closer to the original *Shorter Catechism* than the *Baptist Catechism*, although the latter was employed on the questions and answers on the subject of baptism. A concern to safeguard orthodoxy among future generations can be seen in Spurgeon's commendation of the *Catechism*.

> In matters of doctrine you will find orthodox congregations frequently changed to heterodoxy in the course of thirty or forty years, and that is because, too often there has been no catechising of the children in the essential doctrines of the Gospel. For my part, I am more and more persuaded that the study of a good Scriptural catechism is of infinite value to our children.[9]

2. Historic Calvinism

In the light of Spurgeon's commitment to the doctrines of grace, it may seem surprising to discover that he received bitter opposition from some of his fellow-Calvinists. Recalling his ministry in the later 1850s Spurgeon wrote:

> I did not please everybody even then; and some found fault who ought to have been my best friends. I recollect great complaint being made against my sermon on the words, 'Compel them to come in,' in which I was enabled to speak with much tenderness and compassion for souls. The violent, rigid school of Hyper-Calvinists said that the discourse was

---

[7] C. H. Spurgeon, *A Catechism with Proofs*, 1864; repr. London: Evangelical Press, 1967, p. 3.

[8] It has sometimes been mistakenly described as *Keach's Catechism*, probably because it was confused with the Confession of Faith drawn up by Keach for his church.

[9] Quoted, T. J. Nettles, *Teaching Truth, Training Hearts, the Study of Catechisms in Baptist Life* (Amityville, NY: Calvary Press Publishing, 1998), p. 53.

Arminian and unsound, but it was a small matter to me to be condemned by the judgement of men, for my Master set his seal very clearly upon that message. I think I never preached another sermon by which so many souls were won to God, as our church-meetings long continued to testify; and all over the world, wherever the printed discourse has been scattered, sinners have been saved through its instrumentality; and therefore, if it be vile to exhort sinners to come to Christ, I purpose to be viler still. I am as firm a believer in the doctrines of grace as any man living, and a true Calvinist after the order of John Calvin himself; and probably I have read more of his works than any of my accusers ever did; but if it be thought an evil thing to bid sinners 'lay hold on eternal life', I will yet be more evil in this respect, and herein imitate not only Calvin, but also my Lord and his apostles, who, though they taught that salvation is of grace, and grace alone, feared not to speak to men as rational beings and responsible agents, and to bid them 'strive to enter in at the strait gate', and 'labour not for the meat which perisheth, but for that meat that endureth unto everlasting life'.[10]

The sermon to which Spurgeon referred was preached on 5 December 1858 from Luke 14:33: 'Compel them to come in.'[11] The great sense of urgency in his message can even be felt through reading the printed version of the sermon. He quickly moved to address unbelievers in the congregation: 'And now the plan of salvation is simply addressed to you – "Whosoever believeth in the Lord Jesus Christ shall be saved."' He made it clear that he was 'going after those who will not come'.[12] After showing the impossibility of keeping the law of God or winning salvation by works, he addressed the helpless sinner in these words:

> You are maimed and your arms are gone. But you are worse off than that, for if you could not work your way to heaven, yet you could walk your way there along the road by faith; but you are maimed in the feet as well as in the hands; you feel that you cannot believe, that you cannot repent, that you cannot obey the stipulations of the gospel. You feel that you are

[10] C. H Spurgeon, *The Early Years*, pp. 530–1.
[11] C. H. Spurgeon, *The New Park Street Pulpit*, Vol. 4 (London: Passmore & Alabaster, 1859), pp. 17–24.
[12] Ibid., p. 17.

utterly undone, powerless in every respect to do anything that can be pleasing to God. In fact you are crying out –

> Oh, could I but believe,
> Then all would easy be,
> I *would*, but *cannot;* Lord, relieve!
> My help must come from thee.

To you I am sent also. Before *you* am I to lift the blood-stained banner of the cross, to you am I to preach this gospel, 'Whoso calleth upon the name of the Lord shall be saved;' and unto you am I to cry 'Whosoever will, let him come and take of the water of life freely.'[13]

The stanza quoted in this extract is from one of the hymns of John Newton, himself an Evangelical Calvinist, but the lines have often been quoted by Hyper-Calvinists in a way that excuses unbelief and undermines duty-faith; and to such Hyper-Calvinists Spurgeon was clearly speaking, although not mentioning them by name.

Through the sermon Spurgeon addressed various categories of persons, but was clearly moved by the condition of those before him who remained in unbelief.

> Must I use some other compulsion to compel you to come in? Sinners, this one thing I am resolved upon this morning, if you be not saved ye shall be without excuse. Ye, from the grey-headed down to the tender age of childhood, if ye this day lay not hold upon Christ, your blood shall be upon your own head. If there be power in man to bring in his own fellow (as there is when man is helped by the Holy Spirit), that power shall be exercised this morning, God helping me. Come, I am not to be put off by your rebuffs: if my exhortation fails I must come to something else. My brother I ENTREAT you, I entreat you stop and consider, Do you know what it is you are rejecting this morning? You are rejecting Christ your only Saviour, 'Other foundation can no man lay;' there is none other name among men whereby we must be saved.[14]

Conscious of his critics, Spurgeon eventually turned aside to deal with them.

[13] Ibid., p. 18.   [14] Ibid., p. 21.

Some hyper-calvinist would tell me I am wrong in so doing. I cannot help it. I must do it. As I stand before my Judge at the last, I feel that I shall not make full proof of my ministry unless I entreat with many tears that ye would be saved, that ye would look unto Jesus Christ and receive his glorious salvation.[15]

Spurgeon was aware that so many of his critics, both Arminian and Hyper-Calvinist, were not familiar with the writings of Calvin or aware of the freeness with which he could present the gospel. Commenting on 2 Peter 3:9, Calvin spoke of God's 'wondrous love to the human race, that he desires all men to be saved and is prepared to bring even the perishing to safety'. Calvin had already faced and answered the objection which Spurgeon's critics, from opposite sides of the argument, made later:

It could be asked here, if God does not want any to perish, why do so many in fact perish? My reply is that no mention is made here of the secret decree of God by which the wicked are doomed to their own ruin, but only of His loving-kindness as it is made known to us in the Gospel. There God stretches out His hand to all alike, but He only grasps those (in such a way to lead to Himself) whom He has chosen before the foundation of the world.[16]

3. THE CHALLENGE OF HYPER-CALVINISM

Spurgeon never practised strict communion.[17] He made it clear, however, that he esteemed those who did, although he did not agree with their

---

[15] Ibid., pp. 21-22.

[16] John Calvin, *Commentaries: The Epistle of Paul the Apostle to the Hebrews and the First and Second Epistles of St Peter*, trans. William B. Johnston (Edinburgh: Oliver and Boyd, 1963), p. 364.

[17] Spurgeon did however maintain a disciplined Lord's Table. The American Baptist, A. H. Strong, described the practice at the Metropolitan Tabernacle: 'Baptism is held to precede church membership and permanent communion, although temporary communion is permitted without it.' Strong also averred that after a period of temporary communion those who refuse baptism 'are kindly told that it is not desirable for them to commune longer', *Systematic Theology* (New York: Armstrong, 1899), p. 550. What is not at present clear is whether those thus kindly addressed included conscientious Paedobaptists as well as those who neglected or wilfully rejected baptism.

practice. In 1857, speaking of 'our friends the Strict Communion Baptists', he declared, 'I should not like to say anything hard against them, for they are about the best people in the world, but they really do separate themselves from the great body of Christ's people. The Spirit of the living God will not let them do this really, but they do it professedly.'[18] Such people must have been among those he spoke of 'who ought to have been my best friends'.[19] One outspoken critic who helped rally opinion against Spurgeon was James Wells, pastor of a Strict Baptist church meeting in the Surrey Tabernacle, Borough High Street, less than half a mile from Spurgeon's chapel in New Park Street. Wells was a preacher of great ability who had ministered at the Surrey Tabernacle from 1832 (two years before Spurgeon's birth in 1834). He had originally gathered his congregation through street preaching before taking the Surrey Tabernacle in 1832. Proving too small for his congregation within the space of six years, the Tabernacle was demolished and rebuilt. Further enlargements took place in 1850 and 1853, until the building could accommodate 1,200 people. Further increases in the size of Wells' congregation led, in 1865, to the erection of a larger and much more convenient building in Wansey Street, able to seat up to two thousand worshippers. No other Hyper-Calvinistic Baptist church in London knew such growth. In outlook, Wells was closer to the Stevens group than to Gadsby's, although he always displayed a measure of independence.

In his childhood James Wells experienced crushing poverty and spent some time in the workhouse. Later, making his way to London, he taught himself to read. Here he married and obtained work in a factory; but in December 1824 he was smitten with small pox. While convalescing in hospital, he heard a sermon from the Anglican chaplain on 2 Peter 1:10: 'Wherefore the rather, brethren, give diligence to make your calling and election sure'. He understood little, but the word 'election' fastened itself on his mind. After recovering from his illness, he visited church after church in order to find help, but without success. He later declared:

---

[18] C. H. Spurgeon, *New Park Street Pulpit*, Vol. 4, 1859, p. 23.
[19] See p. 342 above.

I was in my misery beyond the reach of Wesleyanism and Low Calvinism. I was, in my apprehensions, beyond the reach of mercy. Yet as I went on reading the Bible and hearing dead-letter men, I came increasingly to believe that election was a doctrine of the Bible.

Deliverance eventually came when, in desperation, he turned to Isaiah 54 in his Bible:

> I found my guilt depart, darkness passed away, fears removed, my heart enlarged, my mind released, my feelings changed, my soul delivered, and all my powers absorbed in the treasures of the text. I sat and wept and wondered, and said that there was mercy for me after all; that Jesus was certainly my redeemer; that he had shed his blood for me; that he had wrought out and brought in everlasting righteousness for me . . . I looked at election and could rejoice that my name was written in heaven. I looked at predestination and could give thanks unto the Lord that he had not appointed me unto wrath, but to obtain salvation by the Lord Jesus Christ. I looked at my sins and saw that they were all laid upon his dear Son . . . I knew that this God was my God for ever and ever; and that he would be my guide even unto death.[20]

Not long after his conversion Wells joined a Baptist church in Chelsea and was encouraged to preach. He undoubtedly had a preaching gift and gloried in the sovereignty of God in election and predestination, but could not accept that all men have a duty to repent and believe in Christ for salvation. In part this may have been a reaction against the Arminianism that had proved unable to help him when in his deep state of spiritual distress. It is not known what type of ministry he sat under in Chelsea, but he cannot have been a hearer for very long before beginning to preach. Certainly there was always a lack of balance in his preaching,[21] which soon became apparent. Views such as those later expressed by Spurgeon were denounced as 'duty-faith'. W. Jeyes Styles, who heard and admired Wells, says that he seldom preached without attacking

---

[20] *The Earthen Vessel*, 1872, pp, 119, 122.

[21] Many years later he argued for the teaching that Jesus Christ is the Son of God by virtue of his office as Mediator, but not in his divine nature. This view was to bring him into conflict with Philpot.

duty-faith. Typical of Wells' remarks is a statement in a sermon delivered on 11 January 1863: 'You might as well give me heathenism as give me Arminianism; you might as well give me popery as give me duty faithism.'

By the end of 1854 Strict Baptist opinion was divided over Spurgeon. It was clear that the New Park Street pastor preached the doctrines of grace, and did so forcefully in face of a movement towards Arminianism within Baptist circles. On the other hand, his freeness in presenting the gospel to unbelievers smacked of Fullerism. Charles Waters Banks, editor of *The Earthen Vessel*, was among those who were drawn to the young preacher. Banks was opposed to 'duty-faith' teaching, but wrote a lengthy article in the December 1854 issue of his magazine under the title, 'A Brief and Impartial View of Mr Spurgeon's Ministry'. Ever one to act the peacemaker, Banks wrote: 'We are disposed to believe there is truth in the statement of a correspondent – he says – *"I believe Mr Spurgeon is as great a lover of free grace and of real Calvinism, as any man;* but the bigotry of some, who cannot hear the truth unless expressed in certain phrases, seems to put him out of heart; and keeps him walking almost in a separate path."'[22]

While Banks did not agree with Spurgeon's presentation of gospel invitations, he was prepared to ascribe this to the young minister's immaturity and hoped that he would come closer to what had come to be regarded as Particular Baptist orthodoxy. What he, and those Strict Baptists like him, probably had not yet appreciated was Spurgeon's strength as a theologian and his growing understanding of the classic Calvinism of the sixteenth and seventeenth centuries. James Wells, on the other hand, could see that Spurgeon's ministry constituted a major challenge to the prevalent Hyper-Calvinism. He therefore wrote a reply to Banks' article under the pseudonym, 'Job'. After some general consideration of Spurgeon as a preacher, commenting on his abilities as a speaker and the considerable extent of his reading, he made a number of serious criticisms of his ministry:

---

[22] Quoted in Iain H. Murray, *Spurgeon v. Hyper-Calvinism* (Edinburgh: Banner of Truth, 1995), pp. 45–6.

1st. That it is most awfully deceptive; that it passes by the essentials of the work of the Holy Ghost, and sets people by shoals down for Christians who are not Christians by the quickening and indwelling power of the Holy Ghost. Hence freewillers, *intellectual* Calvinists, high and low, are delighted with him, together with the philosophic and classic taste Christian! This is simply deceiving others with the deception wherewith he himself is deceived.

2nd. That, as he speaks some truth, convictions will in some cases take place under his ministry; such will go into real concern for their salvation, and will, after a time, leave his ministry, for a ministry that can accompany them in their rugged paths of wilderness experience.[23]

Wells thus expressed the widespread view among Hyper-Calvinists that a ministry like Spurgeon's was likely to produce a crop of empty professions of faith. Unlike Banks, he did not believe that Spurgeon would change: 'I am nevertheless disposed to believe that we have a fair sample of what he will be even unto the end.'[24]

Wells had expressed himself very strongly, and no doubt expressed the views of a considerable number of like-minded people. It is pleasing to note that with the passing of the years, the two preachers were able to express their mutual esteem. In October 1866, Wells was in the midst of controversy and wrote to the *Earthen Vessel* complaining of the actions of some of his Hyper-Calvinistic brethren, who possessed 'a spirit which has made and still is making sad havoc in the churches, setting brother against brother and despising every minister who does not choose to sacrifice to their net, and burn incense to their drag... Differ as I do from Mr Spurgeon, yet he has shown an independence of judgement, a magnanimity of soul, a nobleness of mind and a range of benevolent feeling, enough to shame the hypers to a man.' It is pleasing also to note that in March 1871, as Wells lay terminally ill, Spurgeon wrote him a beautiful letter of sympathy and encouragement.

Spurgeon outlived James Wells by almost twenty years. Thereafter the opposition to Spurgeon's gospel preaching was promoted by a man of

---

[23] Quoted, C. H. Spurgeon, *The Early Years*, pp. 307–8.   [24] Ibid., p. 309.

very different gifts, William Jeyes Styles (1842-1914). Styles, who began to preach among the Primitive Methodists, is an example of a man who swung from one extreme to the other. Becoming a Baptist he joined the church at the Metropolitan Tabernacle and was trained at Spurgeon's Pastors' College. Adopting Hyper-Calvinistic views, he held a number of Strict Baptist pastorates in the London area, and for some time helped to give ministerial training in the London area to men of like mind. He wrote two very influential books: *A Manual of Faith and Practice* (1887) and *A Guide to Church Fellowship* (1902). Written from an embattled perspective, Styles clearly believed that the Strict and Particular Baptists faced unfair pressure from their fellow Evangelicals and feared that they were ill-equipped to meet the challenge. However, unlike earlier writers, Styles displayed a generous spirit towards Spurgeon and to George Rogers who had tutored Styles at the Pastors' College.

> ... the Minister of the Metropolitan Tabernacle, our first Pastor, the President of the College to which we owe so much; and who still is kind enough to remain our most beloved and esteemed friend. We have quoted him, because we felt it useless to combat with the views of Baxter, Fuller or Hinton, who are not only dead, but perfectly uninfluential as far as modern Christians are concerned. Some living preacher, whose sentiments are a present power, claimed our attention, and we felt bound to select the one we have. We beg that none will charge us with lack of love to him.[25]

Under the heading 'Offered Grace an Ancient Error', Styles disassociated himself from the *1689 Confession* and from Spurgeon's *Catechism*. He contrasted his own teaching with that of the Particular Baptist pioneers and the leading Puritans of the seventeenth century.

> It was through the labours of Tobias Crisp (1600-1642), Joseph Hussey (1660-1726), John Gill, D.D. (1697-1771), William Huntington (1745-1813), John Stevens (1776-1847), William Palmer, (1800-1873), and others, that the truth of God in this branch of the Gospel was

---

[25] William Jeyes Styles, *A Manual of Faith and Practice Designed for Young and Enquiring Christians* (1887; repr. London: Robert Banks, 1897), p. iii.

subsequently elucidated. The question, however, is not whether a doctrine is old or new, but whether it is supported by the word of God.[26]

Throughout Styles's extensive writings on this subject he argued his case against selected quotations from Spurgeon's sermons. He wrote with clarity and vigour. There is little doubt that his books were used extensively by Strict Baptist ministers of various shades of doctrine in the early years of the twentieth century. To sustain his position he insisted that a sharp distinction needed to be drawn between the message preached to the Jews on the one hand, and to the Gentiles on the other. In some respects, the development of Styles' argument appears to be similar to Dispensationalism, a school of thought that was becoming popular among Evangelicals during this period. In other respects, his teaching contrasted with Dispensationalism: he left the Jews with fewer blessings than Dispensationalists have held out to them, and he strongly opposed Millenarianism as 'a dangerous error'.[27] Of the Jews he wrote:

> To them 'He was sent first (in the order of time), to bless them (not by saving them spiritually and eternally, but) in turning every one of them from their iniquities,' (*Acts* 3:26). Their national reformation was His object, and He commenced this branch of His work on earth on the imprisonment of John the Baptist by 'preaching the Gospel of God, (*Rev. Version*), and saying 'The time is fulfilled, and the Kingdom of God is at hand'.[28]

Styles insisted that Christ, 'expressed neither concern nor grief that others did not come unto Him for salvation'. He went on to declare:

> Christ desired the temporal salvation of His own nation; He does not, and never did desire the eternal salvation of any but those whom the Father gave Him. He was grieved when His own nation rejected Him. He is nowhere said to be grieved that natural men continue to live as such. He wept over Jerusalem – as the time of His ministry to the Jews drew nigh to a close; but that He ever weeps now over impenitent men

---

[26] William Jeyes Styles, *A Guide to Church Fellowship, as Maintained by the Primitive or Strict and Particular Baptists* (London, J. Briscoe, 1902), pp. 60, 61.
[27] Styles, *Guide to Church Fellowship*, p. 114. [28] Ibid., p. 28.

who grieve Him by refusing to accept His offered mercy is a falsehood to be earnestly contradicted.[29]

In this context he warns against John Howe's treatise, *The Redeemer's Tears* as 'a work of such high genius, so eloquent and pathetic', but insists that it is 'utterly erroneous'.[30]

Styles was undoubtedly aware that the version of 'Calvinism' he promoted differed radically from that of the Reformers and Puritans and he does not hide this. Philpot was also aware of the differences, although his appreciation of the Reformers' fight against Romanism and the Puritans' experimental theology made him much less critical of them than was Styles. It is apparent, however, that as the nineteenth century passed there was a popular misconception that the true representatives of Calvinism were the Hyper-Calvinists. At James Wells's funeral in 1872, William Crowther one of the officiating ministers stated: 'Mr Wells belonged to what are called the Hyper-Calvinists . . . who could boast some of the greatest names the Church ever had, such as Charnock, Owen, Goodwin, Calvin, Gill, Huntington, Gadsby, Philpot, Foreman, etc.'[31] Such confusion spread widely and was not restricted to Hyper-Calvinists. In 1947 the Principal of a Baptist College could write:

> The truth seems to be that the old Calvinistic phrases were often on Spurgeon's lips, but the genuine Calvinistic meaning had gone out of them. This explains the attacks made upon him as soon as he had begun his ministry in London, by those who had never departed from an unadulterated Calvinism.[32]

4. Final Perseverance

The truth was that Spurgeon consistently maintained his position throughout his ministry. Robert Shindler, a close friend and one of Spurgeon's many biographers, wrote towards the close of Spurgeon's life:

> No change has come over Mr Spurgeon, either as to his sentiments and the faith he has firmly held, and as boldly taught from the very first, nor

[29] Ibid., p.29.   [30] Ibid., p. 29.   [31] *The Earthen Vessel*, 1872, p. 113.
[32] Underwood, *HEB*, p. 204.

as to his love to all the faithful in Christ Jesus. The change has taken place in others, not in him. If any proof were needed that such a change has taken place in others, we might point to the recent amalgamation of the Particular and General Baptists. The name 'Particular Baptist', as representing the Calvinistic view of Redemption has ceased to be acknowledged by the Council and other representatives of the Baptist Union – at least in their official capacity. So far, at least, as distinctive doctrines are concerned, the principles of the fathers of the denomination and the Particular Baptist founders of the Missionary Society are alike ignored.[33]

Spurgeon certainly preached without embarrassment the doctrines of grace to the very end. In one of his later sermons at the Metropolitan Tabernacle, preached in October 1890 he declared:

Now brethren, we are to praise God because all spiritual blessings have come to us in the same way as our election came, 'according as he hath chosen us in him'. How did that come? Well, it came of *his free sovereign grace*. He loved us because he would love us. He chose us because he would choose us. 'You have not chosen me; but I have chosen you.' If there be any virtue, if there be any praise in us now, he put it there. To the bottomless abyss of his infinite goodness we must trace the election of his grace.[34]

Earlier, in an exposition of Scripture delivered in the same service, he referred to a Member of Parliament who had spoken in the House of Commons about 'the gloomy tenets of Calvin'. Spurgeon commented, 'I know nothing of Calvin's gloomy tenets; but I do know that I read here of predestination, and I read here that God hath his own way, and his own will, and that he reigns and rules, and so he will until the world's end; and all who are loyal subjects wish God to rule.'[35]

These comments were made in the aftermath of the Downgrade Controversy. This controversy was not about Calvinism, but was caused

---

[33] Robert Shindler, *From the Usher's Desk to the Tabernacle Pulpit* (London: Passmore & Alabaster, 1892), pp. 271–2.

[34] C. H. Spurgeon, *Metropolitan Tabernacle Pulpit*, Vol. 38, (1892; repr. Edinburgh: Banner of Truth, 1991), p. 355.   [35] Ibid., p. 359.

by the Baptist Union's refusal to confront the liberal theology which was already destroying the testimony of so many of its churches. Men were denying the doctrine of eternal punishment, weakening their teaching on the atonement, and forsaking the authority of Scripture. However, it is of interest to note that the Downgrade Controversy erupted after the appearance in *The Sword and the Trowel* of two articles written by Robert Shindler; in them he demonstrated that the departure from Calvinistic orthodoxy, which took place in the eighteenth century, had resulted in a terrible weakening in the churches at that time. Spurgeon then applied the lessons of Shindler's magazine articles to the situation then current. In a perceptive analysis of the Downgrade Controversy, David Kingdon argues that a weakening of Calvinism in English Nonconformity opened the way to liberal theology and the spiritual collapse that marked the Baptist churches of the late nineteenth century and early twentieth centuries. This tragic development was preceded by a significant period of time when the doctrines of grace gradually passed out of the life of the churches. 'It was not that they [the doctrines of grace] were being openly attacked, but rather they were being quietly ignored.' He writes:

> In the life of the churches, doctrine tended to be depreciated in favour of winning the masses for Christ. Stress was placed upon practical Christianity with the implication that doctrine was relatively unimportant. There was a growing unwillingness to define the Gospel; it was said that Christ must be preached, but few stopped to ask what sort of Christ was being proclaimed. The Christian life was increasingly separated from Christian doctrine, it being assumed that doctrine did not really shape experience, but rather that doctrine was but the formulation of data provided by Christian experience.[36]

While David Kingdon's analysis focuses on those churches that were moving away from the doctrines of grace, it should also be remembered that some Hyper-Calvinists too played down the importance of doctrine in favour of their emphasis on Christian experience. Generally speaking,

---

[36] David Kingdon, 'C. H. Spurgeon and the Downgrade Controversy', in Erroll Hulse, David Kingdon, eds., *A Marvellous Ministry* (Ligonier, PA: Soli Deo Gloria, 1993), p. 112.

Charles Haddon Spurgeon

this was not an age that was doctrinally alert. Kingdon appeals to Willis B. Glover's book, *Evangelical Nonconformists and Higher Criticism in the Nineteenth Century*, to show that 'with the decline of Calvinism there came about the dissolution of a coherent, well-knit body of doctrine. "The general decline of Calvinism", writes Glover, "was not the result of any rival theological system. Its place was taken by the widest variety of theological speculation singularly lacking in intellectual rigour, and in relationship to any well developed system of theological ideas."'[37]

The Downgrade Controversy exposed the extent of Spurgeon's isolation amongst English Baptists. His loyal church stood with him, but sadly his support among the Baptist Union churches was minimal. While Styles wrote pages against the free offer of the gospel and duty faith, declaiming against 'the lie of human responsibility', his *Guide to Church Fellowship* merely skims over the issues for which Spurgeon contended in the Downgrade Controversy, and lacks any reference to Spurgeon's stand. Those who ought to have supported him did not do so. Spurgeon did, however, receive support in the wider Evangelical community. Robert Shindler gave details of a meeting in the Exeter Hall, called by the Evangelical Alliance in order to testify 'to the fundamental truths of the gospel'. Spurgeon was profoundly moved by the support for his stand from an assembly gathered from all the denominations, but reported that 'only a very few of his Baptist brethren were present'.[38] Lacking the dynamism of a vigorous Calvinism, English Evangelicalism entered into one of the most feeble periods in its history. Spurgeon foresaw the difficulties that lay ahead and expressed his concerns when he addressed the Pastors' College Conference in 1889. The need of the day was a powerful ministry of the gospel. He claimed that 'what is being done today will affect the next centuries, unless the Lord should very speedily come.' He urged his men to face their responsibilities in what he called 'a restless time'. He continued:

> I believe that if we walk uprightly and decidedly before God at this time we shall make the future of England bright with the gospel; but trimming

[37] Ibid. [38] R. Shindler, *From The Usher's Desk to the Tabernacle Pulpit*, p. 274.

now and debasing doctrine now, will affect children yet unborn, generation after generation. Posterity must be considered. I do not look so much at what is to happen today, for these things relate to eternity. For my part, I am quite willing to be eaten of dogs for the next fifty years; but the more distant future shall vindicate me. I have dealt honestly before the living God. My brother, do the same. Who knows but what thou art come to the kingdom for such a time as this?[39]

It was exactly sixty years after Spurgeon proclaimed those words that a small group of English Strict Baptists republished the *1689 Confession of Faith* for another generation of Baptists, and in doing so used Spurgeon's edition. But in the decade before its reappearance in 1959, there were already signs of a recovery of the Puritan heritage to which not only English Baptists, but Evangelicals in general, owe so much.

---

[39] C. H. Spurgeon, *An All Round Ministry* (London: Banner of Truth, 1960), pp. 360–1.

APPENDIX A

JOHN COLLETT RYLAND, DANIEL TURNER, ROBERT ROBINSON, AND THE COMMUNION CONTROVERSY, 1772-81[1]

A series of tracts published between 1772 and 1781 turned the attention of the English Particular Baptists to the question of who should be admitted to the Communion Table. Most churches still practised closed communion, restricting participation in the Communion Service to baptized believers.[2] In the 1770s and 1780s, however, three country ministers, John Collett Ryland of Northampton, Daniel Turner of Abingdon, and Robert Robinson of Cambridge powerfully advocated the case for open communion. Their most able opponent was Abraham Booth of Little Prescot Street Chapel, London. Joseph Ivimey referred to the controversy in his *History of the English Baptists*.[3] However, his *History* was written nearly sixty years after this controversy and his treatment of the parts played by Ryland and Turner is not as clear as one could wish, while a mistaken date for Robinson's pamphlet has distorted his account and has led subsequent writers astray.

THE *CANDIDUS-PACIFICUS* PAMPHLET

Referring to the pamphlets of Ryland and Turner, Ivimey wrote, 'The two first of these were anonymous, under the assumed names of *Pacificus* and *Candidus*.'[4] These tracts were probably rare in Ivimey's day. The relevant volume of his *History* appeared in 1830. Subsequent

---

[1] Originally published in *The Baptist Quarterly*, vol. 29, April 1981. Reprinted by permission.
[2] Andrew Fuller, *Works*, London, 1862, p. 855.
[3] Joseph Ivimey, *History of the English Baptists*, vol. 4, London, 1830, p. 35. [4] Ibid.

[357]

bibliographers appear to have relied upon Ivimey's statement for the existence of the *Pacificus* tract. W. T. Whitley listed both, locating a copy of the *Candidus* tract in the Angus Library of Regent's Park College, but appealed to Ivimey as his authority for the *Pacificus* Tract. Edward C. Starr also included both publications, indicating a further copy of the *Candidus* pamphlet at the New Orleans Baptist Seminary, but only referred to Ivimey for *Pacificus*.

A recent search, however, has revealed the existence of a copy of the *Pacificus* pamphlet in the Northamptonshire Central Library. It is a closely printed pamphlet of three pages, measuring 8 by 10 inches and is dated 15 June 1772. The *Candidus* tract, on the other hand, measures 4.5 by 7 inches and consists of sixteen well-printed pages. It is simply dated 1772. Although they are not the same in appearance, their contents are identical apart from two minor differences.

The first difference is in the heading. Daniel Turner *(Candidus)* wrote *A Modest Plea for Free Communion at the Lord's Table; Particularly between the Baptists and the Paedobaptsts.* Ryland appears to state his sympathies in even more catholic terms, writing: *A Modest Plea for Free Communion at the Lord's Table; between True Believers of all Denominations.*

The other difference is found in just one word in the section entitled 'Objections Answered', where the writers are addressing the insistence of the closed communionists that baptism is an initiating ordinance and logically precedes the Lord's Supper. In reply *Candidus* conceded, 'though it be admitted that the order of Churches is of some importance', whereas *Pacificus* wrote 'is of great importance'.

Thus the tracts are really one and must be the result of collaboration between Ryland and Turner. There is no evidence at present to show who took the initiative in writing or whether they appeared at the same time. The work takes the form of a piece of defensive writing to justify the practice of the authors and their churches in the face of criticism from 'several of our stricter brethren of the Baptist denomination'. According to William Newman, later his assistant at Enfield, Ryland had experienced some difficulty with his first church at Warwick because of its closed communion practice.[5] In 1758 Daniel Turner had

---

[5] William Newman, *Rylandia*, London, 1835, p.11.

Appendices

made a cautious plea for open communion in his *Compendium of Social Religion*.[6] In view of their common conviction, their similar titles and pseudonyms, it is perhaps surprising that the fact of the collaboration of Ryland and Turner has been overlooked for so long.

Robert Robinson's Pamphlet

Ivimey mistakenly dated Robert Robinson's *General Doctrine of Toleration, applied to the particular case of Free Communion* as 1771.[7] He proceeded therefore to suggest that Abraham Booth's *Apology for the Baptists* was a reply to Ryland, Turner, and Robinson, stating that 'his masterly work received no reply from his brethren'.[8] At least one modern historian has followed Ivimey at this point.[9] In fact Robinson first published his work in 1781,[10] and while Booth clearly replied to Turner and Ryland, Robinson wrote in the light of Booth's arguments.

George Dyer, Robinson's friend and biographer, declared that the origin of the *General Doctrine of Toleration* was a series of sermons preached in Oxford in 1780 'to a little society of dissenters, then forming themselves into what is called church order'.[11] It was on 16 November 1780 that this little group of Dissenters (Baptists and Paedobaptists) covenanted to form themselves into a church, in which they would receive each other into membership and to the Communion Table, 'because we can find no warrant in the Word of God to make such a difference of sentiment any bar to communion at the Lord's Table in particular, or to Church fellowship in general; and because the Lord Jesus receiving and owning them on both sides of the question, we think we ought to do so too'.[12]

Interestingly it is Daniel Turner, who at this stage appears as a link to earlier developments. Ryland's collaborator was one of the witnesses of the Oxford Church Covenant,[13] which seems to owe something to the preaching of Robert Robinson.

[6] Daniel Turner, *Compendium of Social Religion*, London, 1758, pp. 126-7.
[7] Ivimey, *History of the English Baptists*, vol. 4, p. 35.   [8] Ibid, p.35.
[9] Olin C. Robison, 'The Particular Baptists, 1760-1820', unpublished Oxford D.Phil. thesis, 1965, p. 220.
[10] Robert Robinson, *General Doctrine of Toleration*, Cambridge, 1781.
[11] George Dyer, *Memoirs of Robert Robinson,* London, 1796, p. 197.
[12] Church Covenant of the New Road Baptist Church, Oxford.
[13] Ibid, Daniel Turner, witness.

[359]

Appendix B

Andrew Fuller and the Atonement

Perhaps few theologians have suffered so much misrepresentation as Andrew Fuller. He challenged a number of powerful theological positions and not surprisingly made a number of enemies. On the other hand some admirers have claimed his support for developments that he would have found abhorrent. It has been suggested that he made possible a blurring of the distinction between Calvinism and Arminianism and eventually made possible a union of Particular and General Baptists. Such a suggestion fails to take seriously the words he wrote at the end of his life:

> I have preached and written much against the abuse of the doctrine of grace; but that doctrine is all my salvation and all my desire. I have no other hope than that from salvation by mere, sovereign and efficacious grace, through the atonement of my Lord and Saviour. With this hope I can go into eternity with composure.[1]

It has been objected that Fuller changed his views in the period between the publication of the first and second editions of *The Gospel Worthy of All Acceptation*. Fuller admitted some modification which I have discussed in chapter 8 of this book. However he always insisted that such adjustment did not involve any compromise of the doctrines of grace.

More specifically the charge has been made that to sustain his teaching of a universal and free offer of salvation to all who heard the gospel, Fuller adopted a governmental theory of the atonement, abandoning the doctrine of substitution in the process. The governmental theory of the

---

[1] A. Fuller, *Works*, 'Letter to John Ryland, 28 April 1815', p. lxxxiv.

atonement has often proved attractive to those who have tried to hold a doctrine of general redemption together with an acceptance of the doctrines of God's sovereignty and election, but that was not Fuller's position. The doctrine of substitutionary atonement teaches that the death of Christ removes the great obstacle to salvation – man's sin. B. B. Warfield addressed the problem faced by the teachers of a general atonement:

> But what obstacle stands in the way of the salvation of sinners, except just their sin? And if this obstacle (their sin) is removed, are they not saved? Some other obstacles must be invented, therefore, which Christ may be said to have removed (since he cannot be said to have removed the obstacle of sin) that some function may be left to him and some kind of effect attributed to his sacrificial death ... He removed, then, let us say, all that prevented God from saving men, except sin; and so he prepared the way for God to step in and with safety to his moral government to save men. The atonement lays no foundation for this saving of men: it merely opens the way for God safely to save them on other grounds.[2]

Warfield argues that this is the basis of the governmental theory. It remains to be asked whether Fuller's teaching fits this category.

There are a number of reasons for confusion over Fuller's teaching. Sometimes his statements have been isolated from the wider context of his teaching. In other cases students have not examined with sufficient care the teaching he was addressing. Sadly some critics have savaged his writings when it is clear that they have not read them.

The charge of governmentalism may have first surfaced because of Fuller's criticism of the writings of Tobias Crisp (1600–43) who seemed to teach that Christ became a sinner in order to pay the price of the sinner's guilt. Further Fuller challenged the notion prevalent among some of the Hyper-Calvinists of his day that Christ's sufferings were proportionate to the number of sinners for whom he died. It was being alleged that had he died to save more people those sufferings would have had to be proportionately greater.

[2] Benjamin B. Warfield, *The Plan of Salvation*, Grand Rapids, Michigan, 1942, p. 95.

Appendices

Recently David Bebbington has written that Andrew Fuller was the 'most influential exponent' of the thought of Joseph Bellamy and Samuel Hopkins, both of whom did espouse a governmental theory of the atonement. Bebbington writes:

> Fuller taught that although Jesus suffered the punishment due to human sins, he was not actively punished for them by his Father because guilt was not transferable. The atonement was still a matter of substitution, but, though Fuller insisted that it was in some way penal, it was not penal in the traditional sense. The cross was a display of the eternal principles of justice enforced by the all-wise ruler of the world and willingly accepted by an obedient Son.[3]

Bebbington's statements are less than helpful since he does not sustain them with quotations from Fuller, but immediately appeals to Edward Miall (1809-81), a Victorian Congregationalist, and Edwards A. Park (1808-1900), a New England theologian, neither of whom were contemporary with Fuller as teachers. Bebbington correctly points out that Fuller was impressed by the writings of Bellamy and Hopkins and employed methods they used against liberal critics, but Fuller was using these against Antinomianism and Hyper-Calvinism.

Fuller did create confusion by using the expression 'figurative imputation'. He did this to avoid any suggestion of sinfulness in Christ and to make it clear that the imputation of Christ's righteousness to the sinner did not make the latter purely subjective. As I have already pointed out in chapter 8, Abraham Booth protested against this terminology with good reason. A study of Fuller's writings as a whole indicates that he did believe in a substitutionary atonement and that justification is by the imputation of the righteousness of Jesus Christ. In 1799 a few years before the controversy with Abraham Booth, but at a time when he was reading widely in the New England theologians, Fuller received an enquiry from a person troubled about Crisp's teaching that Christ had to participate in human sin to qualify as a complete Saviour. In his reply Fuller made it clear that the proper way to understand Christ's substitutionary work was in terms of imputation:

[3] David Bebbington, *The Dominance of Evangelicalism*, Leicester, IVP 2005, p. 124.

We have the same authority for believing that our sins were imputed to Christ as that Adam's sin was imputed to his posterity. The word 'impute' is used in neither case, but both are compared to the imputation of righteousness. 'As by one man's disobedience many were made sinners, so by the obedience of one shall many be made righteous' – 'He made him to be sin for us who knew no sin that we might be made the righteousness of God in him', *Rom.* 5:19; *2 Cor.* 5:21. Now will Christopher affirm that Christ was made sin by participation?[4]

There are no grounds for believing that he departed from this position. In a sermon on Justification, he declared:

His obedience unto death was more than the means of salvation; it was the *procuring cause* of it. Salvation was the effect of the 'travail of his soul'. We may be instruments in saving one another; but Christ was the 'author' of eternal salvation'. The principle of substitution, or of one standing in the place of others, being admitted by the Sovereign of the universe, he endured that which *in its effect on the Divine government was equivalent to the everlasting punishment of a world, did that which it was worthy of God to reward with eternal glory not only on himself, but on all those on whose behalf he should intercede* [emphasis in original].[5]

In a second sermon from the same text, he said:

The terms imputed and counted in this connection are manifestly used to express, not that just reckoning of righteousness to the righteous which gives to every man his due, but the gracious reckoning of righteousness to the unrighteous, as though he were righteous.[6]

It may be objected that both of these sermons are undated. This is true, but they were prepared for publication by Fuller himself and published in 1814, the year before his death.[7]

It needs to be remembered that Fuller's writing was occasional, produced over a period of some thirty years and arose from the ever-changing situation he faced as a Christian pastor. Responsible for a large congregation, a travelling preacher, a correspondent of missionaries and

---

[4] Fuller, *Works*, p. 948.
[5] Ibid., 'Sermon on Romans 3:24', p. 610.   [6] Ibid., p. 613.   [7] Ibid, p. lxxxiii.

promoter of their interests at home, he must have been one of the busiest pastors of his day. He was blessed with a remarkably sharp and rapid mind sanctified by grace and a readiness to defend numerous challenges to the faith. His friend and critic J. W. Morris wrote: 'His understanding was not more powerful and rapid in its exercise fixing on the point of an argument with singular precision and accuracy.'[8]

All who knew Fuller spoke of his integrity and open proclamation of the truths he loved. He summarized his own position in a letter to John Ryland in 1803.

> I consider justification to be God's graciously pardoning our sins and accepting us to favour, exempting us from the curse of the law, and entitling us to the promises of the gospel; not on account or consideration of any holiness in us, ceremonial or moral, before, in, or after believing, but purely in reward of the vicarious obedience and death of Christ, which on our believing in him, is imputed to us, or reckoned as if it were ours, nor do I consider any holiness in us to be necessary as a concomitant, to justification, except what is necessarily included in believing.[9]

Over against the suspicion that Fuller intended some union of the Arminian General Baptists and the Particular Baptists, he wrote in the same letter:

> Mr Baxter considers Calvinists and Arminians as reconcilable, making the difference between them as of but small amount. I have no such idea; and if, on account of what I have here and elsewhere avowed, I were disavowed by my present connexions [the Particular Baptists], I should rather choose to go through the world alone than be connected with them [the General Baptists]. Their scheme appears to me to undermine the doctrine of salvation by grace only, and to resolve the difference between one sinner and another into the will of man, which is directly opposite to my views and experience. Nor could I feel a union of heart with those who are commonly considered in the present

---

[8] J. W. Morris, *Memoirs of the Life and Writings of the Rev. Andrew Fuller*, London, 1826, p. 212.
[9] Fuller, *Works*, p. 324.

day as *Baxterians*, who hold with the gospel being a new remedial law, and represent sinners as contributing to their own conversion.[10]

At this point Fuller wrote, 'and here my dear brother I lay down my pen'.

Andrew Fuller was a theologian although he would have disclaimed such a description. In his youth he received a minimal formal education and no theological training. Like Bunyan he wrote under spiritual constraint. The extent of his reading was amazing. Fuller's writings repay careful study. Their sheer bulk may discourage many but he does not waste time, and even topics that do no longer appear to be of general interest may suddenly appear of the greatest relevance to the reader.

---

[10] Ibid.

Appendix C

Letter from Dr J. H. Philpot to Mr Dickinson[1]

25 March 1931

Dear Mr Dickinson,
I am grateful for your letter, and for all the encouraging criticisms of *The Seceders* in the lay and the religious press. I have had to give up any idea of a second volume partly on account of age and infirmity, and partly because I might have had unpleasing things to say of the business side of the *Gospel Standard*. I too remember as a boy enjoying my father's criticisms of Mr Wells, but am very sorry they were ever published in the *Collected Reviews*. As I have tried to explain, W. Tiptaft was an extravert and my father an introvert & of a passionate nature, which, I think, explains many of his self-reproaches. He was in fact half French. Both knew their Bible thoroughly & my father regularly spent two hours a day reading it in Hebrew and Greek.

Personally I believe inward spiritual experience to be the surest foundation of faith, though I have been much blessed myself, yielding to the Lord-instinct, which I believe to be the dominating emotion amongst Roman Catholics in the one thing that is against true religion. Christ said 'Love your enemies'; with St Paul it has already become 'Love the brethren'.

Forgive me if I have not fully answered your questions. I am old and tired & have had a hard-worked life.

Yours truly,
J. H. Philpot

[1] Printed by permission of the Rev. E. E. King of Peterborough.

Bibliography

1. Primary Sources
i. Published Works
(Unless otherwise stated, the place of publication is London)

ABBADIE, JAMES, *A Treatise on the Divinity of our Lord Jesus Christ*, edited by Abraham Booth, 1777.

ANON., *A Brief Memoir of James Jones (Shovers Green)*, Wadhurst, 1889.

ANON., *Memoirs of Mr John Stevens, Late Pastor of the Baptized Church at Meard's Court, Dean Street, Soho*, London, 1848.

ANON., *The Devil and Parson Church*, n.d.

ANON., *The Infamous Life of John Church*, 1817.

BAILEY, JOHN, *The Poor Pilgrim, as Exemplified in the Life and Experience of John Bailey, Pastor of the Baptist Church at Zoar Chapel, Great Alie Street, London, and Late of Wandsworth, London* [1810]; Revised and Corrected by J. A. Jones, 1831.

BAPTIST BOARD, THE, 'Minutes of the Baptist Board from 1724 to 1836', *Transactions of the Baptist Historical Society*, vol. 5, 1916–17, pp. 96–114, 197–240; vol. 6, pp. 72–127; vol. 7, pp. 49–70.

BAYFIELD, GEORGE, *Funeral Sermon of Mr John Stevens at Bloomsbury Chapel, Commercial Road East, October 24, 1847*, 1847

BLACKSTOCK, EDWARD, *Mercy Manifested to a Chief Sinner, or, Autobiography and Letters*, 1853

BOOTH, ABRAHAM, *The Reign of Grace from Its Rise to Its Consummation* [1768]; *Works*, vol. 1.

——, *The Death of Legal Hope, The Life of Evangelical Obedience* [1768]; *Works*, vol. 1.

——, *An Apology for the Baptists, in Which They are Vindicated from the Imputation of Laying an Unwarrantable Stress upon the Ordinance of Baptism and against the Charge of Bigotry in Refusing Communion at the Lord's Table to Paedobaptists* [1778]; *Works*, vol. 2.

——, *Commerce in the Human Species and the Enslaving of Innocent Persons, Inimical to the Law of Moses and the Gospel of Christ* [1792]; *Works*, vol. 3.

——, *Glad Tidings to Perishing Sinners, or the Genuine Gospel a Complete Warrant for Sinners to Believe in Jesus* [1796]; *Works*, vol. 2.

——, *Divine Justice Essential to the Divine Character* [1803]; *Works*, vol. 3.

——, *The Works of Abraham Booth*, 3 vols., 1813.

BROWN, JOHN, *The House of God Opened and His Table Free for Baptists and Paedobaptists, Who are Saints and Faithful in Christ*, 1777.

BUCK, CHARLES, *The Close of the Eighteenth Century Improved: A Sermon preached at Prince's Chapel, Finsbury Square, December 28, 1800*, 2nd ed., 1816.

BURNHAM, RICHARD, *A Scripture Address to Sinners, Shewing that Christ and His Apostles Exhorted Sinners as Such or Sinners of All Descriptions, to Repent of Sin, and Believe the Gospel*. n.d. [1789–95].

——, *A Letter to a Friend on the Law of God*, 1800.

——, *A Sermon Proving the Believers are the Only Proper Subjects of Baptism: with a Few Short Remarks on the Mode. Likewise a Sermon Preached at the Ordination of Mr John Bateman*, 1805.

——, *Five Interesting Letters*, 1806.

——, *Law Spirituality Defended*, 1807.

BUTTFIELD, WILLIAM, *Free Communion an Innovation: or An Answer to Mr John Brown's Pamphlet*, 1778.

BUTTON, WILLIAM. *An Answer to the Question, Why Are You a Strict Baptist? A Dialogue between Thomas and John*, 1816.

CHAMBERLAIN, JOSEPH, *Correspondence and Sermons of the Rev. Joseph Chamberlain*, 2 vols., Leicester, 1858.

CHURCH, JOHN. *The Gracious Designs of God Accomplished by the Malice of His Enemies*, 1819.

Bibliography

COLES, W., W. PIKE, W. BUTTFIELD, T. MARSHALL, AND E. KEACH, *Opposition Opposed, or the Bedfordshire Ministers' Reasons for Not Joining (at their Earnest Solicitation) a Society at the New York Coffee House, London. In Opposition to the Late Application to Parliament in Favour of Dissenting Ministers and Schoolmasters*, Ridgmont, Beds., 1773.

COX, FRANCIS AUGUSTUS, *A Letter on Free Communion from a Pastor to the People of His Charge*, 1818.

CRABTREE, WILLIAM & BOOTH, ABRAHAM, *Encouragements and Cautions for the Household of Faith*, edited by E. Feazey, 1897.

DE FLEURY, MARIA, *A Serious Address to Mr Huntington*, 1788.

——, *An Answer to the Daughter's Defence of her Father*, 1788.

——, *A Farewell to Mr Huntington [Falsehood Examined at the Bar of Truth; or a Farewell to Mr Wm. Huntington and Mr Thos. Jones of Reading]*, 1791.

——, *Antinomianism Unmasked*, 1791.

——, *Divine Poems and Essays on Various Subjects*, 1791.

DISCIPLE OF JESUS, A, *The Voice of Years*, 1814.

DIXON, JAMES, *The Autobiography of a Minister of the Gospel: being Notes of the Life and Labours of James Dixon with Reminiscences of the late Dr Hawker, Mr Fowler, Mr Gadsby, Mr Stevens, Mr Shirley and Others*, 1867.

EDWARDS, JONATHAN, *The Works of Jonathan Edwards*, 2 vols. *[1834]*, repr. Edinburgh: Banner of Truth, 1974.

EVANS, CALEB, *General Letter of the Elders, Ministers and Messengers of the Western Association*, Bristol, 1789.

EVANS, CHRISTMAS, *The Decision of a General Congress Convened to Agree on 'Terms of Communion' occasioned by the Rev. Robert Hall's Pamphlet on That Subject*, 1816.

FOREMAN, JOHN, *Funeral Sermon for John Stevens at Meard's Court Chapel, London, October 24th, 1847*, 1847.

——, *Remarks on Duty Faith*, 1860.

FOXWELL, WILLIAM, *A Letter to Mr R. B. on the Primitive State of Adam, Wherein it is proved the Adam Possessed no Spiritual Blessings of any* kind, and that Adam's Holiness was only Natural, Being what He had by Right of Creation. Being a Reply to his Letters on That Subject, 1807.

——, *A Check for Lordly Pastors. A Letter to Mr John Stevens*, n.d. [1812].

FULLER, ANDREW, *The Gospel of Christ Worthy of All Acceptation, or, the Obligation of Men Fully to Credit, and Cordially to Approve, Whatever God Makes Known, Wherein Is Considered the Nature of Faith in Christ, and the Duty of Those to Whom the Gospel Comes in that Matter.* Northampton [1785]; 2nd edition, Clipstone, 1801.

——, *Remarks on Mr Martin's Publication, Entitled 'Thoughts on the Duty of Man'* [1789]; *Works*, 1862.

——, *Thoughts on Open Communion in a Letter to the Rev. W. Ward* [1800]. *Works*.

——, *Six Letters to Dr. Ryland* [1803]; *Works*.

——, *Dialogues, Letters and Essays on Various Subjects*, 1806

——, *Strictures on Antinomianism in Twelve Letters to a Friend* [1810]; *Works*.

——, *Strict Communion in the Mission Church in Serampore* [1810]; *Works*.

——, *The Admission of Unbaptized Persons to the Lord's Supper Inconsistent with the New Testament* [1815]; *Works*.

——, *Strictures on the Rev. John Carter's Thoughts on Baptism and Mixed Communion*, n.d.; *Works*.

——, *The Complete Works of the Rev. Andrew Fuller.* 1 vol. Edited by Andrew Gunton Fuller, 1862.

GADSBY, JOHN (publisher). *The Rules and Articles of a Particular Baptist Church*, 1852.

GADSBY, WILLIAM. *The Gospel, the Believer's Rule of Conduct, being a Few Remarks upon a Letter written by Gaius and inserted in the* Evangelical Magazine *for December, 1804*, 2nd Edition, Liverpool [1813].

——, *The Perfect Law of Liberty, or, the Glory of God in the Gospel*, n.d.; *Works*, vol. 1.

——, *The Present State of Religion, or, What are the People Miscalled Antinomians?* [1808]; 2nd edition, Manchester, 1809.

Bibliography

——, *'Doctrinal Antinomianism Refuted'*, Entangled in its own Maze, n. d.; *Works*, vol. 1.

——, *Gawthorne Brought to the Test: being a Reply to Mr Gawthorne's Coincidence of Antinomianism and Arminianism, to which is added a Hint to Messrs Bogue and Bennett*, Manchester, 1819.

——, *Sandemanianism Weighed in the Balances and Found Wanting*, Manchester, 1823.

——, *The Nature and Design of the Marriage Union. A Sermon preached at Manchester on 3rd December, 1820. Occasioned by the Proceedings in the House of Lords against Queen Caroline*, 4th edition, Manchester, 1836.

——, *The Works of the Late William Gadsby*, Manchester, 2 vols, 1851.

——, *Sermons, Fragments of Sermons and Letters*, 1884.

GAMBLE, HENRY, *Fidelity Recognized and Rewarded: A Sermon Preached at the Congregational Chapel, Upper Clapton, Sunday, September 18th, 1853, on the Occasion of the Death of the Rev. Francis Augustus Cox, D.D., LL.D.*, 1853.

GIBBS, PHILIP, *General Letter of the Elders, Ministers and Messengers of the Western Association*, [Bristol], 1790.

GILL, JOHN, *The Cause of God and Truth* [1735]; 1838.

——, *The Necessity of Good Works Unto Salvation*, 1739.

——, *The Doctrine of Predestination Stated*, 1752.

——, *An Exposition of the Old and New Testaments*, 1758.

——, *A Declaration of Faith and Practice*, 1764.

——, *A Body of Divinity* [1769]; Grand Rapids, U.S.A., 1971.

GREENFIELD, EDMUND, *'The First Ripe Fruit' Received by God the Father in Eternity and Time, and Given by Him to His Human Election to be Spiritually Eaten as the Spiritual Antidote for 'The Deadly Poison' of the Old Serpent Satan, and his Poisoned Ministers (see James 3:8). Conveyed through, by, and in the Doctrines Denying the Eternal Sonship of Jesus Christ. Especially by the Doctrines of the Recently Deceased John Stevens and his Pre-Existarian Ministerial Confederates*, 1848.

HALL, ROBERT, *Address on Behalf of the Baptist Academical Institution at Stepney* [1812]; *Works*, vol. 4.

——, *On Terms of Communion* [1815]; *Works*, vol. 2.

——, *The Essential Difference between Christian Baptism and the Baptism of John, More Fully Stated and Confirmed in Reply to a Pamphlet, entitled 'A Plea for Primitive Communion'* [1816]; *Works*, vol. 2.

——, *A Reply to the Rev. Joseph Kinghorn: Being a Further Vindication of the Practice of Free Communion* [1818]; *Works*, vol. 2.

——, *Preface to 'Antinomianism Unmasked' by Samuel Chase* [1819]; *Works*, vol. 4.

——, *A Short Statement of the Reasons for Christian in Opposition to Party Communion* [1826]; *Works*, vol. 3.

——, *The Works of the Rev. Robert Hall. A.M.*, 6 vols. Edited by Olinthus Gregory, 1832-3.

HARRIS, DAVID, *Real Facts Stated and Mis-Statements Corrected*, Kingston, 1832.

HASSELL, C. B., *Tidings from the United States of America, wherein Mr James Osbourn's Character as a Citizen, a Christian, a Minister and an Author is Amply Set Forth*, 1847.

HAWKER, ROBERT, *The Works of the Rev. Robert Hawker*, 10 vols, 1831.

HERVEY, JAMES, *The Works of James Hervey*, Edinburgh, n.d.

HINTON, JOHN HOWARD, *The Work of the Holy Spirit in Conversion* [1830]; revised 1841.

HOOPER, EBENEZER. *The Celebrated Coalheaver.* 1871.

——, *Facts, Letters and Documents. An Addendum to 'The Celebrated Coalheaver'*, 1872.

HUNTINGTON, WILLIAM, *The Kingdom of Heaven Taken by Prayer* [1784], Redhill, 1966.

——, *Tidings from Wallingford* [1786]; *Works*, vol. 4.

——, *The Law Established by the Faith of Christ*, [1786]; *Works*, vol. 3.

——, *The Servant of the Lord Described and Vindicated*, [1788]; *Works*, vol. 7.

——, *The Moral Law not injured by the Everlasting Gospel* [1789]; *Works*, vol. 11.

Bibliography

——, *Letter to the Rev. Caleb Evans, M. A.* [1789]; *Works*, vol. 10.

——, *Excommunication and the Duty of all Men to believe weighed in the Balance in a Letter to Mr Ryland, jun.* [1791]; *Works, vol. 11.*

——, *The Broken Cistern and the Springing Well* [1791]; *Works*, vol. 11.

——, *An Answer to Fools* [1792]; *Works*, vol. 11.

——, *Letter to the Rev. Torial Joss* [1794]; *Works*, vol. 12.

——, *The Utility of the Books and the Excellency of the Parchments* [1796]; *Works*, vol. 16.

——, *Letter to Mr Britton* [1801]; *Works*, vol. 19.

——, *The Works of the Rev. William Huntington, S. S.*, 20 vols., 1811.

——, *Gleanings of the Vintage*, 1837.

HUPTON, JOB, *A Blow Struck at the Root of Fullerism*, 1804.

——, *The Truth as It Is in Jesus*, 1843.

IVIMEY, JOSEPH, *A Sermon Preached at Eagle Street Meeting, London, May 21st. 1815, as a Tribute of Affectionate Respect to the Memory of the late Rev. Andrew Fuller of Kettering*, 1815.

——, *The Constitution of the Baptist Churches, etc.* [1816].

——, *A Reply to A Letter on Free Communion by the Rev. F. A Cox, M.A. in Six Letters on Strict Communion to a Young Minister*, 1818.

——, *A Sermon Occasioned by the Death of the Rev. James Hinton M.A. Late of Oxford*, 1823.

——, *Baptism, the Scriptural and Indispensable Qualifications for Communion at the Lord's Table: or Considerations Designed to Expose the Erroneous Practice of Departing from the Original Constitution of the Christian Church by founding Neighbourhoods, where Evangelical Congregational Churches Already Exist. Including Animadversions on the Preface etc. of the Rev. Robert Hall's 'Reply to the Rev. Joseph Kinghorn's Work on "Baptism a Term of Communion"'*, 1824.

——, *Communion at the Lord's Table Regulated by the Revealed Will of Christ. Not Party but Christian Communion: A Reply to the Rev. Robert Hall's Pamphlet Entitled 'Reasons for Christian in Opposition to Party Communion*, 1826.

——, *A Scriptural Manual on the Terms of Communion in the Primitive Church*, 1828.

JAY, WILLIAM, *An Autobiography of William Jay,* ed. by George Redford and John Angell James, 2nd edition, 1855. Reprint of 1st edition, Edinburgh: Banner of Truth, 1974.

KETTERNS, DANIEL, *Maturity in Death Exemplified: A Funeral Sermon Occasioned by the Decease of the Rev. Francis Augustus Cox. D.D., LL.D.,*1853.

KEACH, BENJAMIN, *A Short Confession of Faith, Containing the Substance of All the Fundamental Articles in the Larger Confession Put Forth by All the Elders of the Baptized Churches, owning Personal Election and Final Perseverance,* 1697.

KERSHAW, JOHN, *Memorials of a Covenant God while Travelling through the Wilderness. Being the Autobiography of John Kershaw of Rochdale,* 1870.

KINGHORN, JOSEPH, *Baptism, a Term of Communion at the Lord's Supper,* Norwich, 1816.

——, *A Defence of 'Baptism, a Term of Communion' in Answer to the Rev. Robert Hall's Reply,* Norwich, 1820.

——, *Arguments against the Practice of Mixed Communion and in Support of Communion on the Plan of the Apostolic Church with Preliminary Observations on the Rev. R. Hall's Reasons for Christian in Opposition to Party Communion,* 1827.

LUMPKIN, WILLIAM, *Baptist Confessions of Faith,* Valley Forge, Pa., U.S.A., 1969.

MARTIN, JOHN, *Thoughts on the Duty of Man Relative to Faith in Jesus Christ, in which Mr Andrew Fuller's Leading Propositions on the Subject Are Considered,* Part 1, 1778; Part 2, 1779; Part 3, 1791.

——, *Some Account of the Life and Writings of the Rev. John Martin,* 1797.

MORTON, ELIZABETH, *he Daughter's Defence of Her Father,* 1788.

MURRELL, GEORGE, SAMUEL SHARWOOD, DAVID IRISH, WILLIAM CATTELL, AND THOMAS BONFIELD, *The Friendly Address of Five Country Ministers to Mr John Stevens of London,* St Neots, 1835.

NEWMAN, WILLIAM, *Baptism an Indispensable Pre-requisite to Communion at the Lord's Table,* 1805

Bibliography

———, *Moral and Ritual Precepts Compared in a Pastoral Letter to the Baptist Church at Bow, Middlesex, Including Some Remarks on the Rev. Robert Hall's 'Terms of Communion'*, 1819.

NORFOLK AND SUFFOLK ASSOCIATIONS OF BAPTIST CHURCHES, *Circular Letter on the Work of the Spirit*, Ipswich, 1820.

———, *Circular Letter on the Trinity and Person of Christ*, Ipswich, 1821.

———, *Circular Letter on Church Discipline*, Ipswich, 1822.

———, *Circular Letter on the Sufferings of Christ*, Ipswich, 1823.

———, *Circular Letter on the Sin of Apostacy*, Ipswich, 1827.

NORTON, WILLIAM, *The Churches of God Compared with those which are the hope of some Free-Communion Baptists, who desire union with 'The Existing Great Parties in Christendom'. An Examination of Sentiments Expressed in the Address Delivered by Joseph Angus, D.D. as chairman of the Baptist Union, in April 1865, and in his Prize Essay on Christian Churches. Published in 1862*, 1866.

———, *Responsibility: An Answer to Mr John Foreman's 'Remarks on Duty Faith'*, 1868.

OLD MEMBER OF THE LATE CHURCH, AN, *A Brief Address to the Surviving Members of the Late Church of Christ at Providence Chapel, formerly under the Pastoral Care of the Rev. William Huntington, S.S., with a few thoughts on Mr C. Goulding's Publication*, 1827.

OSBOURN, JAMES. *The Lawful Church Delivered*, Baltimore, 1835.

———, *Gospel Tokens or Letters of Love, Written in a Good Mood*, Norwich [1847].

———, *Liberty Taken Without Grant, or an Experimental, Faithful and Discriminating Letter to the Rev. Joseph C. Philpot*, 1849.

OXFORD, NEW ROAD BAPTIST CHURCH, *The Church Covenant of 1780*.

PALMER, WILLIAM, *A Plain Statement: followed by a Few Reflections upon Mr Philpot of Stamford, as a Christian, a Preacher and a Reviewer*, 1847.

PHILPOT, JOSEPH CHARLES, *A Letter to the Provost of Worcester College, Oxford, on Resigning his Fellowship, and Seceding from the Church of England*, 1835.

———, *New Year's Addresses, etc.*, 1902.

———, *Early Sermons, 4 vols*, 1906.

History of the English Calvinistic Baptists, 1771–1892

PHILPOT, JOSEPH HENRY, & SYDNEY FRANK PAUL, eds., *The Seceders (1829–69)*, 3 vols. Vols. 1, 2, London, 1931–2; vol. 3, Brighton, 1960.

PHILPOT, SARAH LOUISA, *Letters by the Late Joseph Charles Philpot, M.A., with a Brief Memoir of his Life and Labours*, 1871.

[PRITCHARD, GEORGE], *A Plea for Primitive Communion occasioned by the Rev. Robert Hall's Recent Publication on 'Terms of Communion', etc.*, 1815.

REYNOLDS, W., G. PEARSON, G. WRIGHT, J. GOWRING, J. LAY, P. DICKERSON, T. BLUNDELL, S. NUNN, J. WRIGHT, AND S. PLOWMAN, *Letter to the Baptist Churches of Suffolk and Norfolk*, Grundisburgh, 1829.

ROBINSON, ROBERT, *The General Doctrine of Toleration Applied to the Particular Case of Free Communion*, Cambridge, 1781.

——, *Select Works of the Rev. Robert Robinson*, edited with memoir by William Robinson, 1861.

RUSHTON, WILLIAM, *A Defence of Particular Redemption: Wherein the Doctrine of the late Mr Fuller, relative to the Atonement of Christ is tried by the Word of God. In Four Letters to a Baptist Minister*, 2nd ed., 1839.

RYLAND, JOHN COLLETT [*PACIFICUS*], *A Modest Plea for Free Communion at the Lord's Table; Between True Believers of All Denominations: in a Letter to a Friend*, 1772.

RYLAND, JOHN, JR., *The Law Is Not against the Promises of God*, 1787.

——, *Serious Remarks on the Different Representations of Evangelical Doctrine by the Professed Friends of the Gospel*, Bristol, 1818.

——, *Pastoral Memorials*, 2 vols. 1826, 1828.

SAVOY DECLARATION OF FAITH AND ORDER, THE, [1658]. Reprinted, 1971.

SCOTT, THOMAS, *The Warrant and Nature of Faith in Christ* [1797]; *Theological Works*, Edinburgh, 1830.

SHAKESPEAR, H. W., *A Refutation of the Falsehoods contained in Mr Tryon's 'Letter to Mr J.C. Philpot', Containing also Mr Philpot's Letter*, 1847.

SKEPP. JOHN, *Divine Energy, or, the Efficacious Operations of the Spirit of God upon the Soul of Man* [1722]; 2nd edition, with Preface by John Gill, 1751.

Bibliography

SMARDEN PARTICULAR BAPTIST CHURCH, *The Smarden Church Book;* transcribed by K. W. H. Howard, Bethersden, Kent, 1981.

STEVENS, JOHN, *Help for the True Disciples of Immanuel: Being an Answer to a Book Published by Andrew Fuller on the Duty of Sinners to Believe in Christ; which Book is miscalled 'The Gospel Worthy of All Acceptation'*, 1803; 2nd ed., 1829.

——, *Doctrinal Antinomianism Refuted: or, The Prescriptive Will of God in Christ Jesus, the only Rule of Obedience to the Saints*, Boston, [1809], 2nd ed. 1821.

——, *A New Selection of Hymns, Including also Several Original Hymns Never Before Offered to the Public*, Boston [1811].

——, *Verses on the Sonship and Pre-Existence of Jesus Christ*, 1812.

——, *A Scriptural Display of the Triune God and the Early Existence of Jesus's Human Soul*, 1813.

——, *Thoughts on Sanctification and a Glance at Strict Communion*, 1816.

——, *A Religious Catechism*, 7th ed., 1851.

——, *Two Sermons Preached in the Year of 1818, one a few days after the death of Mrs Stevens, and the Other a Funeral Sermon for Mrs Stevens*, 1853.

STEVENS, WILLIAM, *Faith in Christ and the New Birth Connected*, Rochdale, 1821.

STOCKER, JOHN, AND JOB HUPTON, *Hymns and Spiritual Poems*, 1861.

STYLES, WILLIAM JEYES, *A Manual of Faith and Practice*, 2nd ed., 1897.

SUFFOLK AND NORFOLK ASSOCATION OF BAPTIST CHURCHES, *Circular Letter on Prayer*, Ipswich, 1828.

——, *The Divine Obligation of the Sabbath*, Ipswich, 1833.

——, *The Best Means of Promoting Peace and Prosperity of the Church*, Ipswich, 1835.

——, *The Obligation of a Believer to Follow Christ*, Ipswich, 1837.

——, *The Importance of Individual Effort in the Cause of Christ*, Bury St Edmunds, 1838.

SUFFOLK AND NORFOLK NEW ASSOCIATION OF BAPTIST CHURCHES, *Circular Letter on Christian Unity*, Bungay, 1830.

———, *Circular Letter on Adoption*, Bungay, 1832.

———, *Circular Letter on the Covenant of Grace*, Ipswich, 1833.

———, *The Legitimate Consequences of a Spiritual Reception of the Doctrines of the Everlasting Gospel*, Bungay, 1834.

———, *The Means of Grace*, Beccles, 1838.

———, *The Importance of a Revival of Religion*, Beccles, 1840.

TAYLOR, DAN, [*PHILALETHES*], *Candidus Examined with Candor; or, a Modest Enquiry into the Propriety and Force of What is Contained in a Late Pamphlet; Intitled, a Modest Plea for Free Communion at the Lord's Table; Particularly between the Baptists and Paedobaptists by Candidus*, 1772.

TIPTAFT, WILLIAM, *A Letter to the Bishop of Salisbury by William Tiptaft, to which are added Three Letters from the Bishop to Mr Tiptaft, Threatening Him with Legal Proceedings for Preaching in Unconsecrated Places and Mr Tiptaft's Answers*, Manchester, 1834.

TRIGGS, ARTHUR, *A Memorial to the Lovingkindnesses, Tender Mercies and Sovereign Grace of the Lord God of Israel*, 2nd ed., 1840; Part 2, 1860.

TRYON, FREDERICK, *A Reply to a Letter entitled 'A Refutation of the Falsehoods Contained in Mr Tryon's Letter to Mr J. C. Philpot' by H. W. Shakespear*, Peterborough, 1847.

———, *Old Paths and New Paths*, 1847.

———, *Present Tokens of 'Perilous Times', Particularly Addressed to the Readers of the* Gospel Standard, 1847.

———, *Remarks on 'An Address to Our Readers' in the* Gospel Standard, *January 1847 in a Letter to the Editors*, Stamford [1847].

———, *The Single Eye, or, Remarks on Number 118 of the 'Zoar Pulpit'*, 1847.

TURNER, DANIEL, *A Compendium of Social Religion, or, the Nature and Constitution of Christian Churches*, 1758.

—— [CANDIDUS], *A Modest Plea for Free Communion at the Lord's Table; Particularly between Baptists and Paedobaptists*, 1772.

———, *An Exhortation to Peace, Loyalty and the Support of Government*, Abingdon, 1792.

Bibliography

UPTON, JAMES, *Addresses on Practical Subjects*, 1812.

WARBURTON, JOHN, *The Mercies of a Covenant God*, 1859.

WATCHMAN ON THE WALLS OF ZION, A, *An Impartial Review of the Late Mr J. C. Philpot, M.A., as a Christian, a Minister and Editor of the Gospel Standard*, 1870.

WELLS, JAMES, *Funeral Sermon for John Church*, 1833.

——, *A Protest Against the Doctrine of the Pre-Existence of the Human Soul of the Lord Jesus Christ*, 1836.

——, *The Moral Government of God; Wherein it is Shown that the General Exhortations of the Bible are not Founded in the Principle of Man Being in a Salvable State but in the Principle of Moral and Individual Responsibility*, 1840.

WESLEY, JOHN, *The Journals of the Rev. John Wesley, M.A.*, 1837.

WESTMINSTER CONFESSION OF FAITH, THE, [1647]; Edinburgh, 1957.

WHITEFIELD, GEORGE, *The Letters of George Whitefield, 1734 – 42* [1771], repr. Edinburgh: Banner of Truth, 1976.

——, *The Journals of George Whitefield* [1738–41], repr. London: Banner of Truth, 1960.

WILKES, WASHINGTON, *A Fearless Defence of the Leading Doctrines Preached and Received by Modern Antinomians, Succinctly Stated in Seven Letters to His Friends*, 1830.

WRIGHT, GEORGE, *The Power of Godliness* [1829], 1853.

WYARD, GEORGE, *Account of the Ordination of George Wyard at Soho Chapel, Oxford Street, 12th May, 1842*, 1842.

——, *A Series of Pastoral Letters as Helps to Those Who Fear the Lord and that Think upon His Name*, 1859.

ii. Unpublished Material.

BECCLES, SUFFOLK, ARCHIVES OF THE SUFFOLK AND NORFOLK ASSOCIATIONS OF STRICT BAPTIST CHURCHES, *Minute Books of Baptist Association, 1830–78*.

——, *Minute Book of Baptist Home Missionary Society For the Counties of Suffolk and Norfolk, September 13th, 1831–November 18th 1936*.

History of the English Calvinistic Baptists, 1771–1892

London, St John's Wood Road Baptist Church, *Church Minute Book of Blandford Street Baptist Church, London, 1825–63.*

Oxford, Angus Library, Regent's Park College, *The Correspondence of Andrew Fuller.*

——, *The Minute Book of The London Association of Strict Baptist Ministers and Churches, April 3rd 1846–February 9th 1853.*

——, *The Minutes of the London Society for the Support of Students for the Ministry, August 1752 –March 1796.*

——, *The Diaries of William Newman, 4 vols: 7th July, 1808–20th August, 1814; 15th July, 1820 - 10th October, 1833; 10th October 1833–20th May 1834.*

——, *Manuscript Letter, Daniel Turner to Mr Munn, Watford, 14th June 1782.*

2. Secondary Sources
i.Published Works
(Unless otherwise stated, the place of publication is London)

Banks, Adeline Mary, *The Rev. Charles Waters Banks,* 1890.

Barrett, Gladys M., *The Fuller Church, Kettering,* St. Albans, 1946.

Bennett, James, *History of the Dissenters during the Last Thirty Years (1808 - 1838),* 1839

Binfield, Clyde, *Pastors and People:The Biography of a Baptist Church, Queen's Road, Coventry,* Coventry, 1984.

Birrell, Charles M., *The Life of William Brock, D.D.,* 1878

Bland, Samuel K., *Memorials of George Wright,* 1875.

Briggs, J. H. Y., *English Baptists of the Nineteenth Century,* Didcot, 1994.

Browne, John, *History of Congregationalism and Memorials of the Churches in Norfolk and Suffolk,* 1877.

Buffard, F., *Kent and Sussex Baptist Associations,* Faversham, 1963.

Chadwick, Owen, *The Victorian Church,* 2 vols., 1970; 1980.

Chambers, Ralph F., *The Strict Baptist Chapels of England,* 4 vols.

Bibliography

vol. 1: *Surrey and Hampshire*, Thornton Heath, 1952.
vol. 2: *Sussex*, Thornton Heath, n.d.
vol. 3: *Kent*, Thornton Heath, n.d.
vol. 4: *The Industrial Midlands*, London, 1963.

CHAMPION, L. G., *Farthing Rushlight: The Story of Andrew Gifford, 1700–1784*, 1961.

COOPER, R. E., *From Stepney to St Giles': The Story of Regent's Park College, 1810–1960*, 1960.

CRAGG, G. R., *Reason and Authority in the Eighteenth Century*, 1964.

CROSS, F. L., ed., *The Oxford Dictionary of the Christian Church*, 1966.

CULROSS, J., *The Three Rylands*, 1897.

DALLIMORE, ARNOLD, *George Whitefield*, 2 vols. Vol. 1, London: Banner of Truth, 1970; vol. 2, Edinburgh: Banner of Truth, 1980.

——, *Spurgeon, a New Biography*, Edinburgh: Banner of Truth, 1985.

DAVIES, R., AND G. RUPP, eds., *A History of the Methodist Church in Great Britain*, 1965.

DIX, KENNETH, *Strict and Particular: English Strict and Particular Baptists in the Nineteenth Century*, Didcot, 2002.

DYER, GEORGE, *Memoirs of the Life and Writings of Robert Robinson*, 1796.

ELWYN, T. H. S., *The Northamptonshire Baptist Association, 1764–1964*, 1964.

EVANS, J., *Memoirs of the Life and Writings of the Rev. William Richards, LL.D.*, Chiswick, 1819.

FOSTER, F. H., *A Genetic History of the New England Theology*, Chicago, 1907.

GADSBY, JOHN, *A Memoir of the Late Mr William Gadsby*, Manchester, 1844; 2nd edition, 1847.

——, *Memoirs of the Principal Hymn-writers and Compilers of the 17th, 18th and 19th Centuries*, 5th ed., 1882.

GOULD, GEORGE, *Open Communion and the Baptists of Norwich*, Norwich, 1860.

GREENE, J., *Reminiscences of the Rev. Robert Hall, Late of Bristol*, 1832.

GREGORY, OLINTHUS, *Memoir of Robert Hall*, 1831; Hall's *Works*, vol. 6.

HALL, P., *A Memoir of the Rev. Thomas Robinson, M.A.*, 1837.

HALLEY, ROBERT, *Lancashire: Its Puritanism and Nonconformity*, 2 vols., Manchester, 1869.

HARGREAVES, JAMES, *The Life and Memoir of the late Rev. John Hirst, Forty Two Years Pastor of the Baptist Church, Bacup: also an Appendix containing a Sketch of the Rise of that Church, and of the Churches at Clough-Fold, Rodhillend, Rawden, Salendine Nook, Accrington, Blackburn, Cowling Hill, Goodshaw, and a Short Account of Several Ministers*, Rochdale, 1816.

HAYKIN, MICHAEL A.G., ed., *The Life and Thought of John Gill (1697-1771)*, Leiden, 1997.

——, *One Heart and One Soul: John Sutcliff of Olney, His Friends and His Times*, Darlington, 1994.

HAZELTON, J. E., *"Inasmuch", A History of the Aged Pilgrims' Friend Society, 1807-1922*, 1922.

HITCHCOCK, H. T., *Rattlesden Baptist Church, 1813-1963*, n. p., n. d.

HODDY, R., *Memoir of Israel Atkinson*, 1882.

HORNE, WILLIAM WALES, *The Life of the Rev. John Bradford, A.B., late of Wadham College, Oxford; and late Minister of the Gospel, City Chapel, Grub Street, London*, 1806.

HUEHNS, G., *Antinomianism in English History*, 1951.

HUGHES, GRAHAM W., *With Freedom Fired: The Story of Robert Robinson, Cambridge Nonconformist*, 1955.

HULBERT, CHARLES A., *Annals of the Church in Slaithwaite (near Huddersfield) from 1593 to 1864*, 1864.

IVIMEY, JOSEPH, *A History of the English Baptists*, 4 vols., 1811-30.

JEWSON, C. B., *The Baptists in Norfolk*, 1957.

JOHNSON, W. C., *Encounter in London, The Story of the London Baptist Association, 1865-1965*, 1965.

JONES, JOHN ANDREW, *Bunhill Memorials*, 1849.

Bibliography

JONES, W., *An Essay on the Life and Writings of Mr Abraham Booth*, Liverpool, 1808.

JONES, WILLIAM, *Memoirs of the Life, Ministry, and Writings of the Rev. Rowland Hill, M.A., including Fifteen Sermons on Important Subjects*, 1834.

JULIAN, JOHN, *A Dictionary of Hymnology* [1907]; reprinted in 2 vols., New York, 1957.

KLAIBER, ASHLEY J., *The History of the Suffolk Baptists*, 1931.

MACLEOD, JOHN, *Scottish Theology in Relation to Church History since the Reformation*, Edinburgh, 1943.

MANN, AUBRY, *The Old Meeting Church, Bedworth*, n.p., n.d.

MANNING, BERNARD, LORD, *The Protestant Dissenting Deputies*, edited by O. Greenwood, Cambridge, 1952.

MARTIN, ROBERT G., *Zion Strict Baptist Chapel, Bedworth, 1796-1955*, Tunbridge Wells, n.d.

MIDDLETON, JOHN WHITE, *An Ecclesiastical Memoir of the First Four Decades of the Reign of George III*, 1822.

MOON, NORMAN S., *Education for the Ministry, 1679-1979*, Bristol, 1979.

MORRIS, J. W., *Memoirs of the Life and Writings of the Rev. Andrew Fuller*, 1815.

——, *Biographical Recollections of the Rev. Robert Hall, A.M.*, 1833.

MURRAY, JOHN, *The Imputation of Adam's Sin*, Grand Rapids U.S.A., 1959.

NETTLES, THOMAS J., *By His Grace and for His Glory*, Grand Rapids, U.S.A., 1986.

NEWMAN, WILLIAM, *Rylandiana*, 1835.

OLIVER, ROBERT W., *The Strict Baptist Chapels of England*, vol. 5: *Wiltshire and the West*, 1968.

OWEN, J. M. GWYNNE, *Memorial Volume of the 250th Anniversary of the East Midland Baptist Association*, Birmingham, 1905.

OWEN, W. T., *Edward Williams, D. D., His Life, Thought and Influence*, Cardiff, 1963.

PALMER, WILLIAM, *A Brief Memoir of the Late Mr George Murrell, for Fifty Eight Years Pastor of the Particular Baptist Church at St Neots, Huntingdonshire*, 1871.

PARSONS, K. A. C., ed., *History of St Andrew's Street Baptist Church, Cambridge*, Cambridge, 1971.

PAUL, S. F., *Historical Sketch of the Gospel Standard Baptists*, Hove, and Croydon, n.d.

PAYNE, ERNEST A., *The Free Church Tradition in the Life of England*, 1944.

——, *The Baptists of Berkshire*, 1951.

——, *The Baptist Union: A Short History*, 1958.

PHILPOT, JOSEPH C., *Memoir of the Late William Tiptaft*, 1867.

PIGGIN, STUART, *Making Evangelical Missionaries, 1789-1858*, Sutton Courtenay, 1984.

PRITCHARD, GEORGE, *Memoir of the Life and Writings of the Rev. Joseph Ivimey*, 1835.

——, *Memoir of the Rev. William Newman, D. D.*, 1837.

RAMSBOTTOM, BENJAMIN A., *The History of the* Gospel Standard Magazine, *1835-1985*, Carshalton, 1985.

——, *William Gadsby*, Harpenden, 2003.

REYNOLDS, PHILIP, *'These Hundred Years.' A Century Memento of the Suffolk and Norfolk Association of Strict Baptist Churches*, Ipswich, [1929].

RIPPON, JOHN, *Brief Memoir of the Life and Writings of John Gill*, 1838.

RYLAND, JOHN, *The Work of Faith, the Labour of Love and the Patience of Hope, Illustrated in the Life and Death of the Rev. Andrew Fuller*, 2nd ed., 1818.

RYLE, J. C., *Christian Leaders of the Last Century*, 1891.

SCOTT, J., *The Life of the Rev. Thomas Scott*, 1823.

SELL, ALAN P. F., *The Great Debate, Calvinism, Arminianism and Salvation*, Worthing, 1982.

SHAW, IAN J., *High Calvinists in Action: Calvinism and the City, Manchester and London, c. 1810-1860*, Oxford, 2002

Bibliography

SHIPLEY, C. E., ed., *The Baptists of Yorkshire*, 1912.

SLIM, CORNELIUS, *My Contemporaries of the Nineteenth Century. Brief Memorials of More than Four Hundred Ministers of the Gospel of Various Denominations, who have Lived, Laboured and entered into Rest from AD 1800 to 1869*, 1870.

SPURRIER, EDWARD, *Memorials of the Baptist Church Worshipping in Eld Lane Chapel, Colchester*, Colchester, 1889.

STALKER, A. M., *Memorial Sketch of John Stock, LL.D. (Minister of Salendine Nook Chapel, Huddersfield)*, 1885.

STEADMAN, THOMAS, *Memoir of the Rev. William Steadman, D. D.*, 1838.

STEANE, EDWARD, *Memoir of the Life of Joseph Gutteridge, Esq., of Denmark Hill, Surrey*, 1850.

STEVENS, WILLIAM, *Recollections of the late William Huntington*, 1868.

STOVEL, CHARLES, *Preparations for Pulpit Exercises*, edited by W. Willis, Q.C., 1888.

STYLES, WILLIAM JEYES, *John Hazelton*, 1888.

T. A., *A Few Historical Links of Zoar Chapel*, 1889.

TAYLOR, ADAM, *Memoirs of the Rev. Dan Taylor*, 1820.

THORPE, JOHN K., *Other Sheep of the Tamil Fold: The Century Story of the Strict Baptist Mission*, 1961.

TOON, PETER, *Hyper-Calvinism*, 1967.

TRACEY, JOSEPH, *The Great Awakening* [1842]; repr. Edinburgh: Banner of Truth, 1976.

TRYON, M. J., ed., *A Small Memento of Frederick Tryon*, 1904.

UNDERWOOD, A. C., *A History of the English Baptists*, 3rd Impression, 1961.

VAUGHAN, E. T., *Some Account of the Rev. Thomas Robinson, M. A.*, 1815.

WARBURTON, JOHN, Jr., *Memorials of the Late John Warburton of Southill*, edited by C. Hemington, 1892.

WATSON, J. STEVEN, *The Reign of George III, 1760–1815*, Oxford, 1964.

WATTS, MICHAEL R., *The Dissenters*, vol. 1, Oxford, 1978.

WHITE, B. R., *The English Separatist Tradition*, Oxford, 1971.

——, *The English Baptists of the Seventeenth Century*, 1983.
WHITLEY, W. T., *The Baptists of the North West England, 1694-1913*, 1913.
——, *A History of the British Baptists*, 1923.
——, *The Baptists of London, 1612-1928*, n. d.
——, *Calvinism and Evangelicalism in England, especially among the Baptists*, n. d.
WILKIN, MARTIN HOOD, *Joseph Kinghorn of Norwich*, Norwich, 1855.
WILLEY, B., *The Eighteenth Century Background*, 1940.
WILSON, BRYAN, *Religious Sects: A Sociological Study*, 1970.
WILSON, WALTER, *The History and Antiquities of Dissenting Churches and Meeting Houses in London, Westminster and Southwark including the Lives of their Ministers from the Rise of Nonconformity to the Present Time*, 4 vols., 1808-14.
WOLSTENHOLME, S., *These Hundred and Fifty Years. A Commemorative Memento of the Suffolk and Norfolk Association of Strict Baptist Churches*, n. d. [1980].
WOOD, A. SKEVINGTON, *Thomas Haweis, 1734-1820*, 1957.
WRIGHT, THOMAS, *The Life of William Huntington, S. S.*, 1909.
——, *Augustus M. Toplady and Contemporary Hymn Writers*, 1911.
——, *Richard Burnham*, n. d.

ii. Contemporary Periodicals

Baptist Annual Register, 1790-1802.
Baptist Magazine, from 1809.
Evangelical Magazine, vols. 7 & 8, 1799, 1800.
Earthen Vessel, from 1845.
Gospel Herald, from 1833.
Gospel Standard, from 1835.
Missionary Herald, vol. 59, 1844.
Primitive Communionist, 1838-40;
Primitive Church Magazine, 1841-57.

3. Articles

CAMPBELL, K. M., 'Antinomian Controversies of the Seventeenth Century', in *Living the Christian Life*, Westminster Conference Papers, 1974, pp. 61–81.

KIRBY, F. J., '"Gospel Standard" and "Earthen Vessel"', *Christian's Pathway*, vol. 36, 1931, pp. 186–94.

LANGLEY, A. S., 'Baptist Ministers in England about 1750 A.D.', *Transactions of the Baptist Historical Society*, vol. 6, 1918–19, pp. 138–162.

LLOYD-JONES, D. M., 'Sandemanianism', in *Profitable for Doctrine and Reproof*, Puritan Conference Papers, 1967, pp. 54–71.

MANNING, BERNARD L., 'Some Characteristics of the Older Dissent', *Congregational Quarterly*, vol. 5, 1927, pp. 286–300.

NUTTALL, G. F., 'Northamptonshire and the Modern Question: A Turning-Point in Eighteenth-Century Dissent', *Journal of Theological Studies*, vol. 16, 1965, pp. 101–23.

OLIVER, ROBERT W., 'The Dangers of a Successful Ministry. The Life, Teaching and Influence of James Wells', *Bulletin of the Strict Baptist Historical Society*, 8, 1971.

——, 'John Collett Ryland, Daniel Turner and Robert Robinson and the Communion Controversy, 1771–1781', *Baptist Quarterly*, vol. 29, 1981–2, pp. 77–9.

PAYNE, E. A., 'An Elegy on Andrew Gifford', *Baptist Quarterly*, vol. 9, 1938–9, pp. 54–7.

——, 'Abraham Booth, 1734–1806', *Baptist Quarterly*, vol. 26, 1975–76, pp. 28–42.

——, 'Nonconformists and the American Revolution', *Journal of the United Reformed History Society*, vol. 1, 1976, pp. 210–27.

PRICE, SEYMOUR J., 'Dr Gill's Confession of 1729', *Baptist Quarterly*, vol. 4, 1928–9, pp. 366–371.

SELLARS, IAN, 'Some Reflections on the Writing of Strict Baptist History', *Bulletin of the Strict Baptist Historical Society*, 5, 1966.

TOON, PETER, 'The Growth of a Supralapsarian Christology', *Evangelical Quarterly*, vol. 29, 1967, pp. 24–9.

WHITE, B. R.,'Thomas Crosby, Baptist Historian', *Baptist Quarterly*, vol. 21, pp. 154-68, 219-34.

——, 'John Gill in London, 1719-29, A Biographical Fragment', *Baptist Quarterly*, vol. 23, 1967-8, pp. 72-91.

——, 'Open and Closed Membership among the English and Welsh Baptists', *Baptist Quarterly*, vol. 24, 1971-2, pp. 330-334.

WINTER, E. P., 'Calvinist and Zwinglian Views of the Lord's Supper among the Baptists in the Seventeenth Century', *Baptist Quarterly*, vol. 15, 1953-4.

——, 'The Lord's Supper, Admission and Exclusion among the Baptists in the Seventeenth Century', *Baptist Quarterly*, vol. 16, 1955-6.

——, 'The Administration of the Lord's Supper among the Baptists in the Seventeenth Century', *Baptist Quarterly*, vol. 18, 1959-60.

iv. Unpublished Theses

ASCOL, THOMAS B., 'The Doctrine of Grace; a Critical Analysis of Federalism in the Theologies of John Gill and Andrew Fuller', Ph.D. thesis, Southwestern Baptist Theological Seminary, Fort Worth, Texas, 1989.

CLIPSHAM, E.F., 'Andrew Fuller's Doctrine of Salvation', B.D. thesis, University of Oxford, 1971.

COPPENGER, R. A.,'Abraham Booth, 1734-1806. A Study of his Thought and Work', Ph.D. thesis, University of Edinburgh, 1953.

DANIEL, CURT D., 'Hyper-Calvinism and John Gill', Ph.D. thesis, University of Edinburgh, 1983.

HAYDEN, ROGER, 'Evangelical Calvinism among Eighteenth Century British Baptists', Ph.D. thesis, University of Keele, 1991.

MACDONALD, MURDINA D., 'London Calvinistic Baptists 1689-1727: Tensions within a Dissenting Community under Toleration', D.Phil. Thesis, University of Oxford, 1983.

MACLEOD. ANGUS HAMILTON, 'The Life and Teaching of Robert Hall, 1764-1831', M.Litt. thesis, University of Durham, 1957.

Bibliography

MANLEY, KENNETH R., 'John Rippon, D.D. (1751–1836) and the Particular Baptists', D.Phil. Thesis, University of Oxford, 1967.

ROBISON, OLIN C., 'The Particular Baptists in England, 1760–1820', D.Phil. thesis, University of Oxford, 1963.

SCHELL, L. G., 'Robert Robinson (1735-90) with Special Reference to His Religious and Political Thought', Ph.D. thesis, University of Edinburgh, 1950.

SEYMOUR R. E., 'John Gill, Baptist Theologian.' Ph.D. thesis, University of Edinburgh, 1954.

SPARKES, DOUGLAS C., 'Dissenters and the Government of the City of London, 1661–1761', M.A. thesis, University of Keele. 1981.

TAYLOR, ROSEMARY, 'English Baptist Periodicals, 1790–1865', M.Phil. thesis, University of London, 1974.

WINTER, E. P., 'The Theory and Practice of the Lord's Supper among the Early Separatists, Independents and Baptists, 1550–1700', B.Litt. thesis, University of Oxford, 1954.

Index of Names

Abbadie, James [Jacques], 52, 369
Adams, John, 137
Allen, John, 214
Ambrose, Isaac, 264
Ascol, Thomas B., 8–9, 390
Aston, Paul, 176–8
Augustine of Canterbury, 301

Bagster, Samuel, 36
Balls, Roger, 115
Banks, Charles W., 284–6, 348–9
Bayes, Jonathan, 114, 116
Baxter, Richard, 365
Bayfield, Gabriel, 221
Bebbington, David, 363
Beddome, Benjamin, 16–29
Beddome, John, 17–18, 21–2
Beddome, Rachel, née Brandon, 18
Bellamy, Joseph, 94, 108, 363
Bennett, James, 127 n, 144 n, 187 n, 236, 261 n, 382
Berridge, John, 78, 82
Birrell, Charles, M., 251, 259 n, 382
Blackburn, Earl, 8 n
Blackstock, Edward, 179 n, 193–4, 369
Booth, Abraham, 29, 44–7, 60, 65, 70–8, 80, 83–7, 108–10, 112–6, 141, 145 n, 149–67, 168–73, 188, 206, 208–9, 231–4, 237, 244–5, 254, 258, 282, 300, 336, 357, 359, 363, 369–71, 384, 389–90

Booth, Elizabeth, née Bowman, 46
Bowes, W. B., 324
Box, John, 325
Bradford, John, 142–4, 176, 314, 384
Brainerd, David, 94
Briggs, J. H. Y., 200, 382
Brine, John, 10, 12, 28, 32, 90 n, 93, 95, 97–8, 100, 103, 116, 119 n, 142, 181, 203, 205, 264, 268, 320
Brock, William, 251, 258–9, 382
Brook, William J., 144
Brooks, Thomas, 19 n, 27 n
Brown, John, 66–70, 370
Bunyan, John, 58, 71, 89, 91, 93
Burford, Samuel, 53,
Burnham, Richard, 202–3, 211, 218, 223, 370
Butterworth, John, 177
Buttfield, William, 69–70, 72, 370–1
Button, William, 99–102, 104–11, 171, 210 n, 217, 245–6, 370

Calvin, John, 79, 82, 90 n, 132, 170, 205, 231, 312, 337, 341, 343, 345, 352–3
'Candidus' (Daniel Turner), 59–60, 63–7, 357–8
Carey, William, 97–8 n, 109, 118 n, 152, 157, 159
Caroline, Queen (consort of George IV), 196
Castledon, James, 323

[393]

Charnock, Stephen, 95, 264, 352
Church, John, 140 n
Clarke, William Nash, 48, 99
Clayton, Joseph, 204
Clifford, John, xx
Coles, Elisha, 95 n, 205
Coles, Thomas, 28–9
Collins, Samuel, 223 n, 225–6, 263–4, 268, 270, 285, 305, 315, 321, 331
Collyer, William Henry, 214
Comb, George, 323
Cooper, John, 263, 305, 320–1
Cooper, R. E., 257, 383
Cox, Francis A., 251, 254–5, 257–8, 261, 284, 330, 371, 373, 375, 376
Crisp, Tobias, 158–9, 162, 184, 350, 363
Cromwell, Oliver, 109
Crowther, William, 352
Curtis, Daniel, 324, 326

Daniel, Curt, 113 n, 225 n, 390
Darby, John Nelson, 291
Deacon, Samuel, 45
De Fleury, Maria, 133–6, 371
Denham, William, 222
Denney, James, 144
Dickerson, Philip, 266, 317, 321–2, 324
Dickinson, Mr, 367
Diver, Joseph, 92–4
Dix, Kenneth, xiii, 48 n
Doddridge, Philip, 34
Dore, James, 57
Drawbridge, Charles, 277, 297
Dyer, George, 62 n, 78, 79 n, 82–3, 359, 383

Edwards, Jonathan, 13, 42, 55, 91 n, 93, 94, 97, 108, 131, 150–1, 155, 164–5, 235, 371
Edwards, Jonathan, Jr., 150, 163, 166
Ella, George M., 3 n, 90 n
Elven, Cornelius, 316
Erskine, Ralph, 91
Evans, Caleb, 83, 86, 118, 126–7, 132, 138–9, 176, 232 n, 236, 371, 375
Evans, Christmas, 245, 371
Evans, Hugh, 32 n, 85–6, 232
Eve, John, 91–3

Fernie, David, 41
Flavel, John, 173
Fletcher, John, 46
Foreman, John, 212, 225, 266, 270 n, 305, 323–4, 326, 328, 332, 352, 371, 377
Foskett, Bernard, 18–19, 21–2, 28
Foster, Frank Hugh, 114 n, 150 n, 161, 163 n, 166 n, 383
Fox, William, 51
Foxwell, William, 218–20, 371
Franklin, Francis, 177
Franklin, Jonathan, 181
Fuller, Andrew, 11 n, 32, 35, 41–2, 53, 55, 66 n, 67, 70 n, 83, 86–7, 89–111, 116, 118–9, 128, 132, 138, 141–2, 144–5, 149–178, 183–8, 203–10, 213, 218, 225–6, 231–7, 244–5, 252, 254, 258–63, 265–6, 269, 299–301, 308, 314, 326, 329–30, 332, 336, 350, 361–6, 372
Fulton, William, 268

Gadsby, John (father of William), 175

Index of Names

Gadsby, John (son of William), 193 n, 197, 220, 263 n, 272 n, 278, 281, 334, 372

Gadsby, William, 90 n, 91, 144, 171, 173–201, 210–14, 220, 224, 259, 262, 265, 268, 272, 274, 277–80, 285, 296, 301–2, 309–10, 315, 333–4, 346, 352, 372–3, 383, 386

Gawthorne, J,. 186–7, 373

George III, 59, 89, 121, 385

George IV, 196

George, Timothy, 97

Gibbs, Philip, 118

Gifford, Andrew, 38, 49

Gill, John, 3–15, 19, 32–4, 49, 60, 62, 71, 83, 90, 93, 97–100, 102–4, 111, 113, 115–6, 119, 132, 138, 142, 159 n, 181, 203 n, 204–5, 211, 214, 225 n, 244, 260, 268, 277, 320, 329, 337, 350, 352, 373, 378, 384, 386, 389–90

Glover, Willis B., 355

Goodwin, Thomas, 352

Gould, George, 259, 283 n, 383

Gray, William, 56

Gregory, Olinthus, 30, 87 n, 383

Grotius, Hugo, 163, 164 n

Gutteridge, Joseph, 55, 254–6, 387

Gwennap, Joseph, 139

Haley, Robert, 173

Hall, Christopher, 41

Hall, Robert, Jr., 24, 29, 30, 32, 35–6, 37, 55, 77, 87, 119, 122, 144, 231–58, 260, 265, 283 n, 284, 319, 330. 371, 373–8, 383, 385, 390

Hall, Robert, Sr., 32, 38–44, 93, 97, 116

Hall, William, 178

Hart, Joseph, xx, 43, 307

Haweis, Thomas, 201, 203, 211, 223, 225, 388

Hawker, Robert, 143–4, 371, 374

Hayden, Roger, xix n

Haykin, Michael, A. G., xi–xii, 3 n, 13 n, 21 n, 36 n, 39 n, 44 n, 384

Haynes, Richard, 27–8

Hazlerigg, Grey, 281, 334–5

Hazlerigg, Lady, 281

Henry, Philip, 231, 234

Henry, Matthew, 22, 82

Hervey, James, 34, 46, 374

Hewet, Mr (Northampton), 137

Hill, Rowland, 31, 34–5, 78, 140, 142, 385

Hinton, James, 249, 262, 375

Hinton, John Howard, 269, 327, 330, 374

Hoddy, T., 316

Hooper, Ebenezer, 133 n, 140, 374

Hopkins, Samuel, 150, 152–6, 161–2, 165, 363

Horne, William Wales, 119 n, 143 n, 384

Howard, K. W. H., 12 n

Howe, John, 352

Huehns, Gertrude, 113 n, 384

Hunt, Henry, 195

Huntingdon, Selina, Countess of, 34, 45, 48, 116, 176, 201, 203, 225, 314

Huntington, William, 90 n, 119–45, 175–6, 181, 183–4, 186, 192, 198, 210–13, 268–70, 276–7, 281, 297–8, 302, 305, 307, 313, 314 n, 315, 329, 332–3, 350, 371, 374–5, 377, 387–8

[395]

Hupton, Job, 314–5, 375
Hussey, Joseph, 9–11, 98 n, 276

Irving, Edward, 269
Isbell, George S. B., 280
Ivimey, Joseph, 7 n, 39, 50, 53 n, 59–60 n, 69 n, 78 n, 84 n, 98–9 n, 102 n, 109 n, 111, 119, 122 n, 219 n, 220, 231–2 n, 233, 238 n, 244 n, 245, 251–4, 257–9, 282–3, 330, 336, 357–9, 375, 384, 386

Jackson, Alvery, 97
Jay, William, 31, 34, 35 n, 36, 38 n
Jones, John A., 323–4, 331–2, 384
Joss, Torial, 120, 139 n, 142, 375

Kay, John, 280, 295 n
Kaye, Peter, 197
Keach, Benjamin, 5–6, 18, 337, 376
Keble, John, 290
Keeble, John, 264, 266
Kershaw, John, 182, 188, 194 n, 262, 280, 376
Kingdon, David, 354–5
Kinghorn, Joseph, 87, 232–5, 244 n, 245–51, 254–5, 257–9, 283, 319, 336, 374–6, 388
Kiffin, William, 58, 244

Leather, William, 188
Llewellyn, Thomas, 60
Lloyd, Charles, 290
Lindsey, Theophilus, 51
Love, Christopher, 264
Luther, Martin, 113 n, 132

MacGowan, John, 49

Macleod, Angus Hamilton, 231 n, 235 n, 237 n, 244 n, 254 n, 390
Martin, John, 53, 70 n, 93, 99, 102–10, 123 n, 171, 210, 217, 282, 372, 376
Maurice, Matthias, 10, 97
McKerrow, William, 197
M'Kenzie, John, 272–3, 275, 280, 296 n
McLean, Archibald, 153, 187
Miall, Edward, 363
Mileham, C. T., 256
Morris, John W., 98 n, 209, 365, 385
Murray, John, 112
Murrell, George, 225, 305, 376, 385

Nettles, Thomas J., 164, 342 n, 385
Newman, Francis, 289
Newman, John Henry, 289–90
Newman, William, 30 n, 32 n, 33–4, 35 n, 38 n, 49–50, 77, 100 n, 170–1, 232–4, 245 n, 251–2, 254–9, 282–3, 358, 376, 382, 385–6
Newton, John, 37, 344
Nicoll, William Robertson, 144
Noble, John, 10
Norton, William, 282–4, 324–5, 331–2, 377
Nunn, James, 321
Nunn, William, 195 n, 277–8, 280
Nuttall, Geoffrey F., 10 n, 78–9 n, 89, 90 n, 173 n, 389

Oakley, Frederick, 290
Oliver, J., 324
Oliver, Robert W., 3 n, 5 n, 11 n, 44 n, 59 n, 78 n, 226 n, 262 n, 385, 389

Index of Names

Oncken, John Gerhard, 325
Osbourn, James, 285, 297–8, 305–6, 374, 377
Overbury, Robert William, 282–3, 324, 331–2
Owen, John, 14, 27, 49, 55, 95, 151, 162, 165, 205, 207, 352

'Pacificus' (John Collett Ryland), 59–67, 357–8, 378
Packer, J. I., 191
Palmer, Anthony, 20
Palmer, William, 204 n, 209 n, 225 n, 270 n, 296 n, 301–2, 305–6, 322 n, 350, 377, 385
Park, Edwards A., 363
Parry, Joseph, 292–4, 297 n, 301 n
Payne, Alexander, 28
Payne, Ernest A., 44–5 n, 49 n, 58–60 n, 62 n, 70 n, 84 n, 90 n, 111, 122 n, 202 n, 261, 329–30, 386, 389
Pearce, Samuel, 29
Pearson, George, 318 n, 320
Pennefather, Anne, 290–1
Pennefather, Edward, 290–1
Pennefather, Susannah (née Darby), 290–1
Pentycross, Thomas, 142
Philpot, Charles, 288
Philpot, Joseph Charles, 193 n, 194–5, 270, 272–81, 285, 288–311, 330, 333–4, 339, 347 n, 352, 377–8, 380–1, 386
Philpot, Joseph Henry, 193–5 n, 198 n, 272–3 n, 289, 367–8 n, 378
Philpot, Maria (née Lafargue), 288
Philpot, Sarah Louisa (née Keal), 273 n, 303, 378
Pitt, William (the younger), 121
Price, Seymour J., 11–12 n, 389
Priestley, Joseph, 52, 79, 109 n
Pritchard, George, 233–4 n, 244–5, 254 n, 257–8 n, 378
Pusey, Edward Bouverie, 290

Ramsbottom, Benjamin A, 174 n, 179 n, 386
Rawlins, Nathaniel, 28
Relly, James, 114, 135–6
Reynolds, John, 27–8
Rippon, John, 3 n, 11 n, 17 n, 18 n, 21, 39–40, 50–1, 53 n, 57, 62 n, 70 n, 99, 108, 111, 138, 204 n, 261, 282, 313–4 n, 330, 337–8, 391
Roberts, R. Philip, 11 n, 50–1 n, 55 n, 163 n
Robins, Edmund, 181
Robinson, Robert, 59 n, 62, 77–84, 86–7, 236–7, 357–9, 378, 383–4, 389, 391
Robinson, Thomas, 143, 384, 387
Robison, Olin C., 78 n, 359 n, 391
Rogers, George, 350
Rushton, William, 300–1, 378
Ryland, John Collett, 27–8, 30–8, 59–66, 78, 83, 99–100, 133, 136–7, 139, 235, 357, 378, 389
Ryland, John, Jr., 10, 11 n, 12, 34, 37, 39, 43, 53, 67, 83, 86–7, 94, 97, 116–7, 132, 137–9, 142, 158, 171, 177, 254, 262, 365, 372, 375, 378, 386
Ryland, Joseph, 31

Sandeman, Robert, 187–8
Sanderson, Lady Elizabeth, 121

[397]

Scott, Thomas, 153–6
Shakespear, H. W., 303, 378, 380
Shaw, Ian J., xiii, 174 n, 179, 185 n, 196 n, 197, 277 n, 300 n, 386
Shindler, Robert, 352, 353 n, 354–5
Silver, Frederick, 267
Skepp, John, 9–10, 378
Smith, James (Ilford and Shoreditch), 266
Smith, Lady Lucy, 281
Smith, Nathan, 49
Spurgeon, Charles Haddon, 12, 14–15, 130 n, 144, 190, 284, 286 n, 288, 309, 336–56, 383
Spurgeon, James, 339
Starr, Edward, 358
Steadman, William, 171, 232, 236 n, 387
Steane, Edward, 254 n, 256, 330, 387
Stennett, Joseph, 19, 21
Stennett, Samuel, 48–9, 53 n, 83–4, 90, 108 n, 122
Stevens, John, 91, 171, 173–4, 186, 200–27, 259, 262, 263 n, 264, 267, 270–2, 276–7, 282, 285, 296, 298, 305, 315, 320, 321 n, 324, 332, 346, 350, 369, 371–3, 376, 379
Stevens, Thomas, 98 n
Stevens, William (London), 121, 123, 387
Stevens, William (Rochdale), 188–9, 379
Stinton, Benjamin, 5
Stock, John, 265, 266 n, 331–2
Stoughton, John, 261
Styles, William Jeyes, 209 n, 225–6, 266, 347, 350–2, 355, 379, 387
Sutcliff, John, 53, 94, 97, 108 n, 384

Taylor, Abraham, 19, 93, 97
Taylor, Dan, 65–6, 79 n, 84 n, 99, 102, 154 n, 166, 380, 387
Taylor, David, 45
Taylor, Rosemary, 262 n, 281–2 n, 286 n, 391
Taylor, William, 55, 254
Thomas, John, 53–4, 109 n, 151 n
Thornton, John, 281
Tiptaft, William, 273 n, 274, 275 n, 280, 292–3, 295, 311 n, 367, 380, 386
Toon, Peter, 10 n, 11 n, 113 n, 208 n, 214 n, 387, 389
Toplady, Augustus, M., 34, 116 n, 268
Towers, John, 133 n, 134
Trevelyan, George Macaulay, 260
Trinder, Martha, 37
Tryon, Frederick, 280, 295 n, 303–6, 378, 380, 387
Turner, Daniel, 59–68, 70, 78–80, 83, 122, 357–9, 380, 382, 389
Tyndale, William, 301

Underwood, A. C., xx, 90 n, 107 n, 119, 122 n, 200, 259 n, 266 n, 332 n, 353 n, 387
Upton, James, 183 n, 186, 330, 381

Venema, Herman, 165
Venn, Henry, 47, 71
Vitringa, Campegius, 165
Vorley, Edward, 178

Walker, John, 19
Wallin, Benjamin, 48, 99
Warburton, John, 262, 274, 280, 293, 302, 381

[398]

Index of Names

Warfield, B. B., 362
Washington, George, 37
Wassell, David, 331
Watts, Isaac, 62, 82, 214, 339
Wayman, Lewis, 10, 205, 208
Wells, James, 226, 262, 270 n, 276, 277 n, 285, 298–300, 346–9, 352, 381, 389
Wesley, John, 34 n, 46, 84, 114–5, 381
West, Stephen, 150, 163, 166
Whitley, W. T., xxi, 45 n, 104, 116 n, 119, 178 n, 186 n, 200, 223 n, 323–4 n, 327 n, 358, 388
White, B. R., 5 n, 390
Whitefield, George, 20, 30, 34 n, 35, 72–3, 78, 84, 103, 114, 120, 131, 142, 311, 332, 381, 383

Whitmee, John, 203–4
Wickliffe (Wycliffe), John, 301
Wileman, William, 335
Wilkes, John, 58
Williams, Edward, 52, 84 n
Wills, Gregory, A., 13
Wilson, Daniel, 317
Wilson, Samuel, 19, 26
Wilson, Walter, 9 n, 332 n, 388
Winter, T., 331
Withers P., 99 n
Witsius, Herman, 33, 95 n, 162
Wright, George, 315–21, 331
Wright, Thomas, 34 n, 119 n, 388
Wyard, George, 314, 316, 381

Young, William, 113 n
Young, Solomon, 257

[399]

Index of Places

Aberdeen, University of, 4, 29, 235
Abingdon, 60–1, 274, 295 n, 357
Accrington, 180
Alcester, 17–18, 315
Aldwinckle, 201, 203, 223
Allington, Wilts., 274, 292
Annesley Woodhouse, 44–5
Arnesby, 38–41, 93, 235
Attleborough, 175
Aylesbury, 271

Banbury, 271
Barnoldswick, 49, 97
Bath, 31, 174, 331
Beccles, 263, 315
Bedworth, 175–7
Bethersden, 12 n
Birmingham, 79, 83, 121, 142, 176, 271
    Cannon Street Chapel, 29
Blackburn, 180
Black Heddon, 40
Blackwell, 44
Borough Green, 328
Boston, Lincs., 186, 223
Bourton-on-the-Water, 16–17, 20–2, 26–9, 31–2
Bow (Middlesex), 283
Bradford, Wilts. (Bradford on Avon), 28
Bradford, Yorks., 180, 232
Bratton, 28
Brighton, 144, 194

Bristol, 18–9, 20, 21, 26, 28–9, 32, 115, 118, 143, 331
    Baptist College, 32, 85–6, 99, 177, 232, 235, 246, 254
    Broadmead Church, 18–19, 235–6, 254
    Fryers, Pithay Church, 18
Bromsgrove, 28
Burford, 28
Bury, 180
Bury St Edmunds, 316

Cambridge, 9, 10, 62, 77–9, 223, 236, 238, 251, 274, 357
Chatteris, 301
Cheltenham, 28
Chesham, 18
Chester, 177–8
Chesterfield, 47
Chiselhampton, 273, 291–2
Cirencester, 28
Claxton, 314
Coventry, 176–7, 271
Cranbrook, 119

Deeping St James, 295 n, 303
Desford, 178
Devizes, 293, 295 n
Diseworth, 45
Donington Park, 45
Downham, 210
Dublin, 115, 290

[401]

East Anglia, *see* Norfolk, Suffolk
Edinburgh, 25, 187–8, 194 n, 256
Enfield, 34–5, 38, 133, 358
Everton, 82

Foots Cray, 267

Gloucester, 20
Grantham, 210
Great Gidding, 203–4
Grundisburgh, 223 n, 225, 263–4, 315, 318, 321

Hadlow, 328
Hamsterley, 41
Halifax, 180
Helmsley, 121
Henley-in-Arden, 17–18
Hexham, 41
Hinckley, 177–8
Horsleydown, Southwark, 3–5, 12, 18
Horton Baptist Academy, 232
Huddersfield, 47, 180

Ipswich, 174, 212, 263, 314
Irthlingborough, 178

Jamaica, 54–5

Kent and Sussex, 328–9
Kettering, 3, 53, 66–7, 89, 94, 105
Kimbolton, 10, 205 n
Kirkby Woodhouse, 45

Lakenheath, 194
Leicester, 119, 121, 143, 235–8, 330
 Zion Chapel, 334
LONDON:
 Barbican, 133
 Blandford Street, 264, 266 n

Borough, Trinity Chapel, 324–5
Broad Street, 109
Brick Lane, Jireh Chapel, 323
Bunhill Fields, 32 n, 38
Camberwell, 256
Carter Lane, 57, 99, 111, 138
Chelsea Baptist Church, 347
Conway Street Chapel, 181
Cripplegate, 28
Crosby Row, Southwark, 284–6
Curriers' Hall, 10, 97
Dean Street (Southwark), 99, 105, 210 n
Devonshire Square Chapel, 49, 327
Eagle Street, 49, 98 n, 100 n, 283, 331
Edward Street (Soho), 202
Exeter Hall, 355
Goodman's Fields, 48
Gower Street Chapel, 181–2, 193–4
Grafton Street, 70 n, 104, 210 n, 211, 214, 217–9
Great Alie Street Chapel (Zoar), 182, 303
Hackney, Homerton Row Chapel, 324
Hackney, Mare Street Chapel, 251
Hampstead, 323
Horselydown, *see* Southwark
Independent Academy, 19
Keppel Street, 110 n, 282
Little Alie Street Chapel, 181, 324
Little Prescot Street Chapel, 19, 26–7, 29, 47–56, 72, 112–3, 188, 254, 256, 357
Little Wild Street, 19, 48–9
Margaret Street Chapel, 120

Index of Places

Marylebone, Hill Street (Mount Zion), 225, 323
Maze Pond, 48, 57
Meard's Court, Salem Chapel, 222–6, 264
Merchant Taylors' School, 289
Metropolitan Tabernacle, 338, 341, 340, 353
New Park Street, 261, 337–8, 340–1, 346, 348
Petticoat Lane Meeting, 214
Providence Chapel, 120
Redcross Street Chapel, 181
St Paul's School, 289
Shoreditch, Cumberland Street, 325 n, 327–8
Soho Chapel, Oxford Street, 220, 323
Southwark, 3–5, 48–9, 99, 337–8
Stepney Academy, 55, 232, 254–7, 283
Surrey Gardens Music Hall, 341
Surrey Tabernacle, 262, 346
Tottenham Court Road Chapel, 114
Unicorn Yard, 48, 99
Whitechapel, 47–8, 55–6
Whitechapel, Zion Chapel, 226
Whitefield's Tabernacle, 72, 114, 311
York Street Chapel, Soho, 210, 219

Longborough, 45
Lower Ditchford, 31
Lymington, 66 n

Manchester, 174, 178–99, 271–2, 277–8, 285

St George's Road Chapel, 178
York Street Chapel, 179
Maidstone, 265, 331
Melbourne, 45
Meopham, 328

New England, 150, 155–66
Newmarket, 354,
New York, 325
Norfolk, 98 n, 118, 263, 313–22
Northampton, 28, 32 n, 33–40, 60, 94, 99, 133, 137, 178, 271, 357
Northleach, 28
Norwich, 246, 258–9, 283
Nottingham, 47
Nuneaton, 175

Oakham, 274, 303, 311
Oldham, 180
Olney, 37, 94
Oundle, 10 n, 203–4, 223
Oxford, 21, 28, 78, 359
  Regents Park College, Angus Library, 21, 358
  Worcester College, 273–4, 289–94

Pendlebury, 180
Plymouth, 119 n, 120, 122, 143
Portsmouth, 119 n
Preston, 180, 273
Rathsallagh, Ireland, 290
Rattlesden, 337,
Ripple, Kent, 288
Rochdale, 180, 182, 188, 194 n, 262
  Town Meadows Chapel, 188
Rothwell, 10, 97
Rushden, 277

[403]

St Ives, Huntingdon, 223
St Neots, 204, 223, 225, 267
St Vincent, 55
Sheepshead (Shepshed), 103
Smarden, Kent, 12 n, 379
Soham, 91–4
Spalding, 102
Stadhampton, 273, 291–2
Stambourne, 339
Stamford, 274, 311
Stannington, Northumberland, 40
Steventon, 204
Stockport, 180
Suffolk, 98 n, 118, 263, 266, 313–22
Sutton Courtenay, 292
Sutton in Ashfield, 46–7
Sweden, 325

Thorn, Dunstable, 69
Trevecca, 314
Tring, 271

Trowbridge, 28, 193 n, 262, 293
Tunbridge Wells, 328
Tunstall, 317

United States of America, 297–8

Wadhurst, 328
Wallingford, 142
Warwick, 32–4, 358
Warwickshire, 31
Waterbeach, 338
Wattisham, 263, 320
Weston Favell, 34
Wicken, Cambs., 91
Wiltshire, 3
Wivelsfield, 328
Wolverhampton, 194
Woolwich, 325

Yorkshire, 97, 98 n, 119, 121, 174, 180

Index of Subjects

Addresses on Practical Subjects, Upton, 183 n, 186, 381
Admission of Unbaptized Persons to the Lord's Supper Inconsistent with the New Testament, Fuller, 231 n, 234, 372
Aged Pilgrims' Friend Society, 311
American War of Independence, 37, 59, 70, 79, 83–4, 108, 122
Answer to Fools and a Word to the Wise, Huntington, 136, 375
Anti-Corn Law League, *see* Corn Laws
Antinomianism, 7, 10, 39, 51, 86–8, 90 n, 106, 112–31, 133–6, 138, 140–4, 162 n, 173, 175, 178–9, 183–8, 201, 209–13, 251–2, 265, 302–4, 319, 363
Antinomianism Unmasked, de Fleury, 133–5, 371
Apology for the Baptists, Booth, 60, 65, 70–77, 231, 233, 237, 370
Apology for the Freedom of the Press, Hall, 122
Arguments against Mixed Communion, Kinghorn, 234, 250, 376
Arianism, 3, 22, 45, 141, 185, 214, 268, 316
Arminianism, 3, 28, 39–41, 45–6, 55, 90, 97–8, 100, 105, 113, 116, 129, 141, 150–1, 155, 157, 166, 170, 185–7, 204–5, 224, 258, 264, 269, 316, 330 n, 335, 343, 345, 347–9, 361, 365

Arminian Skeleton, Huntington, 129
Assembly of Particular Baptist Churches (1689), xvii, xix, 342
Assurance, 8, 18, 96, 130–1, 143, 189–92, 291
Athanasian Creed, 62, 216, 285
Atonement, controversy on (*see also* Substitution), 157–71, 209, 354, 361–6
Governmental Theory, 150–1, 163–7

Baptism an Indispensable Pre-Requisite to Communion at the Lord's Table, Newman, 77 n, 233–4
Baptism, a Term of Communion at the Lord's Supper, Kinghorn, 245–7, 250, 375–6
Baptism, the Scriptural and Indispensable Qualification for Communion, Ivimey, 233 n, 252–3
Baptist Associations, 262, 312–36
Baptist Board, The, 108, 202, 214, 323
Baptist Catechism (1694), 22, 342
Spurgeon's Catechism, 341–2
Baptist Confessions of Faith:
 1644 Confession, xvii
 1689 Confession, xi, xiii, xvii–xix, 5–8, 11–12, 17, 22, 62, 115, 158, 162, 191–2, 216, 336, 339–40, 350, 356
 Covenant and Articles, Keach, 5–6
 Declaration of Faith and Practice, Gill, 5–6, 11–12, 34 n, 62

[405]

Gospel Standard Articles of Faith, 334–5
Baptist Irish Society, 244, 329
Baptist Itinerant Society, 54, 329
Baptist Magazine, The, 200, 213, 221, 262, 325, 331, 388
Baptist Register, The, 17, 39 n, 108, 204 n, 313–4 n
Baptist Union, 111, 171, 245, 253, 258, 261, 327, 329–32, 335–6, 353–5
Baxterianism, 90 n, 204, 365
Berkshire and West London Baptist Association, 323
Bible Society, 233
Blow Struck at the Root of Fullerism, A, Hupton, 314, 375
Body of Divinity, Gill, 4, 6–9, 373
Body of Divinity, J. C. Ryland, 133
Book of Martyrs, Foxe, 339
Brethren, 'Plymouth', 291, 295
Broken Cistern and the Springing Well, The, Huntington, 124 n, 136

Calvinism, 24, 39, 71, 90 n, 142, 145, 151, 205, 208, 213, 264–5, 295, 300, 336, 338, 341–5, 348, 352–5, 361–6
Calvinistic Methodists, 85, 116, 142
Cambridge and Huntingdon Home Missionary Society, 223
Candidus Examined with Candour, Taylor, 65
Candidus-Pacificus Tract, 60, 63–5, 357–9
Cause of God and Truth, The, Gill, 4
Christology (*see also* Pre-existarianism), 11, 213–7, 224, 311
Church Covenant of the New Road Baptist Church, Oxford, 359

Coincidence of Antinomianism and Arminianism, Gawthorne, 186–7, 373
Communion, terms of, debate, 33–4, 52, 58–88, 193–4, 230–59, 282–4, 313, 319, 323, 331–2, 345–6, 357–9
Compendium of Social Religion, Turner, 61, 359, 380
Congregational Union, 261
Convention of Strict Baptist Churches, 331–2
Corn Laws, 197, 260, 278
Countess of Huntingdon's Connexion, 34, 116, 176, 201, 203, 225, 314
Covenant of Grace, 8–9, 339, 380

Daily News, The, 225
Deacons, 308
Death of Legal Hope, The, Booth, 51, 112–3, 141, 369
Defence of 'Baptism, a Term of Communion', Kinghorn, 250, 376
Defence of Paedobaptism Examined, Booth, 52
Defence of Particular Redemption, Rushton, 300–1, 378
Dissenters (*see also* Religious tests, Toleration Act), 4, 31, 37, 52–4, 58–9, 84–6, 122–3
Divine Energy, Skepp, 10, 378
Divine Justice Essential to the Divine Character, Booth, 158, 370
Doctrinal Antinomianism Refuted, Stevens, 186, 211–3, 379
'Doctrinal Antinomianism Refuted' Entangled in Its Own Maze, Gadsby, 186, 211–3, 373

Index of Subjects

Doctrine of Justification, Gill, 7
Doctrine of Predestination, Gill, 9, 373
Dordt, Synod of, *Canons*, 170
Duty Faith, 10, 95–7, 101, 104–7, 152–7, 317, 324, 326, 332, 344, 347–8, 355

Earthen Vessel, The, 272, 282, 284–7, 347 n, 348, 352 n, 388–9
Effectual Calling, 23
Essay on the Kingdom of Christ, Booth, 52
Essential Difference between Christian Baptism and the Baptism of John, Hall, 245, 374
Eternal justification, 6–8, 19, 314, 323
Evangelical Alliance, 355
Evangelical Magazine, 152
Evangelical Nonconformists and Higher Criticism in the Nineteenth Century, Glover, 355
Evangelical Revival, 20, 59, 71–2, 84–5, 131, 142, 202, 225, 277, 332
Evangelism, 45, 203–4, 222–4, 227, 321–2
Excommunication and the Duty of All Men to Believe, Huntington, 137
Experimentalism, 12–14, 30, 130–1, 140, 144, 189–92, 268–9, 277–8, 295–300
Exposition of the Old and New Testaments, Gill, 4
Exposition of the Song of Solomon, Gill, 12–13

Faith, nature of saving, 96, 153–6, 207
Free Communion, An Innovation, Buttfield, 69–70

Foreign Missions, Palmer, 301–2, 305, 322 n
Free Grace Record, 272
Free offer of the gospel, 6, 8–10, 93, 156, 166, 170, 355
Freedom of the Will, Edwards, 42, 93, 235
French Revolution, 53, 61, 79, 86, 109, 122
Fullerism, 97, 179, 200, 213, 262–4, 267, 300, 314–5, 325, 328, 348

General Baptists, 45, 65, 71, 99, 111, 330, 353
General Doctrine of Toleration Applied to Free Communion, The, Robinson, 77, 80, 378
Glad Tidings to Sinners, Booth, 151, 153–4, 165, 172, 370
Glory of Christ Vindicated, The, Hussey, 276
God's Operations of Grace, Hussey, 9
Gospel Herald, The, 263–72, 274, 280, 282, 285, 287
Gospel Magazine, The, 213, 276
Gospel Standard, The, 198, 225 n, 263 n, 268–70, 272–82, 287
Gospel Standard added Articles, 334–5
Gospel the Believer's Rule of Conduct, The, Gadsby, 183–7, 372
Gospel Worthy of All Acceptation, The, Fuller, 86, 89–111, 149, 152–3, 156–7, 163, 167, 170–3, 188, 204–5, 361, 372, 379
Grace Magazine, 272
Guide to Church Fellowship, Styles, 350, 355

[407]

Heir of Heaven Walking in Darkness, The, Philpot, 278
Help for the True Disciples of Immanuel, Stevens, 204–10, 222, 224–5, 379
Help to Zion's Travellers, Hall, 39, 97, 116
History of the English Baptists, Ivimey, 7, 50, 53, 60, 69, 78, 84, 99, 102, 109, 111, 119, 122, 200, 219–20, 231–2, 238, 384
Homilies, The, Church of England, 162
House of God Opened, The, Brown, 59, 66–7, 370
Huntingtonianism, 118–9, 121, 143–4, 175, 181–2, 198, 212, 268–70, 276, 305, 313, 329
Hymns, 24–5, 48, 60, 191–3, 339, 344
Hyper-Calvinism, 14–15, 23, 32–4, 42, 55, 71, 83, 86–8, 116, 119, 128, 132, 142, 149–52, 156, 171, 173–4, 181, 189, 191, 202–5, 208–18, 222–6, 245, 259, 262–9, 276, 278, 286–7, 300–1, 313–36, 338–54

Imputation, 157–62, 166–70, 363–4
Itinerant Preachers Society, 329

Jacobinism, 122–3
Justification from eternity, *see* Eternal justification

Kent and Sussex New Association of Particular Baptist Churches, 325, 328–9

Law Not against the Promises of God, Ryland, 117

Lawful Captive Delivered, The, Osbourn, 297 n
Letter Addressed to the Bishop of Salisbury, Tiptaft, 275 n, 293–4
Letter on Free Communion, Cox, 251, 371, 375
Letter to the Rev. Mr Huntington, de Fleury, 133–4
Letter to the Provost of Worcester College, Oxford, Philpot, 273–4, 307, 377
Letter to the Rev. Caleb Evans, Huntington, 138
Liberal theology, 354
London Association of Strict Baptist Ministers and Churches, 324–6
London Baptist Association, 323–4
London Baptist Educational Society, 55
London Home Missionary Society, 321

Manual of Faith and Practice, Styles, 350, 379
Memoirs of Mr John Stevens (anon.), 201, 219–21, 369
Methodists, 73, 85, 115, 116, 142, 202
Metropolitan Association of Strict Baptist Churches, 328
Midlands Association of Particular Baptist Churches, 25–6
Mixed Marriages, 303–4
'Modern Question', the, 10, 32, 90 n, 96–7
Modern Question Modestly Answered, A, Maurice, 10
Moral Government of God, The, Wells, 298, 381

Moral and Ritual Precepts Compared, Newman, 251–2, 377

Napoleonic Wars, 289
New Association of Particular Baptists in London, 326–8
New Connexion of General Baptists, 330
New England theology, 55, 150, 155–66
New Park Street Pulpit, 340–1
Nonconformist disabilities, *see* Religious tests
Norfolk and Suffolk Particular Baptist Association (Old Association), 226, 313–6, 319
Northamptonshire Baptist Association, 38–40, 66–8, 104, 117–8

Obligation (*see also* Duty faith, 159, 184, 206
Ordination, 307–9
Ordo Salutis, 153
Oxford Movement, 290, 295, 309

Pacifism, 279
Particular Baptists, statistics, 253
Particular Baptist Fund, 10, 79–80, 119 n
Particular Baptist Missionary Society, 53, 86–7, 107, 151, 171, 221, 222, 260, 322, 329, 353
Particular Redemption, 158, 166–71, 209, 294, 300, 341
Perfect Law of Liberty, The, Gadsby, 186
Pilgrim's Progress, Bunyan, 339
Plain Statement, Palmer, 296, 302–5

Plea for Primitive Communion, Pritchard, 244–5, 374, 378
Politics, 53, 58–9, 108–10, 121–3, 194–7, 309–10
Pre-existarianism (*see also* Christology), 11, 68, 213–7, 225 n, 267–8, 272 n, 276, 373, 379, 381
Present State of Religion, The, Gadsby, 185, 372
Primitive Communionist and *Primitive Church Magazine*, 282–4, 324–5, 331, 388
Protest Against the Pre-Existence of the Human Soul of Christ, Wells, 276

Radicalism, 122, 236, 255
Reasons for Christian in Opposition to Party Communion, Hall, 235 n, 250, 253, 374–6
Redeemer's Tears, The, Howe, 352
Refutation of Arminian Principles, Brine, 97
Reign of Grace, The, Booth, 47, 51, 151, 165, 369
Religious Affections, The, Edwards, 91 n, 131, 235
Religious tests, 58–9, 239
Repentance, 93–6, 107, 343, 347
Reply to 'A Letter on Free Communion', Ivimey, 251, 375
Reply to the Rev. Joseph Kinghorn, Hall, 233, 249–50, 253, 374
Roman Catholic Emancipation, 260
Rule and a Riddle, A, Huntington, 124–6, 128, 130

Sandemanianism, 187–91

Sandemanianism Weighed in the Balances and Found Wanting, Gadsby, 189, 373
Savoy Declaration of Faith and Order, xviii
Scriptural Display of the Triune God and the Early Existence of Jesus' Human Soul, Stevens, 213–6
Scripture Doctrine of the Atonement, West, 163, 166
Scriptural Exposition of the Baptist Catechism, Beddome, 22–3
Seceders, The, Philpot, 193–5 n, 198 n, 272–5 n, 278 n, 281 n, 289 n, 291–6 n, 300–1 n, 307 n, 309 n
Serious Address to the Rev. Mr Huntington, de Fleury, 133–4, 371
Servant of the Lord, Described and Vindicated, The, Huntington, 134
Slavery, 38, 53, 70, 84
Socinianism, 3, 39, 51–2, 72, 118, 141, 149, 164
Strict Baptist, early uses of term, 67–8, 72, 76–7, 87–8
Strictures on Sandemanianism, Fuller, 188
Substitution, 149, 157–8, 160, 162–70, 209, 363
Suffolk and Norfolk Home Missionary Society, 321
Suffolk and Norfolk Strict and Particular Baptist Association (New Association), 318–22, 324

Terms of communion, *see* Communion, terms of, debate
Terms of Communion, Hall, 87 n, 231 n, 234–45, 247, 251 n, 374
Theron and Aspasio, Hervey, 46
Thoughts on the Duty of Man, Martin, 99 n, 104–7
Three Sermons on the Atonement, Edwards (Jr.), 166
Toleration Act (1689), xvii, 59 n, 69
Total Inability, 296
Trinity, the (see also Christology, Pre-existarianism) 4, 8, 14, 51, 68–9, 79, 82, 213–8

Union of Baptist Ministers, 323
Universalism, 114, 135

Verses on the Sonship and Pre-existence of Jesus Christ, Stevens, 215, 379

Warrant of faith, 106, 151–6
Warrant and Nature of Faith, The, Scott, 153, 155, 378
Western Association of Particular Baptist Churches, 22, 118, 138
Westminster Confession of Faith, xviii, 7–8, 115
Westminster Shorter Catechism, 22, 190 n, 342
What is Faith? Gadsby, 189–90
Work of the Holy Spirit in Conversion, The, Hinton, 327, 374

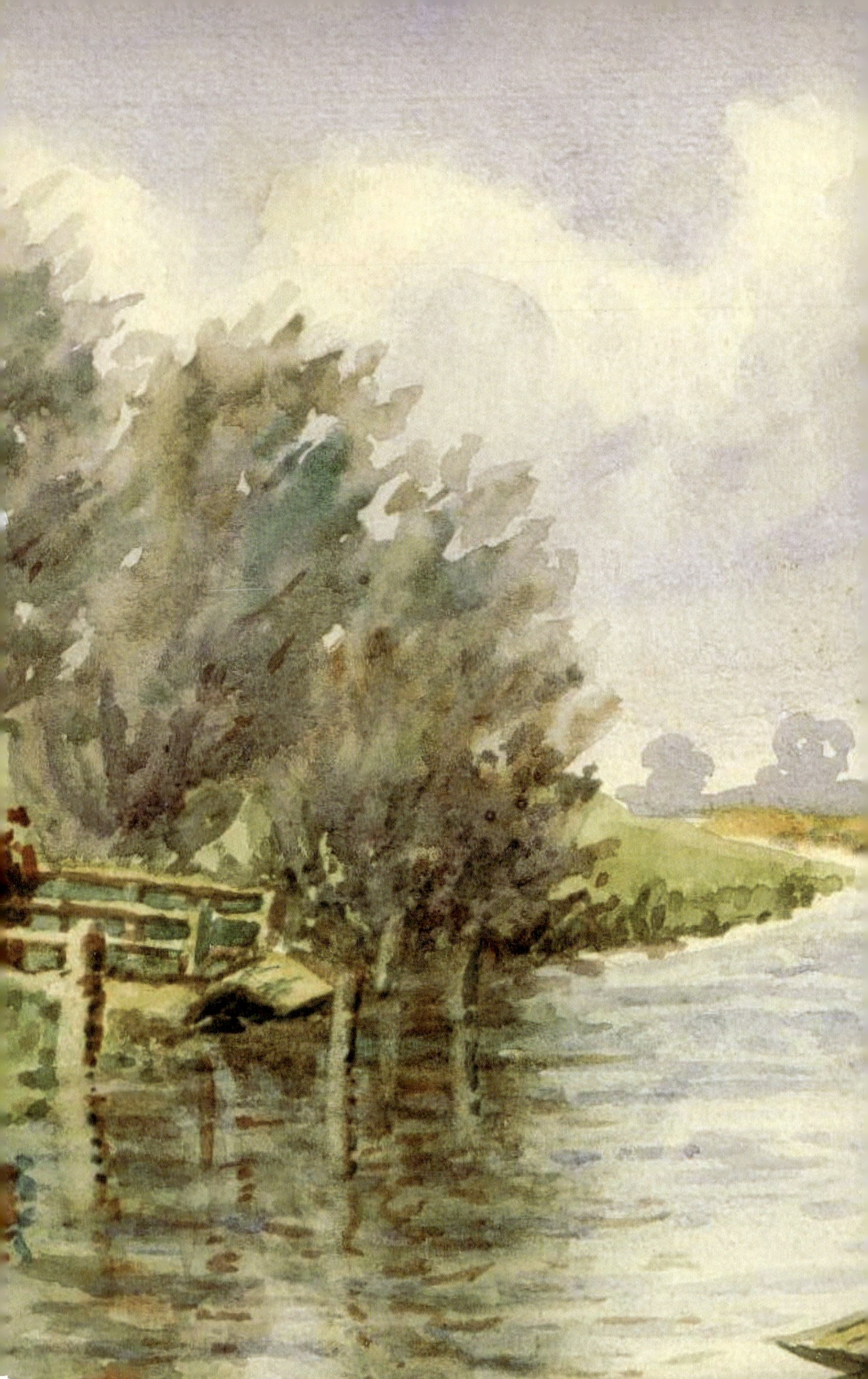